OAKWOOD LIBRARY OF RAILWAY HISTORY OL108

The Schull & Skibbereen Railway

by
James I.C. Boyd

THE OAKWOOD PRESS

© Oakwood Press & J.I.C. Boyd 1999

ISBN 978-0-85361-772-3

Typeset by Oakwood Graphics.
Repro by Ford Graphics, Ringwood, Hants.
Printed by Blissetts, Unit 1, Shield Drive, West Cross Industrial Park, Brentford, TW8 9EX

All rights reserved. No part of this book may be reproduced or transmitted in any form or by any means, electronic or mechanical, including photocopying, recording or by any information storage and retrieval system, without permission from the Publisher in writing.

To
the memory of
DOROTHY

who would have wished me to complete this manuscript
which had occupied us for so many years

God be thanked that the dead have still
Good undone for the living to do,
Still some aim for the heart and will
And the Soul of Man to pursue

Lord Lytton

Published by
The Oakwood Press
54-58 Mill Square, Catrine KA5 6RD
01290 551122   www.stenlake.co.uk

Contents

	Abbreviations	4
	Foreword	5
	Glossary and Notes	6
Chapter One	The Environment	11
Chapter Two	The Main Line Railway reaches Skibbereen	20
Chapter Three	In the Beginning 1860-1883	23
Chapter Four	A Pattern of Progress 1884-1885	31
Chapter Five	A Shaky Start 1885-1886	44
Chapter Six	Nothing but Trouble 1886-1887	49
Chapter Seven	Worrying Times 1887-1888	58
Chapter Eight	Hopes reborn 1888-1892	63
Chapter Nine	Fulfilment in sight 1892-1905	69
Chapter Ten	Consolidation 1905-1916	77
Chapter Eleven	Government Control and State Ownership 1916-1925	92
Chapter Twelve	The Final Years 1926-1956 and after	97
Chapter Thirteen	The Route: Skibbereen to Schull Harbour	107
Chapter Fourteen	Locomotives	167
Chapter Fifteen	Carriages and Wagons	191
Chapter Sixteen	Operating	223
Chapter Seventeen	Permanent Way	245
Chapter Eighteen	Miscellanea	249
Chapter Nineteen	Personalities	255
Appendix One	Waterborne Competition and Coastal Shipping	260
Appendix Two	West Carbery Mining and the Railways	263
Appendix Three	Tickets	265
Appendix Four	Accounts	266
	Sources, Acknowledgements and Bibliography	276
	Index	279

Bi-lingual station name board at Schull. *J.I.C. Boyd*

Abbreviations

BELR	Baltimore Extension Light Railway
C&BR	Cork & Bandon Railway
CB&SCR	Cork Bandon & South Coast Railway
CCR	Cork City Railways
CIE	Coras Iompair Eireann
CL&RLR&TCL *	Cavan Leitrim & Roscommon Light Railway & Tramway Co. Ltd.
C&MLR*	Cork & Muskerry Light Railway
CVT (Later CVR) *	Clogher Valley Tramway (later Railway)
GSR	Great Southern Railways
GWR	Great Western Railway
GSWR	Great Southern & Western Railway
IVR	Ilen Valley Railway
LNWR	London & North Western Railway
SG&UHLR *†	Skibbereen Glandore & Union Hall Light Railway
S&SET&LR *	Schull & Skibbereen Extension Tramway & Light Railway
S&SR (S&ST&LRCo) *	Schull & Skibbereen Tramway & Light Railway
T&DLR *	Tralee & Dingle Light Railway
TCGCL	Tramways Capital Guarantee Co. Ltd.
WCR	West Cork Railway
WCT&LRCL *	West Carbery Tramways & Light Railways Co. Ltd.
BoT	Board of Trade
BoW	Board of Works (Irish)
VRCIR	Vice-Regal Commission on Irish Railways
IRA	Irish Republican Army
RIC	Royal Irish Constabulary
SEYB	Stock Exchange Year Book

† Proposal Only
* 3 ft Gauge

Foreword

In 1964 The Oakwood Press published a small booklet by Alan Newham on this subject, being based on a paper he had read before the Irish Railway Record Society, and which the Society duly published in its Journal.

Like Alan Newham, the writer had visited the Railway in its 'She is not dead but sleeping' phase. Unfortunately, Newham's only visit was after mine and was necessarily short. Neither of us saw the line at work. Attracted by the subject it has taken over 50 years to achieve the aim of writing more fully about it; some of Newham's material appears again, now enhanced by frequent encounters over half a century.

No excuse is made for devoting some space to the historical background of West Cork - what is unnecessary when writing about English or Welsh railways, for instance, is essential for all but Irish readers, for the turmoils that have beset this lovely country and its welcoming people are still with us in 1999.

The basis of this book was written when 'The Tram' had only recently ceased to operate. The district was in decline and prospects miserable; emigration was depopulating town and countryside.

So what of today as the tourist sweeps along the road to Schull which once was bounded by the Tramway on its northern flank? The Irish Tourist Board along with European money has transformed the scene. There is a new prosperity about, and visitors will find little of the background in which the S&SR survived. However, it requires but little imagination in such surroundings to perceive the Tramway which, at a stroke, had lifted the Barony from the donkey-and-cart age and met the aims of the legislation on which it was created.

For all its life The Tram lived under the shadow of the fable, 'Created by the British; misled by a Jew; built by a Welshman; starved of help by the Government', most of which was untrue as the following pages will bear out. Nevertheless, while the Tramway is but memory, the fable lives on . . .

Comic postcard; the sketch was frequently published in connection with other railways and caption amended suitably. *Collection Dermot McCarthy*

Glossary and Notes

Barony. In Ireland, a Baron's demesne, or a division of a county (as in this case). The 'Barons of Carbery' were the Evans-Frekes of Rathbarry Castle, Castlefreke.

Townland. A district or area of country.

Place Names. The Anglicised spelling of Irish place names is frequently based on the vernacular interpretation of the local Irish names given verbally to Englishmen when making the first survey for charts and maps. Apart from inaccuracies which arose immediately, down the years subsequent variations (notwithstanding the recent trend to be 'politically correct') continue to the present day.

The form of spelling used herein is that chosen by the Railway Companies concerned with the subject matter; that used for places off the railway system is, where practical, contemporary with their existence.

Personal Names. For the English reader, it is as well that the present addiction to giving names in Irish (a perfectly acceptable mode) hardly affects the text. However, the same family may be styled O'Sullivan or simply Sullivan; confusingly portions of a family may be Roycroft or Ryecroft. Care and courtesy are needed.

Administration. Both London (Westminster Parliament) and Dublin were concerned in the administration of Irish Railways, the Acts under which they were built, etc. Initially, matters of Inspection and safety were a matter for the Board of Trade in London; appeals for Grants, etc. were made to Dublin. The text attempts to set each event in its geographical place.

Civil Unrest. From origination of the West Carbery Tramway in 1884 to the forming of the Irish Free State in 1925, Ireland was in a persistent state of unrest whilst Skibbereen and around were much to the fore in such matters. This was an ever-present background to the story of the Schull & Skibbereen system.

Events under this heading are known in Irish history under two headings: (a) 'The War of Independence' which stemmed from the burning of the General Post Office in Dublin in April 1916 until the truce of June 1921* (b) 'The Civil War' from June 1922 until June 1923.

During the latter, Munster bore the brunt of the damage. 'The railways suffered heavily - bridges, track and trains were derailed or destroyed. Cork had no railway communication with Dublin'.† The CB&SCR from Cork (Albert Quay) to Bantry and all branches therefrom, was inoperative as was the S&SR. Much of West Cork was in the hands of the Republican Army who controlled land transport and obliged the region to look to the sea for all supplies. Free State Forces were sent by sea from Dublin to Cork and Skibbereen was relieved in July 1922.

Railway Terms. The Standard Gauge of railway track in Ireland is 5 ft 3 in. All references to the 'main line' refer to systems of this gauge and generally to that which connected Skibbereen with Cork city.

---

* Of especial disruption and loss to the S&SR during the War of Independence was that it was situated in an region of unrest termed by the military authorities as a 'Disaffected Area', whereby all markets within that area were ordered to be abandoned. Certain railways were also closed for reasons which included: trains being ambushed, stock destroyed, permanent way removed, failure of local people to support the military . . . By June 1921, 'punishment' had been meted out to five railways, each being inoperative at that date: the S&SR and the Skibbereen-Baltimore main line were among them.

The loss of Fair Traffic, both of livestock and passengers attending those Fairs brought losses far beyond the obvious repercussions.

† See Conroy pp. 323-324 for further detail. Also FREEMAN'S JOURNAL, 13th August, 1923.

GLOSSARY AND NOTES

Government Control. The railways were placed under Government Control on 22nd December, 1916 until 15th August, 1921.

Grand Jury. This was the first-formed Local Authority. It enjoyed legal as well as civil powers and was therefore much more powerful than the present County Councils; the first attempt to reform them was in 1816. See also Grand Juries (Ireland) Act 1836. Discontinued by Courts of Justice Act 1924.

Long Car. The Long Car was an enlarged and elongated version of the Side Car 'on which the tourist can travel cheaply in Connemara and the West of Ireland'. The passengers sit in two rows, back to back; as there was no covering, 'a plentiful supply of rugs and waterproofs should always be included in the traveller's luggage. Umbrellas are of no use in the West of Ireland. Waterproofs are essential'.

Tourists were recommended to choose their seats carefully, so as to be on the side to obtain the best views.*

Bradshaw's Shareholders Manual. The undertaking never submitted matter for this Annual.

Schull & Skibbereen Railway
Outline Chronology

Incorporated by Act	7th December, 1883
Work commenced	July 1885
Opening (Unofficial)	6th September, 1886
Closing 'owing to imperfect construction'	6th April, 1887
Re-opening	2nd January, 1888
Committee of Management formed (First Meeting)	4th August, 1892
Title changed to S&ST&LR	4th August, 1892
Schull Pier Extension (S&SET&LR) (Opened)	October 1893
Vice Regal Commission	1907-1910
Control by Government	22nd December, 1916
Light Railways Investigation Committee	1921
Re-opening after 'War of Independence'†	15th August, 1921
Great Southern Railways (Under Railways Act 23rd July, 1924)	1925
Coras Iompair Eireann	1945
Emergency closure	24th April, 1944
Resumption of services (One daily 'mixed' only)	10th December, 1945
Last Fair Train	16th January, 1947
Limited timetable introduced	20th January, 1947
Last timetabled train	25th January, 1947

---

* See: *Transport in Ireland 1880-1910* (Patrick Flanagan) [Transport Research Associates: 1969] pp. 14-16 etc.

† Civil War began June 1922; Cork city had no rail communication to Dublin. In January 1923 S&SR was one of five railways inactive.

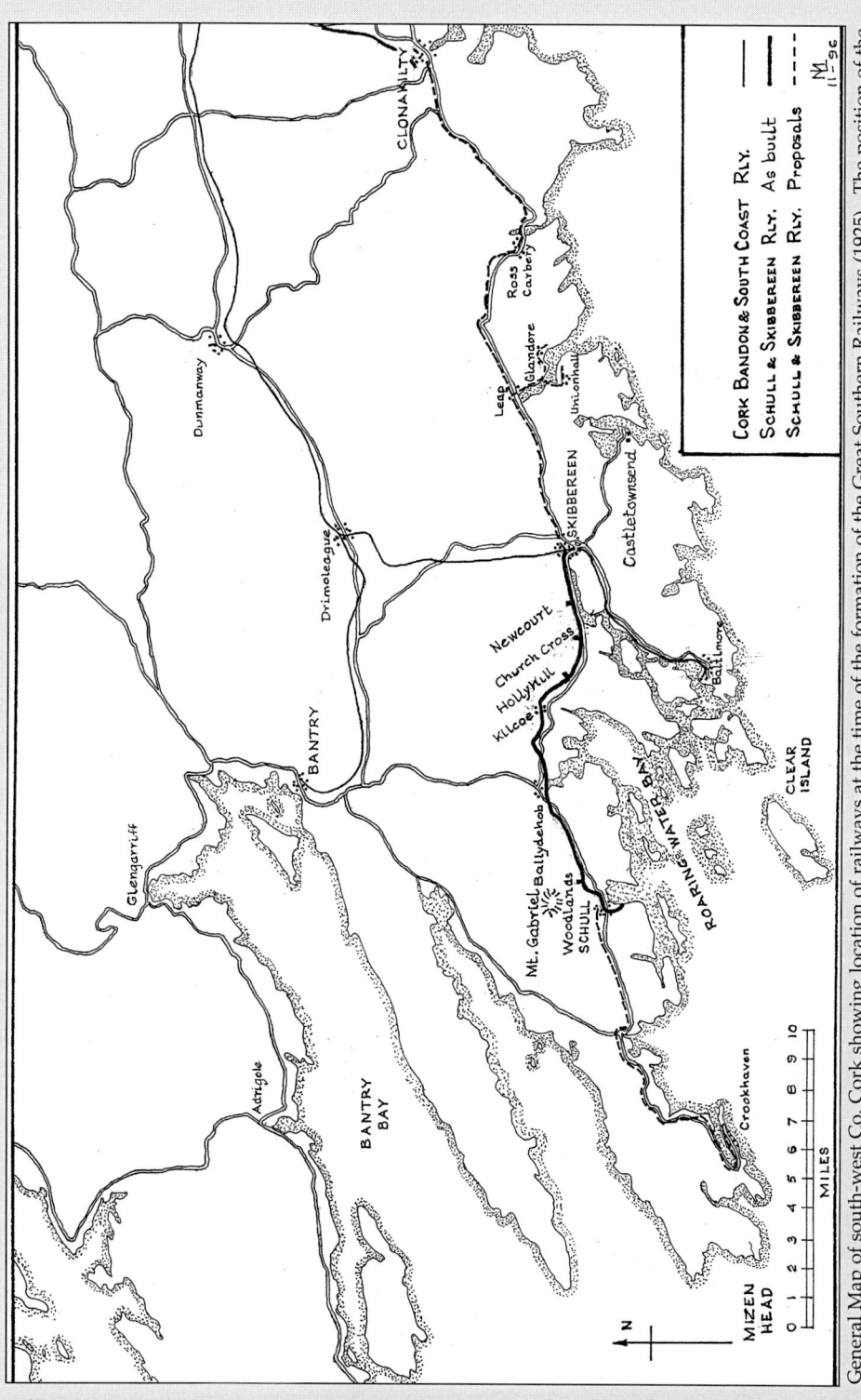

General Map of south-west Co. Cork showing location of railways at the time of the formation of the Great Southern Railways (1925). The position of the then Schull & Skibbereen Railway and the contemplated extensions of its fore-runner, are shown in broken lines.

GLOSSARY AND NOTES

Skibbereen, Glandore & Union Hall Light Railway (Proposal only)
Chronology

An eastward scheme promoted at the same period as that for the system westward of Skibbereen, to reach the fishing villages at Glandore and Union Hall. The idea ran into opposition and although resurrected, never took hold. The failure of the westward scheme on opening, sealed its fate.

Grand Jury sanctions project	29th March, 1884
Grand Jury reviews matter (but strong opposition encountered)	16th April, 1884
Public Meetings to renew powers to build; unsuccessful, so project dropped	8th May, 1884
Meeting at Skibbereen to re-open discussion	26th September, 1889

In 1889 a branch to Castletownsend Harbour was mooted; the destination was then an important fishing centre.

Schull & Skibbereen Tramway & Light Railway
Chronology

Operations of WCT&LRCL taken over by Committee of Management under title S&ST&LRC	4th August, 1892
Order in Council for WCT&LRCL to build Extension to Schull Harbour*	29th December, 1892
Construction complete	October 1893

* An improved pier was provided under the same powers.

Peckett & Sons Ltd., Bristol. Embossed cover of Catalogue.

Typically agrarian housing; relics of the 19th Century are commonplace in West Carbery.
J.I.C. Boyd

Before railways came to West Cork, the Jaunting Car was swift transport for the few.
Collection J.I.C. Boyd

Chapter One

The Environment

A pen-picture of Skibbereen as it was before the Great Famine of the 1840s is helpful to describe the town in the 1870s when the railways came, for little had changed in the meantime:

Thackeray, no mean man with a pen, visited Skibbereen in 1842. He has left us with the following account. 'That light, four inside, four-horse coach, *The Skibbereen Perseverance*, brought me 52 miles today for the sum of 3s. 6d. The coach, like almost every other public vehicle I have seen in Ireland, was full to the brim and over it. For the greater part of the journey the little guard sat on the roof among the carpet bags, holding in one hand a huge tambour frame, in the other a box marked: "Foggarty Matter". Near Dunmanway the great coach: *The Skibbereen Industry* dashed by us at 7 mph, a wondrous vehicle. There were gaps between every one of the panels, you could see daylight through it. Like our machine it was full, with three complimentary sailors on the roof, as little harness as possible on the horses, and as long stages as horses can endure - ours were each 18 mile stages.'

He states 'The hotel had a dirty coffee room with a strong smell of whiskey, a huge kitchen with a peat fire burning and a staircase walking up one side of it, and pantry of "Dan the Waiter" which was the most wonderful thing to be seen in Skibbereen, as every article within is a make-shift and has been ingeniously perverted from its original destination. Here lie bread, blacking, fresh butter, tallow, dirty knives, all in the same cigar box with snuff, cold bacon, brown sugar, broken tea cups, and bits of soap'.

The hotel of which he speaks, you will be relieved to know, has been closed this long while. It was located in North Street, opposite what was the '"Skibbereen Motor Works", and was called the "Becher Arms". The present-day hotels owe their fame to their cuisine and sheer good value. Thackeray describes the scene on Sunday as follows: 'The men came with shoes and stockings today, the women all bare-legged and many of them might be seen washing their feet in the stream, before they went up to the Chapel. The street seemed to be lined on either side with blue cloaks, squatting along the doorways as is their wont. Among these numberless, cows were walking to and fro, and pails of milk passing and here and there a hound went stalking.'

The men of Skibbereen and district are not so chauvinistic now, they provide their womenfolk with shoes nowadays. The cows have gone, but make a comeback on Mart days. Their milk arrives in plastic bottles. The dogs no longer stalk.

Of the town he says: 'The lower street crawls along the river to a considerable extent, having by-streets and boulevards of cabins here and there'.

The layout of the town has changed little since 1842.*

Memories of the line are fast-fading but Ireland is a country where history - true or false - is passed on as if yesterday. Some say that is the cause of Ireland's undoing.

Recently the Tramway was described by one who never knew it but who picked up his information from local gossip:

. . . Although described as a 'tramway', the line carried trains. The early engines, the ILEN, MARION and IDA were tin boxes with funnel stacks. They were superseded by the vastly superior GABRIEL, which was christened by the parish priest of Schull with a bottle of champagne. The ERIN and TRENT followed soon afterwards. These three engines had cowbuffers in front, and drove to the accompaniment of large bells, drawing a line of Pullman carriages whose seats could be reversed at the end of the journey . . . The greatest number of

---

* The foregoing is extracted from the SKIBBEREEN & DISTRICT VISITORS GUIDE, 1987.

passengers ever carried was a record 752 . . . on the hill up to Aughadown third-class passengers were obliged to walk . . .

One can only hope that the remainder of the work from which this largely-imaginative story was extracted, was more reliable.

There are only a few now living who remember The Tram and the customary problems of conflicting stories (sometimes just a little of the local 'Blarney') and the lack of contemporary accounts, bring their own difficulties in a search for facts. One would like to believe all the colourful stories surrounding the Tramway (or Railway, if you prefer) but as they are replicated throughout Ireland, most must be resisted. One undoubted impression is that having its operations in West Cork 56 miles west of Cork city, a considerable distance from Dublin and even further from London, allowed the men on the ground a useful freedom from authority. For this reason the Rule Book, Printed Instructions and the like were looked upon as a hindrance to personal preference.

To build up a mental picture of a time in Ireland when most of the railways were constructed requires some appreciation of the years since 1846; of the Famine, Disease, Poverty, Emigration, Civil Unrest and so on which straddled them. Railways mentioned herein had these for their background and the West Carbery Tramway was no exception.

It requires keen perception to focus on fundamental reasons for the construction of Irish railways serving purely poor agricultural districts in the west, but years of civil unrest made them attractive to move the means of discipline. Though some were financed in such a way that a steady income might be obtained - the WCT was a case in point - only a fool would consider them as an investment to *make* money.

I walked the abandoned rails of the S&SR in 1953; it was all intact and the rolling stock stood as if awaiting for The Second Coming. Though I could piece together the evidence of my eyes, I now appreciate that more than a smattering of Irish 19th Century history was essential to bring the scene to life and to understand the ambivalence with which The Tramway was viewed. Some saw it as a continuing comedy, others as a costly failure imposed on them by the English whilst a few understood they were fortunate to have a rail-way at all. Many parts of Ireland did not.

Readers outside Ireland need a little tuition. During the early part of the 19th Century south-west Cork was adjusting itself to a decline in the dominance of the Protestant minority, for in this part of Ireland the proportion of Protestants to Roman Catholics was greater than in any part of the country; elsewhere the proportion was roughly one tenth. Forty per cent of the Protestants lived in the county's towns (Bandon, Clonakilty etc.); Skibbereen was the most westerly. Contrary to English impression, these Protestants were not all landed gentry, landlords or country-dwellers, but they *were* families of influence. In the countryside they were simply 'Protestant Farmers'. About West Cork their families may still be found; they were the founders and promoters of business, the fishing industry, etc. and of course, railways. They created them, used them and turned away from them when it suited them. When things went wrong they never considered the fault might be their own and when they had built the WCT they tried to blame London for its failure. When ultimately they were given control of the undertaking they fared no better for as they admitted themselves, their upbringing had unfitted them for the task.

But they had no reason to be ashamed; when the line became part of the national system in 1925, things went on much as before.

THE ENVIRONMENT

In England the big landowners hastened the creation of a railway through finance or giving of land for the venture, and so found themselves on the Boards of several railways; in West Carbery the 'Big House' and its owner was not as numerous as further north and east. The climate and rocky terrain did not attract but in the better farms the 'gentry' who dwelled there would employ considerable numbers of local labourers, officially termed the 'peasantry'.

To further assist the reader to set the stage, it should be explained that only when the 19th Century was well established did West Carbery possess all but rudimentary roads, so that both local and long-distance travel was by sea. With Government backing, many small piers and quays were built around the coasts just for this purpose. Most remain today, some unused. Thus the competitor of the railways in those days was the coastal ship.

In the matter of 'link roads', though their condition was indifferent it was better than their contemporaries in England, one reason being that they usually passed close by the big estates and joined them together for security.

The Great Famine of 1846-9 witnessed a big decline in the national labour force and industrial structure; the workforce fell by almost 20 per cent and between 1841-51 three-quarters of a million jobs were lost. West Carbery's agricultural labour force fell by 84 per cent so that the countryside's ability to support a railway was less in the 1880s than it had been forty years earlier. With the effects of emigration over sixty years since then, the circumstances for railways have become even less favourable.* Some historians maintain that the effects of The Great Famine lasted until the Second War, i.e. they spanned the lifetime of the S&SR.

Civil unrest was common in West Carbery and only a few years before the WCT was promoted, the discontent stirred up by nationalist feelings bubbled up again. In consequence, whilst there might be some who would welcome railways which opened the way to new markets for fish or cattle (for instance) there were others who could only see them as the means of imposing law and order; while they had become familiar with gun-boats in Schull Harbour, the military might be dispatched from Cork city by rail in far less time. During the 1880-81 riots by The Land League as a railway westwards from Skibbereen was being contemplated, there was civil commotion in Skibbereen, Ballydehob and Schull. Whether measures to quell it came from London, Dublin or Cork, it did not seem to be a favourable climate for railway-building . . . and with it further restrictions, came added military and, even for the law-abiding, additional taxation to pay for it.†

The main line railways penetrated the South and West very slowly; a reminder of some dates will be helpful:

Dublin to Cork	1849
Dublin to Galway	1851
Waterford to Limerick	1854

South and west of Cork city a line to Bandon was opened in 1851 (an early example of local enterprise) but there it rested. The effects of the recent potato blight were apparent and the larger towns of the county already served, and likely to be served were suffering

---

* The effects of The Great Famine on railway construction were to halt the building of the Waterford & Limerick Railway where labourers were paid in food rather than money. 'A great many men were employed on useless roads which ran nowhere'. The Cork & Bandon Railway benefited from loans made in 1849 to aid construction and mitigate famine. [See Conroy.]
† See MIZEN JOURNAL No. 4 p. 37.

typhus and cholera in consequence. The intermediate country became depopulated as starving people left their homes and flocked to the workhouses; many emigrated and through such events the rural population was halved. Those anxious for railway extension were demoralised and even when the Westminster Parliament brought in legislation to encourage construction, parts of Munster were unable to forward railway or tramway building even though it was obvious such would hasten recovery of afflicted districts.

We must pass on to the early 1880s; the contrary opinions as to their cost and value were ventilated in West Cork. The result on balance would be negative and tramway schemes for and about Skibbereen had to be halved. The few big landowners were unenthusiastic. It would disturb the deer on their estates and interfere with hunting; often living a lonely and isolated existence, the civilised nature of life within their demesne was in utter contrast to conditions without. A railway might be the outrider to ruffle a settled existence and one local landowner moved further deer into his park to make his point.

The Protestant Farmers were concerned about costs but they were enthusiastic for a railway. The period 1865-76 had been one of prosperity for most Cork farmers and the better spirit still lingered on. Tradesmen - almost entirely Protestant - would support anything to assist the backward state of West Cork; it would be gain to them. Opinions ranged from apprehension for the unknown and optimism for the hear-say. The Rt Revd Jagoe, a former Bishop of Bermuda who had retired to Schull, his birthplace, had become the Rector of the Parish. On learning of my interest in the railway he commented, 'People had good reason to be fearful. It was time of light railways and heavy sentences'.

The drawbacks of having no railway are reflected by an account of the pre-1880s: 'To journey 30-40 miles eastwards from Schull entailed a chaise and two horses'. Horses' tails were clipped in preparation for the journey. Experiencing similar privations through a land submerged in a 'deep-rooted famine mentality', where 'the spirit of the area was broken' and Fenian activity was never far below the surface, were barriers which had to be overcome in this inhospitable region. But the opposition of large landowners was weakening; some were leaving the country allowing tenants to buy. None could have foreseen that following the successful defeat of all that mitigated against the creation of a railway between Schull and Skibbereen, a decade of very low incomes from farming would occur, marked by a high emigration rate. This unhappy state would be unhelpful to the struggling tramway enterprise.

The tramway was intended to serve three centres of population, Skibbereen, Ballydehob and Schull, though the later title of the line implied that Schull was the senior. The explanation lay in the desire of Schull to be connected with Skibbereen, thence Cork city and beyond. English markets could be found for cattle, fish and butter. These communities contained buildings whose importance was reflected by the size of the Roman Catholic church, Military or Police Barracks, Workhouse, Mills, Warehouses, the National School and perhaps a recent incomer, the Railway Station.

Something about these three places which were the nerve-centres of the railway will be helpful:

Skibbereen 'The little boat harbour'- formerly Skubbareen or New Stapleton. The town rose from village status after the sacking of the nearby harbour of Baltimore by Algerian pirates in 1631. The Great Famine reduced the population from 4,429 to 3,700. Its business revolved around its wool and linen trades but before these developed the town's position was described as 'in a wild unenclosed part of Co. Cork'. There was a twice-weekly market, a trade in milk and fish, dealings in coal imported by water, and a growing business in butter*.

The town stood on the lowest point at which the Ilen River could crossed; there are two bridges. The upper was of cast-iron girders and adjacent to the town; it was built in 1877 and replaced in modern materials in 1963. The lower is a five-arched stone bridge, 'The New Bridge' which leads into Bridge Street on the west side of the town. When the main line railway reached Skibbereen, it terminated at the riverside close by the cast-iron bridge. When the WCT was built, it passed by the end of the New Bridge; the river is tidal almost to this point.

Transport by water, as mentioned earlier, was the historic means of movement along the county's coasts. It was so cheap and efficient that the railway could only compete in terms of speed. A glimpse at Skibbereen's links with the sea is timely.

From earliest times the town's commerce depended on its links with the sea; waterborne craft such as small boats from the offshore islands, or from Schull or Goleen for instance, which brought livestock to the market, tied up at the Long Quay (or Levis's Quay) by the Saw Mills at the junction of the Ilen River and the small Caol Stream. Lighters, into which cargoes had been loaded from sea-going ships at Old Quay, were man-handled up river to the larger Steam Mills Quay, at the down-stream and south side of the Ilen Street bridge, for it was impossible to bring ships of over 200 tons burden (such as those which carried coal or maize) due to the shallow river.

Furthest into the town was the North Street Quay (the site of the Library today) where Cape Clear Island boats would unload salted fish destined for Cork city. When the advent of a railway to serve the town first became a possibility, it was hoped it would terminate here but in the event, shortage of money determined a less-central terminus.

With coming of the Ilen Valley Railway in 1877 the stage and mail coach era ended, and many new houses were built in this quarter of the town; by the end of the century three independent railways were based on the station. It was many years later however, that the 'port' of Skibbereen became no more, and traces lingered until the Second World War. Old Court still repairs fishing vessels and provides facilities for pleasure craft.

Last century the town boasted a brewery, a distillery, an iron-foundry, ship-building yard and rope-walk - all now but a memory but sufficient then to attract the railway to the town.

When things seemed as if they could not worsen, the privations of the Second War upon Skibbereen showed evidence enough; former shops were becoming private houses and trade prospects were dismal. The main line from Cork into the town was the subject of closure rumours in 1947 and the S&SR's anticipated demise had become a fact, the district was suffering economic depression which was to last well into the next decade. Railways in the area had developed in expectation of growth but as the population decreased by 36 per cent in the period 1911-1951 and emigration continued unchecked, decline affected Schull and Ballydehob equally. Skibbereen had twice the population in 1830 as in 1950; road transport now made the railway quite uneconomic. As one resident said of the town, 'It is a good place in which to commit suicide'. Haughton writes: 'It is clear that the present transport position is unsatisfactory and the lack of any

---

* Irish towns might boast both a Market and a Fair, held on recognised days at calendar-linked intervals. Latterly, most markets were held in place allocated for the purpose. Fairs were usually held in squares or streets according to long custom. Up to c. 1920, Markets gave the railways considerable traffic and their importance to the WCT was vital. Fairs were more informal and localised and were also occasions when men were hired for harvest. Their effect on railway business was small.

'Levis' Quay' off the main street, Skibbereen, with surrounding warehouses and yards.
J.I.C. Boyd

Derelict 19th Century housing, Skibbereen. *J.I.C. Boyd*

town development around the station is indicative of the ineffectiveness of the railway as a transport medium'.*

So much for Skibbereen, an important place for the birth of Irish independence. Although it has an outward likeness to some West Wales towns, it must be seen in its native circumstance by unfamiliar English eyes, (and by the railway historian) as a meeting place of three railway companies whose development was thwarted by a combination of fishing grounds which moved away, famine which impoverished the countryside, emigration which took away the people and civil unrest which caused periods of stagnation . . . and finally, road transport.

So westwards to the-then village of *Ballydehob, 'The Estuary of the Ford of Two Rivers'*, and the focal point of a widespread rural area.† Historically, the discontent of the local people, the appalling poverty and civil unrest were no less than elsewhere - in fact the community acquired a fame unequalled in the-then British Isles and the reputation of acquiring a police force six years before London had the same.# (This was in consequence of Lord Audley working the local mines, then the principal source of employment, in the early 1820s; rumour had gone about that 'a mining machine driven by steam' had been installed and would do away with many employees. Fearing a Luddite-type disturbance Audley sent for the 'Peelers' in 1823 to quell any trouble.)

The land around Ballydehob is of mixed quality; the higher ground contains much thin soil and rock predominates among the gorse and heather. The village nestles at the foot of a shallow valley where the Rivers Bawnaknockane and Rathruane have an outlet to the sea, giving the settlement the advantage of a tidal quay suitable for small boats, well protected from the weather.

Ballydehob has two faces, seaward towards Roaring Water Bay (though the presence of the island Illaunroe hides the Bay from the village), and landward towards the hills where the lower slopes fed cattle which were a considerable traffic to the S&SR. The off-shore islands were served by boats which berthed at the quay. Rail-borne traffic connected thereto was small, though some coal went out: the railway station and quay were not advantageously placed.

Some lime-based sand and kelp from the sea-bed was brought in by 'sand-boats' for spreading on the land, but declined by 1930. The practice was revived by using chemical fertilisers during the Second World War and for a period the railway carried it in bags for hinterland distribution from Ballydehob station. The railway also carried gravel from the beaches of some islands post-World War I which was used for making concrete and house building; the S&SR was the means of transport and a further, logical means for the initial tarring and gravelling of the Schull-Skibbereen road.

On the evidence of the number of wagons provided at the station on Market Days, cattle and pigs were landed from the islands and driven from the quay to the station, ultimately to be loaded with mainland beasts *en route* for Skibbereen. Depopulation of the islands and modern farming techniques extinguished this practice.

Despite the cost and time for handling, in former times schooners would anchor down river and transfer cargoes into lighters which unloaded on the quay. All life's essentials

---

* THE TOWN OF SKIBBEREEN (J.P. Haughton) *c.* 1951.
† By Irish standards it is more than a village; in Smith's HISTORY OF CORK (1749) it receives no mention and may not have existed, but suffice that by 1800 a community known as Swanton's Town existed here. Lewis's DICTIONARY of 1837 states there were 100 houses and the 'new road' from Skibbereen to Rock Island passed through it.
# See MIZEN JOURNAL No. 1 (1993) p. 58.

Ballydehob main street looking west. *Circa* 1898　　　　　*Lawrence Collection*

Main Street, Schull, at the end of the 19th Century, looking east towards the R.C. Church and railway station.
Lawrence Collection

formerly arrived like this - inkwells, sacks of flour, bricks, paraffin . . . Small (steam) coasters could use the quay where a secure and dedicated portion held coal and diesel fuel.

Tradition has it that the S&SR would convey coal which had been landed here from lighters; coal carriers from South Wales ports with Forest of Dean cargoes made regular calls, while other cargoes arrived by weekly steamer service from Cork city. More reliable is the information that this trade had ceased by 1930.

The evidence of mining around Ballydehob may still be seen (1999) but it is unlikely the mines used the railway at all for most of their output left by sea.

So westward to the S&SR's westerly terminus, *Schull (or Skull as frequently used) 'St. Mary of the Schools: Sancta Maria de Scholia'*. In 1749 Smith found it a small and insignificant village; Lewis in 1839 records 79 houses and 385 inhabitants. Small it may have been but it was in the forefront of two considerable anti-tithe demonstrations involving over 20,000 peasants from mainland and islands in June and July 1832 - how many years would pass after The Great Famine before such a multitude could be assembled again?

The 1871 Census reveals how the Famine had reduced the number of houses:

	1841	1851	1861	1871
Ballydehob Townland	128	111	103	115
Schull Townland	104	90	110	109

The place grew up situate at the north-west corner of Schull Bay where the water is deep enough to take larger ships. Below the village is a stone pier which has been enlarged from time to time and onto which the Extension Railway was led. Schull was one of the most important fishing harbours in West Cork in the days when mackerel were abundant; the fishing fleet worked on the basis of one day at sea and one in harbour. Before the Railway Extension was built, ships would deliver empty barrels to be stacked on the pier and foreshore before the arrival of the fishing fleet. The fish would be gutted on trestle tables laid out on the pier; they were then packed in ice or salt inside the barrels and the lid secured. Local women were employed for this work, but Donegal or Scottish girls would also be engaged. In earliest times the loaded barrels left by sea but with a rail access to the pier, the S&SR captured most of the business, the objective being that the catch reached the larger towns for each Friday morning (formerly a meat-less day in Roman Catholic households). Herring and mackerel predominated.

As with Ballydehob, Schull is the centre for a large farming area and the railway carried beasts of all kinds, many having been driven to the station from further west, the day before transit.

Chapter Two
The Main Line Railway reaches Skibbereen

Skibbereen was largest and most important town in West Cork in the early 19th Century ... and before that. As with the English West Country which looked to Bristol as its nearest centre for greater-England so did West Cork look to Cork city as its nearest link with greater-Ireland; so it was from Cork city that the standard-gauge railway stemmed towards West Cork.

Cork city is physically divided, west to east, by the River Lee. This waterway prevented a north-south railway connection over the river until 1st January, 1912 when the Cork City Railways link line was opened. From the river's north bank the GREAT SOUTHERN & WESTERN RAILWAY had connected the outskirts of Cork to Dublin since 1849 (but not until 1855 into the city of Cork itself), and to Queenstown (now Cobh) since 1868. On the south bank the CORK & BANDON RAILWAY linked its starting point on Albert Quay with Bandon in 1851 and could claim to be the city's first standard-gauge railway; in fact construction was begun at the Bandon end in 1845, but the work was lengthy owing to a considerable tunnel and a massive viaduct. The progression of the railway westwards from Bandon (where at first there was no end-on connection between the two railways, facilitated later by the building of the West Cork Junction line) towards Skibbereen was as follows:

Cork & Bandon Railway 20 miles.	Inc. 21st July, 1845	Opened December, 1851
Cork & Kinsale Junction Railway 10 miles.	Inc. 19th April, 1859	Opened 27th June, 1863
West Cork Railway 17¾ miles. Bandon - Dunmanway Ilen Valley Railway 30th July, 1874 by name change of *Dunmanway & Skibbereen Railway*. 16m.	Inc. 28th August, 1860	Opened to Dunmanway 6th January, 1866 Opened to Skibbereen 21st July, 1877

The Ilen Valley system was worked by the Cork & Bandon Railway from the start and retained nominal independence until 1909 but the Cork & Kinsale Railway and West Cork Railway were absorbed by the C&BR on 1st January, 1880. The WCR was in Chancery almost from the beginning.

An Act, 35-36 Vict. cap. 147 of 25th July, 1872, to create the English-promoted Dunmanway & Skibbereen Railway, came about thus-wise: by 1870 the West Cork and the C&BR were at odds over the authorised route of 1866 to extend the WCR from Dunmanway towards Skibbereen. An isolated length of about 4½ m. had been partly built near Skibbereen but the WCR finances being at rock bottom, they asked the C&BR to contribute to the extension but the C&BR refused. Finance for the D&SR was cobbled together with the usual help of a loan from the Irish Commissioners of Public Works, a Baronial Guarantee and a loan from the BoT. (It is impossible to contemplate any railway in West Cork without the backing of English funding ..!) William Barrington of Limerick was the Engineer.* On 30th July, 1874 the name was changed to The Ilen Valley Railway Co. (the valley of the Ilen River from Drimoleague to Skibbereen). Early

---
* For the complex strife, management and financing of the C&BR with its adjacent systems, see IRISH RAILWAY RECORD SOCIETY JOURNAL Vol. 13 No. 72 p. 42-43 & No. 75 p. 200.

THE MAIN LINE RAILWAY REACHES SKIBBEREEN

in 1875 construction was begun by Nixon & Gordon and by contract was due to be finished by early 1876. A further hiccough appeared when the WCR and C&BR dispute over the latter's Bandon station charges came to a head and the former built its own station west of St Patrick's Church (RC), some height above the C&BR terminus. This was almost a mile west of the recently-built West Cork Junction; here there was a single trans-shipment platform with no cover from the weather.*

Although outside the exact title of this history, the calamities which befell the aspirations of uninformed English promoters of undertakings in south-west Co. Cork fall under the umbrella of that dismissive saying by the English, 'How typically Irish'. The position was made more ridiculous by having Governmental departments involved on both sides of the Irish Sea whilst these decision-making bodies clearly had scant idea of the poor nature of the country the further westward as a railway progressed. Whilst the promise of agricultural, livestock and fish traffic beckoned, passenger traffic would be limited. What importance was placed on law and order, the carriage of police and the military? As for those with cash to spare who ill-judged these schemes and lost most of it . . .

We return to the subject of the IVR; the Company had no intention of working the line itself and matter had to come before the Railway Commissioners so that at outset, the WCR did the work. When at last the line reached Skibbereen in 1877 a passenger bound for Cork would pass over the rails of three companies in 61 miles. Whilst this was not 'typically Irish' (there were similar situations in England) one might think that the promoters of a tramway from Skibbereen to Schull would have heeded the problems experienced in bringing the 'main line' to Skibbereen and learned something therefrom. Instead, they were to fall into a trap much deeper than those which had gone before.

Skibbereen was so near yet so far . . . another contractor was obtained and battled with the weather so that on 21st July, 1877 a ceremonial train from Cork was run. After 17 years of waiting, Revd Fr Davis said in a speech that it was a 'Blessed Day'. Public trains began on 23rd July.

It was well known that railway construction out of Bandon had begun at such an early date (1849) (and at such a provincial place) as relief work after the Famine; Skibbereen felt it would not be long before it too would know the benefit of the railway. But almost 30 years later Edith Somerville† noted in her diary the day of Public Opening: 'The arrival of the railway . . . created a sensation. All went up to Skib in honour of the opening of the railway. Great fun and speechifying - ate enormously. Hordes of people. An old man told Papa it was a beautiful vessel he had brought to Skibbereen'.

(The Ilen Valley Railway and the West Cork Railway were worked by the C&BR from 1st January, 1880.)#

For the whole of its life and for long after, these once separate companies in West Cork were known as the 'Cork & Bandon' although in 1880 they were given the status of a single undertaking, the Cork, Bandon & South Coast Railway.§

---

* See IRISH RAILWAY RECORD SOCIETY JOURNAL Vol. 14. No. 81 p. 43.
† Edith Somerville (1858-1949) of Castletownsend, a well-known novelist who wrote in conjunction with her cousin Violet Martin (1862-1915) of Ross, Co. Galway. It is written of them that their novels 'made an unequalled portrait of the collapse of Anglo-Ireland and the rise . . . of the new Irish middle class'. This is also the very period which spanned the life of the S&SR.
# IRISH RAILWAY RECORD SOCIETY JOURNAL Vol. 15 No. 97 p. 382.
§ IRISH RAILWAY RECORD SOCIETY JOURNAL Vol. 15 No. 94 p. 209 and Vol. 15 No. 95 p. 288 (there is but slight reference to the S&SR).

ILEN VALLEY RAILWAY ; (formerly Dunmanway & Skibbereen Railway)
Incorporated 25th July, 1872 to connect Fanlobbus on the West Cork Railway with Abbeystrowry. Length 15¾ m. Baronies to contribute to financing and Commissioner of Public Works to make loans. Initial Directors:

Sir Henry Wrixon Beecher, Bart.
Henry Winthrop O'Donovan, Lissard, Skibbereen
John Warren Payne
Thomas H. Somerville
Daniel McCarthy Downing MP, Prospect House, Skibbereen

For the masses, the lumbering Long Car in its various forms could be seen in West Carbery until the 1890s. *Collection J.I.C. Boyd*

Chapter Three

In the Beginning
1860-1883

The origins of the S&SR lay in two Acts of 1860 and 1862 respectively, (The Tramways (Ireland) Act 23 & 24 Vict. cap. 152) and another of the same title (24 & 25 Vict. cap. 102) which allowed tramways to be built along public roads. In those times, only animal power was envisaged and a maximum speed of 6 mph was imposed and considered adequate. However, second thoughts prevailed and in 1871 mechanical power was sanctioned under another Act entitled The Tramways (Ireland) Amendment Act 34 & 35 Vict. cap. 114 .

There was another Act of the first title in 1881 but under yet a further Act of 1883 (46 & 47 Vict. cap. 43 section 7) all the previous Acts were embodied in it and speed was only restricted where the tramway was less than 30 ft from the centre of the road. In the 1888 Report of the Royal Commission on Irish Public Works, chaired by Sir James Allport, the 1883 Act came in for heavy criticism.

In the 1870s there had been 'talk' - and it was no more than that - of the usefulness of an 'ordinary railway' [sic] if such were to be constructed between Schull and Skibbereen, undoubtedly fostered by the approaching track as it crept westwards from Bandon. (In Cork city, by the way, there was then no physical rail connection with the main line to Dublin which terminated on the further side of the River Lee.) The spur to this incentive had been the incorporation in 1872 of the English-based Irish Tramways Co. Ltd* for the purpose of building a series of horse tramways in Co. Cork to 2 ft 9 in. gauge, a dimension recommended by C.E. Spooner, Engineer to the Festiniog Railway, linking the following:

Clonakilty-Rosscarbery
Schull-Crookhaven (with possible eastward extension to Skibbereen)
Bantry-Castletownbere via Glengariff & Adrigole
Bantry-Newmarket

The major portion of this concept was sanctioned by the Grand Jury of Co. Cork (i.e. County Council) on 22nd May, 1872 but nothing further materialised.

However, on 15th September, 1883 the WEST CORK EAGLE & CO. CORK ADVERTISER published a letter from 'John E. Sloane, late Chief Engineer, Irish Lights Dept., Clontarf, Dublin' suggesting a tramway be built from the existing standard gauge terminus at Skibbereen, westwards to Mizen Head (32 miles), with a branch therefrom northwards to Durrus Road station on the Bantry line. The writer recommends substantial track foundations and the use of 20 ton locomotives. Clearly his interest had been aroused by the first Tramways Act. Portions of the letter may be cited:

---

* This Company had its offices in London, and five London-based Directors. In 1872 it made application for six isolated tramway systems based on existing or intended railheads; only four of these were sanctioned by the Grand Jury. The entry in the Joint Stock Company returns states: 'Objects: Purchasing, laying down and working tramways in Ireland. Office: 6 Queen Victoria Street, Mansion House. EC. Incorporated: 5th March, 1872. Subscribers: Seven, taking one share each. Capital: £100,000 divided into 100,000 shares of £1 each.' (Further reading: GREAT BRITISH TRAMWAY NETWORKS (Bett & Gillham) [1957] p. 188, IRISH RAILWAY RECORD SOCIETY JOURNAL No. 6 p. 150 and THE CAVAN & LEITRIM RAILWAY (Patrick J. Flanaghan) [1966] p. 18 re The Tramways Capital Guarantee Co.)

... a few days ago a gentleman waited on me ... he had had dinner ... in London ... and some conversation on the new Tramways Act ... He had been directed to me as a person who could tell him something about Ireland ... What was my opinion as to tramways for developing the country?
I said that 'tramways' as we understood them, were useless for the people but as light narrow gauge railways they would be the salvation of the country ... the one I would start with would be THAT WHICH WOULD BRING AMERICA MANY HOURS NEARER TO US - A LINE FROM SKIBBEREEN TO MIZEN HEAD. Such a line would be of immense benefit to that vast tract of country almost unknown west of Goleen: it would be available to bring the American mails, passengers and merchandise - weekly - from Crookhaven ... long ago, in 1867, I addressed a letter to THE EAGLE advocating the advantage of the narrow gauge to West Carbery ... it could run alongside the present roads ...

The pre-occupation with the links to America was a natural outcome of immense emigration there during and after the Famine. There is the intriguing reference to the gentleman 'who waited upon' the writer: could this be d'Avigdor, he who ultimately built the Tramway?

As a result of the interest stirred up by the letter a number of local persons met to exchange ideas, *not* for line west of Skibbereen but to the east, serving Leap, Glandore, Union Hall, the slate quarry at Benduff and, if feasible, Rosscarbery. Most of these were little better than villages. John William Dorman, Civil Engineer to the Cork & Bandon Railway, was to make a feasibility survey. Among those supporting the enterprise were:

Thomas Downes	Solicitor & Land Agent	Skibbereen
James Swanton MA*	Merchant	East View, Glandore
G.H. Swanton		Skibbereen
Richard Carey	Manager, Munster & Leinster Bank	Skibbereen

Dorman lost no time: he advised that a line to Benduff Quarry 'should be left in abeyance' and an extension from there to Rosscarbery was unwise due to the heavy gradients and narrow road. (He may have heard about the dangerous underground conditions at Benduff which were to lead to a fatal accident and a period of closure later.) A public meeting was held in the Town Commissioners' Hall, Skibbereen on 20th October, 1883, when Dorman's report was read; Carey was in the Chair and there was a goodly gaggle of clergy from the parishes through which the line might pass. A total expense of £25,000 was envisaged, or *c.* £3,000 per mile for the 8 m. length. Annual expenditure was assessed:

Working & maintenance etc. @ 1s. 8d. per mile	£974
Secretarial, Engineer, Office etc.	£250
Interest on capital @ 4 per cent	£1,000

An annual credit of £144 was calculated if receipts were £2,080; this would be paid to the Baronies.

Several 'Protestant farmers' did not attend the meeting; they were attending the weekly Saturday cattle fair but their backing was expected. A further meeting was held in consequence, only to emphasise that the Rosscarbery scheme was impossible; even if the railway was but 3 ft gauge, the road was too narrow, so the assembly turned to the matter of a line westwards from Skibbereen to Schull.

---

* James Swanton MA JP. A member of 'a notable oasis of culture among a few in the town, The Literary & Scientific Society'. Owner of two stores, a timber yard etc.

IN THE BEGINNING 1860-1883

THE WEST CORK EAGLE & CO. CORK ADVERTISER reported on 27th October on the previously mentioned Skibbereen meeting of 20th October to discuss the eastern project. The article brings new characters onto the stage; special attention was given to a speech made by William Shaw MP in favour of the movement.* He revealed his 'large interest in the Benduff enterprise' but did not wish it to appear that a tramway was to be laid to suit his private interests, so 'Benduff was to be chopped off for the present . . . he and others interested would probably give substantial aid to the connecting branch later on . . .'

A fuller list of names attending is shown than previously disclosed, some additional ones being:

Revd David Fitzgerald, Parish Priest, Leap
Revd T. McCarthy RCA, Castlehaven
Revd John O'Leary CC, Skibbereen
Revd James O'Sullivan CC, Leap
Dr William Jennings MD TC
Cornelius McCarthy, Town Clerk and Secretary to the meeting.

John H. Levis TC
Dr David Hadden MD
Henry St John Wright
William Good TC
G.L. Vickery TC

James Swanton had issued a circular at his own expense recommending that steps be taken to build a tramway to Glandore and Dr Jennings, in proposing a motion to do so, said it was in their 'interest to make Skibbereen the centre of a network of tramways that would spring up, sooner or later, in that part of the country . . .'. James Swanton, who had personal connections both with Skibbereen and Glandore, said the traffic would develop to the extent . . .' that the Barony would have little or nothing to pay in the course of 3-4 years . . . but even if it did, it would be small on the valuation'. John Levis disagreed with him, saying they were 'in the dark on the ground of expense . . . surely they were not going to tax or pledge themselves in the dark'. But he was a lone dissenter.

Fortunately the newspaper article gave full coverage to Dorman's Report (read by the Chairman) for the first time. The principal points were:

---

* William Shaw, of Beaumont, Co. Cork had become Chairman of the Cork & Bandon Railway earlier the same year. The Cork & Bandon Railway had been incorporated in July 1845 for 20 m. of line between the two towns. It purchased the West Cork Railway of 1860, the Cork & Kinsale Railway of 1859 and the Ilen Valley Railway of 1874 (in the last case it acquired certain rights only) in July 1879; an extension to Bantry from Drimoleague was opened in July 1881. The West Cork Railway linked Bandon and Dunmanway. Length 18 m. The Ilen Valley Railway linked Dunmanway and Skibbereen. Length 16 m. (original title intended as Dunmanway & Skibbereen Railway). The combined systems were worked by the C&BR from 1st January, 1880 when it owned 60 miles of line. It terminated on the south side of the river in Cork city and was not then linked to the Great Southern & Western Railway on the north bank at Glanmire. Initially, the C&BR terminated at the east side of Bandon town. When the fledgling West Cork Railway opened, it was from a separate and small terminus on the south side of town, with no rail connection between the two. The offices of the C&BR were at the Albert Quay terminus in Cork and six of its ten Directors lived in the vicinity of Cork city. The offices of the Ilen Valley Railway which reached Skibbereen in 1877, were at 15, Lapp's Quay, Cork city. In 1884 Shaw was a Director (but not Chairman). Shaw was an important character in favour of the project. Born in Moy, Co. Tyrone in 1823, son of Samuel Shaw a Congregational Minister, educated at Trinity College, Dublin. Became Minister of George Street Independent Church, Cork 1846-50. MP for Bandon 1868-74; for Co. Cork 1874-85. Served on several commissions and parties having Irish interests. Nick-named 'Sensible Shaw'. Founded The Munster Bank, Cork in 1864 which stopped payment in 1885. Shaw declared bankrupt in 1886; died at Lislee, Enniskerry, Co. Wicklow 1895.

1) The Mail Coach Road between Skibbereen and Leap was admirably suited to a tramway, and there would be no difficulty in extending from Leap to Glandore.
2) At Skibbereen the tramway terminus would be on the east bank of the Ilen, nearly opposite the National School.
3) From the terminus a branch would cross the Ilen on a 60 ft span bridge to connect with the C&BR.
4) Eastwards from the terminus the tramway would use the public road all the way to Leap except at Derryleagh and Brade to avoid gradients of 1 in 25 and 1 in 30 and ease them to 1 in 40 (permission would have to be obtained from the owners of Brade and Myross Estates to do this). So to Leap.
5) The line to Glandore would be bridged over the stream opposite the Mill, cross over Leap Quay where there would be sidings, so terminating at Glandore.

So far as can be gleaned, Union Hall was not to be served.

As already stated, it was felt a larger public meeting should debate the issue and it was resolved to hold another the next Thursday, 25th October as there was unspoken concern for the absentees who might not give their consent unless they knew what the taxation would be. Shaw made a comment in support of this view, warning that 'there were only a couple of gentlemen present and if they were to pass anything here in the absence of farmers and others interested, deliberately and for the furtherance of private ends, it would be highly dishonourable'. (Hear, Hear). Shaw was at pains to preface his remarks by pointing out that he was not attending the meeting in his capacity as Chairman of the C&BR.

It was explained to those present that the matter would now go before the Grand Jury which would have to bear the brunt of any opposition which a ratepayer wished to make. After that, it would go before the Privy Council; if an appeal was made against it the matter would go before a Judge at the Assizes . . . and might even go before a Committee of the House of Commons. Shaw was determined that everyone present understood there were numerous tribunals to face before the matter reached reality.

Continuing his speech, Shaw was convinced the district would support the measure for a cost of £24,000, '. . . that is to say, the charge would be £1,000 per year. Supposing it paid us nothing but working expenses then, according to the Act, the ratepayers would then only pay half of the £1,000 as the Treasury would pay the rest'. (He continued with a degree of mockery re knocking at the door of the Treasury.) 'Skibbereen is the metropolis of the west . . . a great many business houses in it . . . rely on the support of the C&BR'. There was a good Pig Fair in Rosscarbery 'and they would draw them to the tramway'. He saw boys dragging them from Clonakilty; they must be injured as 'the dragging they received must be enough to drag the life out of them (laughter) but if they were brought to the tramway and so pleasantly carried, the pigs would enjoy coming to be killed' (laughter).

Eventually there was a resolution that a Committee be formed to investigate the matter further, 'watch proceedings and collect subscriptions'; the newspaper said 'During the reading of the resolution the reverend gentleman was repeatedly interrupted by a tipsy-looking person who sat near him, and made use of such discourteous remarks that he only became silent when some parties threatened to throw him out.'

Summarising the event, it must have been a lively one and the clergy had much to say about the movement of fish '. . . if the railway was built to x then the fish would move to y, and vice versa'.

The newspaper had it all, far more than can be detailed here!

A few days later another letter was printed in the same paper: it was from St John S. Broderick, 'a non-engineer' of Cork. 'The rail is what Clonakilty, Skibbereen and Bantry Bay require . . . by establishing baronial tramways on the unused side of public roads, in charge of County Surveyor, magistrates and ratepayers of the district . . . tramways would be regular and most profitable feeders to the trunk line . . . would bring a large traffic in coral sand for manure'.

Once again it is the same paper of 3rd November which keeps its readers to the fore by its editorial:

The Tramway Act in West Cork

A short time ago we referred to the new Tramway Act, with the view of directing public attention to the very important and valuable work that can be carried out under the provisions of this useful measure, being as it is, one of the most desirable Acts of Parliament passed for many years towards developing the various but neglected resources of this country, should it be properly applied and energetically put in force. As Mr William Shaw MP, very tritely remarked at a recent meeting, it can turned into either a blessing or a curse and, by the way, no better guarantee of the utility and excellence of such an enactment could be had than that it should have as a champion a man of such great practical capabilities, surpassing sagacity, and solid common sense as Mr Shaw is deservedly and conspicuously remarkable for. He formed a flattering estimate of the commercial value of Skibbereen and district, and entertained no doubt as to the desirability of introducing a tramway as feeder to the main artery. West Cork, so to speak, revels in minerals of every kind, with its mines and quarries and fisheries in all directions and one of the great drawbacks from which the country has suffered grievously is the absence of light railways, a sorely felt want that can now by energy, spirit, and a small measure of self-sacrifice be effectually supplied. Glandore, Leap and Union Hall, we are pleased to see, are being well brought to the front and the advantages certainly to accrue are many and valuable. Agricultural products would find a readier and more profitable market by means of a tramway, a large tourist traffic would be certain to spring up, and in regards to the transit of slate and other kinds of merchandise there is on every side a vast body of evidence, both as to the necessity and usefulness of tramway extension. Skull too, we understand, is rising equal to the occasion and there is a similarly strong opinion entertained by men most competent to judge as to the facility of establishing a line and the benefits certain to arise from the acquisition of the tram boon. The region of Ballydehob and the district around it is in the centre of the copper mines and besides which is a rich agricultural section of the country with as growing importance in the matter of commerce while Skull, equally so, has a large fish trade to utilise. It is then earnestly to be hoped that an energetic and earnest action will be taken to bring into operation so well-intentioned and beneficial a piece of legislation.

We are glad to be informed, just as we go to press, that the Cork & Bandon Railway have given a handsome subscription towards preliminary expenses, and shares are being taken extensively in the project. We would advise those who wish to help, to do so at once.

As a nice example of flowery Victorian journalism, and scarce-concealed backing, the article could hardly be bettered.

To seek support for this further idea a meeting was held in Ballydehob on 23rd November, 1883, the Parish Priest of Schull, Father Murphy, taking the chair. Also present again were Thomas Downes, the Swantons, Sweetnam and Edward Roycroft. In the discussion that followed it was disclosed that Leahy, the existing contractor for the Mail Car, suffered criticism for the shortcomings of its service but offered an opinion that such a tramway would be heavily trafficked. The Chairman waxed enthusiastically for such an undertaking; he thought the tramway would pay its way, the Company would recoup its shareholders and, carried away in the heat of the moment, recommended that hoteliers should extend their premises without delay!

Despite the cold water which had been thrown on the full eastern project, Glandore - an important fishing port - retained its popularity as an objective and the money for an eastern section was soon promised. For a western section to Schull, the capital required was £57,000 in 5 per cent Baronially Guaranteed Shares (which was contrary to an estimate given by the Public Works Commissioners, namely £61,000). Accounts would have to be kept separate for each section.

On 7th December, 1883 the West Carbery Tramways & Light Railways Co. Ltd was registered under the Companies Act 1862 as a company limited by shares to construct tramways, its place of business to be Skibbereen, Co. Cork. The nominal capital was £90,000 and nine subscribers took 90 shares of £1 each.* Two schemes were projected, entitled:

1) Schull & Skibbereen Tramways & Light Railways.
2) Skibbereen, Glandore & Union Hall Tramways & Light Railways.

The Directors being: John Limrick JP (occasionally spelled Limerick), Dr John S. Levis TCD, Richard Carey, John W. Johnstone [Engineer, West Cork Rly.]: to these were added later Dean Reeves, Father Murphy [Parish Priest, Schull], Captain A. Morgan and others.† Secretary was E.H. Dorman# who held a similar position on the West Cork Railway while Thomas Downes was Solicitor. The personal links with the Cork & Bandon Railway should be noted; it was the Tramway's intention and supposition that their line would be worked by that Railway. Not so.

It was next necessary to lodge the Plans and Sections before 25th December, 1883 with the Secretary of the Grand Juries of both West and East Carbery, together with an Application for Presentments which, if successful, would authorise a Baronial Guarantee: haste was required in order to ensure the Application appeared at the Spring Assizes, 1884. Should the Grand Juries approve, then under the 1883 Act the Baronies involved or parts of the said Baronies (such to be determined by the Grand Juries) would be responsible for the payment of up to 5 per cent dividend annually on that portion of the £57,000 Capital as was paid-up. Baronies, or portions of same involved, were known as Guaranteeing Areas. The arrangement whereby local government could contribute towards tramways or railways (for instance) had been made possible by the Relief & Distress Amendment Act of 1880.

Not until that point was reached could the promoting body make application to the (British) Government i.e. the Parliament at Westminster, through the office of the Lord Lieutenant in Dublin, (he being the representative of the Queen), for an Order in Council which would authorise construction. At this stage, the Grand Juries had the option to appoint a number of Directors.

An attractive feature of the Act was that so long as the undertaking was maintained and operating, the (British) Treasury would repay the Grand Juries half the sum they had paid out under the guaranteed dividend, provided that no more than 2 per cent or the Capital was thereby paid, and that the amount did not exceed more than £40,000 in one year.

---

* The Company was incorporated in Dublin and in the same year 106 companies were incorporated, 68 of which were tramway companies!
† See p. 257 for list of ultimate West Carbery Tramways Directors.
# Brother of J.W. Dorman CE, member of Inst. CE (Ireland).

The Grand Juries would have to be responsible for meeting working deficits, should these occur - which would mean in practice that the *extra charges would be passed on to ratepayers*. And this was not all, for *if losses continued for two years, the Grand Juries might find themselves in possession of the undertaking and not only to meet its costs, but with the responsibility of working and maintaining the system*. In this wise also, ratepayers would be funding the losses and Juries seeking expertise in railway management, etc.

Although the matter of raising sufficient finance was the least of its troubles (many saw the 'guaranteed' Government-backed status of the promotion as an excellent form of security in an age not bedevilled by inflation), the opposition came mainly from ratepayers who saw themselves in a 'can't win' situation, ably headed by officials who, with experience, had found Treasury payment to be embarrassingly tardy. Even after the Schull-Skibbereen section of the scheme had been successfully launched, the eastward proposal to Union Hall and Glandore was dogged by meetings attended by unconvinced farmers who voiced their doubts by interrupting and delaying the business on hand. They had reason for doing so when it became common knowledge that any Treasury benefaction would not become due *until the line was operating* . . . and even then, might not be paid when expected!

The necessary Plans & Sections were deposited before the Secretary of the County Cork Grand Jury (a body which, if the newspapers are any reflection, was held in the lowest esteem by the residents of the county) before the vital date of 25th December; further matter had to be placed before the Lord Lieutenant in Dublin by 8th January, 1884. But on 31st December, a certain Mr Daly gave notice that he would oppose any Baronial Guarantees being sought for either section of the tramway!

The WEST CORK EAGLE* of 15th March, 1884 showed that fervour in Leap was undiminished, even on a Sunday; under the title TRAMWAY EXTENSION IN WEST CORK it detailed a meeting held 'immediately after Divine Service' in Leap. Father Fitzgerald - now in attendance on more earthly matters - was in the Chair. It was resolved thereat to approve the project for the eastern section, to entertain a strong protest against the action of certain parties who endeavoured to mislead . . . 'and impede passing of this most necessary . . . undertaking.'

The meeting was informed that opposition arose almost entirely by the spread of erroneous information regarding the probable amount of the guarantee. 'Mackerel fishing would make it self-supporting from the start even if earnings were nil for the rest of the year'. Clearly the backing of clergy was encouraging a favourable view. The County Cork Surveyor gladdened those present by announcing that the feeble wooden bridge over Leap Harbour and which made a junction with the Leap-Glandore road along which the tramway would be laid, was about to be replaced 'by an iron one'.†

---

* A newspaper considered by many 'as an unchanging advocate for 'Home Rule' and its owner 'Mr F.P.E. Potter as a large employer and ratepayer'.
† Even in 1998 this road reveals its origins as one constructed for Famine Relief in the late 1840s. It is narrow and winding due to its restricted site beside the river. The historic road into Glandore came from the east - useless for the rapid carriage of fish catches to Skibbereen station.

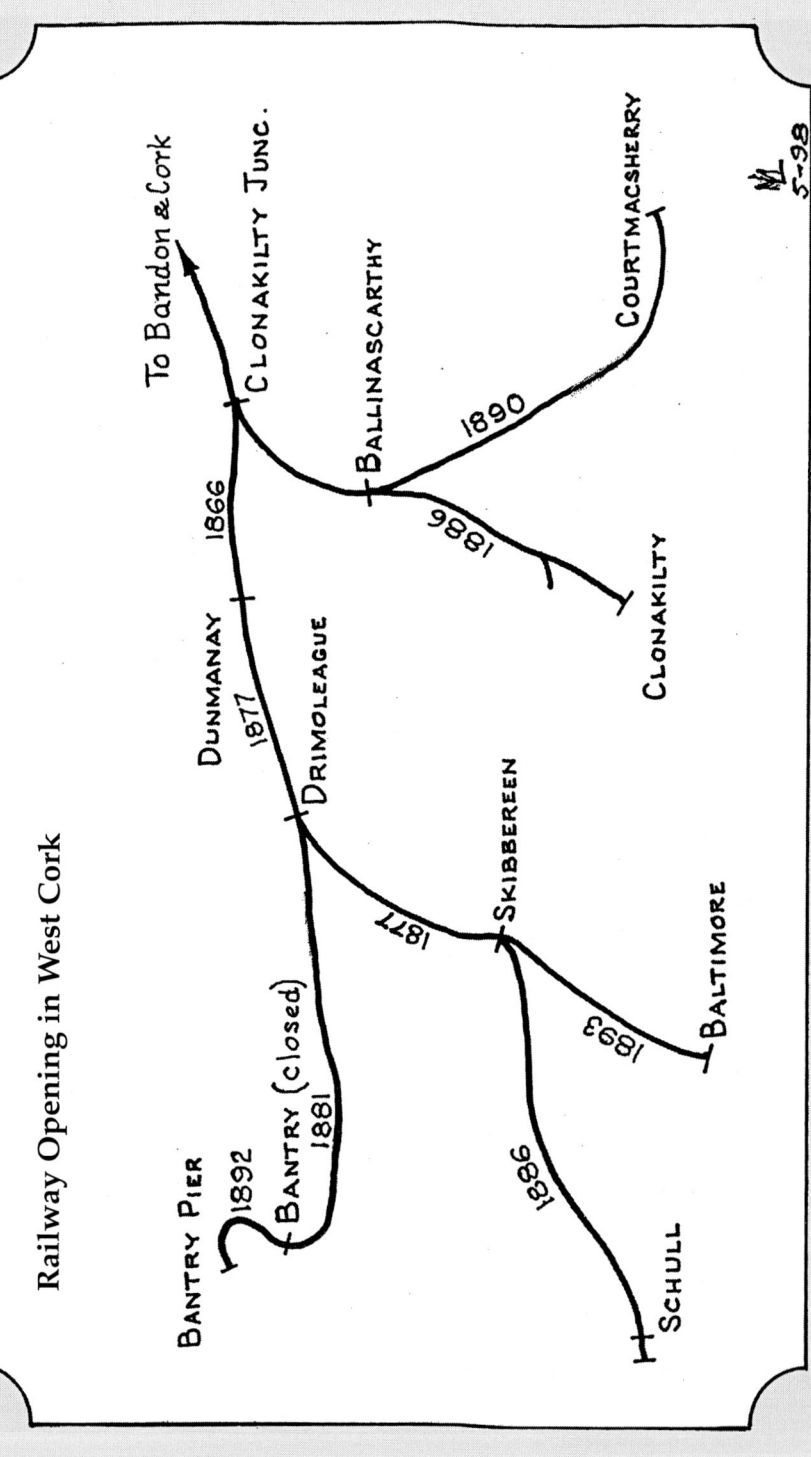

Chapter Four
A Pattern of Progress
1884-1885

The Tramway envisaged would actually consist of two nominal undertakings branching to west and east from Skibbereen station, the terminus of the Ilen Valley Railway (see p. 28). With Skibbereen as their common interchange point, the line to Schull passed through West Carbery and that to Leap, etc. through East Carbery - Carbery being frequently spelled Carberry in those times.

The Commissioners of Public Works in Ireland - with office in Dublin - had appointed H.U. Townsend, a civil engineer, to make enquiry on the scheme, as they were required to do under the provisions of the Tramways Acts. Townsend's job was to report 'on the merits of the undertaking from an engineering point of view . . . and that it can be efficiently constructed and worked in accordance with the Plans & Sections deposited with us'. Any modifications - along with the manner suggested - to be incorporated in the Report.

It will be noted that Townsend's first task was to hold an enquiry in Skibbereen Courthouse on 15th February and at that there was no *engineering objection*.

The Report was dated 7th March, 1884 and endorsed to provide for the protection of navigation and to save the right of the Crown in any tidal lands with which the Tramway might interfere. In due course the Tramways Co., through its solicitor Thomas Downes was obliged to amend the Notice of Application to the Lord Lieutenant in Dublin to read; '. . . to authorise . . . a Tramway . . . commencing in the Townland of Meen Vane adjacent . . . to Schull . . . and terminating in the Townland of Marsh in the Township of Skibbereen . . . three islands in the Ballydehob River . . . belonging to the Commissioners of Woods & Forests . . . so as to protect them'. Although the Tramway was to pass over the river by viaduct at Ballydehob and it would be difficult for it *not* to interfere with navigation, etc., at least the promoters were spared the necessity of providing an opening span . . !

Townsend's work merits its reproduction in full:

Having held an inquiry at the Courthouse, Skibbereen, on the 15th February, 1884, at which no person appeared to raise any engineering objection, and subsequently, accompanied by an assistant of the promoters' Engineers, having inspected the route proposed to be followed by the Skull and Skibbereen Tramway and Light Railway, I have the honour to submit the following report:

By this (a single) line, three feet gauge, the town and harbour of Skull, and the large district around and beyond will have a steam connection with the Ilen Valley Railway (Cork and Bandon) at Skibbereen. The total length is 14 miles 6 furlongs and 9.10 chains. The terminus at Skibbereen is close beside the terminal railway station, and is proposed to be the common terminus of this and the proposed Glandore Tramway. The terminus at Skull is at the Coast Guard Station, in close proximity to the sea, and within a ¼ mile of the town.

It is noted on the plans, 'where this railway is to be laid along the public road the said road shall nowhere be narrowed to a greater extent than will leave a clear width of eighteen feet between the railway and the opposite side of the road'. To avoid the very steep gradients on the public road (in parts one in twelve) three diversions are proposed of a total length of 3 miles 6 furlongs and 1 chain, of Light Railway, the longest of which crosses the estuary below the village of Ballydehob.

There are in all twenty-six crossings of public roads on the level, for each of which a gatekeeper's house is provided. Three public roads are to be crossed by bridges over.

The bridge at six furlongs, which it is proposed to run over by a three feet widening, is not capable of bearing the maximum load. The bridge at 11 miles 4 furlongs is also incapable. The following bridges are adequate, viz., at 2 miles 6 furlongs. 'Meen Bridge' at 8 miles 7 furlongs 5 - one at 13 miles 4 furlongs. 'Keel Bridge' [or Pig's bridge: (Author)] at 11 miles 2 furlongs, is only 17 feet 10 inches wide, and a new bridge outside parapet is desirable.

The flagged culverts will require to be rebuilt for at least formation width of tramway, eleven feet.

The steepest gradient is one in thirty, and the ruling gradient one in thirty.

The sharpest curve has a radius of 2½ chains, and occurs in twelve places, curves of 3 chains radius in eleven.

The country through which the diversions are carried is of a very rugged character, and presents many engineering difficulties, which appear to be skilfully met, except in the matter of curves.

An improvement in this respect is desirable, but would involve much expense.

The following is the description of permanent way furnished by the Promoters' Engineers:

The permanent way will consist of forty-five pounds per yard steel flange-rails, thirty feet long, laid on red wood Baltic creosoted sleepers, six feet long, eight inches wide, four inches thick, to which they will be fastened, usually by one five eight inch fang at each end, and eighteen dog-spikes, except on steep gradients on the 'straight' where two intermediate fangs will be used. On sharp curves there will be no fang-bolts used, but grooved soleplates to take the flange of the rail, with a clip at each side secured to the sleepers by fang-bolts, will be as follows:

Curves of over 10 chains radius will have two soleplates and clips, with sixteen dog-spikes; from 4 to 10 chains radius will have three soleplates and clips, with fourteen dog-spikes; curves under 4 chains radius will have four soleplates and clips, with twelve dog-spikes to each length of rail.

The ballast will be 10 feet wide at base, and 8 feet at level of sleeper, being 2 feet deep from top of rail, the lower portion being usually composed of shingle, and the upper of gravel. Wherever the line is on the level of the public road, there will be a guard-rail; the space between the rails, and for 2 feet at each side, being paved, and the line will be laid on cement concrete, either with or without the sleepers, as the county surveyor may desire.

I would recommend that the formation width be not less than 11 feet in cutting and 12 feet in embankment.

Where the tramway runs at the side of the public road, and 18 feet clear is left between the line and opposite footpath or fence, the railway will be raised 1 ft 6 in. above the level of the road, and a stone curb placed on the outside, to prevent cars getting on to it.

List of Gradients

Mileage		Radius in Chains	Rising or Falling	Gradient
M.	Ch.			
0	7	2½	falling	1 in 82
0	30	2½	rising	1 in 30
0	55	3½	falling	1 in 76
0	75	4	rising	1 in 119
1	26	4	rising	1 in 38
1	32	3½	rising	1 in 38
1	39	2½	rising	1 in 30
3	56	4	falling	1 in 30
3	69	3	falling	1 in 30
4	0	3	falling	1 in 30 and 1 in 89
4	10	3	falling	1 in 89
4	20	2½	rising	1 in 30
4	68	3	falling	1 in 30
5	32	3	falling	1 in 30 and level
5	45	3	rising	1 in 30
5	51	3	rising	1 in 30
6	47	4	rising	1 in 186
6	78	4	falling	1 in 32.5
7	24	4	falling	1 in 30

A PATTERN OF PROGRESS 1884-1885

Mileage M. Ch.	Radius in Chains	Rising or Falling	Gradient
7 38	2½	falling	1 in 30 and level
7 48	3	falling	1 in 30
7 72	4	horizontal	-
7 76	2½	horizontal	-
8 0	2½	rising	1 in 30
8 20	2½	rising	1 in 30
9 29	2½	rising	1 in 30
9 32	3	rising	1 in 30 and 1 in 40
9 45	2½	rising	1 in 81
10 3	4	falling	1 in 30
10 7	4	falling	1 in 96 and 1 in 30
12 7	2½	rising	Level, and 1 in 30
12 10	3	rising	1 in 30
13 3	3	falling	1 in 30
13 42	4	rising	1 in 2,170
13 50	4	rising and falling	1 in 2,170 and 1 in 1,373
14 40	4	horizontal	-
14 69	2½	horizontal	-

The distance from Mrs Driscoll's Pro Dominan and Kirkley.
I would recommend that the curb be not higher than 8 inches, and the remainder of the slope be secured with a stone pitching, a surface channel being found on the road side and the water led off by pipes at intervals, and that in all cases such protection and walling be provided as the county surveyor may require.

Signed, H.U. TOWNSEND, Inspector.
Maryborough, March 6, 1884.

W.B. Soady, esq., Secretary,
Office of Public Works, Dublin.

Attached to the Report was a detailed estimate of expense for building the undertaking, prepared by the Board of Works, and an 'opinion' by Nathaniel Jackson (Surveyor), the latter addressed to the Grand Jury for the Spring Assizes 1884.

This will be a very useful line as it will open a large district at present landlocked.
As it will join the Cork and Skibbereen Railway at Skibbereen, it will greatly increase the traffic on that railway, and be one of the means for reducing the baronial guarantee.
The road over which it is proposed to construct this rail or tramway is well suited for the purpose.
The steepest gradient is 1 in 30 for not more than 3 furlongs in two or three places. If possible, I think it would be advisable to improve this gradient, as in my opinion, the extra outlay would be amply compensated for in the facility it will give in working the line.
When the fishing trade has been properly developed on this coast, this line will enable the fish to be carried direct to Cork and the neighbouring towns without any delay, and be one of the means of cheapening this valuable food.
There are no engineering difficulties in connection with the bridges, &c., to draw your attention to.
I have the honour to be,
Your obedient servant,
NAT. JACKSON

To the Foreman and Gentlemen of the Grand Jury Spring Assizes, 1884.

MEMORANDUM.

THE WEST CARBERRY TRAMWAYS AND LIGHT RAILWAYS COMPANY.

FROM SKULL TO SKIBBEREEN.

ENTIRELY IN THE COUNTY CORK.

Length of Line—14 Miles, 6 Furlongs, and 9 Chains. Single Line.
Gauge—3 Feet.

Promoters' Estimate of Expense, ... £57,000

Presentment of Grand Jury for guaranteed dividends at £5 per cent. on so much of the Share Capital of the Company as shall for the time being be paid-up Capital, as defined by the Act of 1883. *by £ — £57.000.*

Chargeable on the Baronies of—
West Carberry, W.D., and West Carberry, E.D.

The Board of Works estimate the amount of paid-up Capital necessary for construction at . . . £61,000

(Copy of detailed Estimate annexed)

The Board of Works recommend certain modifications in the undertaking as suggested in their Report, and that Clauses be inserted in the Order in Council—I. to provide for the protection of Navigation; and II. to save the rights of the Crown in any tidal lands which may be interfered with by the proposed works.

The Commissioners of Woods and Forests request that a Clause be inserted in the proposed Order in Council providing that no property belonging to the Crown is to be taken possession of, or interfered with, without consent in writing from their department.

Copies of the Reports of the County Surveyor and Board of Works are annexed.

Name of Line—Schull and Skibbereen Tramway and Light Railway.

Length of Line—14 miles 6 furlongs 9·1 chains; Double or Single—Single; Gauge, 3 feet.

Detailed ESTIMATE OF EXPENSE OF UNDERTAKING. *by Board of Works.*

		£ s. d.	£ s. d.	£ s. d.
Earthworks, &c., forming—including earthworks under 2 feet,	10¾ miles, at	100 0 0	1,075 0 0	
Excavation in Rock,	18,460 cub. yds. at	0 2 6	2,308 0 0	
Do. in Clay,	15,786 ,, at	0 1 1	855 0 0	
Embankment in Road approaches, &c., from side cutting,	1,690 ,, at	0 1 6	127 0 0	
Metalling of Roads and Level Crossings,	1,305 ,, at	0 3 6	228 0 0	
Public Road Level Crossings,	3 ,, at	170 0 0	510 0 0	
Farm Road Crossings on Roads,	10¾ miles, at	15 0 0	161 0 0	
			5,264 0 0	5,264 0 0
FENCING—				
Ditch and Mound and 2 Wires,	14,467 lineal yds. at	0 1 10	1,326 0 0	
Setting Back Fences on Road,	18,927 ,, at	0 0 11	867 0 0	
				2,193 0 0
BRIDGES, &c.—				
Public Road Bridges,	3 at	300 0 0	900 0 0	
Accommodation Works through fields,	4 miles, at	150 0 0	600 0 0	
Viaducts or River Bridges,	—	—	3,300 0 0	
Lengthening Viaducts or River Bridges,	—	—	400 0 0	
Culverts and Drains in fields,	4 miles, at	100 0 0	400 0 0	
Lengthening Culverts and Drains,	—	—	600 0 0	
Gatekeepers' Houses at Level Crossings,	3 at	120 0 0	360 0 0	
	Total,		6,560 0 0	6,560 0 0
PERMANENT WAY—Cost per mile.				
Rails and Fish Plates (weight per yard, 45 lbs.),	74 tons, at	7 0 0	518 0 0	
Fastenings,	6 ,, at	17 0 0	102 0 0	
Sleepers,	2,200 at	0 2 6	275 0 0	
Laying Way,	1,760 yards, at	0 1 6	132 0 0	
Ballasting and Boreing,	2,200 at	0 2 0	220 0 0	
Permanent Way, for 14 miles 6 furlongs 9·1 chains,		1,247 0 0	18,535 0 0	
Ditto in Sidings and Junctions, 2 miles,			2,494 0 0	
			35,046 0 0	
Stations, including Signals,	—	—	4,450 0 0	
Purchase of Land and Buildings,	37 acres at	90 0 0	3,330 0 0	
Telegraph, Mile Posts, and Gradient Boards,	14¾ miles at	45 0 0	664 0 0	
Law Costs, Engineering and Cost of Order in Council—				
In fields,	4 miles at	300 0 0 }	3,350 0 0	
On roads,	10¾ ,, at	200 0 0 }		
Contingencies, 10 per cent.	—	—	4,684 0 0	
Engines,	3 at	1,250 0 0	3,750 0 0	
Passenger Carriages,	6 at	240 0 0	1,440 0 0	
Goods Waggons, &c., &c.,	40 at	80 0 0	3,200 0 0	
			8,390 0 0	
Management of Company, including Office expenses, Secretary, Directors' Fees, and Remuneration to County Surveyor till opening of Line, say,			1,000 0 0	
	Total Estimate of Expense,		£60,914 0 0	

During March 1884 the Grand Jury had had only the Schull & Skibbereen section before it, in length 14 m. 6 furs. 9 chs. The promoters had suggested that the Barony of West Carbery should be taxed for the Guarantee as, on the current rating, the district could produce £2,859 on its valuation of £6,470. To further support the case, a table of traffic returns of goods carried by the C&BR from Cork to Skibbereen was submitted by its Manager, Alexander Gordon, showing a tonnage of 7,000 per annum; half this was estimated as bound for destinations further west representing an income to the tramway of £3,000. Gordon's view was that the fish traffic, now largely shipped from Schull 'by steamer', would benefit by rail carriage on the tramway and so onto the C&BR; he reckoned that 54-75 per cent of it could be diverted to rail. Father John Murphy - as ever the spokesman for Schull - felt that farmers were willing to pay a Baronial Tax of 7d./£1 for the use of the line for travel to local Fairs and Marts. Mr Young, a local trader, said he spent £80 per annum on cartage.

The Grand Jury gave the project its blessing on 29th March, 1884, giving a Baronial Guarantee in perpetuity on £57,000 capital. Including a proportion of Stock unsupported by Guarantee, this brought the total capital to £95,000. [Of Mr Daly's opposition nothing more is recorded.]

In time to come, the S&SR thus came to be looked upon as a guaranteed investment, the shareholders not having to concern themselves with efficient (or otherwise) management.*

Following the Grand Jury's approval of the scheme, no time was lost and a Memorial was sent by the Promoters to the Lord Lieutenant on 12th April 'praying for an Order to authorise construction of the Tramway', the 'Promoters' being the WCT&LRCL. The Lord Lieutenant granted the Order with certain interesting provisions:

1. The gauge shall be 'three feet'.
2. The axle loading limit was 8 tons.
3. The speed limit through any town or village to be 6 mph and 12 mph elsewhere. If the track should be at a greater distance than 30 ft from the centre of the public road, the speed could be increased up to 25 mph.
4. Vehicles shall not exceed 20 ft length, 6 ft width and 7 ft height. [These limits were imposed to obviate the risk of derailments in high winds; they could be exceeded if the means was found to resist wind pressure of 'at least 25 lbs. per sq. ft' in which case the width (only) might be increased to 6½ ft.]†
5. Three years for completion from date of the Order were allowed.
6. Where the Tramway was laid at the side of the road on a footpath, a new footpath was to be laid on the opposite side.
7. In the event of an alteration in road level by an authority, the Promoters were bound to bring the Tramway rails to that level (liability for expense is not stated).
8. Should part of the Tramway 'be removed' for repairs, a temporary tramway may be laid on adjoining land during the discontinuance.
9. A list of tolls and charges to be exhibited in every carriage.
10. No passenger or goods shall be carried on the roof of any carriage.
11. Baronies may elect a Baronial Director to be a Director of the Promoters, to hold office for one year.#
12. The County Surveyor shall inspect the line and all equipment at least once a year, sending an Annual Report to the Grand Jury and the Board of Trade.

---

* for detail see Conroy p. 260.
† Rolling Stock see Chapter Fourteen on.
# Directors were 'not to exceed six in number'.

A PATTERN OF PROGRESS 1884-1885

13. Twenty ratepayers in any one Barony liable to make payments under the Baronial Guarantee may call for a BoT Inspection if they feel that the Promoters are at fault in building or operating the Tramway.
14. If the BoT notify the Lord Lieutenant that the Promoters have failed to comply with the BoT Certificate in respect to the Order, the Lord Lieutenant may direct the Grand Jury to appoint a Committee of Management to work and maintain the undertaking.
15. On completion of five years of payment by the Baronies concerned for maintaining and working the undertaking, it shall become the property of the Grand Jury who may appoint a Committee of Management. Such Committee members to be paid by the Grand Jury.
16. The Tramway shall carry mail as the Postmaster-General shall require.

There are many other provisions but only those which have interest to the general reader or which bear on the later history are mentioned. Some (such as carrying passengers on the roof) are simply historical and not reference to the behaviour of Irish travellers in particular!

The draft, first laid before the Grand Jury on 29th March, 1884, at the Spring Assizes, was not finally signed until 26th July, a delay which no doubt irritated the Promoters and pleased the protesters.

Finally: the precise situation of the undertaking was appended:

A Tramway and Light Railway (being partly one and partly the other) commencing in the townland of Meenvane . . . adjacent to Schull at a point 33 yards along the public road measured north-easterly from the northern end of the Coastguard Buildings . . . to a point on the east side on the public road in front of the entrance of the Skibbereen station of the Ilen Valley Railway . . . 133 yards from the Ilen River bridge in Ilen Street.

And thereabouts it duly proved to be!

It was now the turn of the eastern section to go before the Grand Jury. Having noted previously that Union Hall had been omitted from the deliberations, mention of it was now restored. Ironically, despite the earlier promise of some funding, there was further opposition when the Grand Jury reviewed the matter on 16th April and the application was rejected.

True to form, the EAGLE had carried an article on 26th April, 1884 revealing that the Grand Jury's decision had not deflated the protagonists for an eastern section who had held another public meeting at Rosscarbery to promote a yet-farther extension from Rosscarbery - which had already been condemned as a terminus - to Clonakilty. Because the meeting was called at short notice, there was meagre attendance, the whole idea being dependant on a C&BR branch to Clonakilty; such a branch was opened in 1886 . . . but by then, tramway schemes were in the past.

Striking west from Clonakilty, such a tramway would pass by Sam's Cross - Ballinavan Church - Quaker's Cross to Rosscarbery Chapel, a distance of 7½ miles at an estimated cost of approximately £5,000 per mile. The steepest portion would be 1 in 50. The new pier at Rosscarbery (actually one mile south of the village on the west side of Rosscarbery Bay) would develop the fishing trade.

The meeting appointed a committee to further consider the matter.

[There are documents in the Cork Archives Institute (Christ Church, South Main Street, Cork) under the title Skibbereen, Glandore & Union Hall Light Railways Nos. 1 & 2 in the Cork Council County Survey Collection, being Plans dated 29th May, 1884 by Surveyors/Engineers J.W. Dorman and S.A. Kirkby. Also OS maps 3 m./1 in., 1 m./1 in., Plans & Sections of 24th December, 1883 and 29th May, 1884, enlarged plan of Skibbereen terminus, etc.]

The same edition of the EAGLE brought to a head a row which had developed behind the scenes concerning opposition to the tramway in general and the eastern section in particular to the effect of condemning that section. The EAGLE was anxious through its columns to be seen to uphold any scheme which would benefit the district and by the same token, to expose any opposition. Here, Mr Daly re-appears and is roundly condemned under a column SKULL UNION along with his friends - said to be The Skibbereen Board of Guardians - for opposing the tramway. The paper nails its colours to the mast with, 'Skull should appreciate support for the district is always sponsored by the WEST CORK EAGLE'.

And that was not all, for on another page it was reported that the Skibbereen Town Commissioners had criticised the action of the Board of Guardians regarding the EAGLE's support for tramways generally and the Board's opposition to them. As the two parties bared their teeth, censure of the EAGLE came from an unexpected quarter when Daly addressed the Board of Guardians. His case was that while supporting the tramway cause, the paper had suppressed criticism of it; he recommended that the Board should withdraw its advertisement from the paper in protest.

The divided merits and degree of support which the Schull Union reflected (the title now changed from Skull Union) were encapsulated in its resolution of 25th April:

> We, as Guardians of the Schull Union, having learned that the West Carbery Tramway are renewing the application for the line from Skibbereen to Glandore Harbour and Union Hall, . . . express approval of the Barony of West Division of West Carbery being included in the Guarantee, but on the same principle as to the proportion between the baronies adopted between the Schull line being in the case, that our barony shall only bear ⅔ths of the Guarantee.*

Some opinion was that though they 'wanted to break the transport monopoly' (presumably the local road carriers were charging what the traffic would bear), they wanted a tramway *but not* at the expense of higher taxation. Others warned that now 'Schull and Ballydehob have got their tramway, Skibbereen will suffer'.

The last forecast was based on the experience of the Cork & Bandon Railway as it had probed further west; when the C&BR main line had reached Dunmanway, Clonakilty had declined. The consequence was a branch to Clonakilty was being built - the effect on Rosscarbery and Skibbereen might prove detrimental.† A more-light-hearted view was that '. . . the line could be useful; were it only to prevent people having to drive home in their carts - perhaps drunk - on market and fair days and get them and their families upset'.

That the meeting became a little passionate is shown by speakers who contended 'Parties are going round advising against it', and 'Some against it have gone up to Cork with a tissue of lies'.

There was some disturbance at the back of the hall. Many questions had little bearing on the subject . . . order was restored. Potter of the EAGLE could not resist making it a political platform: 'To kick out the scheme would be as kicking out Mr Parnell'.# The Chairman, fearing the vision of a political affray, told him sharply to confine himself to the subject.

---

* i.e. Schull was only prepared to pay ⅔ths of the 'Eastern Guarantee'.
† This is an issue not encountered before. The rural economy of the period could only produce a finite tonnage in any area which it could bring to the railway; falling rural population and emigration were largely responsible. If a railhead in one town was more convenient, an established railhead in another might suffer an eclipse.

A PATTERN OF PROGRESS 1884-1885

Overall, it was not politics which were foremost. It was the problem of gainers and losers both as a district and individually. Basically, private opinion was that a tramway would be beneficial but if it was going to hurt them in the pocket, they would have second thoughts. And who could blame them for who among their number had first-hand experience of a railway, its initial and on-going costs and what risks it would bring to their way of life?

So what progress had been made to date? The western section had been Registered but the Grand Jury's support for the remainder of the project did not appear very strong; the EAGLE was a useful ally and its propaganda could sway the waverers.

On 30th April, 1884 the Office of Public Works, Dublin, having costed for the building of the line, advised the Under Secretary at Dublin Castle that the Commissioners of Public Works estimated it would require £60,914; a copy of this was sent to Thomas Downes (this account was reduced to £57,000 upon revision).

The Parish Priest of Leap, Father Fitzgerald, dismayed by the rejection of the Grand Jury called another public meeting on 8th May, 1884 when, despite a single opponent, contended that the application be reviewed at the summer assizes on 14th June, 1884. The support of the clergy was again evident, the Very Revd Dean Reeves (Dean of Ross, original supporter and shareholder), Revd S. McConnell (Rector of Leap) and Father J. O'Sullivan CC were noted among those present.

All to no purpose, the application was rejected but the district was still obliged to pay Baronial Tax towards the cost of the western section! Hereafter, the authorised section would be known as the WCT&LRCL (S&S Branch); its 5 per cent Guaranteed £1 shares would be 'guaranteed in perpetuity by the urban & rural districts of the West (⅖ths) and East (⅗ths) Divisions of West Carbery'.

Fred Potter's hand can be seen clearly in the EAGLE's editorial on 31st May, 1884; headed OUR TRAMWAYS, he had much to say about the prejudice which had prevented Leap, Glandore etc. enjoying the benefit of a tramway, and the opportunities these villages had lost thereby. Of course he was right and although he undoubtedly knew who was behind the opposition, he could not spell out in print the private interests responsible. What made the situation intolerable to those who felt that public good was the first fruit of a local rail system, was that hardly a month went by when some new system in the county was at the proposal stage - it seemed that every small town would soon be served by a light railway!

In the foregoing newspaper, under WEST CORK TRAMWAYS, is reported an 'enthusiastic meeting at Glandore in Keenan's Hotel', with the Dean of Ross again taking the Chair. Among those attending were Potter, P. Hegarty (Cork), J.K. Levis, (Glandore), Fitzjohn de Burgh, M. de Burgh, James Keenan (Glandore) and the usual gaggle of clergy. The object of the meeting was to raise again the matter of a line to Glandore which the Grand Jury had failed to accept at the recent assizes - and for which a guarantee of financial support for the *whole venture* would also be rejected at its next meeting on 14th June!

From their May 1884 meeting the Board of Guardians of the Skibbereen Union sent letters dated 24th May to the Lord Lieutenant and the Cork Grand Jury protesting

---

Parnell, Charles Stewart (1846-1891) Irish Nationalist politician committed to attaining Home Rule. President of the Nationalist Party 1877 and supporter of the illegal Land League. MP for Co. Meath 1875 but exchanged for Cork City 1880. (It was alleged locally that his career, ruined in a divorce case in 1890, was also blighted by being involved in the over-running of a passenger train in (old) Bantry terminus station when he was found in a derailed carriage in the company of a lady.)

THE SCHULL & SKIBBEREEN RAILWAY

Name of Line, *Schull and Skibbereen Tramway & Lt Railway*

Length of Line: Miles *6* fur. *9* / *1* chains,

Double or Single: *Single*

Gauge: *3* feet *0* inches

ESTIMATE OF EXPENSE OF UNDERTAKING.

	Cubic yards.	Price.	£	s.	d.	£	s.	d.
Earthworks, &c. *Forming including earthworks under 2-10¾ Miles @ £100*			*1075*	.	.			
Excavation in Rock,	*18460*	*@ 2/6*	*2308*	.	.			
Do. in Clay,	*15,786*	*@ 1/1*	*855*	.	.			
Embankment in Road approaches, &c., from side-cutting,	*1,690*	*@ 1/6*	*127*	.	.			
Metalling of Roads and Level Crossings,	*1305*	*@ 3/6*	*228*	"	"			
Public Road Level Crossings		*3 @ £170*	*510*	"	"			
Farm Road Crossings on roads		*10¾ Miles £15*	*161*	"	"			
			5264	"	"	*5264*	"	"

	Description of Fence	Lineal yards.	Price.					
Fencing,	*Ditch and Mound and 2 wires*	*14467*	*@ 1/10*	*£1326 . 0 . 0*				
	Setting back fences on road	*18,927*	*@ 11d*	*867 . 0 . 0*		*2,193*	"	.

				£	s.	d.			
Bridges, &c.—			Number.						
Public Road Bridges,			*3 @ £300*	*900*	"	.			
Accommodation Bridges *works through fields*			*4 Miles @ £150*	*600*	.	.			
Viaducts or River Bridges,				*3,300*	.	.			
Lengthening Viaducts or River Bridges,				*400*	"	"			
Culverts and Drains, *4 Miles in fields @ £100*				*400*	.	.			
Lengthening Culverts and Drains,				*600*	.	.			
Gatekeepers' Houses at Level Crossings,			*3 @ £120*	*360*	.	.			
			Total,	*6560*	.	"	*6560*	"	.

				£	s.	d.			
Permanent Way—Cost per mile.		Price.	Tons.						
Rails, Weight per yard, *45 lbs.* *and fishplates*			*74 @ £7.0.0*	*518*	"	.			
Fastenings,			*6 @ 7.0.0*	*102*	"	"			
Sleepers,	Number. *2200*	*@ 2/6*		*275*	.	.			
Laying Way,	Price per yard, *1760*	*@ 1/6*		*132*	.	.			
Ballasting and Boxing,	*2200*	*@ 2/-* Cost per mile.		*220*	.	.			
Permanent Way, for	*14* Miles, *6* Furlongs, *9 . 1* Chains.			*1247*	.	.	*18535*	"	"
Ditto in Sidings and Junctions,	*2* "	"	"				*2494*	"	"
			Carried forward,				*35046*	"	"

Schull and Skibbereen Tramway & Light Railway

	£	s.	d.
Brought forward,	35046	"	"
Stations, including signals	4450	"	"
	A. R. P.		
Purchase of Land and Buildings, 37. 0. 0 @ £90	3330	"	"
Telegraph, Mile posts and Gradient boards 14¾ Miles @ £45	664	"	"
Law Costs, Engineering and Cost of Order in Council, 4 Miles in fields @ £300 }	3350	"	"
10¾ " on roads @ £200 }			
Contingencies, 10 per cent.	4684	"	"
Number. Price			
Engines, ... 3 @ £1250 £3750.0.0			
Passenger Carriages, ... 6 @ £240 = 1,440.0.0			
Goods Waggons, &c., &c. 40 @ £80 = 3,200.0.0			
	8390	"	"
Management of Company including office expenses, Secretary, Directors' Fees and Remuneration to County Surveyor till opening of Line. Say	1000	"	"

Signed { Engineer. TOTAL ESTIMATE OF EXPENSE **60914 : 0 : 0**

The same details for each Branch and General Summary of Cost. The spaces are left for any items of Cost that may be special to some of the lines.

Dublin: Printed by JAMES WALKER & Co., 94 Middle Abbey Street,
For Her Majesty's Stationery Office.
(1782). 400. 2. 84.

against the financial guarantee now being demanded for the Union Hall/Glandore line. The Board held that such a line would never pay expenses and that a further addition to the rates 'which are already too high' would not be met. 'The ratepayers are determined more than ever to renew their opposition should the promoters renew their application for a second guarantee for the construction . . . of a Tramway from Skibbereen to Schull.'

Owing to the infrequency of its meetings, these letters were not posted until 4th August, only two days before a resumed application for a guarantee was to be heard. When the Judicial Committee heard it, they upheld the application but limited the capital to £57,000. A footnote stated, 'The application was not opposed'.

In consequence the Solicitor General was given leave to settle the Draft Order which, having been prepared beforehand, was dated 25th July.

Styled the Skibbereen, Glandore and Union Hall Light Railway, it was essential that a new survey be made after the March 1884 meeting, and Messrs Dorman and Kirkby produced one on 27th May, 1887, eliminating some of the problems which had arisen at the promotional gatherings. The eastern section was to start a few yards west of Skibbereen station at a point on the Schull line - which is shown on the Plan as running along the *south* side of the Schull road. To enter Skibbereen station itself, an eastern section train travelling west, would have had to reverse.

From this junction with the Schull line, the eastern line would have curved almost 180 degrees round the end of the station, and by this means proceed northwards along the east of the station before curving eastwards to cross the Ilen River. To achieve all this, according to the Plan, the tracks of the Ilen Valley Railway would have been crossed on the level: the IVR Engineer would hardly have accepted such an arrangement . . !

Once over the river, the route now easterly, would have crossed the present Athletic Ground and paralleled the Cork road on its north side and at some distance. At 2 m. the line would climb at 1 in 40 for almost a mile and between 3-4 miles there were reverse curves to avoid hummocky ground; the route then passed round the north side of Shepperton Lakes.

It continued to follow the Cork road at some distance from it and with gradients no steeper than 1 in 40 and 1 in 60. To cross the Mullaghnagowan River on entering Leap a bridge 12 ft span x 12 ft high was envisaged. At 7 m. the rails would pass along the village street for a short distance, then beneath it by a bridge of 25 ft span and 16 ft high. The course would make two sharp reverse curves as it headed southwards; the second, through the Drom townland, would have required a 2 chain radius curve, the sharpest on the section.

Thereafter, the line was intended to follow the edge of the Famine Road along the east shore of Leap creek (a very narrow site), pass the wooden Poulgorm Bridge and end above the shore close by the Church of Ireland and right above the foreshore of Glandore Harbour - an exposed but picturesque site.

The scheme's antagonists would be naturally alarmed at the proposal to carry the line along the narrow Famine Road for it was bordered on one side by rocky cliff and on the other by a seawall. The Plan* here is marked 'Terminus of Light Railway No. 1. 8 m. 6 fur. 1 ch.'

The proposal to serve Union Hall was by 'Light Railway No. 2. 0 m. 7 fur. 8 ch.' and would have involved a train re-tracing the line from Glandore terminus so far as the east end of the Poulgorm Bridge, a rickety timber affair. Sharp curves at the bridge ends would carry it over, then southward along the west shore of Glandore Harbour to end

---

* Cork Archives Institute: Copy of Plan - Item 24B (211-216).

A PATTERN OF PROGRESS 1884-1885

at it most westerly extent; oddly, this was somewhat short of the village and fishing pier, a shortcoming the branch shared with that to Glandore and maybe intended to avoid conflict with the landowners . . .

All to no avail. The eastern section was never achieved and reports of its demise were not published. Its source of traffic would have been fish and when, as happened elsewhere along this coast, the fish swam away, it could not have been sustained.

(As for the weak Poulgorm Bridge, this was to be 're-built in cast-iron' and raised 4.20 ft'; its length was 590 ft. Rebuilding *did* take place *c*. 1890 with a swing portion towards the west end. Today, a replacement stands in its place.)

The Manx fishing fleet was off Glandore at the time and Skipper James Quirk attended the meeting, giving a timely first-hand account of the benefits to fishermen which had been brought by the opening of the Isle of Man Railway in 1873. The local farmers agreed with the fishermen - they would all obtain higher prices for their output if it could reach the Skibbereen market.

The promoters of the Clonakilty-Rosscarbery scheme had had another meeting too; they had dropped the idea of a tramway in favour of a physical extension of the proposed Conakilty branch of C&BR (opened 1886).

West Cork was much in the British news that same month when the Channel Squadron of the Royal Navy assembled in nearby Bantry Bay under the command of the Duke of Edinburgh; the illustrious event somewhat overshadowed the futile efforts of the 'eastern section party ' by comparison, who felt they were being by-passed in their modest efforts to bring a tramway to the district while Bantry, possessor of a railway since 1881, took the accolades!

The Order in Council for the section between Schull & Skibbereen was issued on 26th March, 1885 having only reached the Privy Council earlier that month. Some of the delay was due to the number of presentments received by the Grand Jury which failed to state the maximum sum on which dividends were guaranteed, even though the amounts were clearly stated on the applications, resolutions, etc. named in the Schedule to the Tramways Act of 1883. [An amendment to the 1883 Act was required, and it received Royal Assent on 14th July, 1884; one project named in the Schedule was 'A tramway and light railway from Skibbereen to Ballydehob and Schull'.]

A plaintive letter from Thomas Downes on 21st September (and 7th October) explains why he was unable to prosecute the Clauses suggested by the Grand Jury for inclusion in the Order 'owing to the absence of Directors and Counsel at this time of year . . .' - obviously Dublin Castle would be similarly placed with the drawbacks imposed by the gentry who had more pressing matters on their hands, viz. the Shooting and Hunting Seasons. A period of gestation from July 1883 to March 1884 was inevitable!

Chapter Five

A Shaky Start
1885-1886

The West Carbery Co. lost no time in finding a contractor to build its tramway though how the Board became aware of them is one of the many intriguing mysteries of the story. Messrs McKeon, Robinson & d'Avigdor of 13, Victoria Street, London SW were chosen and contracted on 6th July, 1885; (by 1896 they had become McKeon & Robinson of the same address and among their work in 1898-1900 were extensions to the Demerara Railway in British Guiana and the Easton & Church Hope Railway in the Isle of Portland. No other contracts have been traced).

On the West Carbery contract the firm appears to have left the whole assignment in the hands of d'Avigdor, a truly remarkable character whose links with the West Carbery were but a small event in a life full of excitement and interest such that it would seem his short sojourn in West Cork only appealed to him for the opportunities it would give for indulging in pursuits quite separate from railway construction.*

To enable the new venture to obtain the necessary finance, the West Carbery was directed to the Tramways Capital Guarantee Co. Ltd., incorporated on 29th January, 1884 with a share capital of £100,000 in £10 shares all of which had been taken up. The TCGCL's object was to subscribe for all or part of the capital of companies incorporated to construct light railways in Ireland. The companies named in the Schedule to its Act

---

* Some extended notes on d'Avigdor will be found in MODERN ENGLISH BIOGRAPHY (Frederic Boase) Vol. IV from which the following is taken:

Elim Henry d'Avigdor, Engineer and Communal Worker, was the eldest son of Count Salamon Henri d'Avigdor and Rachel, the second daughter of Sir Isaac Lyon Goldsmid. He was born in 1841 and educated at University College, London and matriculated at the University of London in 1860 and graduated BA in 1861. He was a member of convocation. He was articled to Hawkshaw the civil engineer and after qualifying he went to Hull to work where he married a daughter of Bethel Jacobs by whom he had one son and five daughters. The son Osmond Elim d'Avigdor Goldsmid inherited the Goldsmid estates on the death of Sir Julian Goldsmid, assumed the name Goldsmid and was created a baronet in 1934 (the baronetcy appears to be extinct now). Elim Henry then went to work in Rangoon and later supervised the construction of railways in Syria and Transylvania and waterworks in Vienna. He formed the Tyrian Construction Company.

He was a member of the Council of the Anglo Jewish Association from 1871 until his death and he was a warden of the Spanish and Portuguese Synagogue. He joined the Chovevi Zion Association in 1891 and was chief of it until his death. It was apparently his concern with Syrian Railways that brought about his interest. He bought THE EXAMINER and edited it and brought out THE YACHTING GAZETTE. He was master of the West Surrey Staghounds in 1895. He wrote many hunting stories of merit for which he was well qualified being himself an intrepid rider to hounds.

He was the author under the pseudonym 'Wanderer' of ACROSS COUNTRY in 1882, FAIR DIANA in 1884, GLAMOUR in 1885, A LOOSE REIN in 1887, WHIMS in 1889, LADY HETTY in 1895 and other novels and HUNT ROOM STORIES AND YACHTING YARNS in 1885 and ANTIPODEAN NOTES in 1888. In the professional field he translated Friedman's DESIGNS FOR THE CONSTRUCTION OF MARKETS, WAREHOUSES AND SHEDS in 1877, wrote WATER WORKS ANCIENT AND MODERN in 1876 as well as DER WIENFLUSS UND DIE WOHNUNGSNOTH published in Vienna in 1873 and DAS WOHLSEIN DER MENSCHEN IN GROSSTADTEN published in Vienna in 1874.

He died at 35 Lancaster Gate, London on the 9th February, 1895.

There is no mention of his death in any engineering periodical and the 1885 Directory only gives 'McKeone & Robinson, Railway Contractors, Westminster Chambers, Victoria Street, London'.

were the West Carbery and the Cavan Leitrim & Roscommon Light Railway & Tramway Co. Ltd both of which had been sanctioned and possessed baronial guarantees given in perpetuity at 5 per cent. The TCGCL had acquired (at 112.5 per cent) £56,750 in £1 shares in the West Carbery and £99,000 in £5 shares in the CL&RLR&TCL. In turn, the cash raised by the Guarantee Co. had been obtained by an issue of Trust Certificates. Without adding further detail, the end-result was that the Trustees held the shares in both railway/tramway undertakings and could use the dividends from them to pay the Trustees and their Auditors fees, for the payment of interest on the Trust Certificates and lastly, to pay any surplus to the TCGCL. It was something of a tangled web.

The Act forming the TCGCL anticipated a financial return for that concern - the details are not essential here - based on the expectation that the Tramways Act of 1883 would give birth to many new systems. This expectation proved groundless as the dividends on the tramway company shares went to pay either fees or interest to the Trust Certificate holders. There was no surplus to pay to the TCGCL.

The idea of the TCGCL was that shareholders might spread their risk over several Irish tramway companies; a doubtful light had been thrown on certain such operations by the RAILWAY TIMES who referred to certain slick operators as 'The Tramway Ring'.

While Newham maintains that the TCGCL was wound up in 1885 having advanced the necessary capital to the West Carbery beforehand, this was not so and further reference ensues. Suffice to add that Skinner's Register of Defunct Companies records that the Company went into voluntary liquidation on 4th March, 1932 without any capital being returned to the members; there was a final meeting registered on 18th June, 1932. Of interest is that the Company was a promotion of Sir John Lubbock, a former Lord Mayor of London; as regards the West Carbery, it was simply a financial exercise and appeared to be a water-tight investment. The Company did not concern itself with technical matters or events on the ground.

There was some difficulty in raising the balance of the money which comprised Stocks unsecured by guarantee.

And so to matters down in West Cork; a man named Woods was appointed by the contractors as their Agent and Engineer while d'Avigdor took on the role of a dilettante, a now-you-see-me, now-you-don't character. Father Bernard, Curate-in-Charge, cut the first sod at Ballydehob and blessed the undertaking, and there appeared this embellished reference in the MINING JOURNAL for 4th July, 1885:

Skibbereen & Schull Tramway - Operations have been commenced on this important and beneficial work. In a few days Mr Avigdor, the contractor, will have 100 men at work. Many hands are already at work at Ballydehob. Skibbereen and Bantry are already connected by rail with Cork and the tramway from Skibbereen to Schull will open up a valuable mineral district . . . . the little town of Schull is most pleasantly situated and affords delightful sites for miners' villas and cottages . . . become a fashionable watering place . . . no winter is known in Schull . . .

At least the MINING JOURNAL supported the Tramway (for the obvious reasons) whilst it was passing through a period of uncertain promise but with hindsight the local mines, which had been such a large employer of native labour, had passed their peak and in any case, would hardly have been wooed from their traditional transport means, the cart, aerial ropeway and ship from the nearest inlet.

Actual construction began at three points - Skibbereen where materials could arrive by C&BR; Ballydehob where the principal civil engineering work of the system was to be found - a viaduct of considerable proportions; Schull where the most convenient place for landing materials was situate (although at that time there was no permanent rail connection from the pier).

Thomas Downes, with offices at 81, Gardiner Street, Dublin and North Street, Skibbereen, as well as being solicitor to the West Carbery, also acted for the contractor . . . a most uncomfortable arrangement, however convenient, when it was alleged the contractor's work was faulty.

For the Tramways Co. Messrs S.E. Kirkby and John William Dorman were in partnership as civil engineers, the latter having appointed one Percy (later replaced by Kenny) as Resident Engineer-in-Charge; both partners were only in their early twenties.*

d'Avigdor soon fell foul of the local people as he had an unfortunate ignorance of (or chose to ignore) native aspirations, the activities of the Land League and the bitterness incurred by evictions, etc. He was utterly naive in such matters and committed the cardinal sin of buying property offered at auction which had in the first place been seized for rent arrears (no Irishman of any standing would be forgiven for such an act). Almost immediately he was indiscreet enough to purchase a small farm and put himself at odds with the local community. As the history unfolds, many references will be made to his (alleged) activities and it is sufficient to leave the subject there for a moment.

It must not be assumed that the faults were all on one side. In drawing up the contract between the WCT&LRCL and its builders, the advice given to the Promoters was faulty and in due course was to underline the most serious omission of all, that is to say a clause requiring the contractor to work the Tramway for a specified time after opening (and so eliminate any shortcomings) was omitted with disastrous - if not comic - results. Another shortcoming manifested itself immediately when Dorman pointed out that no Agreement had been made as to who was the owner of materials delivered to the site: however it was agreed they were the property of the Tramways.

As each section of line was completed and inspected to Dorman's satisfaction, he issued a Certificate to the Company who allotted shares to the contractor against it; under the Agreement such shares were passed in turn to the Guarantee Company.

It appears that civil engineering aside, the track itself was laid from the Skibbereen end of the line. This is the only instance where d'Avigdor is recalled as personally involved; his 'economies and short cuts' in laying down the permanent way so as to save on materials were often related to the Author over forty years ago. Such accounts were so vivid that one might be led into thinking they were witnessed by the speaker . . . they were made all the richer with the help of a good imagination and a well-filled glass! Be that as it may, there is little doubt that d'Avigdor acquired a reputation for cost-cutting.

The Tramways Co. letterhead now gave the Registered Office as 54, South Mall, Cork with J.W. Dorman, Secretary. He was also Secretary of the Ilen Valley Railway Co. Ltd, (see p. 20) with RO at the same address. Col J.L. Somerville JP, was appointed Chairman of the Tramways Company on 29th February, 1886.

On 23rd June, 1886 d'Avigdor sent notice to the Board of Trade (the second such notice - the first is missing from File MT6/1764/1 at the Public Record Office) intimating that the line was ready for inspection. Apparently he owned no official notepaper as the letter was sent on plain paper 'on behalf McKeone, Robinson & d'Avigdor; contractors for construction and equipment'. The change of spelling will be noted.

---

* S.E. Kirkby MA (Cantab.), became County Surveyor, East Riding, Co. Cork.

A SHAKY START 1885-1886

Major Gen. Hutchinson* was appointed by the BoT to inspect but no sooner was this done than a letter dated 30th June arrived from d'Avigdor at Skibbereen withdrawing the notice 'owing to the requirements of the County Surveyor & other causes'. This time some official notepaper was used, headed, SCHULL & SKIBBEREEN TRAMWAYS etc.

A little later the BoT received a communication of 4th July from Bernard Fleming† of New Court (3 miles west of Skibbereen, bounding the line on the north side of the river: the house is now demolished). Fleming was a strong opponent of the Tramway. He requested

... close and accurate inspection of the line as the curves and gradients are perfectly appalling ... many others share the same apprehension ... there have been three derailments on curves of wagons behind the locomotive and one on a holiday trip given by the contractors ... deeply concerned in the success of the line, of which there can be no chance unless the permanent way is safe ... I have been and am still opposed to the line as are - with very few exceptions - the farmers and gentlemen, landowners in this Barony, and have refused to accept a Directorship in this so-called Company ...

... The promoters are secured against loss in case of total failure of the line and in case of gain (which must be small, if any) they have no profit as the surplus must go to the Guaranteed Money ... .If it should fail, responsibility falls on the Grand Jury, a transitory body and quite unsuitable for the management of such an undertaking ...

... It was the intention that the Cork & Bandon Railway should work it for 10 years unaided by the Baronies, but this was struck out by the Privy Council in Dublin ...

Fleming's letter shows his extra-ordinary ambivalence; having stated his opposition, his continues by asking the BoT 'to come to their aid to prevent the line becoming a failure ... We have had several accidents already from horses being terrified by the engines, and traffic in consequence has been diverted from this (main) road to a circuitous hilly road'.

* Hutchinson, Major-General Charles Scrope. RE, CB. b. Hythe, Kent, 8th August, 1826. d. Blackheath 29th February, 1912 aged 85. Was Inspector of Railways to BoT 1867-1895. He served at Woolwich: posted to Ireland 1844-45 and in charge convict labour at Spike Island, Cork Harbour, 1848-51 (time of Famine); Professor of Fortifications at Royal Military Academy 1862-67. Retired 1877 as Hon. Major-General. See: RAILWAY ENGINEERING (No. 16 February 1895. p. 38).

† The Flemings were one of an inter-related group of Protestant 'landed gentry' families in West Cork. Lionel Fleming (I) attracted much unpopularity during the Great Famine. There was much intermarriage between them and they seem to have little disposition to find marriage partners elsewhere. New Court was a big Georgian House, the centre of extensive local property and further west, to the Mizen; Lionel Fleming of Aughadown acquired New Court in 1776, but the family may have come from Biggar in Scotland. Their relations in other parts of Co. Cork included Roman Catholics. On the roadside just outside the main entrance were two 'Gothick' water-gates which could be seen from The Tram as it passed New Court Halt; one still survives (1998). The Flemings are given the credit for the building of the main roads in the district by persuading the Government of their necessity and in drawing attention to the corrupt ways of the repairing contractors who did not fulfil their task. Roads before then were unfit for carriage or cart and if small children needed to travel 'they had to be packed into panniers on either side of a horse'.

The Great Famine had struck New Court a blow from which it never recovered: three soup kitchens were set up in the area. To feed the starving Lionel John Fleming put men to work to make a road from New Court to Church Cross which at the time was simply a bog-track. Stone was obtained from a quarry set up on the hill, and carts used to transport it.

Nearly forty years later, The Tram travelled along the edge of that same road; today tourists of world-wide origin speed along its straight and level course without any knowledge of its history. [Source; THE FLEMINGS & REEVES OF CO. CORK. (Lionel T. Fleming). Published privately. - Copy loaned to the Author by Captain Paul Chavasse, Castletownsend.]

In considering Fleming's outlook it must remembered that contemporary West Cork was extremely isolated and in attempting to set the stage as has been done previously herein there was obviously opposition to developments which would bring an idyllic rural riverside setting - as it was clearly recalled - into an English 19th Century scene. To have a smelly, noisy machine passing along the northern boundary of his estate was unacceptable. Fleming's supposition that the landed gentry was opposed was not entirely true and there is wide evidence that many farmers welcomed it; the finish of his letter appears to accept the railway was a *fait accompli* and he genuinely wished to see it perfected.

His observations on the capabilities of the Grand Jury in this responsibility were to prove largely correct.

On 31st July, 1886 the BoT instructed Hutchinson to make the inspection but hardly had he 'girded up his loins' when d'Avigdor's frantic letter of 3rd August was received: 'Line not ready for Inspection due to bad slip; not ready until end of month'.

Writing in 1926, Conroy (p. 261) made the following observation on the Tramway as things were in 1886:

> It would not have happened if the shareholders had had any interest in the railway as a commercial concern. In the case of the Baronial Guaranteed railways, the rails might have been pulled up and cattle housed in the Waiting Rooms, yet the capitalists would have dealt merrily in the phantom Stock of the undertaking, knowing that they had the local and Imperial guarantees at their backs . . .

Sketch of Ballydehob Viaduct.   *Southern Star*

Chapter Six
Nothing but Trouble
1886-1887

Hutchinson was instructed to travel to Skibbereen on 13th August and reported to the BoT on 2nd September. A précis of his Report reads [the numbers in parenthesis have been added by the Author and refer to the notes which follow]:

. . . This Tramway and Light Railway is the first constructed under the powers of the Act of 1883 which has been completed (1) . . . the authorised length is 14 m. 69.1 chains but is 14 m. 23 chains actual, a saving of 46.1 chains by improvements effected in the laying out of the line. (2) Enough land is available for 18 chains sidings at the termini and interim points . . . at entrances and exits to public roads and private lands, gates and gatehouses have been provided. (3) Parts of the line are laid along the side of the public road, and parts on private land.

The authorised steepest gradient is 1 in 30 and there are app. 3¼ m. at this inclination. The sharpest curve is 2½ chains radius; six of these were authorised but by improvements the number is reduced to three. All have check-rails.

The permanent way consists of flat-bottomed steel rails, principally 30 ft long, weighing 45 lb. per yard, fished at the joints with fishplates 18 in. long, of transverse sleepers of Irish larch 6 ft (minimum) long x 8½ in. x 4½ in., ten to each rail length, the central intervals being 2 ft 3 in. at the joints and 3 ft 1 in. elsewhere. The ballast is principally of broken stone, 8 in. deep. Dog spikes are used except on gradients steeper than 1 in 70 where fangbolts are placed at the end of each rail. (4)

On curves of radius 5 chains or less there are two pairs of soleplates under each rail. On gradients of less than 1 in 70 with curves less than 5 chains, there are four pairs of fangbolts and two pairs of soleplates to each rail.

The width of the formation level is 10 ft and there is 6 ft 8 in. between the outside rails of parallel tracks.

There are two overbridges: a footbridge of 26 ft span formed of trussed rails (5) and a roadbridge of 16 ft span wrought-iron girders supported on stone abutments. (6) The girders are sufficient to support 15 ton locomotives.

There are three road underbridges and three river underbridges. Four have wrought-iron girders on masonry abutments - the widest span is 21 ft. (7) Girders - see above. The remaining two are entirely of masonry with spans of 20 ft. (8)

Ballydehob Viaduct has 12 masonry spans of 20 ft (one being included in the foregoing item. (9) It is a fine piece of work, built on rock foundations.

The seven large masonry culverts (widest 12 ft) are substantially constructed.

Fencing is of post and wire, or drystone wallings, sod-packed.

There are fixed stopping places at app. 2 m. intervals. At Skibbereen the existing station has been made available, the new line being brought along the back of the platform. (10)

There are small engine turntables at each terminus.

Facing points are locked by the Train Staff as the line is to be operated by One Engine in Steam or two coupled together. Speed is very limited, and the usual erection of signals and interlocking . . . is dispensed with. The line is divided into two sections; locomotives will carry the Train Staff.

There is a list of rolling stock inspected:

Three small 4-wheeled engines of tramway type weighing 15 tons each.
1st-3rd Class carriages with doors at ends. (11)
Break Vans [sic], Cattle Waggons [sic] and Open Trucks.

Continuing the précis of the Inspector's Report:

The engines are fitted with steam and hand brakes . . . there is automatic vacuum on carriages and break van. The waggons and trucks have handbreaks, and are also piped. (12)

49

The County Surveyor of the West division of Cork attended the inspection and informed me he was generally satisfied with the conditions of the line except as regards some few matters which were in course of completion and had no objection to opening. (13)

Hutchinson further required:

1. The buffer stop beside the road at Skibbereen, strengthened. (14)
2. The finishing of the fence at 12¼ m. beside the Slea River.
3. 'It must be impossible to remove the keys from the locks of facing points unless the points are locked for the main line'.
4. The urinals at Schull and Skibbereen to be properly screened.
5. Engines to be fitted with speed indicators.

The Report was completed by the addition of conditions contained in the Regulations. At a later date the Inspector was informed that traffic would consist largely of mixed trains. Consequently he stipulated that when purely goods, mineral or cattle trains were run, these must be two brake vans. (15)

Author's Notes on Hutchinson's Report
(1) A list of tramways/railways built under the 1883 Act appears on p. 51.
(2) Shortenings which d'Avigdor is said to have achieved at the expense of steeper inclines and sharper curves.
(3) Not all of these have survived (1999). Some gatehouses were based on the standard Board of Works design. Gates were removed at an undisclosed date, probably pre-1910.
(4) Fangbolts were to prevent rails moving down gradient due to braking on wheels.
(5) At Laurel Hill Farm.
(6) At Laurel Hill Farm.
(7) (See description under 'Route').
(8) (See description under 'Route').
(9) The viaduct still stands, a memorial to excellent worksmanship.
(10) Stations (i.e. stopping places) were; Skibbereen; New Court; Church Cross; Hollyhill; Kilcoe; Ballydehob; Woodlands; Schull (see 'Route' for details). None save the terminii and Ballydehob had platforms but these were subsequently built at Church Cross, Hollyhill and Kilcoe. ['Cross' in a name means a road intersection.] Between Kilcoe and Ballydehob a stopping place named 'Crooked Bridge' is said to have existed at first (see also 'Route' chapter).
(11) Hutchinson does not quote quantity. (See 'Rolling Stock' chapter.)
(12) 'Piped' vehicles were fitted with 'through' vacuum pipes but they themselves did not have the appropriate vacuum brake gear.
(13) The 'few matters' are not listed.
(14) This was a most vital fixture, as it prevented trains from over-running the Station when entering Skibbereen.
(15) The vacuum brake on such goods etc. trains would operate on the engine and the two vans (both presumably, at the rear - though this is not stated). The vacuum brakes on the vans would be actuated per the through-pipes fitted to the intermediate vehicles. The mandatory instruction to have *two* vans in a train underlines the very severe gradients involved.

Railways built under the 1883 Act

Title	Incorporated	Opened
Clogher Valley	26th May, 1884	2nd May, 1887
West Clare	15th December, 1883	27th July, 1887
South Clare	9th June, 1884	3rd August, 1892
Cork & Muskerry	12th December, 1883	8th August, 1887
	6th June, 1890	-
Cavan & Leitrim	3rd December, 1883	17th October, 1887
West Donegal	21st July, 1879	16th September, 1889
Tralee & Dingle	4th June, 1884	31st March, 1891
West Carbery (S&S)	7th December, 1883	6th September, 1886

All the foregoing had a reserved track/roadside sections except the Clare and Donegal lines which ran entirely on their own right of way.

A Sealed Undertaking was received from the Company at the BoT dated 6th September, 1886 regarding the Staff working with One Engine (or two coupled together) but without a Staff Ticket. The heading is expressed in the plural as 'Tramways' and 'Railways' but on the seal is in the singular, which was incorrect - though the title was to become singular in 1892.

The seal itself shows the nearby Fastnet Lighthouse upon its rock (upper half) and two clasped hands (lower half) encircled by the erroneous title.

On 28th September, 1886 the BoT sent the Company its Regulations prefaced by: 'Safe working of the line will, to a very great extent, depend on the observance of a very moderate rate of speed . . .'

A summary of the Regulations is:

A. *Locomotives.*
   Each coupled wheel must have a break block operated by steam, treadle (or) and by steam.
   Each locomotive must be numbered conspicuously.
   Each locomotive to be fitted with speed indicator, a fender to push off obstructions, and a bell.
   Engine to be arranged for driver to have fullest view of the road before him.
   Engine machinery to be concealed from 4 in. above rails.
   Fire to be concealed from view.
B. *Carriages.*
   To be so built as to protect passengers from the machinery of the engine (etc.).
C. *Board of Trade.*
   May inspect from time to time.
D. *Single line working.*
   As Undertaking given.
E. *Speed Limits etc.*
   12 mph at roadside and elsewhere a 15 mph speed limit to be observed. 4 mph over facing points.
F. *Couplings.*
   All vehicles to have double couplings.*
G. *Locomotives.* (Further to the foregoing)
   To carry conspicuous lamps in front.
   To sound special bell as warning from time to time.
   Not to emit smoke or steam sufficient to cause complaint.

---

* Central buffer/coupler and side chains (J.I.C.B.).

H. *Speed Limits.* (Further to the foregoing)
On all descents of 1 in 35 or less: 6 mph.
On curves at 12 m. 39 ch. and 12 m. 76 ch: 6 mph.*
On curve of 2½ ch. at 1½ m. (1) from Skibbereen. At 4½ m. (2) and 7 m. 38 ch. (3): 4 mph.
I. *Train must stop to avoid danger.*
Train must make Absolute Stops at:
Schull level crossing in either direction.
From Skibbereen at:

68 ch.	Road intersection:	New Bridge
1 m. 60 ch.	Road intersection:	Abbey Cottage
7 m. 65 ch.	Road intersection:	Ardura Beg
10 m. 40 ch.	Road intersection:	Shanvanagh†

From Schull at:

4 m. 43 ch.	Road intersection:	Shanvanagh
10 m. 50 ch.	Road intersection:	Church Cross

11 m. 40 ch. Crossing Gate in either direction. Watergate. Approaching Skibbereen in either direction - at crossing gate.
J. A copy of these Regulations to be placed in each carriage in a conspicuous position.

[For an official document the general layout of the Regulations is extremely poor and confusing. In particular the section applying to Speed Limits, the special limits on certain curves, whether the distances quoted were measured from Schull or Skibbereen (it appears they might be measured from either but this is not always clear), makes the interpretation of the locale a puzzle. The distances quoted do not always tally with the position of a hazard; in one case there is no hazard and one must assume a misprint. Sufficient to add that men of experience operated the trains and for their well-being, did so in the every-day knowledge of its dangers and without need of 'Authority' . . !

When the Great Southern Railways became owners of the system in 1925, their Working Timetable (Appendix) p. 208, dated 1st March, 1935 simplified the location of Speed Restrictions by applying, place-names. Unfortunately some of the personal names applied have now passed from local memory and our knowledge remains incomplete.

The Author has used the oldest-available 25 inch/1 mile Ordnance Survey Plans for reference. Assuming Datum Point to be the S&SR buffer stop at Skibbereen, in some instances a slight variation in distances occurs between Railway Company published figures and those of the Plans.]

It cannot escape notice that the BoT recognised the dangers inherent in this tramway and it is to the credit of its operators that there were no serious accidents which could be blamed on the owning Company. Accidents there were, and plenty of incidents - not every one reported! When ownership of the line changed no alteration was made to the Regulations, (except in the matter previously mentioned) though the Author does not recall their display in the carriages. An unusual requirement?

The Rules and Regulations as approved by the Company on 17th August, 1886 were combined into a pocket-size book. A copy of the original has not been seen but a re-print of 1899 by Purcell & Co., Patrick St., Cork is headed THE SCHULL & SKIBBEREEN & LIGHT

---

* Woodlands Bridge.
(1) [Not found].
(2) Laurel Hill summit.
(3) Below, and west of Kilcoe Cross.
† later amended to 'both directions'.

RAILWAY (Offices: North Street, Skibbereen)* The Rules are the standard format. The edition is dated 11th July, 1890.

But the narrative proceeds too quickly. On the day the Seal Undertaking was signed the tramway saw its first official train though to show goodwill, the contractors had run a pre-opening train on which the locals were invited to ride. Regrettably it left the rails and the day finished with disappointment for the participants and the anger of the critics.

Under the terms of the Agreement, the contractors were to supply the rolling stock, these listed as three locomotives, five carriages and sixty other vehicles; to save money in the event four coaches and forty-nine wagons were supplied. Three tram engines were delivered, the most striking feature being the small size of them all - even for a tramway. They were similar to those supplied to a local street tramway in England, e.g. Huddersfield.

On Tuesdays there was a monthly Pig Fair in Ballydehob and on 7th September, 1886, a special train ran from Schull (where the engines were shedded) to Ballydehob, and loaded pigs for Skibbereen market. A higher price for the animals was obtained rather than if they had reached Skibbereen 'on trotter' by the road. To celebrate the official opening two days later, Ballydehob held a 'Monster Sports Meeting'. This proved too much for one of the three tram engines, which broke down. It was not a helpful augury.

Whilst there seems to be no actual ceremony to report, the SKIBBEREEN EAGLE & COUNTY CORK ADVERTISER reflected the pride which it felt upon the completion of the Tramway and at the same time, cautioned the authorities in the manner for which it was to become celebrated.

From the statements made in various places this week the benefits of railway extension would seem at length to be appreciated in fair, if not adequate measure. For our part, we have at all times, whether it be in Mayo or Skull, strongly and earnestly advocated an enterprise of the kind for which we are convinced that it proves an invaluable factor in the promotion of civilising influences and the development of a country's resources. This week the Skull & Skibbereen Light Tramway opened what is fondly believed will be a profitable and useful carrier . . .

(The completion of the Tramway and also the standard gauge branch line to Clonakilty had thrown many labourers out of work at a time of agricultural depression and the paper backed an appeal to the Government for a loan which would enable a railway from Ballinscarthy to Timoleague to be built.)

For the opening, Woods, who had been agent to the contractor, was appointed Manager. While receipts rose to £45 per week by mid-November, expenses plus the Manager's salary gave very little profit margin. Unprovided-for costs were rising due to the frequency of derailments, said to be due to a badly-constructed system; with hindsight, whether such an accusation could be supported by the evidence, or whether derailments came through other causes, is a matter for further investigation. At least one issue became clear from the start, the tram engines were almost useless and could not make sufficient steam to hold off the vacuum brake, so trains ran with the brake disconnected. One aspect of the engines' troubles was removed when at his last inspection, Hutchinson had agreed that the mandatory condition for them to 'consume their own exhaust' was un-necessary and so the steam-driers were removed.

Evidently Woods thought that as Manager, he was underpaid, for he resigned on 18th December. The position was not filled; instead, J.W. Johnstone was taken on as Traffic

---

* Kindly loaned by Tom Kelly, Ballydehob.

Manager and Locomotive Superintendent at £11 per month.* He was later, General Manager.

During the year just ending considerable settlement of the earthworks had occurred but Woods had dealt with those. He made the excuse that shortage of funds had prevented him from keeping up to scratch with the maintenance and also revealed that funds prevented insistence on a year's maintenance by the builders, as the latter would not sign an Agreement containing this provision. An instance of subsidence was that at Crooked Bridge, where the line descended to cross the Lleamawaddra River; it had sunk three inches and required 300 tons of ballast to raise it.

Between the date of opening and the half-yearly meeting on 26th December, £251 6s. 5d. had been taken in passengers, parcels etc. and £202 14s. 7d. in goods, cattle etc., with passengers numbering 6,828 in total (while of these those passing through Skibbereen were 4,436). In the period, an average of approximately 72 passengers was using the tram each day (there was one train on Sundays). Owing to heavy initial expenses and repairs, the Grand Jury called on the Baronies to pay out £692 3s. 4d. expenses, in addition to the guaranteed dividend.

This demand raised the temperature even further and when news came through that services had ceased on 6th April, 1887 as no locomotive was fit enough to operate the service, it had the effect of stirring up a hornets' nest. Bernard Fleming of New Court complained to the Board of Trade at once, pointing out initially that the Board had not replied to his previous letter. Under the Agreement between Tramway Company and the contractor, Fleming continued, the latter was due for payment as soon as Hutchinson's approval to open the tramway was received. The Company, compelled to pay under the circumstances, was now informed that 'd'Avigdor was now in Australia'. (This is hardly likely in the time involved!)

Fleming had interviewed the County Roads Inspector† ('Whoever he may be', reads a marginal note added by the BoT) who found the following defects:

1)   In five locations the curves are too sharp.
2)   The stated gradients are incorrect.
3)   The flanges of the wheels are too shallow.

The result is that there are three new engines broken down and the line is closed, the men are discharged. The immediate cause is the engines' vital defect - steel being used instead of brass - expansion of steel caused leakage which clogged the machinery and extinguished the fires. If the line is to re-open a new engine must be bought and the old engines repaired at a cost of at least £2,000 . . . there is a renewal fund lodged in the Court of Chancery to meet such defects in the contract, but the contractor, *relying on your inspector's certificate, has brought an action to recover that sum*.

---

* Johnstone was the son of J.J. Johnstone, a Director. He had served a fitter's apprenticeship at the Inchicore Works of the Great Southern & Western Railway, Dublin. He was employed by Dick, Kerr & Co. Ltd of Britannia Engineering Works, Kilmarnock, when they were building the three tram engines for the West Carbery. At the time of his appointment as engineer to the C&BR he was so youthful-looking that the Board ordered him to grow a beard to 'instil respect and discipline'.

† The IRISH DAILY TELEGRAPH's correspondent, writing almost a decade before the Tramway was built, had this to relate: 'Ballydehob . . . there is a monthly Fair at which an enormous amount of business is transacted . . . Sanitary Inspectors, if any, would find full employment in the back yards, many of which are in an abominable state of filth; the streets are also in a disgraceful state of mud. Where are the road surveyors? Are there any for West Cork? . . . I never saw one but he is much wanted . . .' Could there be any link-up, some years later, with the apparent indifference of the responsible Surveyor to his duties to inspect the building of the Tramway in the same district?

My property pays 7d. in £ per ½ year for the bare construction of the line, and over £45 *per mile* is required by the Company for *working of the line for the last six months* . . .

Fleming concludes by adding that the service stopped on 6th April and calls for intervention by the BoT.
On 11th April, 1887 the following appeared in the newspaper:

The Directors have most unhesitatingly felt compelled to stop for the present the traffic on the Skibbereen and Schull Tramway, the entire breakdown of the engines rendering it absolutely necessary to take this course. From the time the Tram was left to them, those engines were continually going out of order and in two months after it had opened it had to be closed for some little time, and even then portions of the engines were under repair. As a rule, the engines have not had sufficient power to do their work, and unfortunately the public lost confidence in them, but with great efforts, they struggled on. Now the break down is complete, and until certain repairs are executed, which would cost £300, nothing can be done. Those engines were never really capable of doing their work properly. The Directors have also been grossly hampered for want of funds, as on starting they had only £200 to begin with, and, as they had to keep up the line from the commencement, and that at great cost for labour, coals, oil and the numberless necessary outgoings. They would never have since been able to go on but for the Munster & Leinster Bank which gave them a handsome advance . . . this has come at an unfortunate time as, during recent weeks, the traffic had considerably increased . . . English shareholders are considering their position . . . if they gave sufficient help to get a new engine and repair the old ones . . . The Directors are being sued by the Master of the Rolls for the deposit money, about £2,000. The contractors are trying to force them to draw it for them . . . the engines are incapable, the stations unfinished, particularly the Schull one which is in danger of being swept away by the sea . . . the secondary sidings have not been put. The Directors hope that things may mend, and the line begin again in good working order.

The Tramway Directors were also spurred into action, and a letter over the names of John Limrick of Union Hall, and Dr John Levis of Glenview, Skibbereen was sent to the Governor General on 16th April. It is long and laboured with complaint, but its flavour is too good to resist some quotation:

We most respectfully beg to lay before (you) . . . the miserable state of this undertaking . . . we are not answerable for its present condition . . . no Baronial Director could be appointed . . . for nearly eighteen months after the Company was formed. Mr Limrick . . . could not legally act as the entire sum granted for making the line was allowed to the contractors . . . nothing to enable working to proceed. There was nothing . . . for the keeping of the line in order by the contractors for a specified time . . . we had no control over the Engineers appointed by the Company. Since our appointment to the Board we saw one of these Gentlemen but once or twice and the other not at all . . . their remuneration £1,000 was paid by the contractors . . . and they had their money but paid no attention . . .
Mr d'Avigdor, a very able and clever man, was completely allowed his own way . . . some of the Directors was in on the Shares was in on the Syndicate . . . and others may not have known much of Railway Works or Management . . . At one meeting Mr d'Avigdor handed in claims for extras over £3,000 . . . done to terrify members of the Board . . . this could not be enforced . . . then a demand made to take the line from the contractors, open to the public and one of Mr d'Avigdor's Engineers engaged for four months to work and arrange it . . .
(On satisfactory certification) £9,000 in Shares, were handed to the contractors, Mr Limrick objecting that . . . Schull station was totally unfinished and in dangerous condition . . . carriages continually going off rails . . . portions of the engines . . . in England . . . under repairs. A large number of people had to be employed (to renew the line).
. . . It was early found the engines were not equal to their work . . . confidence was greatly shaken and buyers from the fairs . . . afraid to send pigs and cattle for fear of not reaching in time . . . Our

> financial condition is most deplorable . . . we have not one penny or chance of getting it; the English Shareholders will not give assistance . . . the Baronial Presentment will only settle until the end of December . . . and in West Carbery can hardly be collected at this time of year, the Collector stated that there was over £1,600 arrears due to him on that wild and poor Barony and at a crushing rate in addition will be difficult to get. Unless we can manage to buy two sufficiently powerful steam engines or Bogie Trams . . . to put a guard rail at the sharp curves . . . we cannot go in . . . it is really pitiable . . . traffic was just beginning to develop. . . If we could master our work we could . . . cover our working expenses and be a great boon and a blessing to that wild and extensive country at its back . . .
> . . . We have been served by the Contractors with a writ to draw out the deposit which is about £2,800 . . . we have resisted this demand. . . . The contractors are now at work at the Schull station and have not finished . . .
> . . . The Line is now closed . . . something over £4,000 to put us in fair working order . . . £2,000 would get us new engines to draw 50 tons . . . If some help cannot be given the Grand Jury will have to take it up . . .

The appeal to the Lord Lieutenant reveals the agony of those who had promoted a railway that they imagined would be a god-send to a very impoverished part of Ireland, had fought against protest and carried out the significant quantity of Governmental requirement. They had received their Order, and engaged a Contractor who appears to have taken advantage of their ignorance and gullibility; they were now in a straight-jacket of singular Irish making.

Alerted by this information, the BoT wrote to the Grand Jury in Cork and asked their agreement to a request that Nathaniel Jackson, County Surveyor for the North Riding of Cork, visits the tramway and reports to the Grand Jury. On 23rd April the Grand Jury advised the BoT of the subsequent findings;

> The stipulated gradient of 1 in 30 has been faithfully carried out except at New Court where the line rises 14 in. in 30 ft, but can easily be altered. Several embankments have sunk. Ballast packing under the track on non-roadside sections' inclines is slack, especially in a rock cutting between Schull and Ballydehob. [This would be at Laurel Hill. Author.]
> Five curves are under 2½ chains; one of these is only 2 chains and none has been properly check-railed as required by Hutchinson. Checkrails are not carried far enough nor properly fastened, being spiked only and not bolted nor tie-rodded.
> Recommendation that a 'good bogie engine' be purchased at a cost of c. £1,250 - it is useless to make the present engines equal to the heavy traffic.* The cost of altering the present engines would be equal to the cost of a new engine: a good make could be guaranteed to last 4-5 years: the present engines could be put to light work.
> Recommends 'two tie byes' between Skibbereen and Ballydehob to make stations 3 m. apart. This will enable an extra train to run on Fair Days - cost would be c. £300. Carriages flanges are two shallow and the wheelbases too long for the curves. A seawall is needed at Schull station. Fencing is still unfinished, the level crossing road approaches are too steep and poorly finished.

On the face of it, such a Report is considerably at odds with Hutchinson's findings and his Certificate; could things really have become so bad between Hutchinson's last visit and Jackson's? On the face of it, they could.

Jackson concluded that 'three-fold traffic is offering'. He opined that the line could be put into good order under J.W. Johnstone, the Manager, and the track into working

---

* If this statement is taken at face value, despite what may seem a paltry number of passengers on mixed trains (unsurprising in a, by then, lightly-populated district), other traffic was not disappointing - and Jackson envisages potential increase. Income from traffic would therefore be satisfactory but outgoings on locomotive repairs and track maintenance were insupportable.

order with Thomas Creedon as Superintendent of Permanent Way.

It would seem that Bernard Fleming had taken it upon himself as a self-appointed 'Our Man on the Ground', indeed his correspondence tells us more than the official scriptures. But on 28th April - three weeks after the cessation of trains - the Company gave the BoT their explanation of the stoppage:

> The locomotives failed because the firebox plates are ¾ inch steel instead of copper of ⁷⁄₁₆th inch. Expansion has opened the seams and tubes have leaked. The firebox plates around the firedoor ring have split from the rivets outwards, in one case so badly that water cannot be kept in the boiler. On the locomotives the tubes leak to such extent so they could not operate without losing time and using an enormous amount of fuel. Irregular stoppages have become so frequent that we have no other course than to suspend traffic.

What would we give for a sight of the lone fitter struggling to keep his charges railworthy in that lonely engine shed on the shore-line at Schull! And more valuable, for a sight of his Maintenance Book. He must have become almost a stranger to his own bed. Basically the trouble appears to centre around the tram-engines' fireboxes. Were they made of steel because the West Carbery Co. was pruning costs and therefore agreed a substitute for copper? Was steel preferred for reasons of delivery? Knowing the other steel materials used in the boiler, was there excessive expansion/contraction? Did in fact, the nominal builders of the engines actually make the boilers and fireboxes themselves, or was such put out to contract? There is no clear answer but one thing is certain, it would be beyond the facilities at Schull to do much more than remedy tube defects.* An extra hand, from the Cork workshops of the C&BR, would assist but nothing short of loading the complete engine onto a C&BR flat wagon at Skibbereen and forwarding it to Cork would meet the problems.

On 6th May, 1887, the 'Baronial Directors of the District' laid before His Excellency the Lord Lieutenant & General Governor of Ireland the miserable state of the undertaking, for which 'the entire sum for making the line was granted to the contractors'. (The Directors' complaints were supported by Nathaniel Jackson who wrote from the County Surveyor's Office at Bandon to the Under Secretary at Dublin Castle on 7th May. He felt that a sum of £3,000 would enable the Company to fit new fireboxes, lay two sidings and spend £1,000 on a new locomotive, and end the impasses. The Under Secretary's re-action was to put the matter in the Pending Tray: 'Put by for the present', he wrote in the margin.)

They then appealed to the Lord Lieutenant for help. It was a desperate situation.

The failure of the Tramways Company to come to an Agreement with the 'Cork & Bandon Railway' - as it was known locally - to work their line was a fatal flaw from the beginning but the terms offered were not acceptable; the Cork concern had demanded a guaranteed traffic of £4 per mile, or £40 a week. This stipulation was quite beyond the Tramway to consider.

However, it was agreed the C&BR Skibbereen Station Master should do duty for both concerns.

---

* At first there were no shed or workshop facilities at Skibbereen.

Chapter Seven
Worrying Times
1887-1888

It was now the Tramways Company's turn to complain. The BoT received a letter from them dated 9th May, 1887 saying that the Grand Jury had not sent them a copy of Jackson's Report and they could make no further comment, but meanwhile 'all three fireboxes of locomotives *supplied by the contractor* were completely done up and they had no funds for repair or a new locomotive'.

The BoT must have wondered how it was going to rid itself of this disastrous and irritating concern, for the next missive arrived, dated 7th May. Under Clause 45 of the Order in Council, twenty ratepayers had applied for a BoT Enquiry into the troubles besetting the Tramway. Their Memorial, submitted by John Levis of Glenview, Skibbereen, required Hutchinson 'to make enquiry into any default in making and maintaining the line'. The BoT replied by pointing out that their powers were limited by the Order in Council but Hutchinson *would* hold an Enquiry in Skibbereen on 30th May.*

Hutchinson reported on 13th June; it is fascinating to see who attended, and in what capacity having regard to what had happened previously:

Dr Levis and Mr Limrick	Baronial Directors
Mr Carey and Mr Johnstone	Promoters' Directors
Mr Downes	Company Solicitor
Mr Nathaniel Jackson	County Surveyor: W. Riding of Co. Cork
The O'Donovan	(representing ratepayers of the Eastern Division of West Carbery)
Mr Fleming	(representing ratepayers of the Western Division of West Carbery)
Col Somerville	former Baronial Director
Mr Marmion	Chairman: Skibbereen Board of Guardians
Mr Dorman	formerly one of the Promoters' Engineers
Mr J.W. Johnstone	General Manager of the Tramways Company

There were others.

Hutchinson took an engine and carriage and inspected the line before the event. The O'Donovan and Mr Marmion said at the outset that the Enquiry was not sufficiently publicised and should be adjourned, but Dr Levis said the EAGLE had carried a notice, so Mr Fleming said in effect, 'Let's get on with it'. And they did.

As is the way of things, the Enquiry was to reveal some odd goings on. Despite the legal dispute with the contractor - whose whereabouts they had failed to trace (in modern times, Lord Lucan disappeared similarly) - the Tramways Company was negotiating with William Martin Murphy, 'that well-known public man', to overhaul the line and that he would 'likely work it himself as a contractor's line'. Thomas Downes (Company Solicitor) testified that when he put it to the shareholders in London, whose chief was Sir John Lubbock, their reply was, 'We have given sovereigns per Share to the contractor; why should we pay?' Downes added that when Kenneth Bayly, Engineer of the G&SWR since 1878 had inspected (informally, it is presumed) and he himself visited the tramway 'a very heavy 40 ton train was working satisfactorily'.

Hutchinson also interviewed J.W. Johnstone, Manager (who had been appointed on 18th December, 1886), Augustine Cruise, engine driver (appointed August 1886),

---

* The Memorialists included Revd T.C. Abbott (Rector), the RC Parish Priest, a Justice of the Peace, the High Constable of the Barony, the Head Constable, the Clerk of the Union, McCarthy (butcher), T.P. Somerville (farmer), J.T. Wolfe (Solicitor), James Swanton; a broad spread of local worthies!

WORRYING TIMES 1887-1888

Thomas Creedon, foreman-ganger (appointed 26th November, 1886) - the last-named had come from the Cork & Muskerry Railway, also of 3 ft gauge and opened 8th August, 1887. Hutchinson presented his Report on 13th June; his findings were:

LOCOMOTIVES: Their failure was responsible for the cessation of services.
TURNTABLES: Owing to their failure, locomotives could not be turned in observance of the BoT conditions.
CHECK RAILS: These were only 30 ft long; this was insufficient, especially on long curves. They were improperly secured.
BANKS: These had settled and then slipped, becoming too narrow on the formation.
SLEEPERS: Untreated Larch had been used whereas creosoted Baltic Redwood had been specified.
RAIL FASTENINGS: Their application on curves was erratic.

Hutchinson concluded the Promoters had failed in maintaining and working the line. He recommended repair of the existing tram engines and the fitting of copper fireboxes. 'A new locomotive should be obtained, consistent with the nature of the line'. And he gave the Company four months to remedy the defaults.

It fell to the former Engineer to the Company, J.W. Dorman, to reply to these criticisms during a Vice-Regal Commission review of Public Works (including certain Irish railways) during the latter half of 1887. He blamed - previously - the shortage of money for poor condition of earthworks. The centrepins of the turntables were screwed up so tightly that the tables arched giving them excessive drop at each end; when an engine's weight was put on the table, the guide rollers fractured in consequence. The ultra-sharp curves were due to trains on straight sections causing the track to edge forward (in part due to brake application) to the effect that an ensuing curve was sharpened and became dog-legged.

Dorman preferred to use untreated Larch for sleepers which, if cut in the correct season, lasted three times as long (16 years) as Redwood: creosoting was the C&BR practice.

Dorman opined that it was the expansion of the brick arches which caused the fireboxes to leak* and that the engines had not been fired correctly.

By September 1887 the superheaters ('Steam Driers') had been taken off, but without much improvement.

The troubles of this insignificant railway system in an unheard-of and remote part of Ireland had come to a head when Mr James Gilhooly, the member for Cork West, asked the Secretary to the Treasury in the House of Commons on 16th May -

Whether it is a fact that the line of tramway between Schull and Skibbereen has become a complete failure owing to the manner in which it has been constructed; and whether, considering, the fact that a Government Engineer has certified that the line has been properly made, the Treasury will come to the relief of the ratepayers who are liable for the money advanced for the promotion of the scheme?

He was later to ask the Secretary to the BoT the same question and, (not withstanding the BoT Certificate) if it is a fact that all traffic has been suspended? If so, who is responsible?

In reply to Gilhooly's question in the Commons, the Secretary to the BoT (Baron Henry de Worms: Liverpool, East Toxteth) replied;

---

* This was hardly a tenable argument as brick arches had become the common practice.

An inspecting officer of the BOT reported . . . the railway was fit for public traffic . . . in September a certificate was issued . . . in consequence of representations made by 20 ratepayers . . . BoT have given orders for an enquiry at early date.

Locomotives: Dick, Kerr: had not been enthusiastic about the boilers and thought tubeplates were too thick. The fireboxes had been fitted with 'superheaters' which were actually steam-driers for the riddance of exhaust steam. They leaked from the start, eventually burning out (and were removed).

In October 1886 traffic was stopped for ten days whilst the engines were being repaired but recovery was short-lived and none could climb the frequent sections of 1 in 30. True, under the terms of the contract they were specified to haul 30 tons; this they were *just* able to do when in first-class condition but even then they were forced to a standstill at the breast of every summit to build up sufficient steam to proceed. In an attempt to conserve all steam for haulage, the vacuum brake had been disconnected [a circumstance which disturbed Hutchinson considerably].*

Turntables: Adding to their problems, three months later the turntables had become so unreliable that the engines could not be turned and they made one journey with chimney leading [the design of a tram engine was such that it could be driven with the men and controls at the leading end - some were designed (when running with chimney leading, and the driver's view ahead was obstructed) to be driven from either end . . . but not in this instance].

Formation: The formation works were in a wretched state: owing to slippage the width at the top of embankments was too narrow. Embankments had sunk thus increasing the gradient to 1 in 28 in places. The whole route was short of ballast; rock had not been cut away to sufficient depth below the sleepers, so that in places the track rested on bare rock and there was no space for ballast. Curves had been forced out of shape. There was a deficiency of spikes to hold down the rail.

There was no seawall at Schull station which was endangered by every high tide. Neither were there any sidings for Fair and Market workings. [Were these omissions the fault of the promoters or were they features which the contractor ignored? Were they left off the contractor's schedule by oversight? There seems to be a lamentable lack of foresight - Author.] 'The promoters have made defaults in working the line; they must make them good', the Enquiry was told. It began to look as if the *promoters* must now take all the blame!

Rectification: This must include the fitting of copper fireboxes to the tram engines and the purchase of a new engine best suited to the conditions, having an 8 ton axle loading. Turntables must be put into good order. Additional sidings must be put in, and the Schull seawall.† £3, 000 would be needed to effect these, and three months allowed to complete - in the event the Tramways Company was given four months.

The deliberations of the Enquiry did not satisfy. In the Commons on 17th June the Chief Secretary to the Lord Lieutenant of Ireland asked if 'the BoT Inspector was the same person who two years before had inspected and passed the line? Will the Government now conduct a careful, independent Enquiry, by a different Inspector, into the causes . . .' etc.

---

* When steam pressure falls below a certain point, the vacuum brakes 'leak on' and stop the train; the brake is only held 'off' if there is adequate steam to maintain a vacuum.
† The building of extra sidings at Skibbereen, Hollyhill, Ballydehob and Schull will be found under 'The Route described', p. 107.

The pencilled, marginal notes on the documents at the Public Record Office testify to the confusion among civil servants called to rule on a matter which had no precedent. Was a BoT Inspector responsible if a railway undertaking which he had found to meet his strictures and for which he had sanctioned a Certificate, then proved faulty? There was no doubt in West Carbery that the BoT and its Inspector was to blame for being unaware that the engines and stock were incapable from the outset. (One has to read into this the traditional Irish trend to blame anything of this nature on the Government of the day.) Clearly Mr Hunter was one of these - in his mind the fault lay with the BoT and not the local promoters. Where did an Inspector's responsibility end?

The Revd T.N. Townsend of Kilcoe Rectory put his concerns onto paper by writing to the BoT on 24th June:

> ... to inform you in the strongest possible manner to discontinue this terrible invasion of the inhabitants here - first of all it is quite clear that it will never pay them, there will continue to be the half-yearly tax on the poor about here who are already taxed higher than their means will allow ... the line is a constant danger to all horses ... it is a crooked, bad road so that the carriages fall off the line ...

But he was told that the BoT had no authority whatsoever over the contractors to do either of these things.

Gilhooly had already made a name for himself by asking frequent questions in the Commons concerning Cork-related railways. More widely, he had earned the reputation as having 'fought for the rights of a down-trodden people in an alien Parliament'. Born 1847 as James Peter, son of Peter Gilhooly of Bantry, he married a local girl, being imprisoned several times for political activity. Meanwhile he became Chairman of the Town Commissioners, of the Rural District Council and President of the local National League. He served on Cork County Council and was twice MP for North Co. Cork; he died on 16th October, 1916. In West Cork he was especially concerned with the Bantry Bay Extension Railway and the similar sea-seeking extension line to Baltimore.

The weeks passed and now it was August; in the Commons James Gilhooly asked the President of the BoT if he will *compel* the contractors to repair the line and supply locomotives? On 9th August an internal memo at the BoT seems to have summed up the situation; it concluded the line *was* fit for traffic at the Inspection, but it is not *now* ... and this was to be the official reply.

At Skibbereen, Col Somerville proposed that the Grand Jury (who agreed and acted on the proposition) send a strongly-worded note to the Treasury stating that it had been moved that the Government should pay £2 per cent per annum of the dividends due from Tramways Company, and so give nominal relief to the rate-payers of West and East Carbery, on grounds that the BoT Inspector certified that the line was fit for opening ... and now admits it was not (9th August, 1887). This was certainly a new twist to the story.

Being much behind with reparations, the beleaguered Tramways Company (who had managed to cobble together £3,000 for the purpose) sent a pathetic letter to the BoT on 28th October to ask if an extension of time would be given for locomotive repairs and suggesting that a further six weeks would be needed. The BoT acceded to a new date of 21st December and on 28th December, 1887 the Company advised that it was intending to re-open to traffic on 2nd January, 1888.

The Treasury was not inclined to take heed of the Grand Jury's intimation of the previous August, and had not replied, so on 15th March, 1888 its Secretary (Capt H.F. Townsend) was instructed to write again ... 'Government should pay £2 per cent for which cesspayers are now liable . . . had not the Government Engineer certified the line was fit for traffic?'.

So the cat-and-mouse play continued, repetitive arguments and Reports proliferated. The Tramway Company persisted while Government departments no doubt prayed that this irritating and obscure concern had died at birth.

60, North Street, Skibbereen, for many years the Company's Registered Office. *J.I.C. Boyd*

Chapter Eight
Hopes reborn
1888-1892

West Cork was in an unsettled state, even as a tramway between Skibbereen and places to its west was under consideration. In the known perception of the time, a railway could bring the forces of law and order as well as more peaceful benefits. 'To quell flash-points and rioting a large military force arrived in Skibbereen by rail in June 1881 and the gun-boat ORWELL followed by the BRITOMAR, anchored in Schull Harbour.'

At this time, James Gilhooly of Bantry and MP for North Cork was serving sentence in Naas Gaol; he became an enthusiastic protagonist for railway schemes in the district. Gilhooly was to become very familiar with Ballydehob and Schull shortly after the Tramway was re-opened: he addressed public meetings in support of The Land League on behalf of Castle Island tenants (and other islands affected) who had been evicted in the summer of 1890. The uneasy state of things was worsened by the news that the potato failure in the Schull area was causing great distress, and fears of a further famine were expressed.*

No account of the WCT situation at this juncture can ignore the events which were occurring on its doorstep; ignoring the problems in which it found itself, both as an engineering disaster and financial failure, it was likely to be the target of vandalism as a transport venture which, though promoted for peaceful ends, could just as easily bring the instruments of law and order. Little could it be imagined that it would be in the centre of civil unrest until the mid-1920s.†

When the line re-opened in the following January it was in no better position regards motive power save that the tram engines had each had considerable overhaul and replacement so that they were able to maintain a service until they were joined by a four-coupled tank engine with leading bogie obtained from Nasmyth, Wilson & Co. Ltd later in the same year (see Chapter Fourteen for details).# This carried the name ERIN.

The Company had been able to borrow £1,600 to put both track in order and reduce the initial cost of ERIN. Urged on by the crying need for passenger stock which would remain on the rails (!), they extended a Hire Purchase Agreement which covered the balance of ERIN's cost and that of a new coach, the locomotive and coach totalling £1,818 9s. 6d. Wisely, a bogie carriage (the first on the system) was preferred so that undertaking had now taken the first steps to operational reliability. The critical stage to enable the Company's impasse was now past; the ability to borrow £1,600 had followed a Vice-Regal Enquiry in 1887-88.

Even now, the Tramway deigned to provide essential links with the rest of Ireland north and east of Skibbereen, by failing to make useful train connections with the Ilen

---

* Railways were being encouraged by the Government to bring forward any scheme which would offset the effect of famine. A local construction which fulfilled the Government's wishes exactly was the building of the Baltimore Extension Railway, a Light Railway begun in May 1891 which extended the C&BSCR from Skibbereen to Baltimore Pier.

† More detail may be found on p. 116 of the MIZEN JOURNAL No. 6, 1998: 'The Castle Island evictions - 1889-90' (Liam O'Regan).

Nasmyth, Wilson was established in 1836 as the Bridgewater Foundry, Patricroft, Manchester by James Nasmyth; the title Nasmyth, Wilson & Co. Ltd. was adopted from 1882. From 1873-1938 most of its locomotive production went overseas.

Valley workings; this may be due to a continuance of unreliability felt by the Tramway management . . . understandable!

John Limrick now took the chair; the Registered Office was at 60, North Street where the Skibbereen Gas Co. met. Its Boardroom was hired at £10 per annum. C.T. Oliffe became Secretary while J.J. Johnstone, a promoter and original Director, died. P. Slattery was the Skibbereen Station Master.

In October 1886 a Royal Commission on Irish Public Works had been appointed, with Sir James Allport, then age 74, as Chairman.* Its terms of reference were; 'Whether increased facilities could be afforded to trade or commerce by any changes, legislative or otherwise, in the organisation or management of the Irish Railway system . . . etc.'

The Commission reported in 1888 and began by criticising the Act of 1883 in no uncertain terms in that it was too cumbersome, expensive and involved many counties and baronies, too many engineers and perhaps more than one Grand Jury. Though not suffering under all these drawbacks (as had the Clogher Valley Railway, for instance), the S&SR had laboured under its weight. There were other faults, one pertaining to the S&SR being the excessive responsibility thrown on the local ratepayers if the Promoters made default. Moreover, the Grand Jury was composed in the main, by owners of the land 'while the County cess falls principally on the ratepayers'.†

Furthermore, no provision was made for any margin of capital to serve as working capital (except in a few cases not including the S&SR) where all capital was used in construction and nothing was left available for repairs and renewal of permanent way, stock etc.

'The danger was that lines might simply be a means of investing money on the strength of the guarantee, and that the shareholders would have no interest in the management of the concern.' This defect was brought to the notice of the Commission by a firm of London solicitors.#

The absurdities which the Enquiry had highlighted were partially remedied - especially the impoverishment of ratepayers called upon to underwrite losses to the extent that few proposals were now coming forward - by the Light Railways (Ireland) Act 1889 52 & 53 Vict. cap. 66 of 22nd August. With this measure, the Lord Lieutenant could declare that a light railway was required for the development of 'fisheries or other industries' but Government financial help would be needed to create it; the Treasury could meet that need. The S&SR did not, in fact, qualify for help but the change in Government attitude to assisting backward districts was an enabling influence to its future developments: under the Act some 236¾ miles of railway were built, but only 43¼ miles was of 3 ft gauge.

All this Government support for rural tramways and light railways - not necessarily of narrow gauge - gave a great boost to the protagonists for the narrow gauge and for about forty years of the late 19th century their merits were claimed by book and periodical. While a few systems proved profitable, many others failed for three reasons; (a) they should have been standard gauge extensions of an existing line; (b) they were financially vulnerable having cost too much to construct; (c) transhipment costs and wear-and-tear renewal was excessive.

The S&SR did not conveniently fit these categories but it carried the distinction of being the least-successful promotion in Ireland. That however, is to deny its usefulness to the community once the enormous teething-problems were overcome. Writers of technical

---

* Sir James Allport, formerly with the Birmingham & Derby Railway; later, General Manager, Midland Railway.
† Second Report on the RCIPW 1888. (Parliamentary Papers 1888 Vol. 48. p. 28).
# Conroy: p. 254 *et seq.*

HOPES REBORN 1888-1892

railway books of the period who leaned heavily for their source material on English or Irish Government activities, either through ignorance or in the knowledge that mention of the S&SR would hardly be a supportive example, make scant reference to it.*

In the Summer of 1889 Jackson had made his Annual Report to the Grand Jury (dated 15th July). He found the original tram engines in 'good order' but we are left to speculate exactly what had transformed their performance. The new 'bogie engine' had been delivered and was expected to be running in a few days. Clearly, the management was in high hopes of fewer sleepless nights.

While 'good order' was found in the track, Jackson wished to 'earnestly impress upon the Directors the necessity of erecting a tank at Ballydehob whatever the cost (which in my opinion will not be much). It will be better than running the constant risk of having the engines disabled and that at the most critical period of traffic'. [From this remark it may be assumed that the engines' tanks were insufficient in size and that, although there was a tank at Kilcoe station, a second intermediate one would save the engines having to drop the fire *en route* owing to shortage of water.]

Traffic was steadily increasing and better by £16 6s. 3d. than the corresponding half-year previously. Jackson recommended the building of a pier at Schull in connection with the tramway and opined that this would readily reduce the Guarantee on the line 'as the Harbour is of the best and easiest approach on this coast'. A copy of this Report was sent to the BoT as required, who forwarded it to the Directors.

Seeing the 1889 Act as an unexpected lifeline, the supporters of the Eastern Section of the Tramway - who had been obliged to lie low after their last unsuccessful attempt - lost no time in calling a meeting of ratepayers at Skibbereen Town Hall on 26th August, 1889 with a view to applying for a grant under the Act to build the intended line to Glandore and, a fresh inspiration, a branch to Castletownsend Harbour.†

On 17th August Downes had written to the Lord Lieutenant's Office, in the knowledge that an Act which would benefit the Glandore scheme was about to receive Royal Assent, to accompany a Petition ' to develop the fishery trade . . . for Mackerel, Cod, Ling, Haak, Sole, Plaice . . . and Herring . . .' After waxing lyrical on the potential of Glandore Harbour with its 'splendid site for a pier' written testimonials were added in support.

Downes had done his work well; there was praise for the now tramway-served Schull whilst the disadvantages of tramway-starved Glandore were emphasised. It appears that before the opening of the Tramway, Schull Harbour had only been used by French fishermen yet now further development of the trade was hampered by locomotive breakdown and shortage of rolling stock. In 1888 the Tramway had carried 1,850 boxes of mackerel each containing 60 fish; in April-June 1889 it carried 6,189 boxes.

Traffic receipts spoke for themselves:

1886	6th September-31st December	£454	1s.	0d.
1887	1st January-6th April (Line closed)	£313	2s.	3d.
1888	Half year to 30th June	£736	16s.	3d.
1888	Half year to 31st December	£877	3s.	8d.
1889	Half year to 30th June	£993	10s.	1d.

* The contemporary and definitive publication on LIGHT RAILWAYS (J.C. Mackay): [1896], is a case in point.
† Castletownsend Harbour. In absence of any supporting map, it is assumed the branch would have served the east side of the harbour where there is a short pier, currently used. A photograph of this narrow sheltered bay shows the coast-wide and primitive arrangements for landing fish; here they were landed on a projecting spit of land ('The League') and packed in the open in boxes or barrels, delivered by ship. Loaded, these containers left by horse and cart.

The objective was to load fish directly from a pier into tramway vans which, with closed doors, would keep ice packed among boxes, etc., free from melting until they trans-shipped at Skibbereen station. At present the warm air melted the ice before the boxes reached Skibbereen station. Cork was the immediate goal for the haul: here there was an immense demand, especially on Fast Days. There was evidence that Cork was already selling fish to the Irish hinterland or consigning it to the 'great Fish purchasing centres in England' (Birmingham, Liverpool, Manchester, London etc.). After the season ended, salted fish were sent to markets in the south of Ireland by rail. And this, years before refrigeration became widespread . . . !

It is not difficult to imagine the enthusiasm for a tramway which would raise the standard of living through the proven trends of the fish trade. Directors Limrick and Carey signed the Petition. Fitz John Hussey de Burgh (Kilfinnin Castle), said a sudden large catch would leave them short of carts, so that the fish was already bad before it arrived at Skibbereen station. 'The landing place at Union Hall is a miserable slip.' 'Loaded fishing vessels pass Glandore which has no landing and no supplier of ice; the Manx and Irish fishing fleets avoid it and prefer Baltimore or Kinsale instead.' William J. Limrick, Michael Crowley, Thomas Fuller and other fishermen gave evidence.

Richard Carey, Manager of the Munster Bank at Skibbereen these last 15 years, added that £4,664 was paid in for fish brought from Glandore and Castletownsend in 16 weeks. He had personally founded the Baltimore Fishing Co. with the arrival of the Ilen Valley line.* This Company served several harbours but carting to Skibbereen ceased about 10th July annually as fish went bad in the carts.

Not content with the Glandore Petition, a second concerning the Western Section was prepared and copies were sent to the Lieutenant General and the Rt. Hon. Arthur J. Balfour MP, Chief Secretary for Ireland. To the former Petitioners was added the name of John S. Levis.

The value of the second's content is that d'Avigdor's *coup de grace* is revealed; during the period of traffic suspension and 'as a result of a suit instituted by them' (the Petitioners)

> . . . against the Contractors, they enforced from these Gentlemen a Sum which enabled them partly to cope with their difficulties in getting the engines repaired and defects in the permanent way, partly remedied. Petitioners were further assisted by the holders of the Tramway Stock who guaranteed for Petitioners the repayment by instalments of £1,200 the price of an additional engine.

The Petition then introduced further 'fishy business'. It complained that 'the Engineer who planned the Line did not extend the same to the Pier at Schull where there is deep water', which pier was a recommendation of the recent Royal Commission. They explained that with about half a mile of extension, the railway could terminate on such pier and boats load directly into a Train, 'bound for the Cork, Bandon & South Coast Railway, Cork, Dublin and the English Markets . . . an enlargement of the pier would also be necessary'. They also pleaded for their own station at Skibbereen in view of the cost of sharing one with the CB&SCR.

In seeking 'favourable consideration' of their Petition, it was considered that £5,000 would be adequate; the Petition asked that it be recalled that the ratepayers were also taxed in respect of the guarantees for the Ilen Valley Railway and Bantry Bay Extension 'at 2s. in the £'. A contribution from 'State Funds' was sought . . . 'No more eligible place for judicious expenditure . . . could be found in Ireland'.

---

* Baltimore was then the most important fishing harbour in all Ireland.

One body which supported the proposal to build an extension to Schull pier was the Congested Districts Board for Ireland which came into existence in 1891 'to ameliorate the conditions of life of the inhabitants of certain of the poorest districts of the western coast of Ireland . . .' This identified certain areas where the quality of the land was insufficient to support the population at its existing density; 'the great want is not more land but more *good* land'. The vital part played by fishing in the coastal areas was recognised as even in a good year people lived on the edge of starvation.*

The countryside at the western end of the S&SR was designated a Congested District, while there were pockets of land around Skibbereen also named.

In consideration of the aims of the Board in relation to improving the fishing *industry*, (rather than just as a means to stave off starvation), increased profitability would only be achieved if better transport was available; in particular, Co. Cork needed more landing facilities for its existing markets in towns where up to now, only smoked and salted fish was available. With rail connection, fresh fish packed in ice could reach a Dublin dining table.

In West Cork the major response to these observations was the emergence of Baltimore as a fishing capital and, to lesser extent, the rail extension to the pier at Schull.

[The emphasis on fish traffic in promoting the conception of an extension to Schull pier must not mislead one into believing that in event, fish would be the lifetime root of its traffic. In the heady enthusiasm of the times for social improvement by means of encouraging the trade, none at that time could envisage that a century later, fishing would be controlled and subject to quota. Even within memory, the fishing grounds had moved so that boats from Schull had to go further and look for other forms of catch.

Ultimately, as fish landings at the pier decreased, Extension loadings were more of grain, domestic and railway coal, and sea-sand which was widely used to improve the land. Such hard economic realities must be considered as they explain why 90 per cent of the S&SR goods traffic was carried in those covered vans, whose contents were otherwise a mystery to the onlooker . . !]

By 1894 the fishing fleets on which the trade relied were of 'immense size'; their origins included Ireland, the Isle of Man, England, Scotland and France. Most mackerel went to America, with approximately 300 fish in each barrel.

Evidently Nathaniel Jackson felt it was prudent for him to inspect the Tramway again soon, for he sent a letter to the Grand Jury on 17th March, 1890; it 'was in good working order'. A water tank at Ballydehob 'has been attended to with the best results as no engine has been disabled since the want of a full water supply'.

He drew attention again 'to the great injury done to the rails on the quick curves by the long wheelbase of the four-wheel carriages causing too great a strain', pointing out that they could be altered at little cost (as he mentioned in previous Reports, but they had ignored his recommendation). Whilst more fang bolts and tie bars had been put into the track, many more were needed.

At Skibbereen inspection pits should be built to 'enable the carpenter and painter to clean and paint beneath carriages'. And one was necessary at Ballydehob too . . . 'I have mentioned that before'. He reminds the Board that when an accident had occurred 'to one of the connecting links of the engine, for want of a small pit the driver was unable to get under the engine and the train was delayed for fully two hours'.

'It is no use my mentioning these things . . . if they are not carried out.'

'Some minor repairs are wanted to the engine shed at Skibbereen. These should be attended to at once as great inconvenience arises from the neglect of trifling things.'

---

* Ref: THE GREAT IRISH FAMINE (R.T.E.), Mercier Press, Cork, 1995.

Clearly, Jackson had lost patience and communications were poor.

In due course the BoT received copies of Jackson's work; alerted to the shortcomings, they asked the Company why the work had not been done? The Directors blamed a shortage of funds, 'It would cost £40 to alter each carriage': as to tie bars, many had been added.

Either passenger traffic had increased considerably or the Company had become tired of putting the carriages back on the rails, for in June 1890 they told the BoT - doubtless with the ploy of shocking them into action - that they 'were using goods trucks converted into carriages . . . would the Board lend them any money?'. The BoT put the matter to the Treasury who recommended that the Company incurred expense on putting matters to rights, and then the County would be bound to re-imburse it!

And so the matter went on another 'Departmental Tour' and there is no evidence that carriage wheelbases were altered but plenty that they continued to leave the rails. The Company's solution was to acquire bogie carriages as cash allowed; the first was bought in 1890 for £465. It was composite and carried 40 passengers.

Under Section 6 of The Regulation of Railways Act 1889, the Company would be required to write or print fares on tickets issued after 1st January, 1891: the Company asked the BoT if it could use unpriced stocks and hand write the fare thereon? This was acceptable.

The Petitions to connect the tramway with a pier at Glandore and a rebuilt pier at Schull had mixed results; Glandore was refused again but on 29th December, 1892 an Order in Council was given to the Tramway Company to extend their line as requested. The Government gave a grant of £750 under the 1889 Act for the purpose; under the title The Schull & Skibbereen Extension Tramway & Light Railway, the line was to be 42 chains in length and to commence at an end-on junction with the existing system on the north edge of the highway immediately to the rear of Schull station (see plan p. 156). For most of its length it was on private right-of-way. The Extension was opened in October 1893; it fell all the way to the pier.

The narrative has run ahead somewhat in order to conclude the effects of the 1889 Act; changes resulting from the Spring Assizes 1892 would end the life of the Tramway Company and bring problems for the Extension, not to say other developments. But of them, more later.

An example of the S&S Tramway being involved in local unrest (just the kind of incident which the local people had anticipated and feared), occurred in unusual circumstances:

> On June 20th, 1890 the trial of Father Crowley was due to take place in Schull. He was charged with having used intimidation towards Reverend E.H. Hopley, Rector of Toormore. Feelings in Schull were running high and hundreds had travelled up from Goleen with Father Crowley and hundreds more assembled in Schull.
>
> A large force of police arrived by train (said to be about 200 men, of whom some came on 'Long Cars'). The Court assembled and heard that a 6 cwt. stone had been placed on the rail lines just west of Ballydehob.
>
> After some discussion the case was adjourned to Bantry . . .

In due course Father Crowley was convicted and sent to prison in Cork. On release he returned to Schull by train, accompanied by cheering crowds *en route* and at stations. At Schull he was met by hundreds of well-wishers who walked to Goleen with him.*

---

* The writer is indebted to Mrs Mary Mackey of Schull for this account.

Chapter Nine

Fulfilment in sight
1892-1905

At the 1892 Spring Assizes a Committee was appointed 'to inspect both the main line and the extension', but as the Extension was, at that stage, simply a worthwhile intention, presumably the Committee - which inspected on 9th June, 1892 - was basically assessing the potential of one. On the 'main line' it had been necessary to replace 3,000 sleepers with new creosoted ones at a cost of £384 during 1891 but 10,000 still needed changing - this amounted to almost 6 miles of the line's 14 miles 600 yds length.

After inspecting the layout at Skibbereen station, the Committee condemned the dangerous practice of reversal into the station which all arrivals were obliged to perform. It was recommended 'that negotiations be opened with the Cork & Bandon Rly Co. for the building of a new platform further south'. (Nothing was achieved in this connection and the layout remained unchanged: a more notable Irish station legendary for even more reversing movements was Limerick Junction.) The Committee also noted the limited accommodation for rolling stock, a legacy of the idea behind the creation of a tramway whereby the line was considered as commencing at Schull and such limited facilities as existed, were concentrated there.

The Committee urged the immediate construction of 'shelter-stations' or Halts, at Church Cross and Kilcoe as there were no stopping places between Skibbereen and Ballydehob. This circumstance should not have arisen; Baronial Capital had been provided but after all the money had been handed over to the contractors on condition they provided Halts, they had not done so.

There followed an important change in the life the Company. Under the terms of the Order in Council and in consequence of 'two years or more' working losses incurred by the West Carbery Tys & LRCL, a Committee of Management* was appointed by the Grand Jury to take over the operation of 'the main line' - an important definition in time to come. In consequence, the last meeting of the original company took place on 26th June, 1892. The Committee of Management's inaugural meeting was on 4th August following under the banner, 'The Schull & Skibbereen Tramway & Light Railway'.

There was no provision for extinguishing The West Carbery Tramways & Light Railways Co. Ltd under these arrangements, so it continued to exist until the railways of southern Ireland were nationalised on 1st January, 1925, its meetings being held in Dublin. Thereby, shareholders continued to receive their guaranteed dividend from funds provided by the Grand Jury of Co. Cork, the only change being that these were passed through the Committee of Management. (In 1898, the Grand Jury became the County Council.)†

---

* Consisting of six Baronial Directors and six representatives of the Grand Jury.
† Under the Local Government Act of 1898, Grand Juries were to be superseded by County Councils. So far as baronially-guaranteed railways were concerned, the right of appointing Directors to represent ratepayers simply passed on to the new Councils. Members of Grand Juries tended to be landed gentry. In the matter of the S&SR, the Directors and Committee of Management seem to be from the same cadre of persons throughout.

It is not apparent whether the Grand Jury involved with the S&SR did exactly the same as was done on the CL&RLR&TCL - to re-appoint the existing Directors before the dead-line of the new Act in mid-1899 and thus postpone the risk of any new blood being voted onto the County Council for the time being, which might have upset the status quo! This was demonstrated on the CL&RLR&TCL when in mid-1902 a shareholder wrote to point out the inadequate representation of shareholders on the Board. It is now impossible to find out if a similar position obtained on the S&SR; the CL&RLR&TCL Order in Council omitted to expressly define the shareholders' representation. (*continued over*)

An early view of The Tram after arrival at Schull. Driver Cruise leans nonchalantly on his engine.
Collection Mrs E. McCarthy

It was soon perceived that the situation of the Schull Pier Extension was, by virtue of these manoeuvrings, unworkable; while the S&ST&LRCL had authority to operate over 'the main line' it had none to work over the Extension. (It was argued that only the WCT&LRCL had authority to do *that*!). Much time was lost in acrimony but by an Agreement of 1894 the Committee of Management was permitted to work it on behalf of the WCT&LRCL.

It had required the seven years between 1886 when the Tramway opened, and 1893 before the problems that had dogged the undertaking from the start might be seen to be overcome. There were still doubtful features which the Committee of Management inherited about which little could be done; the tortuous track and saw-tooth gradient profile would remain to plague the Committee into modern times, and cause it to curse its progenitors and builders without compensating appreciation of the benefits a railway had brought.

The narrative has again overtaken events on the ground. A meeting at Skibbereen of the West Carbery Presentment Sessions reported in the EAGLE for 13th May, 1893 is worthy of note. Its findings were highly critical:

[The S&SR was not the only system to have a Committee of Management imposed upon it; among others were the Timoleague & Courtmacsherry Light Railway, the Tralee & Dingle Light Railway, and the Donoughmore Extension Light Railway (see Conroy p. 250).]

(See also Flanaghan p. 36 for the near-parallel case of the Cavan & Leitrim Railway.)

FULFILMENT IN SIGHT 1892-1905

1) The line did not yet connect with Schull Harbour.
2) There were many sleepers lying on the lineside.
3) Too many of the line's administrators had a self-interest in the CB&SCR; the CB&SCR influence should be curtailed.
4) The Grand Jury was not giving enough attention to the Tramway.
5) The Tramway Directors were held in disrespect. 'They only attended a Board Meeting for one hour in Skibbereen; they left immediately afterwards and as soon they had collected an attendance allowance of One Guinea'.
6) The ratepayers were unrepresented at every level.
7) There were no local men among the Directors.

The meetings of Presentment Sessions were held in Skibbereen on the first Thursday each month with powers to fund certain public works, i.e. road repairs. Their deliberations concerned the Tramway only so far as it was adjacent to the highway and one of its number (a Mr Notter) caused laughter when he admitted 'I do not know any more about the Tramway than if I was living in Africa'. The meeting had before it an official request for 'Special Presentment' of £300 towards the Extension.

The Board replied to the Sessions' criticisms as follows:

1) The CB&SCR was ready to take over the Tramway management.
2) The sleepers at the lineside were rotten and had been taken out of the line; many more needed replacing.
3) The vehicle wheels 'were worn to a thread' and required replacement.

In 1894 the Stock Exchange Year Book contained an entry concerning the July 1886 issue of £155,100 Perpetually Guaranteed 5 per cent Trust Certificates at the then-price of 112 per cent; the face value was £100 with interest payable on 15th January and July each year. (In those days of near nil-inflation this was an attractive and guaranteed yield.) The Trust consisted of guaranteed shares in the S&ST&LRCL and the Cavan, Leitrim & Roscommon Light Rly & Tramway Co. Ltd, the amount of shares in the former being £56,827 and the latter £99,000 . . . dividend guaranteed by the Tramways Capital Guarantee Co. Ltd. Shares were quoted on the Stock Exchange under 'Financial and Land' as 'Irish Light Rails'. The 1894 price was 107.

By Act of Parliament 57-8 Vict. cap. clxxxiii of 1894, holders of the Certificates were enabled to exchange them for an equivalent amount of shares deposited with the Trustees. By 1st October, 1896 out of a total value of £155,100 Certificates issued, £151,300 had been exchanged. (The last entry in the SEYB for the Certificates was for 1900.)

Some random musings on the 1894 Act are pertinent; the Act does not make it clear as to whether the holder of a £100 Trust Certificate was allocated *all* S&SR shares or *all* CL&RR shares or (most likely) *pro rata c.* 36 Schull shares and £64 of Cavan Stock.

[The risk of the Capital Company having to make up the interest on the Trust Certificates was low because there was both the Baronial and Treasury guarantee on the Tramway Company shares in order to secure the interest on the Trust Certificates. Had there been surplus dividends from the Tramway Companies the Capital Company shareholders would have done well, bearing in mind that they had only subscribed £20,000 for an interest in the surplus on combined Tramway Company capital of £155,750.]

In the end it would seem that when the Capital Company was ultimately wound up in 1932, there was no money left for the shareholders in the Capital Company. (The holders of shares in the S&SR when it was absorbed by the Great Southern Railways in

1925 received £125 of 4 per cent Preference Shares in the GSR for every £100 held in the S&SR.)

One other interesting question emerges; did the contractors - if paid in shares - receive £100 of shares for £100 of work and thus sold out at a profit of £12.50 per share, or had they to take £100 for £112.50 of work?!

The Annual Inspection in late 1895 revealed that an 'unknown action' was eroding the webs of the rails and so something over two miles of line would have to be replaced. The cause may have been that ballast (or whatever had been used instead) had been brought up to the level of the rail surface - a common practice in those times - and so the webs were always wet; the coastal atmosphere was also unhelpful.

At Schull there was provision to store the locomotives under cover but all the rolling stock there stood in the open, virtually at the water's edge. Weathering was accelerated so a Carriage Shed was built over the siding which extended eastwards from the Station House. As was the Irish practice at the time, the sides were not carried down to the ground, allowing air to circulate.

A new bogie carriage to seat 8 persons (1st Class) 32 persons (3rd Class) was delivered in 1890, carrying No. 5.

The developments continued: the layout of Skibbereen yard was altered and extended, including the replacement of the turntable. As well as the new carriage, a new locomotive (GABRIEL) was bought from Peckett & Sons Ltd for £1,220; under hire purchase terms the Company had three years to pay. Another wagon was acquired (details are not given) and 62 tons of new rail to replace that with deteriorated webs. The reasons given for these purchases were that the original rolling stock was now 20 years old and *all* required replacing. And for the same cause, all rails needed renewal. The latter may have been the case, but the former suggests that wagon upkeep had been neglected - perhaps due to lack of money . . .

The Managing Committee echoed the Engineer's opinion; a new and bigger locomotive was needed and to meet increasing traffic for which the original small wagons were inadequate, larger stock of greater capacity was essential. Nor did they omit their annual bleat - 'sharp curves and steep grades need removing'.

Attention was now paid to the 'lop-sided' accommodation of the undertaking, wholly as a result of it being deemed to commence at Schull. In consequence, the exchange station at Skibbereen hardly had any facilities at all, all repairs being done in the open air or in a small workshop adjoining the Locomotive Shed at Schull. It was patently obvious that this was the reverse of desirable arrangements and in 1898 construction was begun on a new Engine Shed (later extended) and Fitting Shop at Skibbereen. Just as urgently needed was a new Carriage Shed and Repair Shop for carriages and wagons, and these followed.

John George McCarthy, now surveyor for the West Riding of Co. Cork, had made his annual inspection of the county's tramways and in September 1899 reported to Cork C.C. that 'all the Tramways in his area satisfied him, except the West Carbery Tramways'.

[At this time the Surveyor brought to the new Council's attention, a new competitor with steam power for transport in West Cork, the road steam traction engine. In consequence all bridges which were the responsibility of the Council, including a number on and surrounding the S&SR, were given restricted weights; in the next few years quite a number were found to be too generous. Offending locomotive operators were seldom caught at first but the Carberys were now truly in the Steam Age.]

By the turn of the century Timothy Creedon (Manager) and William L. Carey (Secretary) continued to serve, with the Registered Office remaining at 60, North Street,

Skibbereen. The Committee of Management included Florence McCarthy (Chairman), Henry Cullinane, Daniel Burke, Timothy Hayes, Edward Roycroft and John H. Kelly.

In Autumn 1899, the shareholders having complained about the late payment of the guaranteed dividend, an investigation took place. It appeared that with the Grand Jury, whose responsibility it was to pay it from their funds, becoming the County Council in 1898, a new brush was sweeping clean and Counsel's Opinion was sought on the matter. Counsel's reply was that 'the County Council should not pay dividends to the West Carbery Tramway until it was satisfied that the previous dividend had been properly applied'. This was an extraordinary utterance as the dividend was paid to shareholders who took no part in the administration of the railway; possible it was a continuation of the proper lack of knowledge by the Committee of Management?

In August 1899 'an Act to facilitate the construction of Light Railways in Ireland . . . with particular reference to the fishing industry' was passed and on 26th August some ratepayers from Glandore met in Skibbereen Town Hall to promote - not for the first time - an eastward extension of the Tramway from Skibbereen to Glandore with a branch to Castletownsend Harbour under the terms of the new Act.* Although the scheme enjoyed approval and the instance of the Baltimore Fishing Co. was quoted the idea came to nothing once again.

Bearing in mind the criticisms of the original tram engines, the decision to buy a new boiler for IDA must have been prompted by Armstrong, the Engineer, that such would be worthwhile; an order was placed with Nasmyth, Wilson & Co. Ltd in May 1901 at a cost of £403. Was this connected with Armstrong's dismissal on 8th July: he was replaced by Richard Evans of 53, South Mall, Cork (who was Engineer to the Cork & Macroom Direct Railway)? Two months later, sanction was obtained to roof-over the S&S platform at Skibbereen, and give it a brick facing.

The year 1901 saw the Irish Board of Works examining the accounts of the Committee of Management.

Richard Evans, whose appointment dated from 3rd December, 1901, was also to be responsible for the 'Architectural Department' and was retained on a consultative basis at £30 per annum. His reign began with a further inspection of the Permanent Way at the Board's direction, and a critical Report and recommendation dated 29th November, 1902. His findings do not surprise, and can be summarised, using his own vernacular:

a) The average speed of travelling, including stoppages, is 10½ mph.
b) Ruling gradients are 1 in 30; sharpest curves 300 ft radius.
c) Some of these curves are badly sited on gradients, and at considerable distance from the summits.
d) Steep gradients occur at - New Court, Church Cross, Hollyhill, Meen Bridge, Crooked Bridge, Ballydehob, Woodlands, near Schull.
e) Quick curves entail much additional wear to the rails, sleepers and fastenings, all of which must be kept in better condition than would be necessary if the curves were easier.
f) Wheel flanges become quickly worn from grinding against the outer rails of the curves, and must be kept in exceptionally good order to take the curves safely.
g) The engines are strained to their greatest capacity while hauling comparatively small loads up the gradients, and brake power has to be used on the downgrades. The result is that there is slow travelling, large consumption of coals, wear and tear of stock, and small carrying power.
h) Liability to accidents is greatly increased because of the gradients and curves and slight carelessness on the part of the driver on a down grade will cause the train to be out of control.

---

* Such a branch must have had The League on the eastern shore of Castletownsend Harbour, in mind. A terminus at Castletownsend itself would have involved considerable civil engineering.

Slippery rails and brakes out of order would have similar effect. If the curves were removed on or near down grades, a runaway train would not have to traverse a sharp curve at high speed but could be pulled up on the level.

i) The contractor laid out the line without avoiding the hilly parts of the County Roads and should have taken advantage of the contour of the country. At the expense of some additional cuttings and embankments, gradients would have been reduced to 1 in 50 or 1 in 60 and sharp curves could have been avoided. These advantages would have been very great and resulted in greater safety and earning power while reducing expenditure on traffic and maintenance.

j) To make changes to the course now and provide diversions to avoid curves and gradients would entail a collective length of seven miles i.e. half the length of the line at a cost of app. £25,000 and its length would be increased by 500 yards. Had this necessary improvement been carried out when the line was built, only a small portion of this cost would have been entailed.*

The Committee of Management having Evans' Report before it, and supported by resolutions from local bodies, approached the Lieutenant Governor again for a Grant towards improving the line on the basis of a scaled-down Estimate which Evans had been asked to submit; this time the amount came to £10,000 which would cover only the worst curves which would be increased to 10 chains radius. An appeal towards further rolling stock was also made. (In later years it was acknowledged officially that 'train speeds on the S&SR are the lowest in Ireland': in some measure this was true.)

When in 1905 Evans had occasion to refer to his 1902 Report, he added that to flatten curves would reduce costs to £10,000 and that 'the present situation threatens the type of derailment as had occurred on the Tralee & Dingle Railway if a runaway train, even if check rails are used . . . would topple over at the first sharp curve'.† (Evans understood that the T&DL received £23,000 from the Government towards improvements.)

During 1902 'Cheap Day' tickets were introduced; these were available on the 7.15 am train from Schull and by the same train from Ballydehob. Passengers east of Ballydehob to Skibbereen found them only available on the following train due out at 10.20 am from Schull; was this a ploy to prevent overcrowding - and a load which might be too much for the engine to haul - of the first train?

Up to now the Registered Office had had to serve as a Board Room and general office - it was in North Street and some way from Skibbereen station. During the summer of 1903 tenders were invited for new premises in the 'Tramway Yard' with the sanction of the CB&SCR. This proved to be a small cement-rendered single-storey building with slate roof, having a central front door flanked by a single window each side. It fronted Marsh Road facing west, and had the 'main line' of the Tramway passing to its rear. (Road junction improvements here have altered arrangements here from those shown on the diagram p. 111.) When S&SR traffic ceased, the internal shutters were closed as if in mourning, and the building survived until auctioned in 1964.

In the thirteen years from 1890, the four four-wheel carriages were supplemented by three bogie vehicles; there is no formal list but from the conflicting sources, many without date, the following seems to be pattern of purchase:

---

* It is notable that Evans did not recommend the improvements and so eliminate the shortcomings of the Contractor; perhaps he realised the finance could not be raised? Apropos wear and tear due the necessary heavy braking, there would be a constant need for changing worn-out brake blocks; does 'brakes out of order' suggest slackness in this regard? - Author

† This spectacular accident, known as The Camp Disaster, took place on Whit Monday 1893 and stemmed in part from a driver not being familiar with all the line's hazards. A pig train ran away down the infamous Glenagalt Bank and derailed on a 2½ chain curve over the Curraduff Viaduct. [For a racey account see NARROW GAUGE ALBUM (P.B. Whitehouse), 1957: Ian Allan Ltd.]

FULFILMENT IN SIGHT 1892-1905

No.	Date purchased	Builder	Type	Cost
5	1890	Gloucester Carr. & Wagon	Compo./40 seat	£465
6	1903	Gloucester Carr. & Wagon	3rd/	£350*
7	1903	Gloucester Carr. & Wagon	3rd/	?

By 1904, the wretched carriage situation was relieved somewhat but the initial No. 5 needed 'new bogies, sides and ends' and a new coach similar to it was urgently needed even before the two almost identical Nos. 6 & 7 were delivered.

In November 1906 the Chairman, Edward Roycroft JP, prepared a statement for the Royal Commission regarding the carriage position:

Each carriage (of the original delivery of four-wheeled vehicles) held 18 passengers but as business improved there were not enough seats so the Directors turned some wagons into something like passenger cars, but this was not enough, and in 1890 they got a bogie composite carriage for 40 passengers for £465.

The BoT would *not* have been happy to learn of the expediency!

The Gaelic Athletic Association and its strong nationalistic undertones was keenly supported in Skibbereen and in February 1904 the Skibbereen Football & Hurling Club had a special train and set a trend whereby there was a regular Sunday train from 1906.

A significant occurrence took place when on 25th April, 1904 The Clyde Shipping Co. Ltd gave notice that its weekly steamer from Cork would no longer call at Schull. In times past it was the coastal trader which was the most convenient and economical bulk carrier around the shores of Great Britain and had retained its importance wherever there were no hinterland railways. The curtailing (but not cessation) of Cork coastal passages took place over a long period, but this event marked a 'bull's eye' for the S&SR and its rail connections with the rest of the country.

One such traffic, now lost to ships, was the carriage of about 300 tons of meal weekly, from Russell's Mills at Limerick via Cork, bound for Schull, whence it was carried by rail to Ballydehob and Skibbereen. Most other goods from Cork city came likewise. In consequence the most economical route was per CB&SCR/S&SR.†

Newham suggests that at this time the S&SR carried 'heavy machinery for the local mines' but this is difficult to sustain as mining had practically ceased.§

It could be said that the S&SR had now reached a 'plateau' in its history. True, it had inherited the most appalling route with which any driver of a steam train conveying passengers would have to contend, and there was little the Company could afford to do about it. Yet on the whole, prospects were brighter as new motive power, better carriages and goods stock were procured. Skibbereen station was more workable and it was infinitely easier to work the system from a terminus now equipped with repair facilities and covered storage for stock. It will be seen that the new goods vehicles were larger and carried a greater load to tare weight; the bogie engines treated the track more kindly whilst having sufficient tractive effort. In fact it was commented that the 'broad gauge stock is off the track at points more frequently than ours, despite our notorious curves'.

This stage of events seems to be an appropriate place to conclude this chapter.

---

* Also given as £300.
† See Appendix One on Coastal Shipping & Competitors.
§ See Appendix Two on West Carbery mining.

Train at Skibbereen with rebuilt tram engine IDA. 1906.

H. Fayle

Chapter Ten
Consolidation
1905-1916

While it might be expected that the three tram engines would be a very poor investment so far as further expense was concerned, surprisingly a decision to rebuild IDA in 1905 was made. Notwithstanding that alterations had already made to this machine in 1886 (see p. 60-on), at the same juncture it was revealed that MARION had received a new domed boiler at a previous date (not disclosed in the Minutes) and that this domed boiler 'was now on its last legs', so the rebuilding of IDA would prove to be even more drastic than MARION.*

It is obvious that the first boilers did not produce enough steam and were probably prone to priming as the water level changed considerably within the boiler on the steeper pitches. Clearly the fitting of the new boiler to MARION had brought improvement, as the fact that the engine had been used to the extent that its boiler was life-expired proves. A more drastic rebuild of IDA would seem a natural step, allowing that finance was not available for a new locomotive of different type; virtually the whole locomotive above the frames was discarded so that when a new domed and larger boiler with alterations to the fittings, cab and side sheets was added, it bore little resemblance to its sisters.

A new locomotive to work alongside ERIN and having the same wheel arrangement, was ordered from Peckett & Sons Ltd of Bristol,† also in 1905. Ostensibly, this was to replace MARION. H. Coggins (a curious misnomer; his name was William Goggin) the Company Secretary, wrote to the BoT pointing out that the byelaws did not reveal that the title of the undertaking had changed, and that he was now the Secretary. The BoT thought he should be sent a copy of the current model byelaws 'without the byelaws on spitting which we did not approve for Irish railway companies'. [This sounds like discrimination!] Goggin clarified that the Company was now based in Dublin, 'where the seal is'.

When in 1906 the new Peckett made its first run to Schull, an interesting ceremony took place 'behind' the station on the Pier Extension. On mounting the footplate before the smokebox, Father John O'Connor, the Parish Priest of Schull, broke a bottle of champagne over it and christened the engine GABRIEL.# (Whether this was a 'baptism' or a 'launch' is open to question.) A newspaper account recalls those present: they included

Members of the Committee of Management	
Richard Evans	Engineer (and his son)
John W. Loane	Station Master, Skibbereen
Jack Daly	Engine Driver
James McCarthy	Fireman
Jim Stack	Guard

---

* Names only were carried until 1925.
† Peckett & Sons Ltd. Began as Fox, Walker & Co., Atlas Engine Works, St George, Bristol. Began locomotive building in 1864: taken over by Thomas Peckett in 1880. Two almost identical engines to the S&S delivery of 1905 were built for the 3 ft gauge Sarawak Railway in the same year. There was to be a further 4-4-0T supplied in 1914, a similar but smaller type.
# GABRIEL was not named after the Archangel but is that of Mount Gabriel, the 1,339 ft high 'mountain' which overlooks Schull from the north.

77

GABRIEL, as yet un-named, before it left Bristol for Ireland. *Collection J.I.C. Boyd*

GABRIEL is officially named at Schull before entering traffic. *Collection G.R. Thomson*

CONSOLIDATION 1905-1916

The years 1906-1907 were important ones for the Company. On 15th May, 1906 Evans sent a further Report to the Directors, along with costings, regarding the state of the Permanent Way; this Report could be condensed by saying he found there was little 'permanent' about it. A copy of Evans' findings, together with an explanatory letter from the Management Committee, to the Rt Hon. James Bryce, Chief Secretary for Ireland, accompanied an application for a Government grant to put things into order. Bryce wanted more information so a more detailed document headed 'Proposed Improvement of Permanent Way - CONDITION OF THE LINE - August 1906' left the 'Skibbereen Offices' on 9th August. Much of this repeated earlier applications, but new material was:

1) T.M. Batchen, Chief Engineer of the Board of Works, inspected the line on 19th July, 1906; his Report is awaited.
2) The loss on working since the line opened was £80,114. The Treasury contribution has been 2 per cent towards the interest on Capital, making in all £21,600. About £4,000 has been paid out of the Local Taxation Account under Section 58, Sub-section 4 of the Local Government Act, 1898. There is a balance of over £54,000 which has been borne by the ratepayers of the Guaranteeing Area, and which has fallen exclusively on the occupiers of land and houses.
3) These districts already make guarantees to two other railways:
   Ilen Valley Railway. Skibbereen-Dunmanway. 16 miles.
   Bantry Extension Railway. Drimoleague-Bantry. 12 miles.

At this point the appeal sets out the rates payable for each district and ends '. . . they had the enterprise and spirit to impose on themselves a heavy tax for the development of the country and the promotion of public welfare and deserve to be rewarded for their progressive action'. Strong stuff.

The Traffic Receipts showed promise:

	£	s.	d.	
1897	2,279	5	1	
1898	2,283	2	8	
1899	2,392	6	9	
1900	2,350	2	8	
1901	2,449	7	0	
1902	2,741	12	2	
1903	2,711	15	9	
1904	2,756	12	6	
1905	2,826	2	9	
To June 1906:	4,473	11	5	(the highest half-year to date)

It was costing more and more to maintain the condition of the line, viz: 1900 £787 12s. 5d., 1904 £1,076 4s. 10d., 1905 £1,036 13s. 4d. That was a matter for concern.

To increase the traffic as is wished, new and better rolling stock is needed. These are our costs of renewals and repairs to carriages and wagons:

	£	s.	d.
1900	188	4	10
1901	146	9	7
1902	157	14	2
1903	277	8	2
1904	541	13	7
1905	397	10	8

A new engine costing £1,220 has just been bought (GABRIEL) to be paid for by instalments over three years.

Mr Armstrong, then our Engineer, in July 1900, found that the number of worn rails was rapidly increasing; since then a large portion of the line has been relaid. Since 1903, 6,150 sleepers and 3,000 paling posts have been bought, offices built at Skibbereen, the retaining Wall at Clashmore Lake has been taken down and rebuilt. Recently the BoT made an Order and check rails had to be placed on all curves - all have incurred heavy outlay.

[All of which might have been summed up as 'Small railways can have large expenses'.]

The application closed by saying that the Committee hoped extra expense would not be incurred by a request for the Company to supply maps, etc. to back their case. 'The Railway has already been, and still is, a very burden on the ratepayers of this poor, remote and congested district'. So wrote William Goggin, the Secretary.

Appended was Manager Creedon's 1906 Report, terse and to the point:

CARRIAGES.

No. 4 3rd Class. Requires new roof, platforms, end and sidepanels and floor.

No. 5 Composite Car. New bogies, panels on sides and ends, doors, 1st Class compartment newly upholstered. You also require a new composite bogie carriage to interchange with No. 5 carriage.

A New Guard's Van for Passenger Train, as our present vans are worn out, and also are too small for the conveyance of passenger's luggage, which entails the putting on of an extra covered wagon on nearly every passenger Train, of which wagons we have not enough for our goods traffic.

Nos. 47, 48, and 49 Guard's Vans require a thorough overhaul, No. 49 especially, as the frame work at sides and ends is loose, and crumbling to pieces. Nos. 47 and 48 are now generally used instead of covered wagons for goods.

COVERED WAGONS.

You have 12 covered goods wagons of which 4 have, during the last 18 months, got a general overhaul, leaving 8 which badly require to be put in a satisfactory condition, as I am constantly receiving complaints about goods damaged in wet weather through leakage at sides and doors. You require at least 4 more wagons, of 6 tons each, to cope satisfactorily with our present goods traffic, the bulk of which is made up of mill stuff.

OPEN GOODS WAGONS.

You have 5 open goods wagons and 4 ballast wagons, each of which requires a thorough overhaul.

TIMBER WAGONS.

There are two wagons for the conveyance of timber, which are always run together, the timber lying on two bolsters, one on the middle of each wagon. Sometimes these require a ballast wagon between for the conveyance of long timber. These wagons require to be repaired very badly, as, in consequence of their every day in use, we cannot afford to take them off the road for any length of time. If we had one open-ended wagon for the conveyance of timber, about 14-16 ft long, it would save the running of the other two very often, and would give a chance of carrying out repairs from time to time.

CATTLE WAGONS.

You have 22 cattle wagons, one of which has been rebuilt in the past half year, and another taken into the workshop to rebuild [sic] it. Of the remaining 20 wagons, 18 require to be renewed altogether, with the exception of the ironwork.

(It must be concluded that the system was carrying traffic quite beyond its ability to keep up with renewals and repairs to its rolling stock in terms of time . . . and possibly without funds to buy sufficient materials or labour. In the West Cork climate there is rapid deterioration of woodwork which is not adequately protected. The Manager's experience of the weight and types of traffic reveal that the forecast made in the 1880s of traffic patterns - if in fact, one was made at all - may not have provided enough wagons of suitable types but as the final arbiter was d'Avigdor himself (who failed to complete delivery as contracted), the likely answer is that Kerr, Stuart would provide stock which experience had shown would meet the needs of their customers . . . perhaps no one warned them that Irish needs were different while the guidance given to the promoters was either nil or faulty!

So it was the Manager and employees who had to wrestle with the difficulties which the Report scarcely hides. If the woodwork of stock suffered the worst, we learn that the running and braking gear was in a poor way on a railway which by its faulty construction, was the last situation on which such could be tolerated. In short, the originators of the undertaking had promoted a Tramway, which despite its drawbacks, had become a *successful* transport medium, more akin to a Railway. So much for its latter-day critics.)

The emergence of Railway Status from Tramway Perception is subtly demonstrated by the discarding of the Tram Engines in their delivered condition and attempts to improve their performance by inexpensive rebuilding. Then came the first locomotive of Railway type. Next it was the substitution of four-wheel carriages for bogie stock. By 1906 the bijou dimensions of the goods stock meant that it might be running 30-40 per cent more mileage over that switchback route than it would had the wagons enjoyed greater carrying capacity . . . an argument then recently put forward - but lost - in favour of the Great Western Railway's Broad Gauge.

The West Carbery Tramway had been a victim of its own success. Metamorphosis into the Schull & Skibbereen Railway, easily achieved by giving it a new title, was hampered by the inevitable shortage of money. The appeal now being described, was for a Government Grant of £10,000 by which it was confidently assured the undertaking would be on a firm footing. After these necessary considerations, Manager Creedon's Report can be resumed:

STATIONS.
The goods stores at Schull and Ballydehob require to be renewed. These were built 20 years ago and consisted only of ¾-inch boards nailed on to a timber framework, which is all rotten. It would be better renew these with corrugated iron sheds, and a concrete floor, which would save a lot of damage to Goods by getting rid of rats.

You also require a crane at Schull station capable of lifting 3-4 tons weight; and a turn table at Ballydehob Station is urgently required as, when working Ballydehob Fairs, we have to run the Engine, with the large wheels leading, from Skibbereen to Ballydehob, which, owing to our sharp curves, is a continual source of danger, besides causing extra wear and tear on the Permanent Way and Engines.

I might also bring under your notice that you must very soon make provision for the purchase of a new Engine. No. 3 Engine* (ILEN) will very soon be worn out - in fact, it is not fit to work the traffic on the road at present, and is scarcely ever at work more than a day or two at a time, while another engine is being washed out, and then it entails the lighting of a special Engine to work the Goods Traffic.†

---

* Creedon meant the third Tram Engine.
† Creedon's Report is quoted exactly as it was presented.

Up to the time of GABRIEL's delivery, materials for the four existing locomotives had cost £800 per annum, or 7d. per train mile. Maintenance of carriages and wagons was averaging £172 or 8½d. per train mile. The Committee of Management, in supplying these figures to the Chief Secretary, Dublin, added, 'These figures are enormous . . . come to our aid'.

Richard Evans was then asked to comment on the provision of a new engine as outlined by Daniel Creedon. He (Evans) pointed out there was little that could be done as regards a more powerful design:

> Nothing could improve haulage capacity save by using heavier locomotives with more coupled wheels, but this is unacceptable as the rails would not take heavier weights. The present locomotives are already at maximum wheelbase owing to the quick curves prevent us adding more coupled wheels. For the same reason, weights could not be added to existing locomotives.

His reply suggests that wheel-slip had proved to be the 'bottom line' and in certain conditions, lack of adhesion could make a mockery of the larger engines' extra hauling capacity.

On the Chairman's evidence in November 1907 before the Vice-Regal Commission, one engine (probably MARION which was still in 1889 condition; see above) had been sold for scrap for £25.

According to Roycroft, the 'ordinary timetable was worked by the best engine we have [available]' in winter but a second one was necessary on Fair Days. There was nothing in hand.

Though over-running the narrative somewhat, we continue into 1908 in order to follow the activities of the Commission for in that year certain members made a personal inspection of the Railway. It must have been a sobering experience for they concurred that it was impossible for the driver to observe the mandatory speed limits when the rails were greasy after rain; they admitted that under such circumstances there was great danger in passing over the sharp curves.

And what of the grant the S&SR so assiduously sought? None was forthcoming and no action was to be taken until after the Final Commission in 1910, when a Grant *might* be considered. It could have been that the Commission was influenced by the opinion of their member W.M. Ackworth* who advised improvements to the coast road and the substitution of road transport in view of the meagre tonnages carried by the railway. His view was supported by the 1904-1908 figures showing average weekly takings of £4 3s. 4d. a mile when operating expenses were £5 14s. 7d. The employees were working a 12-hour day - more if it was demanded, and there was no overtime.

Ackworth's concern was that whilst a grant in the sum of £10,000 had been suggested initially, this was now boosted to £30,000 to ' provide for complete re-construction, including seven miles of deviations'. His view that road transport would do the work more economically seems ill-timed; road vehicles were then more prone to failure than the tram engines whilst the coast road was quite unsuitable for commercial traffic. But then, Ackworth is unlikely to have visited West Cork . . !

Roycroft's evidence on these occasions is certainly vivid and supported the Railway's case admirably; the trouble was that it did not always agree with that of the Manager or Engineer. He mentioned a payment of £12 to the CB&SCR for a second-hand turntable

---

* Ackworth was described by Joseph Tatlow in 50 YEARS OF RAILWAY LIFE as 'a well-known writer on railway economics and a keen but friendly critic of railway affairs.' He was a great traveller, a competent linguist and Secretary to the English Section of the International Railway Congress.

for Ballydehob - which Creedon observed was badly needed: Newham states that the one replaced went to Schull. Confusion here; the original turntables at the terminii had been replaced with improved type, but there is no evidence that Ballydehob ever possessed one.

The Vice-Regal Commission 1906-1907

During 1906-7 a Vice-Regal Commission sat in Dublin to examine Irish railways, the Schull & Skibbereen being one of those concerned. Examined was the Company's Chairman Edward Roycroft JP, and its Engineer Richard Evans CE (on 20th November, 1906 and 2nd March, 1907 respectively).

The examinees sought to pin the blame for faulty construction on the failure of the BoT to supervise, but early in the Enquiry it was pointed out that the Board's interest was confined to reporting on the feasibility of the scheme from an engineering point of view, preliminary to it being brought before the Grand Jury of the county, the Privy Council and the Lord Lieutenant of Ireland for their respective roles.

It was recalled that after a recent Report on the line's unsatisfactory position, the BoT had sent an engineer to inspect and report back to it. Anger was scarcely concealed by the Grand Jury in that no copy of the Report had been received in Cork.

In 1906 the Managing Committee had applied to the Irish Government for £10,000 ' to improve the line'. In consequence, a BoW engineer made a further inspection and report at the request of the Governor. Copies of his Report were sent to the Under-Secretary and the BoW on 2nd August, 1906 but the S&SR had had no communication and were ignorant of any findings.

As has been said, the examinees' intention was to place the blame on the BoT and they quoted the considerable correspondence with the BoT, who had been sent copies of the Accounts. But it appeared to the Managing Committee that their submissions only found their way into the filing tray. Roycroft referred to an exception when, during 1899, the BoT (possibly wearied by letters from Skibbereen) had written recommending:

1) That from 1901 a third daily train be run.
2) That the S&SR timetable be re-cast so as to make connections with the CB&SCR.
3) That from 1904, through rates be available to CB&SCR stations.
4) The adoption of new and improved goods rates from 1900.

At the same opportunity the BoT had disowned any responsibility for the design and construction of the line; 'the plans were the province of the promoters'. Furthermore, under the Act of 1883 there was no provision for Government supervision over works constructed with state aid. (The subsequent Allport Commission found this to be a very serious defect of the 1883 Act.)

It is notable that Roycroft - true to character - did not accept either this formal explanation of the BoT's limitations or a repetition of them which the Commission were at pains to repeat at the start of his evidence: throughout his examination he continuously hints that the BoT should be held responsible.

More colourful was Roycroft's account of the affair, though whether he was able to vouch for the truth personally cannot be verified entirely; at any rate, these matters have now become local folklore and some recount them today as if they were personally witnessed!

'... The contractor rented a very big mansion in the neighbourhood, and kept a pack of hounds and a very excellent table, and did extremely bad work* ... The railway was badly designed and the work was even worse, but he entertained all the Authorities in the most sumptuous fashion, and not withstanding all the defects, the line was duly passed.
 - Did the price you speak of, include all the rolling stock?
 - Yes, the rolling stock included three engines which struck work from the first, however. They seemed to have a constitutional objection to hill-climbing of any kind.
 - Was it the engines or the men that struck work?
 - The engines. They defied all the laws of motion, and instead of going forward they imitated the crab and began to go backward.
 One has now disappeared into space, and was sold for £25, and degenerated into scrap iron... The legend the engines bore was 'S&SR' which meant Schull & Skibbereen Railway, but the people of the district, on account of the state of the engines, interpreted it as the 'Sick & Sore Railway'.
 - Have you done anything to improve the rolling stock?
 - We have done a great deal ... General Hutchinson (who came down in March after it had opened the previous year) said everything had been done wrong by the contractor ... he who had passed the line 5-6 years earlier ...
 - You have improved the rolling stock out of earnings?
 -There are none ... the money came from ratepayers. Last year the actual loss was £4,092 3s. 4d. By virtue of the Act the [British] Government pays 2 per cent on the capital of £57,000 ... the working expenses of the line were £1,242 3s. 4d. and in addition there was £2,580 for the 5 per cent guaranteed on the capital ... in the town of Skibbereen the rate is about 7½ in £ ... in the last five years, though the actual baronial contribution was only £1,710, owing to the loss on working expenses, they have been called upon to pay £2,858. All this is paid by the farmers, the occupiers and none of it ever fell on the landlords (the Act having provided that it should be paid by the occupiers, who could claim no deduction from the landlord for this rate) ... The line broke down owing to the bottom of one of the engines tumbling out, and they could not go up the steep gradients.
 - There are gradients of 1 in 30 or less?
 - Yes, all holes and hollows.
 -Was the tramway built and financed by a London Company?
 - Sir John Lubbock's Company financed it. The local people had no voice in the matter. The Board of Management took over in 1891; it has six members, five County Councillors and one Skibbereen merchant. They have no experience or practical knowledge of railway management ... they are as experienced as their predecessors.
 - Then they cannot be expected to promote the efficient working of the line?
 - I cannot disagree with you.
 - It is of the greatest importance to remedy the sharp curves and gradients, and to provide proper rolling stock?
 - We have a new engine to haul 60 tons ... bought with a loan from the Bank and repayable in three years, and costing £1,220. It was made by Pickett's [sic] of Bristol.

Under further question Roycroft submitted that the S&SR 'was a pretty bad railway, it had two trains each way each day except one day in the week when we get three. It costs so much because ... so much coal is required and the wear and tear on the curves and gradients ... we work it has cheaply as we can'.

 - Do the Managing Committee of the County Council pretend to be railway experts?
 - I do not want to say anything about them ... they are all doing their best ... and compare favourably with the old Grand Jury Committee.

---

* There was a marked decline in Irish hunting in the '80s after restrictive legislation. Many households took up residence in England and on the Continent in consequence.

- Does it seem to you . . . to be an economical way of running a railway?
- It would better if it were in the hands of some railway experts.
- Why is it not worked by the C&BR? Do you run into their station?
- Yes, and pay a rent of £125 a year . . . Obviously because they do not want to lose £1,200 a year . . . We would make them a present of it . . . I would rather the thing be torn up. The baronies have put £80,000 into it already.
- If anybody would take it off your hands, free, gratis and for nothing, and work it for you, would you be glad?
- We would give them our Benedicamus.*
- At the time of construction, the Grand Jury gave a guarantee on the understanding that the C&BR would work the line . . ?
- There was one of those vague promises which mean anything or nothing. The C&BR gave a vague promise.
- Mr Avigdor was the contractor?
- He was everything; he was the promoter. He said the ratepayers would not be called upon for anything but if it were, it would only be 2d. or 3d. in the pound.
- Who supervised the construction?
- Mr Avigdor had an engineer of his own. The Committee of the Grand Jury were supposed to look after construction and keep the contractors up to the mark.
- Did they do it?
- They did not. The contractor tipped the Inspector . . . the men did what they liked. Though nominally supervising the line, they did nothing.
- Under the Agreement the contractor had to supply four locomotives and twenty-four wagons . . . rails of 56 lbs/yard?
- I think so; our Engineer has not got the original specification; we applied for it but could not get it. It appears there was a burning in Cork and this specification was there and it was burned.† . . . The engine came off the track the third day after opening . . . the engine and carriages would not run safely on the line?
- That is a most extraordinary story.
- That is a fact. The line was closed so the Committee borrowed £1,600 to put it right again . . . there was no arrangement for the contractor to keep the line in repair for a certain period after opening . . . he ran away the moment it was passed and we have not seen him since.
- Where did he come from?
- From London, I think. He went back to Australia then, and we have heard no more about him . . . He wrote a pamphlet and said he had bamboozled the Irish people, and that he was taking £23,000 over with him.
- With the borrowed money they got another engine and some rolling stock on the hire system?
- Yes.

Roycroft's further evidence may be paraphrased; he said that:

a) The contractor had used bad sleepers; Baltic wood was specified but soft Larchwood was used, and fewer of these than proper. 'The Grand Jury's surveyor looked after it; he passed it, as did the BoT Inspector'.
b) The contractor agreed to supply five passenger carriages and sixty other vehicles but supplied only four (eighteen passengers each) coaches and forty-nine wagons. Owing the passenger traffic increase, 'we were obliged to pay £465 for new carriages in 1890'.#

---

* Benedicamus - Blessing.
† This a typical example of native strategy; true or false, to fall back on 'a burning' is often quoted as a reason for loss where lack of will, shortage of time or staff, poor access or sheer carelessness can be covered up. The ploy is not confined to Ireland but is encountered there in all forms of circumstance.
# Roycroft is frequently questioned on historical, financial or engineering matters where his replies rely on hearsay or memory. These questions would have been better addressed to the Secretary, Engineer: in this instance for example, he gives a slightly erroneous reply and an inaccurate impression.

Roycroft confirmed that yet further stock was needed in 1898 when the Managing Committee took over.

> We built a new engine recently costing £1,300 [GABRIEL built by Peckett in 1905] the old ones are practically of no use. Wagons have had to be renewed; I believe the first ones were partly second-hand and they are constantly breaking down.
> ... We have built four wagons; we are building them ourselves, getting carpenters and carriage to construct them on our premises now ... Every one of the old stock requires renewing; they are practically valueless ... We are using them for all they are worth and getting the timber work done ourselves. All that is after only 21 years' wear. ... There is much wear and tear, the steam pipes burst frequently - and that sort of thing.

Almost all the remainder of the interrogation was repetitive and along the same lines. Unfortunately the evidence was frequently stated in a vernacular mode such as, 'steam pipes burst frequently', when the discussion concerns wagons! This may be due to the confused mind of the examinee or shortcomings in the short-hand account. Some remarks shed a little light on events not described elsewhere, but they are not always clear. However, doubtless the witness 'knew what he meant'.

To summarise: the VRCIR would be given the impression that an unscrupulous Jew had persuaded sufficient influential residents that he could build a railway in West Cork which would be a profitable venture or at the worst, the ratepayers would have to meet a small loss in exchange for its advantages. Competition for the contract had been bought off and secured by bribery, while the proposer proceeded to ingratiate himself among the neighbourhood by high living, entertainment and largesse. (Though not forthcoming before the Commission was the suggestion that he bought up properties vacant as a result of eviction; this would be ignorance of disastrous portent.)

To continue the summary: it was alleged the contractor had bribed those responsible for monitoring construction. He did not adhere to the Plans he had himself drawn up and had had approved. No one had questioned his alterations which curtailed some civil engineering, shortened the course, sharpened curves and increased gradients in order to save materials, etc. Furthermore, by his contract the Company could not hold him to his commitments once a BoT approval was obtained.

Did d'Avigdor take advantage of goodwill of the Irish and its unfamiliarity with matters of this nature? Did they accept him as a trustworthy man and leave him 'to get on with it'? The contract was far from watertight too. Was d'Avigdor the rogue suggested and did he 'buy his way' so that the completed railway was a victim of bribery in the vital places alongside some who had no experience of the 'bargaining' which is a customary process in certain countries. No doubt would be left in the Commission's mind that the Company felt d'Avigdor had cheated it and the BoT had a responsibility to which it did not admit. Worse, when it asked for financial help from the Government it was informed 'The time is not opportune'. Roycroft's bitterness is understandable but there is no *evidence* that d'Avigdor had criminal intent.

Allowing that Roycroft was determined to demonstrate the bitter cup which he and his fellow Directors had been handed and accepting that his evidence was couched in that vein and had included certain errors of fact, the condition of the undertaking had not been overstated. The management, staff and employees continued to carry out their tasks with the skill and loyalty which was expected of railwaymen in those times; perhaps they were unaware that in the circumstances they were operating 'the worst railway in Ireland'?

There were financial aspects aired before the Commission.

Apparently when Rt Hon. James Bryce, the late Chief Secretary for Ireland was down in Schull (the exact date is not recorded), he had said that an application for a grant would be dealt with sympathetically. When £10,000 was suggested, the Chief Secretary wrote saying the time was not opportune. Whatever sum would have been granted, the Directors would have had no influence on the matter themselves, and the 'poor ratepayers could not help it'. (Roycroft inferred that the railway had been imposed on the ratepayers from the first; they had no control over the creation and were bound to support it financially thereafter.) 'The ratepayers were helpless . . . Between 1897 and 1907 traffic has nearly trebled but expenditure is such that we have paid more against the guarantee than it cost to build the line altogether'.

Roycroft agreed that the six Grand Jurors had been imposed upon from the first by an enterprising contractor with their only professional advice coming from the County Surveyor who probably knew nothing about railways in particular. The Irish Board of Works Engineer, T.M. Batchen, had also been negligent in checking that the construction was being done in a proper manner. He was only seen once, yet where the Board had advanced money it bound its Engineer to make frequent inspections. On the morning the Board of Trade Inspector was to make inspection, 'The contractor had a lot of men with oil-cans oiling the rails to make things go smooth'. Roycroft was certain that no supervision had been exercised during the building of the railway.

Roycroft could list nine places *en route* where the engine was halted to built up steam pressure for the gradient ahead; 'Very often the passengers had to get out and shove it up the hill. There were some Englishmen in Skull and they wrote all about it in the London papers'.

It was alleged that 20 per cent of the capital had been spent on promotion and legal charges, and that the Grand Jury had hushed up the amount - the ratepayers could extract no information from the Grand Jury as to how the railway was being managed. The Enquiry concluded 'the ratepayers had manifestly suffered a very great hardship: the net loss had been £56,963 in 21 years, and the gross loss £86,000'. A reflection of the Guarantee embodied in the financial structure was that in 1907 the £1 shares stood at £1 5s. - a useful premium. (There was then a discussion regarding a possible redemption of the Guarantee by the Treasury.)

A deputation had waited upon the Chief Secretary in Dublin. In consequence, the Board of Works Engineer had inspected the railway in 1905, but the BoW had subsequently failed to send a copy of their Engineer's Report to the S&SR.* The County Surveyor was still (1907) making inspections twice a year as required by the Act, noting defects and complaints and making representations to the County Council.

The Enquiry learned from Roycroft of their continuing grudge against the BoW for the amount of grant they had allowed to the Tralee & Dingle Light Railway to upgrade the safety of their route following the accident in 1907.†

The Enquiry of that day finished on a more positive note when told the County Council administration now in being was a far more representative body. There followed more facts from the two examiners which are pertinent to train working, costs and timetables.

---

* It is small wonder that administrative affairs in Ireland gained a laughable reputation in England, frequently reflected in the cartoons of PUNCH at that period. Not so frequently recalled was that certain administrators responsible for Irish affairs were Englishmen sent over by the Westminster Parliament for whom there were sufficient attractions within the Pale as to make familiarity with the hinterland beyond completely unnecessary!
† In that year a livestock train had become out of control and left the rails on a sharp curve, with fatal results.

Continuing the Enquiry and the search for blame, and what bodies should be held responsible, the investigation pinned down the examinees with a now more searching quest for the culprits: at every turn the examinees stressed the injustice which had been meted out on the locality. The Minutes of Evidence return again and again to the same subjects; though they become tedious, who would have held his peace when such an opportunity to vent anger was afforded? It was held by the examinees that guilt should be shared along the following lines - note that the Board of Works was an Irish Institution, and the Board of Trade was London-based but had responsibilities in Ireland: it was a convenient circumstance for filibustering:

1) In view of local and Treasury guarantees, both BoW and BoT should have been responsible for ensuring the line was properly built.
2) Both BoW and BoT had failed in discharge of their duties.
3) Based on the above, the Commission must infer that the British Government had incurred a special responsibility to the ratepayers of the district.
4) It was accordingly, the responsibility of the British Government to provide them with a 'proper railway' [sic] now.
5) Such was the 'pretty result of wise and careful Government in the late nineteenth century?' posed an Examiner.
   Reply: 'It was'.

Other facts arose during an interesting interrogation: rumour had it that d'Avigdor had been killed in Australia, but that before he reached there he wrote a book stating that he had taken away £23,000 with him. It was he who had persuaded the Grand Jury of the scheme who then gave a Guarantee upon which the contractor raised the capital. The contractor had decamped with the whole of the capital (£57,000) on completion. 'There was not one penny left.'

When the line opened the contractor had not installed a turntable; the Company had bought one themselves: the Minutes do not make it clear whether d'Avigdor should have built offices, sheds, workshops and a Boardroom - the inference was that he had contracted to do so.

Because of the lack of turntables,

> the trains on some occasions had to go large wheels first [i.e. the 4-4-0 tank engine had to travel cab-first . . . down those steep gradients, past those sharp curves . . . and we have worse curves than Camphill . . . We have careful drivers and they slow down, but if the brakes give way, they refuse to work . . . We should not wait for the Government's 'auspicious moment'- there may be an accident first.*

At this stage the Enquiry's tone takes the complaint of the protesters; they question the BoT, BoW and County Surveyor's lack of concern at what must be, in view of the condition of the line, a cause for public concern. The view held is that the BoT was given 'some palm oil', and that it would liable for damages if it was a private trader and there was an accident. The Commissioners were tending to the opinion that Government departments 'were screening themselves behind their immunity'. For example, the Treasury maintained it had received so many applications for money grants from the South and West of Ireland that an application at this time would have no chance of a favourable reception. The Hearing was told the 'auspicious moment' to apply for a Grant would only receive fair consideration after someone had been killed.

---

* The reference to Camphill is the scene of the T&DLR accident.

CONSOLIDATION 1905-1916

A spokesman for the Examiners then declared that most of them were Englishmen, 'anxious to do what they can for Ireland'.

Richard Evans the Engineer had calculated what the engines could pull in comparison with another line. The 'new engine' on the S&SR 'carries very little more than the weight of the driving wheel. The driving wheels are twenty tons [i.e. the weight available for adhesion was 20 tons]; she carries little more than sixty tons, whereas on another line on which I am engaged, the engines will carry twelve or thirteen times the weight of the driving wheels. That is four times more than we carry'. He attributed this to the steep gradients and the risk of accident where a fall a 1 in 22 and 1 in 25 lasting half a mile would end in a two-chain curve ('or less').

He added that the driver 'cannot keep the speed down if we have got a slippery rail - the speed gets more than we want sometimes . . . we have been fortunate in having no accident'.

He said that had the line been taken through the fields instead of beside the road, its length would not have been increased. His estimate for putting the whole line 'into order' was £25,000: he thought that extra land to improve the route could be bought cheaply and by compulsory purchase; the contractor had followed the roadside to save the cost of buying land.

Asked if he thought a grant would better be spent on improving the road, he said that as they already had a railway, and they were obliged to operate it, such money should be spent on improving the railway.

(The Committee next examined Patrick McCarthy, General Manager of the Lartigue-system Listowel & Ballybunion Railway. Although a useless comparison with the S&SR, he confirmed that its financing was mainly private and that the Lartigue-system had its faults, and was not found elsewhere in Ireland.)

A Table was published showing Working Results of Irish Light Railways from 1900 with an average working expense of 1s. 8d. per mile; this is valuable for making comparisons:

Railway	Length	Train miles	Receipts per mile/year £	Receipts per train mile s. d.	Expenses per mile £	Expenses per train mile s. d.
Donegal	106	288,788	345	2 6	274	1 6
Londonderry & Lough Swilly	99	237,102	453	2 7	274	1 7
Cavan & Leitrim	49	100,059	234	2 3	207	2 0
Clogher Valley	37	103,006	227	1 7	223	1 7
Cork & Muskerry	27	113,516	413	1 10	368	1 9
Schull & Skibbereen	14	23,648	192	1 10	273	2 8
Tralee & Dingle	37	76,851	209	2 0	389	3 6
West & South Clare	53	155,898	366	2 6	396	2 8
Averages*			305	2 1	298	2 2

* Making allowances for the exceptional financing of the Clare Railways, the true average cost would be £285 1s. 8d.

All the above are 3 ft gauge. The foregoing Table taken on its own, discloses some interesting facts for the brief period shown: there were the following number of train-miles each day (exc. Sundays):

Donegal	184.5 miles
Clogher Valley	65.8 miles
Tralee & Dingle	49.1 miles
Schull & Skibbereen	18.3 miles

which suggests that during the period, there were days when a S&S train ran in one direction only, or not at all!

The high annual earnings of the Lough Swilly show its earnings to be well ahead of the Donegal with its greater mileage. Disregarding the West & South Clare (which was financed differently) it will be seen that only the Tralee & Dingle with its formidable route, cost more per train-mile than the S&SR - hence one reason for the comparisons during the Commission.

This Table was submitted by William Barrington M.Inst.CE who was Engineer to the West & South Clare Railways. When examined he pointed out that the T&DLR and S&SR had both received free grants from the Treasury to improve their systems but that the Clare lines had not been so fortunate.

The average cost of these nine railways had been £3,999 per mile; the Clogher Valley had been the cheapest, and like the S&SR, was largely a roadside line but differed in parts by running on the road, rather than roadside, in built-up areas. Comparative figures were:

West Clare	£4,844 per mile
South Clare	£3,692 per mile
Cavan & Leitrim	£3,889 per mile
Clogher Valley	£3,332 per mile
Cork & Muskerry	£4,166 per mile
Schull & Skibbereen	£4,071 per mile

The Board of Works agreed that many minor branch lines and feeders were needed in various parts of Ireland in more or less backward districts, but felt that in the first instance would be better developed by a motor service. 'Our experience of branch lines has not been financially satisfactory'.

On a final note concerning the Commission, the deliberations were protracted, the matters concerning the S&SR extending from October 1906 to November 1907. Its final Report was presented in 1910, resulting in the S&SR receiving a free grant of £12,000, the highest amount of the four grants given. This was based on a deficit every working year, averaging £1,307 per annum over 1886-1916. The Report stressed that unification of Light Railways was more urgently needed than ordinary railways; the grants were to be recognised as given 'pending the amalgamation of Irish railways'.*

From 1906 the Railway played a useful role in early experiments with wireless telegraphy by Guglielmo Marconi, who had set up a transmitting station on Brow Head, on which a tall mast was erected. The Head is the most southerly point in Ireland and among the most westerly; to reach it from the train arriving at Schull, Marconi would have to travel by road through Goleen, along Crook Haven and so to this bleak and isolated promontory, reaching out into the Atlantic (14 miles from Schull). Writers

---

* See Conroy pp. 284-87, also: FINAL REPORT OF THE VICE-REGAL COMMISSION ON IRISH RAILWAYS Parliamentary Papers 1910. Vol. 37. pp. 74-75.

maintain that 'he travelled frequently on the Tram' and certainly memories of his visits were vivid until recently, viz.:

At Schull station he would be met by 'Pats' Hennessy, jarvey at Duggan's Hotel, who drove him to Crookhaven, where he stayed at Nottage's. The mast was set up during a very bad winter, the local people attributing the unseasonable weather to his activities . . .

So writes Newham.

Marconi sent the first message to Cornwall in 1906 and he made about three journeys along the Railway until 1914 when the Brow Head installation closed. It remained thus until 1922 but was burned down then by 'Irregular Republican Forces, probably to prevent its use by the Royal Navy'.* Crook Haven was to remain a Lloyd's Signalling Station for many years.

It may be noted in 1852 there was a scheme for a 'Bandon & Crookhaven Railway & Trans-Atlantic Packet Station' which would give certain harbours in south-west Ireland a railway connection.

It was rarely that some detail of locomotive up-keep found its way into the Minutes, but in 1912 - a year in which the Book is helpfully detailed - we learn that Patrick Murphy the fitter reported that GABRIEL, IDA and ERIN 'were in good working order' but that the ejectors were giving trouble (this would mean that the vacuum brake might be unreliable). This Minute would verify that GABRIEL and ERIN were taking the Lion's Share of the traffic, leaving the tram engine IDA as 'spare'.

Be that as it may, the Company had the good fortune to pension off IDA (but not to scrap it) when in 1914 a new locomotive KENT was purchased.

The goods shed at Schull stood on a platform above the shore line where rats who lived along the seashore could raid the shed; problems with salted fish and foodstuffs stored there were commonplace. At Skibbereen the goods store was the property of the CB&SCR and rodents would be frequently disturbed.

More serious were the losses on working at this period:

1908	£1,490	
1909	£2,683	
1912	£1,807	
1914	£1,221	(Jan-June)

The traffic receipts for September 1912 were £322 1s. 9d. (an average of £80 weekly when the tourist season was over) but without any comparative figures between goods/passenger, no conclusions can be made. Newham writes that up to the 1930s, the special cheap fares attracted about 500 passengers on Saturdays and 100-200 on other days of the week.† Even having in mind the seating capacity of the bogie carriages, such figures would make Saturday travelling horrendous, many would be standing within and on balconies.# Whether the locomotive could cope with such loadings and the factors which induced people to travel are as yet to be researched . . . (see also Schull Regatta working p. 233).

* Memoirs of the late Bernard O'Regan.
† Newham does not quote his source, but the figure for *Saturday* travel must be erroneous.
# It is alleged that the public was accommodated in open wagons if the carriages were full; this may have been the case before the Company was absorbed by the Great Southern Railways but even allowing for purely local indulgences, the new owners would hardly risk such practices or condone same if carried out.

Chapter Eleven

Government Control and State Ownership 1916-1925

During these troubled years, the S&SR's lifeline, the CB&SCR connection to Cork, was often out of action with consequent knock-on effect. The events can conveniently be summarised:

1st January, 1917	Railways under Government control
December 1920	Due to military action, service restricted to movement of goods only. Skibbereen-Baltimore was closed completely
5th November-9th December, 1921	All traffic suspended due to unsettled state of country, and GS&WR workshops' strike in Dublin
26th January-14th February, 1922	All traffic suspended due to a GS&WR employees' strike

It was impossible to predict what daily service could be run under these conditions, as any connection with Cork and beyond depended on circumstances prevailing. However, sea travel was largely unaffected and Schull received the benefit.

As if this was not enough, Civil War broke out in June 1922 and the conflict between Free State and Republican Forces was extremely bitter in the South West. The S&SR was again prey to what occurred in the vicinity, even though the new Free State Army had formed a Railway Protection Brigade; in August the vitally-situated Chetwynd Viaduct, five miles out of Cork towards Bandon, was seriously damaged by malicious explosion and the CB&SCR closed the system completely. Creedon* describes it:

> This resulted in West Cork being virtually isolated from the city .. as many road bridges were damaged ... In January 1923, several bridges and station buildings had been damaged or destroyed, and ten signal cabins burned down.

On 1st January, 1923 the CB&SCR Board stated the Railway was officially closed but repairs to the Chetwynd Viaduct allowed a limited timetable from 20th February; Skibbereen continued to have no trains.†

Gradually repairs to bridges and stations westward from Bandon were taken in hand but the Drimoleague-Skibbereen-Baltimore line was the last to open - on 23rd May, 1923. Much of the rehabilitation work was done by railwaymen under the new Irish Government's body recruited for the purpose, the Railway Defence & Maintenance Corps.

Business on the S&SR continued to be hampered by affairs far from its doors; a dockers' strike in Cork affected shipments for four months in 1923 and while this was good for West Cork ports, the S&SR received only a little benefit. Fish traffic north of Cork was resumed from Carbery ports by the opening of a new railway bridge across the Blackwater River at Mallow in 1923; the original had been destroyed in August 1922. Dublin was an important destination for fish landed at Schull.

An example of two-way generosity arose from the previously recorded GS&WR strike and S&SR subsequent closure in late 1921; taking advantage of the unemployment of the S&SR men, the Board considered their hardship at the approach of Christmas and offered the men three days' track-work from 20th November. It was some financial

---

* CORK BANDON & SOUTH COAST RAILWAY. (Vol. 2) p. 49.
† Dunmanway-Bantry re-opened; isolated section worked by one of the CB&SCR 4-6-0 tank engines.

recompense for the Company itself when, under the Irish Railways (Settlement of Claims) Act, 1921,* it was entitled to £15,716 in respect of compensation for the effects of Government control during World War I.

This sum seemed pitiful when the Board Meeting of 3rd May, 1922 discussed the proposed unification of railways in Ireland and the drawbacks inherent in systems other than of 5 ft 3 in. gauge. Goggin, the Secretary, reminded the members of the losses incurred to perishable goods by delays in transhipment at Skibbereen. The financial gloom was further darkened when he pointed that the loss on working, together with interest on the Baronial Capital, amounted to £152,755 5s. 3d., being the gross total since opening. The system had lost money from the start.

The official Stock Returns for 1922 showed: four locomotives, ten carriages and forty-five wagons.

There were numerous incidents in which the railway was involved during the War of Independence. Certain of them are recalled only by patriotic legend, a notably unreliable source. One such which appeared in print was the sacking and burning of the RIC Barracks at Schull by the IRA in 1920. Police Stations (Barracks as they were known) were local centres for the British to keep law and order and their intelligence. They were prime targets for the local 'volunteers' whose 'A' Company was based on Skeaghanore, centrally placed for observing the Barracks at both Ballydehob and Schull. Before arrangements could be made to attack the former, the Barracks at Ballydehob was evacuated to Schull.

Of similar importance to the IRA were Coastguard Stations and that at Schull was occupied by forty Royal Marines at this time but it does not appear to have been a prime target for arms.

It was the practice for five men from the Barracks to leave the premises at 7.30 pm each evening for Schull station, to meet the Down train and collect the mail, newspapers etc.; they would be out of the Barracks for half an hour on this mission.† The IRA had obtained the pass-word from an informer and while the station party was away, easily infiltrated the Barracks, set it on fire and locked the divided RIC men in the local hotel. Throughout the affair, no word had reached the Marines who never left the Coastguard station. The incarcerated men were released the next morning.

It was a common practice of the IRA to sterilise a railway by running a locomotive (or complete train) off the rails. The crew of the engine were usually well informed and would co-operate by starting the victim from rest and then jumping off and leaving the engine to make a spectacular crash, frequently where rails had been taken up. Such an occasion took place on the Schull Pier extension when KENT was sent down the steep gradient and left the rails, falling off the bridge which carried the branch over the stream opposite the Harbour Master's office, and ending on its side.

During this troubled time Kilcoe station was the scene of a skirmish and the building there was burned. A similar fate befell Hollyhill building to prevent it being used by the British and for the same reason, the IRA burned down Skibbereen workhouse in June 1921 to prevent its occupation by incoming troops. All this resistance was centred on Skibbereen, a stronghold of eighteen RIC and fifty military; the IRA felled trees over roads, and the railways were halted by obstructions and the rails taken up. The S&S was affected similarly, all to prevent the movement of troops.#

---

* 11 & 12 George V cap. 50. See also Conroy pp. 228-9.
† At this date there were no passenger services.
# For an incomplete account of this period, 1916-1921, see TOWARDS IRELAND FREE (L. Deasy) [Mercier Press, Dublin: 1973]. No other source for involvement of railways in West Carbery has been traced.

With rear sanding gear now added, GABRIEL is seen at Schull. *Circa* 1924.   *Collection J.I.C. Boyd*

KENT has pulled IDA from Skibbereen shed - note coupling bar, with pin/tongue' beneath smokebox door, and spark arrester. 1924.   *Collection J.I.C. Boyd*

GOVERNMENT CONTROL AND STATE OWNERSHIP 1916-1925

A regular driver on the S&S section was Dan Hallihane from the main line. He had the reputation of innocently misleading British forces when they stopped his train and an ambush was intended. Equally innocent was his disclosure to S&S driver Curly Hegarty that working west on an early morning Fair Special, they had hit and killed his donkey which had been put to graze on the line.

The closure of the S&SR - one of five systems so affected - was due to it being located in a area proscribed as a 'Disaffected Area' in 1921. This action was to 'prevent ambushes, derailments etc. and was a punitive measure aimed against the inhabitants for their failure to support the military'.

An example of the knock-on effect upon the railways in which the S&SR was a victim during those miserable times, took place in Skibbereen in 1921. It was anticipated that British troops were to be sent from Cork by train to seal off the town; to forestall this national factions removed the rails to the north of the main line station. As an additional block, 'railway carriages were carted from the station and placed across North Street outside St Fachna's School'. (It is suggested that the 'carriages' were in fact, goods wagons and being more easily handled along the street, were off the S&SR.)

The Civil War came to an abrupt end on 22nd July, 1921. A Truce had been drawn up; it was a sudden and unexpected event. On 21st December, 1921 a Treaty creating the Irish Free State was signed. Michael Collins, founder of the Irish Republican Army, signed for the State, declaring 'I have signed my own Death Warrant'. The Irish Parliament voted to accept the Treaty on 21st January, 1922. Royal Assent was given to the Westminster Parliament's Irish Free State (Agreement) Act on 31st March, 1922.

In retrospect, the railways did not wholly benefit from the period of Government control. Wages, which had been stable for so many years, began to rise - in particularly during the period 1917-21 - but meanwhile the railways received no compensating increase in rates and fares. To make matters worse, where rates rose in situations where the distance hauled was short, customers began to transfer their allegiance to the road.

A casualty of the Civil War 1922; KENT - unattended - is maliciously run down the Schull Pier Extension to fall into the stream-bed after the small underbridge there had been destroyed.
Collection W. McGrath

The new Irish Government,* on the Commission's recommendation, brought out a Bill to merge all the railways in the country with the exception of those wholly in Ulster or spanning the border between. The consequent Act spawned the Great Southern Railways and came into force on 1st January, 1925. It was necessary to assemble the Railway Tribunal on 2nd March, 1925 to cover the complications of lines affected by a Baronial Guarantee, of which the S&SR was one. So the system passed into the GSR fold; had it not done so, it would probably have suffered an early eclipse.

S&SR shareholders were allotted £125 4 per cent GSR Preference Stock for every £100 shares held in the S&SR (being £71,250 for the original £57,000 of 5 per cent Guaranteed Shares).†

There was little evidence of new ownership on the line itself. Regular Sunday trains were discontinued but Sunday workings were available in season and for special occasions. The sharp-eyed might have noticed the suffix 's' now added to the engine and rolling stock numbers.

In due course the engines appeared in the unlined all black paint adopted by the GSR, but somewhat remarkably the nameplates were retained and numbers given. ERIN, which never boasted a nameplate but had it painted on the side tank, lost it under a coat of black. The GSR claret colour and crest appeared on the coaches and some stock retained it until the early 1950s. By then it had become so weather-worn that certain coaches were given CIE colours and the 'Flying Snail' device - it may have been thought appropriate . . ! On carriage No. 2s the Skibbereen painter applied the 'Snail' transfer the wrong way round.

Goods stock continued to be painted grey, with characters in white: the numbers (+ 's') now appeared on each end.

The stations and halts revealed their new owner when enamelled sheet-metal nameplates were put up, having a black ground with white margins and letters.

The Company's independent workshops at Skibbereen operated on much reduced status henceforth; locomotives were sent on low-loader wagons for heavy repairs to the Inchicore Works of the GSR in Dublin. On the evidence, it was seldom necessary to despatch a *complete* locomotive, an obvious latter-day exception being No. 6s. The excellent woodworking skills of the existing staff kept carriages and wagons in sufficient shape to cope with the traffic then offering, though the number of semi-derelict vehicles in Skibbereen yard evidenced decreasing demand.

---

* The Dail Eireann.
† Ref: STOCK EXCHANGE OFFICIAL YEARBOOK.

Chapter Twelve

The Final Years
1926-1956 and after

In the preceding chapter the various small outward changes under the new owners are mentioned. The fact that operating practices, the labour force and timetable remained largely as before the take-over did not surprise for the circumstances in the country entered a more settled period under its changed political status. Economy remained the watchword but as the S&S had always watched the expenses, the new owners could hardly trim down costs any further.

One advantage arose in that men from the main line could now be booked for S&S section duties so relieving the strain. Wages continued to rise slowly whilst legislation prevented employers from requiring railwaymen to work long hours. If West Carbery people expected great improvements to follow they would be disappointed and would hardly be fooled by the emergence of trains in new paint or colours.

In short, things continued much as before except the political background was calmer and therefore local unrest ceased: the new Free State was finding its feet. The S&S section had the benefit of a concern behind it with apparently unlimited resources for its needs such as rail, sleepers, coal . . . everything from office stationery and passenger tickets to steam oil and uniforms.

The commencement of World War II in September 1939 changed all this. Though now an independent country and not involved directly, a universal shortage of items which everyone had taken for granted, became acute. Priorities for essentials such as locomotive coal, were drawn up and the S&S section was *not* on any such list . . . not for nothing was it known nationally as 'The Emergency'. Newham writes of 1944-45:

> During the Second World War, the fuel situation caused much anxiety in Eire; by early 1944 the position was so serious as to demand drastic reductions on passenger travel, trains being totally withdrawn on many branches, those on the Schull section being suspended on 24th April, the Company undertaking that, with the return of normal conditions, services would be resumed; the SOUTHERN STAR recalled that the line passed alongside a bog, and that, during a critical fuel situation in 1942, the engines had run successfully on turf (peat).*
>
> During 1945 the local inhabitants wondered when the line would re-open, a question in Dail Eireann† not eliciting a satisfactory reply. However, in November a large body of men were observed clearing vegetation and overhauling the track, which gave rise to hopes of an imminent resumption of services, which were confirmed when on 11th December the first train - a 'mixed' - left Schull with a full complement of passengers and livestock, the return working likewise well patronised.

A new owner of the system appeared on 1st January, 1945 following the parlous financial situation of the GSR, largely due to road competition. Together with the Dublin United Transport Co. it would now operate under the title Coras Iompair Eireann. So far as the S&S section was concerned, this development was merely superficial and did nothing to ease the fuel crisis which was largely due to the purchase of coal from mainland Europe in the 1930s, which source was now closed. The goodwill previously existing with South Wales suppliers had thus evaporated.

The closure of 1944 brought second thoughts to the mind of Daniel Ducey, the Ballydehob Station Master, who clearly thought his opportunities lay elsewhere. In

---

* The newspaper was ill-informed: attempts to mix coal with turf had never solved railway locomotive problems.
† The Irish Parliament in Dublin.

At noon the first Down train leaves for Schull. 1938.   *R.W. Kidner*

A surprise working; No. 3s comes out from Skibbereen with extra vans for the next day's Schull Market. 1938.   *R.W. Kidner*

THE FINAL YEARS 1926-1956 AND AFTER

The afternoon working from Schull enters Skibbereen with a considerable train. 1938.
R.W. Kidner

Whilst at Hollyhill, the crew attend to a leaking piston packing. 12th September, 1938.
H.C. Casserley

West of Church Cross, there comes the awesome section on the climb to Hollyhill. Bravely, the engine staggers up the slope with considerable smoke effect. 1939. *W.A. Camwell*

The attempt which failed (*see page 103*). Cyril Fry's unfulfilled venture; locomotive No. 6s with a stubborn door on carriage No. 6s. 1950. *Ivo Peters*

THE FINAL YEARS 1926-1956 AND AFTER

consequence, before re-opening the CIE Fortnightly Notice advertised the post and gave detail of the official house and the number of rooms.

The hoped-for easing of coal imports did not materialise, rather the contrary was the case. A severe cut in railway services became inevitable and services between Schull and Skibbereen were withdrawn entirely. From now on, passenger public transport would have to rely on the 'bus, as the Cork-Skibbereen service had been extended to Schull.

It is not necessary to detail the last train journeys as some of their features are covered (see p. 231-on). These dying moments are not without some of the mystery which had clung to the line since its conception.

Surviving Notices give the flavour of a Cattle Special which ran on Friday 10th January, 1947, to serve Schull Market. This left Skibbereen for Schull at 6 am with eight empty vans and a carriage for the Buyers. Twelve further vans had been sent down to Schull previously. The loaded train left Schull at 10.30 am. The carriage for the Buyers only ran on the outward journey.

On Thursday 16th January, 1947 a Cattle Special ran to Ballydehob, leaving Skibbereen at 7 am; it consisted of ten empty vans and a carriage. After loading it left Ballydehob at 11.15 am to return to Skibbereen (no extra vans had been forwarded beforehand).

The last Working Timetable operated from Monday 20th January with a train running from Schull on Monday, Tuesday, Thursday and Saturday, the very last train ending at Schull as customary. It is probable that engine No. 6s worked all the traffic. The official date for cessation of services was 'on and from Monday 27th January' but as there was no Sunday working, Saturday's train was the last.* The occasion was not marked in any way, as it was assumed that services would be resumed when fuel became available.

By that fateful Saturday night, a number of vehicles would be left standing in Schull yard, to be worked back to Skibbereen by locomotive(s) as opportunity offered. One mystery of the situation lies in a blizzard of such intensity that Cork city was completely paralysed that same week-end. How did the Schull line fare?

It seems that the working(s) which must have collected all the stock from Schull (and any at Ballydehob) passed un-noticed for every vehicle ended up in Skibbereen yard, with No. 6s, which would have worked such trains, left outside the engine shed. In that shed were No. 4s and KENT, nearer the door, but it would be folly to surmise which of the two had last seen service. Clearly, No. 6s had been the only inhabitant of Schull shed.

In passing, such Fortnightly Notices as quoted above give insight as to the loop line at Ballydehob; it was not a recognised passing place but must have allowed Cattle Special's locomotives to run round the train - Specials between Skibbereen and Ballydehob (only) were commonplace. All the same, whilst the passing of *trains* at Ballydehob is not recalled, there would be occasions (for instance on Thursdays and for the Schull Regatta etc.) when it came into its own. The division of the line into two Staff Sections supports the contention.

The Public Timetables never gave hint of special goods workings but the Working Timetable for 1943 records a Cattle Special for Goleen Market on Tuesday 6th April; this would take the form of empty stock worked to Schull on that day. The cattle would be driven on foot from Goleen to Schull (9 miles).

---

* The official closing date is sometimes given as 1st February. The official authority for closure was The Railways Act of 1933 (Section 9).
See THE MILNE REPORT 1943 (IRRS Journal Vol. 19 No. 131 p. 274).

Right: KENT shunting stock into the Carriage Shed, Skibbereen. Edmund Daly, porter. Note double brake hoses.   *A.P. Hughes*

Below: Inside Skibbereen engine shed, Nos. 4s and 3s, looking somewhat unloved but still usable, await their last journey. April 1953.   *J.I.C. Boyd*

THE FINAL YEARS 1926-1956 AND AFTER

There was one final and amusing scene in July 1950. Cyril Fry of Dublin, formerly a railway employee himself and therefore enjoying a good relationship with the powers-that-be, arranged for a 'last steaming'. Not surprisingly, it took rather more time than expected to raise steam in No. 6s (in this day and age, had No. 6s been left outside for three years in England, it would probably have been rendered useless by vandals); the near-by water-tank was unusable and resort was made to a hosepipe to fill the side-tanks. Rather later than sooner there was sufficient steam to move one of the derelict bogie coaches - and then to drag out the two inhabitants of the engine shed. By then, any thought - had there been a secret proposition - to attempt a short run was out of the question and perhaps the day ended with mixed emotions.

The Frys had planned the occasion to be a private one, conducted with much secrecy, so there was consternation when another well-known railway figure who happened to be passing in his car and saw smoke rising, alighted to witness this unexpected scene, thinking that the gods must be on his side that day. There was a nasty squabble and when the organisers told him to put away his camera and leave the site, he was afflicted by a sudden form of deafness . . .

On 29th September, 1952, CIE applied to the Transport Tribunal for an Order to abandon the Section, which was sanctioned in due course. Opportunity was given to hear any objections to the closure, and the County Council was ready to consider making representations. However, on learning of the strength of local indifference to the continuing existence of the line, they desisted.

In Autumn 1954 (Newham gives 1952, incorrectly) the passenger and goods stock - mainly in the form of bodies-only - was sold off to farms, etc. where the skeletal remains of some may still be seen (1999). Track lifting began from Schull, again attracting no printed witness. By August 1954 only the rails at the road crossings remained.*

The three locomotives never turned a wheel again until April 1954 when a breakdown train arrived and with the assistance of a mobile crane, they were loaded onto suitable main line wagons and made a last journey to Inchicore for scrapping. It is said Inchicore wasted no time in cutting them up. No. 4s left Skibbereen in a partially dismantled state so as to clear the overbridges; were there insufficient suitable wagons?

On 17th August, 1956 Public Notice was given re the making of an Abandonment Order for the Schull & Skibbereen section of CIE. This Order was a pure formality as virtually all the track had already been lifted, and such stock which had not found its way to the surrounding farms for use as outbuildings, etc., had been broken up.

The official reason for the cessation of services was that although a train had run on 25th January, 1947, from Monday 27th January the service would be suspended due to the fuel shortage. This implied that services would be restored again when the crisis ended. They never were.†

This procedure had the effect of legalising the position but only as it affected the original West Carbery section. The Pier Extension at Schull was overlooked and

---

* There was one curious exception to the general disposal of the carriages; an Englishman, one R.W. Winn, of Winn Technology Ltd, Kilbrittain, Co. Cork, bought and removed No. 7s, a bogie saloon, 'for restoration' there in the early 1970s. It was a futile project as for almost quarter of a century the vehicle had stood without protection and in the paintwork of the 1925 period. When photographed at Kilbrittain some years later some misplaced optimism still surrounded the decaying remains. The project expired and a further scheme was conceived - it would be brought home to Skibbereen and restored by the Technical College. But, tired of misplaced zeal, No. 7s disintegrated on the return journey.
† IRISH RAILWAY RECORD SOCIETY JOURNAL (No. 19 p. 195 & No. 20 p. 246).

No. 6s (*left*), No. 4s (without chimney, *right*) are finally loaded in Skibbereen yard. No. 3s awaits in the background. The cortège will leave shortly for Cork. Note the unsuitability of the wagon carrying No. 4s; it has no adequate well. April 1954.
Collection J.I.C. Boyd

Far from a railway, the Gloucester-built bodies came to rest in a field beside Bantry Bay; this specimen had been sawn in two. 1967.
J.I.C. Boyd

THE FINAL YEARS 1926-1956 AND AFTER

required separate authorisation. Actually, the track on the pier itself had been removed before January 1947 but much of the remainder was then intact though overgrown.

The curtain fell on the *whole* railway system of West Cork on 1st April, 1961 after many objections and political incrimination. It left that part of the county with inadequate main roads, narrow and over-loaded, so that its transport arteries were appalling. The roads have but recently received the benefit of 'European Money' whilst in the intervening thirty-five years one heard, 'Bring back the railways'.

Today, West Cork has a thriving tourist industry and the cry is, 'What a pity we have not got The Tram today'. It appears the lessons have not been learned.

Between 24th-27th October, 1986 the centenary of Ballydehob Viaduct was celebrated and an article of 8th November in the SOUTHERN STAR does a little to redress the criticism which surrounded the S&SR during its lifetime.

A more balanced view reminds the paper's readers that the coming of the Tramway 'was perhaps the brightest phase in the economic and social history of the Mizen Peninsula'. Pat Cotter of Ballydehob had worked on the building of the bridge and his grandson Den Cotter switched on floodlighting of the viaduct to mark the occasion. A suitable plaque had been affixed to a road-side arch and this was unveiled.

The same paper had said:

> The tram brought many benefits to the area. Before its advent Skibbereen was a faraway place for many from the peninsula. It played a major role in the post primary education for the Schull area as it was then the only means of transport to Skibbereen schools . . . It became the subject of laughter in the British House of Commons when Tim Healy, MP for West Cork, said, 'The line is so curved that at one point the driver can light a cigarette for the guard though they are at opposite ends of the train' . . . [After closure] . . . It was running again at Christmas 1945 and only after considerable agitation by Patrick O'Driscoll TD. This operation was short-lived - already CIE buses were running from Cork . . .

With hindsight there will always be endless speculation as to why the S&SR was among the costliest failures in these Islands. At the same time, the factors which made it the eccentric concern it was, make it a fascinating study. Had it been nearer centres of population it would have become better known and less worthy of belated interest.

It suffered from lack of planning, poor civil engineering and lack of supervision during building and afterwards. And was the Board of Trade Inspector negligent? The promoters' contract was weak and permitted the contractor liberties and loopholes through which - it is alleged - he gladly slipped. The contractor was also accused of bribery though there seems no proof of it; whatever took place was not witnessed.

Faced with a completed railway of startling configuration, the contractor failed to supply locomotives and stock which were adequate for the conditions.

We have no proof that the contractor was a rogue but much evidence that inspection and supervision was inadequate. The promoters had little or no railway experience and those who managed the Railway afterwards were no better. It would seem that at every stage reliance was placed on those who proved untrustworthy or inadequate for the work to which they had been assigned.

Shakespeare had some words for it: '. . . I wonder men dare trust themselves with men' (*Timon of Athens*).

Public Sale of Skibbereen Railway Station

OUTSTANDING AND EXTENSIVE PROPERTY, INCLUSIVE OF STATIONMASTER'S RESIDENCE, STATION OFFICES, VARIOUS OTHER BUILDINGS, AND CAR PARK, FOR SALE BY PUBLIC AUCTION, ON THURSDAY, AUGUST 20th, 1964, AT THE STATION PREMISES.

J. HEGARTY

Is instructed by The Board of Coras Iompair Eireann to sell, by Public Auction, on the above date, this most outstanding and valuable property in three lots.

LOT 1—Spacious Cark Park, adjoining the public road.

LOT 2.—Stationmaster's Residence, with large adjoining spaces, both front and rear.

LOT 3.—Station Offices, former Schull & Skibbereen Tramway Offices, Signal Cabin, and various other buildings. The area of the 3 lots is—1 acre 2 roods 2 perches.

The extensive Cark Park, which adjoins, and is approached from the public road, would constitute a most valuable property to owners of business establishments and others for the erections of Garages, or parking spaces for fleet owners, it being already developed for such purposes. As well, this and the other sections of the property, provide an opportunity for an industrialist, or factory promoter, to acquire a well laid-out site.

The Station Residence, which is 2-storeyed, is most suitable as a suburban, permanent or summer residence, having all the services installed, and having ample space for external extensions.

The Station Offices, which include the former spacious passengers' Waiting Room, would be ideal for conversions into a restaurant, or residence, and overlook a wide and pleasing landscape. Likewise, the former Offices of The Schull and Skibbereen Tramway Company would be ideally suited as a residence. Full sanitary arrangements are on the property.

☞The Auctioneer directs the attention of the public to the outstanding possibilities of the specified sections of this well-situated property, close to the business centres of the town and with ample space for extensions of the existing buildings. They constitute those of one of the principal Stations on the former, what was known as The Cork, Bandon and South Coast Railway, and served a most imporant commercial West Cork centre. He will point out each Lot to intending purchasers.

Further particulars and Conditions of Sale from:—
BRENDAN A. McGRATH, ESQ., SOLICITOR, ISLANDBRIDGE, DUBLIN. Tel. 75661.

Or: **J. HEGARTY, AUCTIONEER & VALUER, SKIBBEREEN.**
Tel. 17.

A newspaper advertisment for the sale by public auction of Skibbereen station on 20th August, 1964.

Chapter Thirteen

The Route
Skibbereen to Schull Harbour

The route described as in the late 1930s

Skibbereen Station*

The Ilen Valley Railway had ended on the north bank of the Ilen River immediately opposite the town of Skibbereen on the south bank. Here it was in the Townland of Marsh, and 54 miles from Cork city where the IVR had its parental-commencement at the Albert Quay station, on the south bank of the River Lee. (Until 1912 the vital rail connection to the railway on north bank of the Lee was denied to it and this must always be borne in mind when considering through traffic from off the S&SR to Cork.) The essential rail connection was by means of the Cork City Railway, a linking railway through the streets and over the river incorporating several interesting civil engineering works. Although the passage of a passenger train along it was irregular (excursion traffic being foremost), freight, etc. workings made frequent movement, trains being preceded by a flag-man who walked in front. This outcome was in poor contrast to the hoped-for Rosslare-Bantry through carriages which the newly-opened Rosslare route would permit.

This system was authorised by the Cork City Railways Act (4th August, 1906): the Great Western Railway of England and the Great Southern & Western Railway of Ireland were among contributors to the cost, and the line was to be worked by the GS&WR. The line was opened on 2nd January, 1912, and right from the start the S&SR cattle traffic benefited, for which the CB&SCR had built fifty new vans since 1910.*

There was no necessity for the IVR to go further. Cash was tight and the essential bridge to cross the Ilen would not have been economically viable. In any case, Ilen Street/Marsh Road lay north-south just outside the terminal station and a cast-iron bridge by Bickley, an Englishman, had been built in 1877 by which that road crossed into the town itself.† Here the river was tidal but small vessels and barges could pass underneath the bridge to reach the various quays and warehouses in the town (see p. 15).

The first terminus stood on a low embankment to keep it above the surrounding meadows and river floods. There was a single platform facing east with run-round facilities; behind the platform was a covered carriage shed. The engine shed was served by a small turntable which also accessed the run-round. At the river bank, the track terminated in a wagon turntable from which riverside sidings were led. At the north end, a long siding served a goods platform and shed.

From the Plan of the proposed West Carbery Tramway of May 1884 that Tramway's course would have involved a right-angled crossing on the level between the station platform and the engine shed (see plan p. 110, upper).#

---

* See also THE CORK, BANDON & SOUTH COAST RAILWAY Vol. 2: 1900-1950. (Colm Creedon) [Cork, 1989].
† The old cast-iron lattice-girder structure (visible on page 120, lower) consisted of two spans carried on masonry abutments, the centre support being three cylindrical steel piers with the roadway carried on ¼ inch steel troughing plates fixed on the main girders. It had a total span of 120 ft. When the WCT was opened it was less than ten years old. Its successor, opened in June 1964, cost as much as the *whole* West Carbery Tramway did eighty years beforehand.
\# For assistance in this respect the Author is indebted to the Cork Archives Institute in Cork city.

107

South end of Skibbereen main line station looking towards river bridge; narrow gauge out of sight to the right.
J.I.C. Boyd

Drimoleague-Baltimore mixed train at Skibbereen.
J.I.C. Boyd

THE ROUTE - SKIBBEREEN TO SCHULL HARBOUR

Train with through Cork coaches departs from Skibbereen. The branch engine was shedded here. 1953. *J.I.C. Boyd*

Baltimore-Drimoleague mixed train shunting at Skibbereen; narrow gauge station off right. 1934. *J.I.C. Boyd*

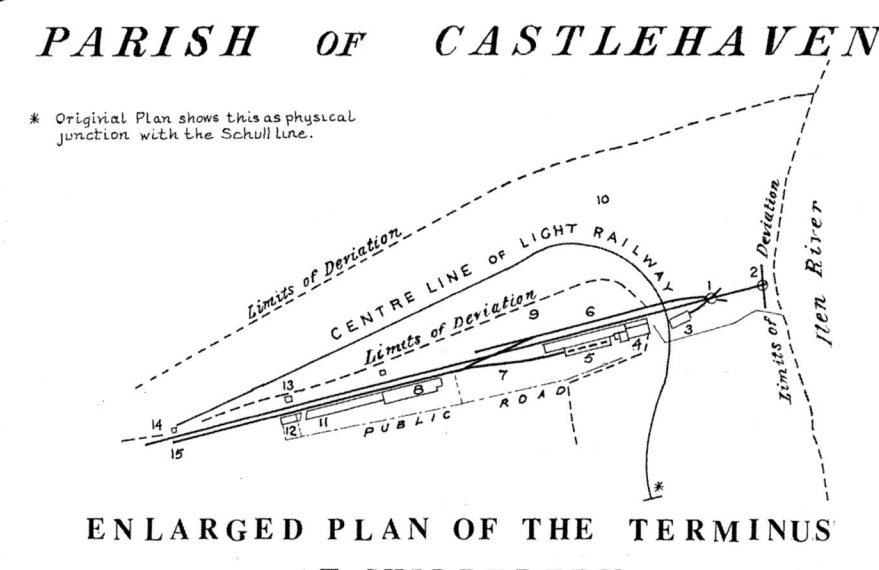

ENLARGED PLAN OF THE TERMINUS AT SKIBBEREEN.

Copy of Deposited Plan of part of proposed eastern section showing Skibbereen standard gauge station as built and opened in 1877. Key: 1. Turntable, 2. Wagon turntable for Ilen Quay wharves, 3. Engine Shed, 4. Station Master's House, 5. Passenger station and Carriage Shed, 6. Run-round loop, 7. Goods Yard, 8. Goods Shed, 9. Boundary fence, 10. Land to be taken for Tramway purposes, 11. Goods platform, 12. Signal Cabin, 13. Boundary fence, 14. Railway to Drimoleague, 15. Headshunt.

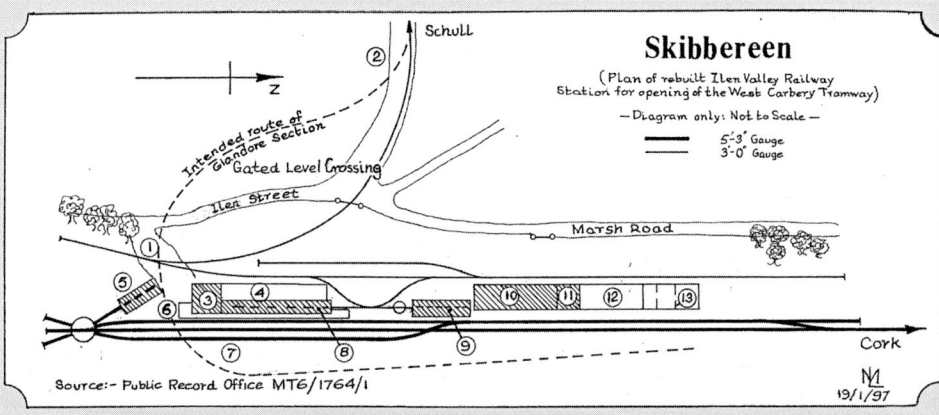

Skibbereen (Ilen Valley Railway station) as re-organised for opening of the West Carbery Tramway in September 1886. Note that Deposited Plan of Skibbereen layout shows standard gauge on both sides of the station platform, but the above taken from the Official Plan shows that between 1877 and 1886 the standard gauge had been moved to accommodate the WCTy. The standard gauge had been re-located entirely to the east. Key: 1. Headshunt to accommodate Schull trains WCTy, 2. Junction Schull line with proposed eastern (Glandore) section WCTy, 3. Station Master's House, 4. Original west-facing standard gauge platform constructed at rear of original station, 5. Engine Shed - standard gauge, 6. New standard gauge platform, 7. Run-round - standard gauge, 8. Carriage Shed WCTy, 9. Engine Shed WCTy, 10. Goods trans-shipment Shed, 11. Goods Shed dedicated for WCTy, 12. Goods trans-shipment open platform, 13. Cattle Dock.

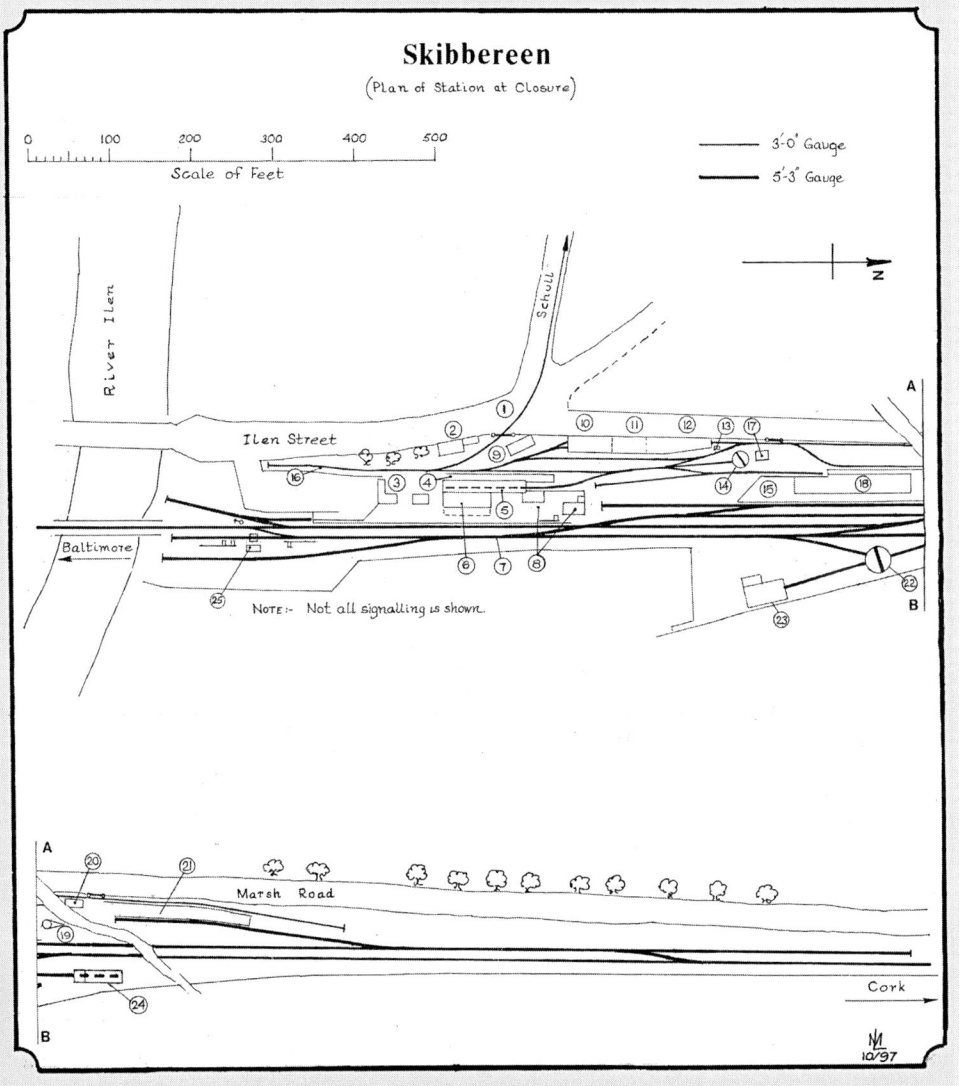

Skibbereen in 1953, intact and complete but with narrow gauge out of use and before a certain amount of simplification was done to the standard gauge tracks. *Key*: 1. Road crossing of Schull line, 2. Ex-S&SR Office, more recently the section office, 3. CIE Station Master's House, 4. Narrow gauge platform, 5. Narrow gauge Carriage Shed - then roofless, 6. Standard gauge station building, 7. Standard gauge layout following revision after building of Baltimore Extension, 8. Standard gauge platform and signal cabin, 9. Narrow gauge stores shed, 10. Narrow gauge Carriage Shed, 11. Narrow Gauge Carriage & Wagon Repair Shop, 12. Narrow gauge Shed for two engines, 13. Narrow gauge Water Tank, 14. Narrow Gauge Turntable, 15. Trans-shipment Goods Platform, 16, Re-positioned headshunt arrival/departure spur: Schull line, 17. Narrow gauge Coaling Stage, 18. Trans-shipment Goods Shed (replacement of earlier building), 19. Crane, 20. Cattle Dock (moved from earlier site), 21. Materials etc. trans-shipment platform, 22. Standard gauge turntable, 23. Standard gauge stores etc., 24. Standard gauge Engine Shed combined with water tank.

THE SCHULL & SKIBBEREEN RAILWAY

Mixed train for Schull reversing out of Skibbereen platform; locomotive No. 4s. *Circa* 1930.
Collection J.I.C. Boyd

Schull train awaiting departure (in reverse), Skibbereen. Note 'express' headlamps. Locomotive No. 3s.
Collection J.I.C. Boyd

THE ROUTE - SKIBBEREEN TO SCHULL HARBOUR

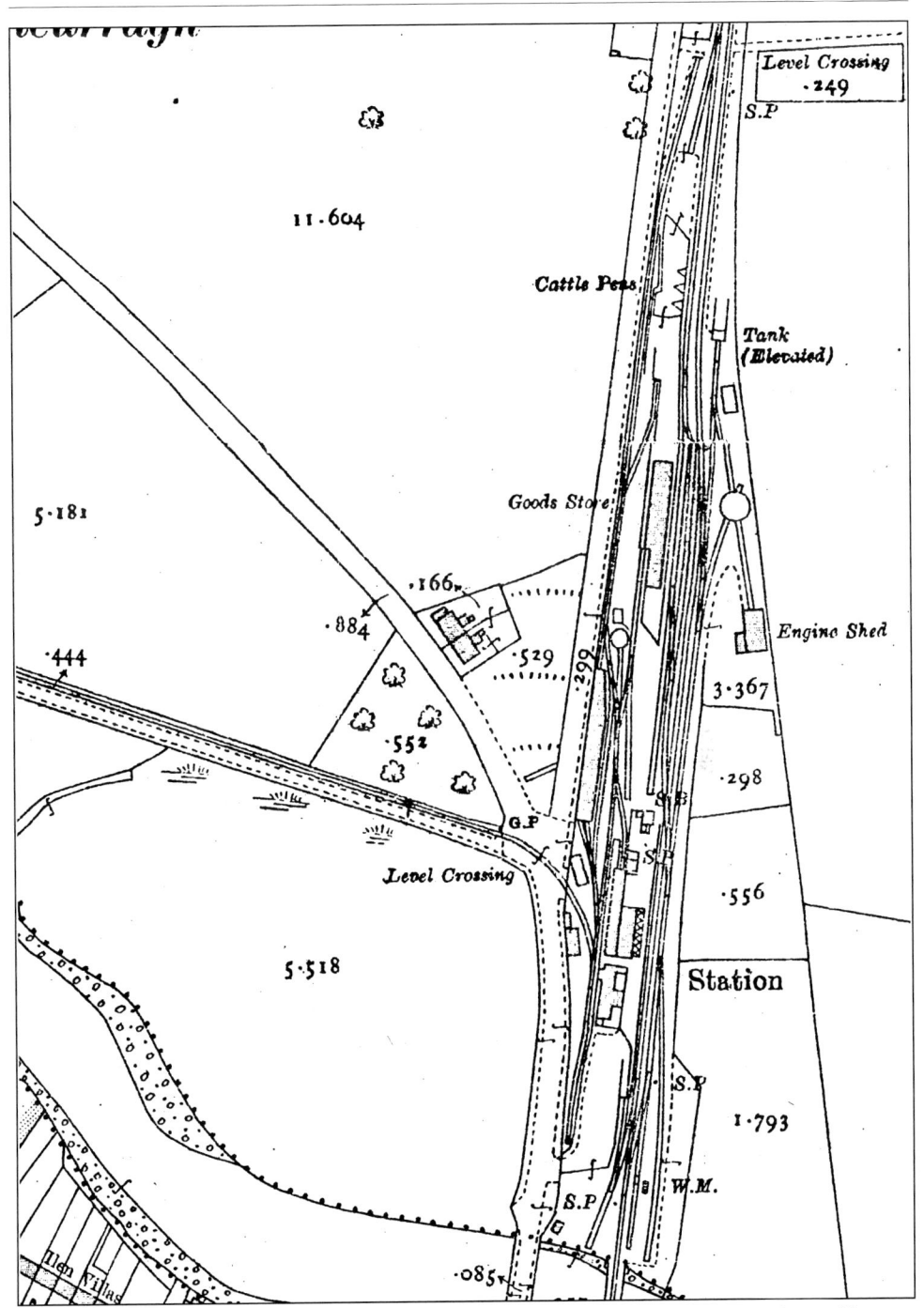

Skibbereen station. *Reproduced from the 25", 1941 Ordnance Survey Map*

Train from Schull passing rear of Office and entering Skibbereen reversing neck; locomotive No. 4s. 1938.
H.C. Casserley

Skibbereen (S&SR section) looking towards reversing neck. Main line station to left; carriage shed etc. on right. 1938.
H.C. Casserley

THE ROUTE - SKIBBEREEN TO SCHULL HARBOUR 115

The forecourt and station entrance faced west and were but a stone's throw from the north end of the river bridge. The entrance to the small goods yard lay a short distance up north on Marsh Road, to its right. The station building was two-storied and cement-rendered; the Station Master was accommodated therein.

The whole formed a basic country terminus, of very limited accommodation but adequate for the times. This left the nearest centre of population without railway connection as Baltimore, an important fishing harbour, eight miles to the south-west.

The second enlargement of the station was due to the building of the western project of the West Carbery Tramway, the eastern project having been dropped. No provision was made for such an eastern project, but its promoters were still hopeful that such would eventually come to fruition.

Baltimore demands mention in that in 1892-1893 Skibbereen station was enlarged for a third time to become a through station when the line was extended over the river and, cutting deeply through rock at the west side of the town, eventually reached Baltimore. A number of poor dwellings were demolished in the process.

The building of Tramway facilities and terminus on the west side of the existing station created a curious situation as it was now necessary for the public to cross the West Carbery Tramway rails sited across the forecourt to reach the standard-gauge station. The WCT arrangements were simple in the extreme (see plan p. 110, lower). They included usurping the carriage shed which was now put to Tramway use, and installing a small turntable and engine shed. Goods and cattle facilities were added on a lengthened platform flanked by a transfer siding. These curious arrangements prevented a locomotive from running around its train! The sparse layout suggested to the on-looker that a more extensive scenario might exist elsewhere - perhaps at Schull?

On the standard gauge side there was little change save for an extra engine release line off the turntable (see plan p. 111).

From 1886 and for the next seven years this second Skibbereen station layout served as terminus for two railway systems in juxtaposition, until the Baltimore Extension Railway opened on 2nd May, 1893; thereby the standard-gauge crossed the Ilen River from the point where it had terminated on the north bank.

It was to be almost two decades later when, following a further extension on to the new fishing pier at Baltimore, this most south-westerly of point of railways in Ireland was connected to the remainder of the Irish rail system by the building of the Cork City Railways. It was a significant date for the S&SR too, but in contrast to the excitement which attended the opening to Skibbereen, the Baltimore opening caused '... absolutely no interest ... (in Skibbereen) ... at Baltimore it was no better', so reported the CORK CONSTITUTION.

This change of attitude can almost certainly be traced to a bursting of the optimistic bubble which preceded the coming of the railway to West Carbery, specifically to the fiasco and misery attending the collapse of the eastern section plans of the WCT and the diabolic problems of the line to Schull. The district could be forgiven if it looked upon railways as the precursors of trouble and expense.

The increase in the station's business, mostly in the goods side, grew as did the amenities for passengers and freight occasioned by it. A Plan of the arrangements in 1953 (see p. 111) stresses the alterations and especially the additions to the narrow-gauge portion. Whilst no change was possible to the awkward narrow-gauge entrance/exit, by the end of its life the narrow-gauge could boast its own office, new Engine Shed and Carriage Shed (both on new sites from the originals), Workshop, passenger platform,

Narrow gauge station, Skibbereen. No. 4s running round its train. *Circa* 1930. *per R.S. Carpenter*

THE ROUTE - SKIBBEREEN TO SCHULL HARBOUR 117

North end of narrow gauge terminus, Skibbereen. Turntable behind No. 4s: goods transfer shed to right.
H.C. Casserley

A view of Skibbereen goods yard, west side, with No. 4s shunting wagons. 1938.
W.A. Camwell

Cramped conditions in Skibbereen workshops; No. 1 without its boiler. (The boiler was condemned when it reached Inchicore.) 1938.
W.A. Camwell

The Company's Office at Skibbereen.
J.I.C. Boyd

replaced turntable, water tank, coal stage, enlarged goods/transfer arrangements etc. Taking these in turn:

Company Boardroom & Office. In stone, with cement-rendered facing, tile roof, red brick chimneys with salt-glazed pots, red brick quoins to sash windows. Facing forecourt of station with line to Schull at rear. Later extension to north end in corrugated-iron, possibly for storage of office equipment etc.

Carriage Shed. Double-track, with wooden doors. A basic and cheap agricultural-type building, originally door-less, in corrugated-iron with curved roof. Situated inside of and parallel to boundary fence with Marsh Road. Date 1898.

Workshop/Carpenters' Shop. Situated north of and contiguous with the Carriage Shed, but having interior stone dividing wall and one through line fitted with heavy timber partition. Built in the same materials as Carriage Shed so externally appeared to be undivided. Date 1898.

Engine Shed. [Capacity: two 4-4-0 tank locomotives.] North of and continuous with Carriage Shed and Workshop. Built in corrugated-iron also, but having ridged roof made of small iron sheets. West side only partially of corrugated iron as there was concrete walling to six feet from ground. Building slightly tapered at north-east to accommodate vehicle-clearance without. Single track with pit. North end appears to have been heavily repaired (extended?) with good quality timber doors and replacement gable. [1906-period photographs reveal different roofing and smoke ducting.] Date 1898.

Water Tank. At north-east corner of Engine Shed, supported by heavy timber baulks. Extremely small diameter discharge pipe demanded long periods to fill locomotive tanks!

Turntable. Removed from original position to centre of yard, and probably of improved design to replace unsatisfactory specimen. Perhaps second-hand from CB&SCR. Brick pit, diameter 22 ft 0 in.

Passenger platform etc. Covered section converted from original Carriage Shed having curved roof supported by heavy timber uprights; sides partially clad with corrugated sheeting. Roof ends finished with highly-decorative deckle boarding (origin uncertain). This covered section largely disused and periodically had obsolete carriages, dog-carts, wheelbarrows etc. stored therein.* Platform itself low and brick-faced, having two sides. This work was carried out in August 1901. Transhipment platform with goods shed & cattle pens; hand crane. Extension and enlargement of standard-gauge arrangements. Large hand-crane (Capacity Five Tons). Buildings in corrugated-iron (still extant). Further transhipment sidings to north of station.

Stores Shed. Built in corrugated iron, CB&SCR pattern.

The whole area was bounded on the west by a stone wall or stockade built of old sleepers. The Schull line entered it from the road outside through a pair of timber gates.

Owing to the situation of the station, the angle of the road to Skibbereen, the proximity of the river bank and the intended eastward projection from Skibbereen station, the roadside location of the Tramway forced it enter the premises by one of those arrangements which seem typical of Ireland but which more truthfully are found the world over. The site necessitated a reversing movement for every train, whether arriving or departing.

A departing train would be drawn up at the platform and when given the 'Right away', would drop back carefully onto the stop-block which marked the limit of headshunt. After the Foreman had changed the points in front of the engine, the train would draw out noisily and slowly across the road junction, beckoned by that same gentleman's hand-signal to assure the fireman the road was clear. (The curve denied the driver this luxury.) As if to emphasise its right to precedence, the engine whistle would blow continuously, the cylinder drains would remain open; the safety valves would be lifting and the wheels

---

* Roof removed 1941.

While waiting on the roadside outside Skibbereen station, the morning train from Schull approaches. *Circa* 1930.
Collection R.S. Carpenter

Skibbereen from the west; road with tramway to Schull in foreground. Main line station in background. Ilen River in floodtide. *Circa* 1898.
Lawrence Collection

of the train would be squealing with complaint on the sharp curve. Who needs a flagman under such circumstances? Almost the whole town could hear 'The Tram' departing! But it was all according to the Rule Book: the speed limit here was 5 mph.

Skibbereen-Church Cross

Once the footplate crew had ensured that the van at the rear had cleared the station gates and the guard had waved to indicate he was on his van - occasionally a train left without one! - the train could begin to gather speed. A few late-comers might run alongside and leap onto the coach steps, having assumed they would have had 'Time for one more' and the usual reliability for The Tram to depart late.

So the train would take up its position on the north verge of the dusty Schull road and begin to clank amicably at something akin to 12 mph.* This was an easy stretch, almost level, with flood-meadows down to the river's edge on the left and a low range of hills to the right.† Although it was tempting for the driver to open the regulator even more, it was fair to give a 'laid-back' appearance to this first stage of the journey so the going was confined to a gentle canter. After all, the fire had not fully burned through, the engine was still 'cold' and the skills of the crew would be tested enough in the miles to come. So past the ¼ m. post. On the hillside to the south across the Ilen, Upper Bridge Street was marked by a thin row of houses until it petered out and the town was lost to view, while the tall Steam Mills building# and chimney, and the prominent West Cork Hotel, opposite, were the last to disappear.

Here on the north side, local folk, well-used to the vagaries of the river, would avoid this waterside stretch of road in times of Spring Tides and high winds as it was known to flood in places; the alternative was a parallel but more winding and hilly partner up the hill on the right. The telephone poles were placed beside the tramway here and this part of the country road possessed a high pavement so that the clear highway was limited in width. The Tram just ploughed through any flood water; it was seldom deep enough to quench the fire.

The ¾ m. post is passed and the line bears left here and meets the river which flows immediately beside it and the road. The hill to the right has closed in leaving a narrow gap at its foot for the highway. At 1 m. the level crossing and road junction at New Bridge is reached. Here is a five-arched stone bridge built about 1826, which pre-dates the Ilen Street bridge in the town so making it the lowest point at which the Ilen can be crossed. Also here are the ruins of the ancient Abbey Strowry (there are various ways of spelling) and a grave yard where many of those who died in the Great Famine were buried.§

In former times the level crossing had a hut for the attendant, and gates, but neither can be recalled. The tramway is 16 ft above sea-level here.

And so continuing westwards: the hillside forms the view to the north, but the river on the left (south side) is full of interest with its many states of the tide. At slack water

---

* The official limit.
† The Ilen River - Eibhlie - 'the Sparkling Stream'. It source lies six miles north of Drimoleague and the railway follows its course to Skibbereen. Below that town it is tidal and navigable.
\# The Steam Mill opened in October 1846 and almost immediately became a 'Soup House' to serve the starving of the Great Famine. It contained the first stationary steam engine in West Cork.
§ The Great Famine and its after-effects are considered in Chapter One. Cromwell's soldiers are supposed to have camped here.

there is little movement of the flow, but a surge of water comes with changes of the tide. There is not much commercial traffic these days, but an occasional pleasure or multi-oared craft preparing for the several regattas hereabouts, will be seen at practice. There is a multitude of seabirds, with swans nesting on the occasional island, their habitat at risk when Spring Tides come.

Salmon and other fishermen (legally or otherwise) wade waist deep from the banks; winged fishermen (such as herons) having dived from the surface for a catch, now line the shores of tidal mud with wings outstretched to dry them. It is an engaging scene whose peace is shattered by the on-coming clatter of the train. Grazing horses and cattle take fright and the fields are momentarily obscured by drifting smoke, for the coal supplied for locomotive use may create some heat but for the passengers the desire to dissipate the cosy fug within the train is tempered by long familiarity of the risks of a continuous shower of small hot coals and soot from the engine's chimney . . . and the engine has not been put to real work as yet!

The river slowly widens to embrace two small low islands where wildfowl gather; on its far bank there is a pleasant slope of hill, and a small quay below Deelish House. Between, a country road runs parallel to the river, connecting Skibbereen with Old Quay, an important berth for ships unable to negotiate the river any higher. At low tide, the skeletons of abandoned river barges poke up through the mud. On the right the old Schull road drops down from the hillside, crosses the line and joins us (1½ m.). A sharp rise gives the engine some real work for the first time but the effort is short-lived and a fall ensues where the old road branches off again to the right. Here is Abbey Cottage, pleasingly built above the riverside with view up and down the valley; it was once the home of 'Mick the Fox', the Ganger for this section, where he could command the scene of his labours.

(This is a suitable point to mention the adjacent roads: the 'Mail Coach Road' to Skibbereen from Cork via Clonakilty was building in 1813 and finished in 1816; Stage Coaches used it until 1877 when the railway came.* Westward the road to Ballydehob and beyond is dated about 1826 though there have been many improvements to it since then. For instance, immediately west of Skibbereen the former course took the high way above the flood meadows.

It should be appreciated that when West Cork came to be served by the railway, the pattern of road transport changed. Hitherto the fastest transport was the horse and the landed gentry and wealthier farmers - though owning horse-drawn vehicles themselves - preferred horse-back to being thrown around in a Covered Car. The proliferation of hunting and horse-racing meant that even gentlewomen took to the saddle for winter journeys which would not be tolerated today. The railway changed much of this, and vehicles would be sent 'with a man' by the better houses to meet the train, the man to handle the luggage and wrap up any visitors against the weather. Around the early 1920s when miles of Co. Cork's railways were closed, uninhibited families avoided 'such nonsense' and made stoic passages of over 100 miles with their own horses and carriage.)

The junctions with the old road required two sets of crossing gates in close proximity, and for the second time on the journey the countryside is deafened by the shrill whistling demanded by the Rule Book. Though not 'official', it was usual for local

---

* See THE STORY OF WEST CARBERY (W.J. Kingston) [The Friendly Press, Waterford, 1985.] p. 97. In the interests of tourism, the road as described herein can hardly be recognised today (1998) such are very recent alterations.

people to alight or board at these level crossings, for the days of the intimate railway still existed, where every passenger was known and the carriage would be a veritable 'Gossip Shop' and the atmosphere thick with burning plug. The cutting-back of the rockface along here was essential to accommodate road and rail.

Not even yet would the passage of The Tram affect the road traffic. Drivers would rein-in their nervous horses until it had passed, and wisely hold their heads to the roadside fence. As a pedestrian, only the chronically deaf could fail to hear an oncoming train. Cars were the province of the wealthy; delivery vans, lorries and the bus were seen and sufficiently frequent to have taken some business from the The Tram. Unusual occasions when steam encountered steam were when one of the traction engines from Crookhaven Quarry made a sortie off its usual beat. The road surface was not good however and much of it contained loose limestone chippings, and the screening plant being inefficient, passed much dust which, dropped on the road, caused every motorised vehicle to be followed by a dust storm.* To a lesser extent, The Tram was also responsible. (It does raise the question of whether the bogie coaches were fitted with dust blinds as a standard overseas specification or not - on dry windy days they would come into their own.)

The line continues level and by riverside without much change of view; it is now in the Townland of Rossnagoose. At 2 m. there is a sudden rise in the road and the Tramway follows it obediently. The rise is 11 ft in a quarter mile, and makes the engine blanket the surroundings with smoke: the line falls as suddenly, and the 'pattern' of the railway's building becomes clearer.

The level, almost river-clinging section is behind us and the driver prepares to begin work with steam regulator and reverser, and the fireman, with shovel. The rails lead in modest switchback fashion while the road has twists and turns which they follow obediently; the Tramway passes through a pleasant tree-lined stretch. Three minor roads join us from the right, the last at 2¾ m. serves Mohanagh Lodge; the family here are regular users of The Tram. Through the trees to the left can be seen the big, curving sweep of the river, now flowing away due south past New Court.† Note on the south bank, the small Deelish Pier, suited to small craft only.

The Tramway, now at 35 ft above sea level, is about to climb at 1 in 47, making the first of many diversions from the road in order to avoid a bend in it; here Mohanagh Dispensary was sited. On the opposite side of the road to the Tramway begins a considerable stone wall built as famine relief and marking the boundary of the New Court demesne. There is no sign of New Court from the train as the old house has long been a ruin among the jungle where had been gardens.

The track has now climbed to a summit of 63 ft; the curve demands a speed limit of 8 mph and the engine, which has made a vociferous ascent of the recent incline, rolls down the steep slope to the gates of New Court, an official halting place marked only by a sign on the roadside. It is locally known as 'Young's House' from the nearby farm and the official Regulations use this title to define it as a point where speed must not exceed 8 mph. Two small level crossings appear here, the adjacent roads being but bohreens.#

---

* To avoid chewing mouthfuls of grit thrown up from the back of his Land-Rover, on intending to stop the Author would try to find a place to pull in *off* the road and so let the rushing dust-cloud travelling behind his vehicle, 'overtake' him.

† New Court. In a ruinous condition, the remnants were demolished to allow a new farm to occupy the site, and the surrounding plantation was felled.

Boreen. Irish term to describe what in England would be a fourth-class road; rough, un-metalled, narrow, boscage-encroached but not necessarily twisting or hilly. In the Author's experience it was used loosely to describe any vehicular road not maintained by the County Council.

No. 4s, westward bound, hustles its train along the riverside section, 2½ miles out of Skibbereen. 1939.
W.A. Camwell

A sylvan scene; a train stops momentarily at New Court Halt for a woman and child to board. 1939.
W.A. Camwell

Hereabouts is the 3 m. mark; the rails are 10 ft above the road and a stone wall separates them from the farm all on a sharp curve. We have made a short, dramatic drop to 46 ft. We cannot fail to notice the Watergate opposite.*

The fireman makes the most of this brief respite, turns on the injector to top-up the water-level and counteracts its steam pressure loss by turning on the steam blower. The firedoor can now be opened and the sound of the ring of a shovel indicates that coal is being added to the fire. A cloud of black smoke rises energetically from the chimney and dissipates among the tree tops.

All this takes place in a short space of time for there is seldom need for a prolonged stop here. A short blast on the whistle and the equipage moves off slowly as if time was inconsequential, but more accurately because the driver knows he has time well in hand . . . emergencies permitting.

There is a run of almost three-quarters of a mile ahead, virtually straight, slightly undulating and scenically unremarkable. The fireman can sit back and the driver allows the engine do the work as economically as a railway like this allows. Both men face only one hazard - the sudden appearance of a cow from the railway-side hedge or the impetuous urge of a solitary donkey wandering on the highway to use the Tramway route instead, or the occasional instance of a passing horse-drawn vehicle whose steed takes fright and bolts. In such cases the animal may end its life under the wheels of the train, possibly derailing it as well. The engine crew must keep a keen lookout for Tramway and road are unprotected from each other.

We are now travelling almost due west through the Townland of Gurteenroe; from a point where the line is separated from the road and in a coppice, and actually several feet below it; it reaches road level again and gains the roadside just prior to the cross roads which heralds the scattered hamlet of Church Cross (3 m. 70 ch. 55 ft asl). There follows a long slow fall to this little community, a fall which ends at a crossing of the Keal Stream at the quaintly-named Pig's Bridge where the track begins to climb again and enters the Townland of Knockaraha.

There is no actual station here; The Tram draws up outside the Post Office & General Store situated beside the line. It is an un-prepossessing place. Behind stands the Creamery (a local co-operative), as usual surrounded by small two-wheel carts pulled by diminutive donkey or horse: occasionally there will be a motorised float too. Each carries the milk in churns. Their drivers are unseen - mostly in the adjoining Bar for the daily exchange of gossip. Some milk churns are exchanged with the train, and the van unloads deliveries for the Store. Sadly, the days when The Tram delivered the Mail are over.

Church Cross-Hollyhill

Pig's Bridge (only *one* pig, be it noted) is officially 3 m. 49 ch. from Skibbereen but as yet, The Tram's engine has not yet been called upon to work hard. Now all is to change; The Tram is about to embark on what is possibly the most bizarre piece of railway engineering in Ireland.

---

* Watergate. There were formerly two brick arches - one each side of the road, but that on the north edge was demolished by a lorry - erected by Lord Riversdale who then owned New Court, to mark the entrance to the estate; they were copies of the Watergates at Hampton Court.

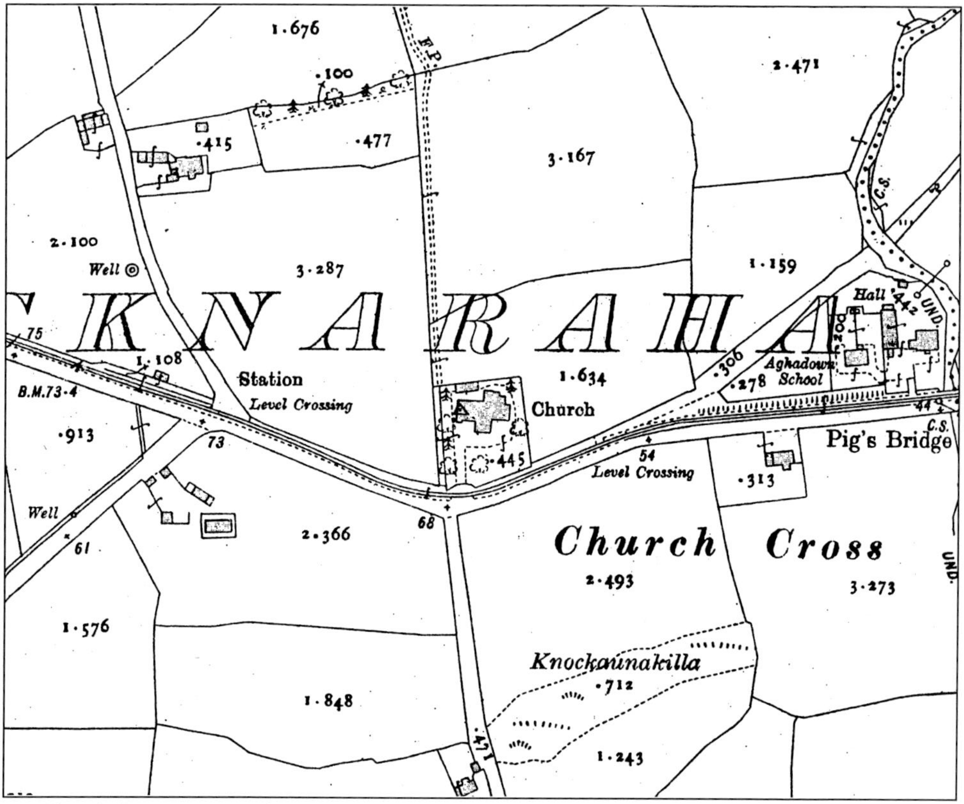

Church Cross station and Pig's Bridge.   *Reproduced from the 25", 1941 Ordnance Survey Map*

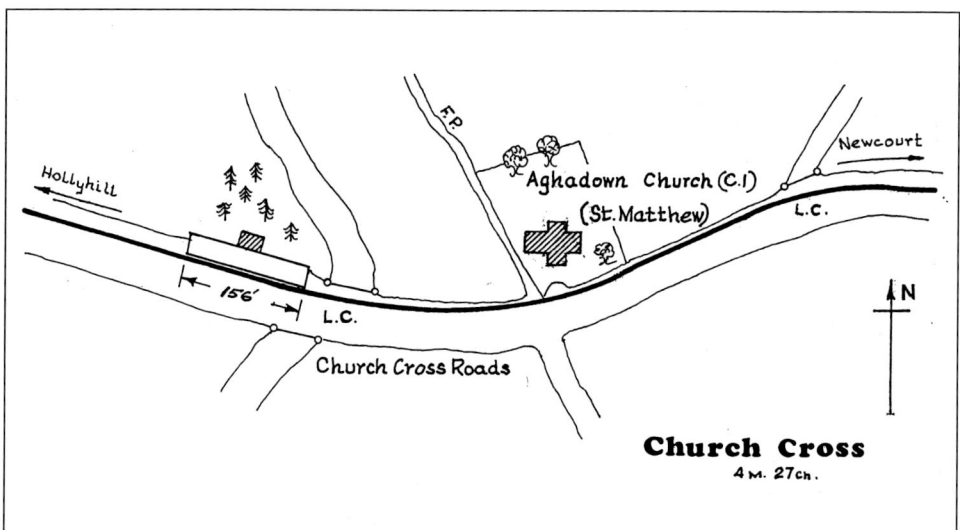

Church Cross
4 M. 27 CH.

THE ROUTE - SKIBBEREEN TO SCHULL HARBOUR

Pig's Bridge itself is constructed in the same way as are most of the other underbridges - it is of 16 ft span comprising 1 ft 6 in. deep rolled steel joists carried on stone abutments. In normal weather, this gives a 6 ft clearance above the water. However, West Cork has a wet climate and flooding is to be expected.

There is a steep pull from the Post Office. The regulator is opened wide for The Tram to make a spectacular start from rest. Aughadown School (4 m.) will be smothered in smoke as it passes and there is a fierce but short climb to Aughadown Church which stands at the cross roads and gives name to the community; in 260 yds the line rises by 25 ft (1 in 31).* Speed must be kept down as on the curve beside the church gate in the wall there is a restriction of 8 mph. (Aughadown Church (Church of Ireland) is dedicated to St Matthew.)† The level crossing is monitored from the station 110 yds beyond where there is another road crossing.

The 'official' station for Church Cross is adjacent, and boasts a 52 yds-long concrete-faced platform on the off-road side just over 4½ m.# 'Official' because the Powers-that-Be are unaware that the locals prefer equally the Post Office and School stop; the Tramway's management will turn a blind eye to activities which generate business . . . furthermore the guard will not re-start the train if he knows there are customers who have the last swallow to make in the bar or crack to finish in the shop . . . for he may be among them.

So The Tram halts a second time for such as those who live in this upper part of the village. Clearly there was no platform in the early years, nor any covered accommodation, but both now exist to the convenience of railway-user or bystander for it can be awfully wet in this exposed situation. The shelter is a simple concrete but windowless building with single-pitch roof of corrugated-iron; it is more akin to a farmyard than to a station platform. However, it serves.

The Tram leaves the station; the driver 'opens up' the regulator and prepares to storm the steep hill ahead. From a height of 74 ft the incline increases in severity; road and rail pass a side road to the ancient landing-place at Reenmarish on the left, before both turn north-west. The 4¾ and 5 m. posts are passed and from the latter the line rises with incredible steepness, ultimately supported on embankment above the road to maintain an even rise to reach a summit at 187 ft; here there is a road crossing with a route to the south serving Aughadown House. Here are the ruins of old Aughadown House with Aughadown Castle and Tower remains, close by.§ The Tramway has climbed at 1 in 30-24 for the last half-mile and fortunately there are no curves in the course until the culmination. The locomotive has been tested to degree by this effort, and the blast from the chimney heard far around; (small wonder spark arresters were fitted to protect crops, meadow and coppice).

---

* Aughadown or Aghadown
† This is a replacement for the now ruined church of 1812.
# A.P. Hughes of West Winds, Bantry asserted many times that 'an old 25 in. Plan shows a passing loop here'. The appropriate Plan before the writer shows no such feature. Lesser evidence is that field-work does not support the contention.
§ Aughadown House. Only ruins mark the site of the 'strong castellated mansion' with its entrance by drawbridge and other features which allowed visitors to feast their eyes on the scene below Aughadown Townland, the Bay and the Fastnet Rock way out to sea. Photography could seldom do it justice as the sun tends to throw its delights into shadow. Aughadown ('The Field of the Fortress') was built by the Bechers in the early 17th century; the Castle ruins stood a single field away. [More intimate detail is in THE COAST OF WEST CORK pp. 95-6.]

After a steep pull up from Pig's Bridge, No. 4s stops at Church Cross. With the blower on, the fireman takes the opportunity of adding coal to its tortured fire. 1939.   *W.A. Camwell*

No. 4s, somewhat winded, stops at Church Cross. The safety valves start to blow re-assuringly. 1938.   *H.C. Casserley*

THE ROUTE - SKIBBEREEN TO SCHULL HARBOUR

While there is no recognised stop here, the train is brought to a stand for any 'regulars' to alight or embark. The fireman, meanwhile, must refill the boiler for the gradient has reduced the water level while the needle in the steam pressure gauge has sagged alarmingly. The injector is turned on and plays its tuneful sound which is music to all enginemen: the blower is turned on too, to keep the fire bright and restore the fallen pressure. The fireman now looks to see how much damage has been done to the fire - the blast caused by the need to work the engine hard has played havoc with the coals in the box - some of them have been shot into the air, half burned, and the rest is in sorry state. So thin is the layer of coal in places one can see the firebars. A few moments with a pricker sorts the errant fire to order, and a few deft rounds of coal restore it to normality; the fireman may now straighten his back and perhaps lean from the cab to inhale a helpful breath of sea air. A heavy pall of black smoke bears witness to his labours.

Inside the train the passengers are oblivious to all this. The initiated have wisely had the windows closed but the stranger among them will have been alerted to what is now the broad and breathtaking vista of Roaring Water Bay from this point (the name is said to be taken variously from the sound of the Atlantic Ocean breaking on the strands of many foreshores or that of the Roaring Water River).

By long experience, The Tram may be 30 minutes or more late by now but the gradient is now in its favour and there is a steady fall at the roadside for ⅜ mile to Hollyhill station (155 ft) at the crossroads of that name. Still aiming north-west, the line makes a curve through the station, which is preceded by a 25 yds-long goods siding facing Skibbereen to its east side. There is a tiny goods store beside it built in dressed stone, and having a convex roof of corrugated-iron. As is commonplace, there may be confusion in place names, for Holly Hill House (spelling different) was passed near the *previous* level crossing - one becomes used to such anomalies in Ireland.

According to the Regulations, there was formerly a crossing keeper's cottage here, the official distance from Skibbereen being 5 m. 860 yds.* The 50 yds-long platform is probably an original feature; it is curved and surmounted by a neat cement-rendered building with slated roof giving limited but adequate accommodation to the former staff (it is now unattended). It is a replacement for the original burned down in 'The Troubles'. The views to the south and west still open up scenes of the Cork coast, with larger hills rising in the near background; further towards Mizen Head more high ground beckons. When sunshine obtains, it reflection on the sea and shore is almost dazzling; during rain there is no view whatsoever and all is shrouded in a jacket of saturated cloud and mist. One is constantly reminded in such bleak weather of the miseries suffered by hundreds hereabouts during the famine before the countryside was denuded of human life by starvation, disease and emigration. Perhaps the local passengers show these past endurances in their faces, but the tourists among them, mesmerised by a combination of sunshine and beauty, are unlikely to recall them.

During the interregnum at Hollyhill, the driver has descended and with oil-can in hand, has encircled his engine and lubricated all accessible bearings . . . and some not so convenient. The injector has been working again, and a great stream of water now flows down the road from its overflow.

---

* Now given as 5 m. 45 ch. This crossing is not marked on the 25 in. 1899 OS Map.

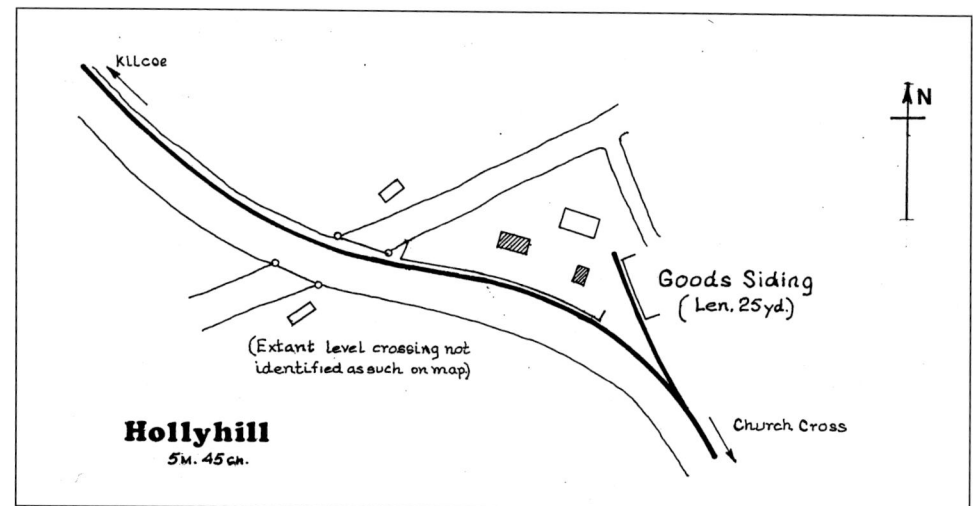

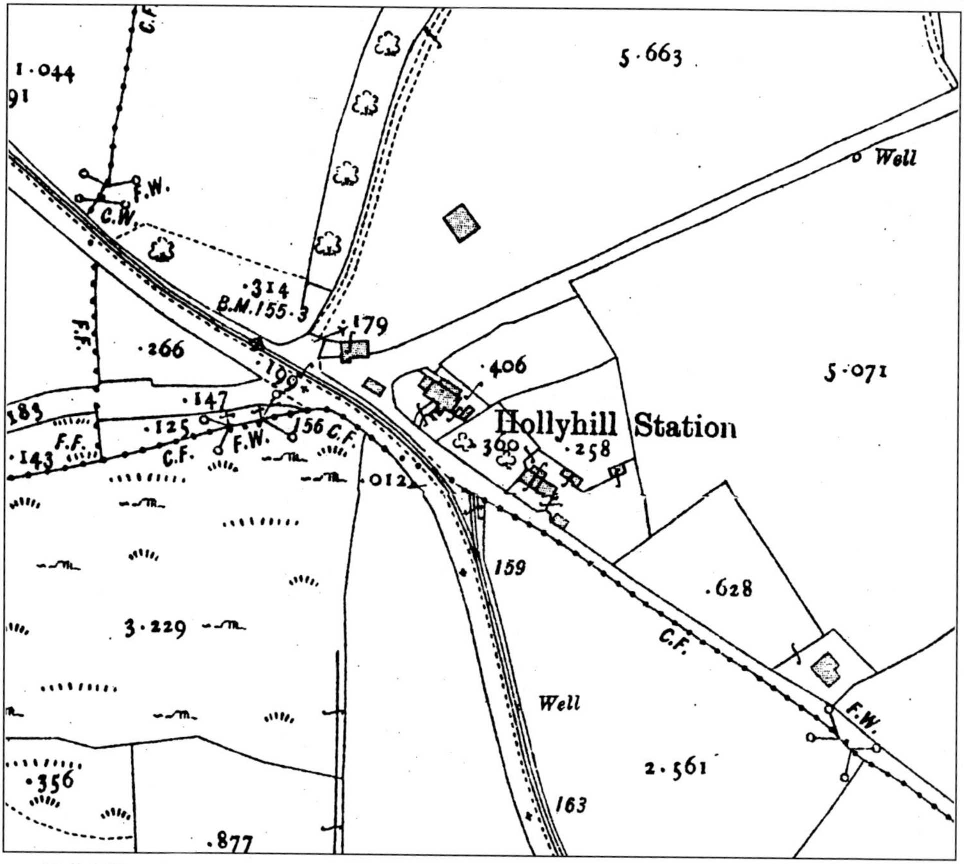

Hollyhill station. *Reproduced from the 25", 1941 Ordnance Survey Map*

THE ROUTE - SKIBBEREEN TO SCHULL HARBOUR 131

With KENT at its head, the noontime departure from Skibbereen leaves Hollyhill. Carriage No. 5s is next to the engine, behind come three of the large vans followed by the 'mystery' wagon (possibly a former ballast wagon). Note the two vans in the siding (*extreme right*). 1938.
W.A. Camwell

The 1.45 pm from Schull pauses at Hollyhill. 'Curly' Hegarty is the driver. 1938.
H.C. Casserley

THE SCHULL & SKIBBEREEN RAILWAY

The 1.45 pm ex-Schull simmers quietly in a sylvan setting at Hollyhill. 1938. *Eric Hannan*

After some energetic climbing, Hollyhill is reached. 1938. *H.C. Casserley*

THE ROUTE - SKIBBEREEN TO SCHULL HARBOUR

Hollyhill-Kilcoe

A short blast on the whistle comes in answer to a wave of the guard's hand; he stands in the road so as to be seen from the engine. Steam is put on gently, and the equipage begins to drift down the hill through Hollyhill Townland. There is rough, rocky high ground behind the train but ahead a useful valley opens out and assists the line to descend.

The fall in the adjacent road is now too steep for the Tramway which diverges to the right at 5¾ m. and there is another 8 mph curve. The railway's descent becomes steeper; the train passes 'Allen's House' (once the Aughadown Post Office) sandwiched between road and railway, and one of the standard Board of Works' dwellings once so common throughout Ireland.

The course runs north here, falling through boggy ground surrounded by overgrown hedges. There are two level crossings which give access to the higher ground on the right; the first rejoices in the title 'Kilcoe No. 1 & Cottage' (5 m. 1,650 yds) and here rail and road enjoin again. The Cottage was again a BoW type and probably housed a lengthman rather than a gate-keeper; gates are non-existent anyway.

The railway and road passes together through low, swampy ground covered by bog-heather in season. The train passes the 6th milepost as a left-hand curve carries the track up onto a low embankment where the falling gradient ends; the brake blocks smell hot under the carriages for the driver has made a cautious descent from Hollyhill. On top of this low embankment is a gated level crossing and almost immediately the Roaring Water River is crossed at Meen Bridge (100 ft, two spans with a central stone pier) on an 8 mph curve and there is a road junction to the south (gates were un-necessary here as the Tramway is still embanked and separated from the highway).* A small crossing house stands adjacent; it supervised several road junctions nearby.

Close by is Kilcoe National School and next to it, a fine church (RC). Meen Bridge is the foot of a dip; now the line turns west and there is a short, straight run up the 'impossible' hill ahead lifting the track from 100 ft to 122 ft at Cross House, the last section being at 1 in 25. Meen Bridge being a small settlement the train would halt there occasionally but the driver preferred to press on and have a brief 'run' before hitting the foot of the gradient.

Cross House stands beside the line, and this *is* an important stop. You will not find this substantial double-fronted house in the timetable but on the largest maps it *is* marked 'P.H.' and the opportunity for passengers and crew to adjourn 'for a short delay' (as it is described locally) is not to be missed. This ritual applied particularly to the train carrying the Directors back from their meetings in Skibbereen. Other reasons for the stop are the unloading of barrels, groceries, etc.

The next bit is easy; gradually climbing yet still beside a straight road, The Tram reaches what the map says is Kilcoe Cross Roads (the summit of this section at 147 ft) and Kilcoe station. The Regulations term it 'Kilcoe No. 2 & Cottage' 6 m. 1,015 yds from Skibbereen - it was very precise. Not bothered so much about the niceties of its former title which began, 'Schull & . . . ' the operating owner since 1925, The Great Southern Railways, considered Skibbereen to be superior and measured distances therefrom.

Despite the liberties exercised only half-a-mile back, the engine seems to be winded and the driver conducts the now-routine ceremony with the oil-can while the fireman

---
* The Roaring Water River is also known as the Meen (or Mean) and 'roars' at its confluence with the sea.

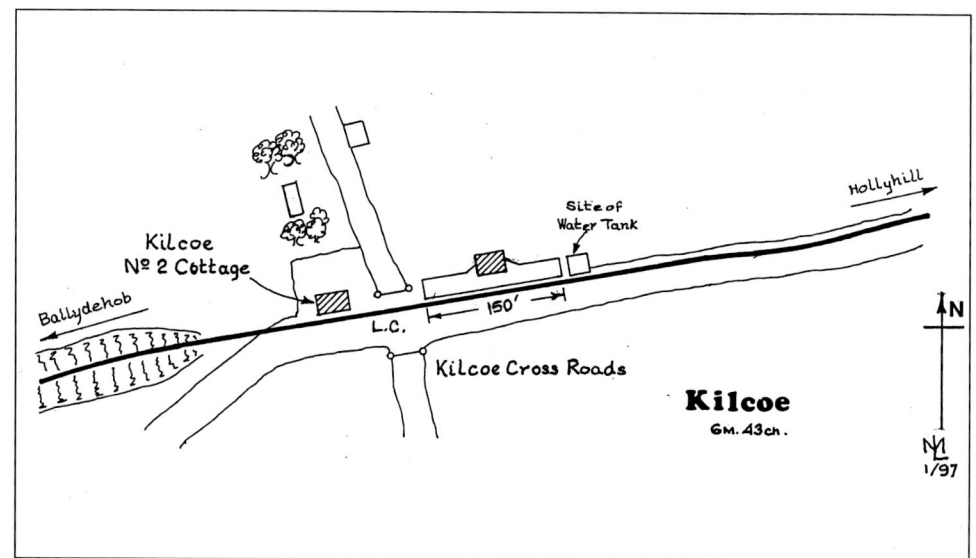

Further west, on another occasion, the 1.45 pm from Schull is found at Kilcoe, recovering from the climb up from Crooked Bridge. 1938.
H.C. Casserley

THE ROUTE - SKIBBEREEN TO SCHULL HARBOUR 135

Another frightful climb for Schull-bound trains precedes the station at Kilcoe - here hidden by the train. 1939.
W.A. Camwell

Kilcoe Halt and crossing-keeper's cottage; the track had been lifted six months previously. 1954.
J.I.C. Boyd

No. 3s and train cautiously descends to the Crooked Bridge. 1944. A.P. Hughes

A Down train stands on the Crooked Bridge to take water. The ganger stands at the pump-house door below the tank. 1938. H.C. Casserley

smoke-screens the vicinity with clouds having a slightly greenish tinge - for they are now burning Polish coal landed at Schull. The injector leaves its calling-card on the road again but this time the procedure has been interrupted by a woman appearing with a wicker-basket of washing and setting it down in the road while the injector 'obliges' with a drench of water and steam.

Kilcoe station resembles Church Cross, but in fact, each station is different. The concrete-faced platform is 49 yds-long (extremely generous in fact) and backed by a fence of old sleepers which speak for themselves! The station building is superior, entirely of corrugated-iron with convex roof so frequently seen in Ireland. There was a small waiting room with fireplace. The 'cottage' beside the crossroads at the west end is based on the BoW design and adopted for each Tramway level-crossing worthy of the name. A water-tank once stood at the east end but its supply was said to be unreliable. The station was the centre of an ambush during the Civil War.

Again, views come into prominence at this lofty point almost bereft of habitation. To the west, ahead, stands Mount Gabriel and to the south features in the bay are clearer; Cape Clear Island to the south, the string of islands off the mainland shores, and here and there the ruins of further castles, churches, graveyards, farms, houses, hovels and copper mine buildings and chimneys, spelling out the history of West Carbery.

Kilcoe-Ballydehob

But even The Tram does not halt here long enough to digest all there is to see. With a short whistle it is off and lost to view from the road which descends sharply to cross the Leamawaddra River at the Crooked Bridge. The railway has other ideas, entering an entirely new terrain with much gorse-covered hillock, rocky outcrops and a fall in the quality of the land generally.*

By means of curvaceous descent, passing through rock cutting, along shelf and embankment formation, and with check-railed curves having 8 and 10 mph limits imposed, and with notable smells and noises coming from protesting brake blocks, the rake will twist its way to the edge of the Leamawaddra River ($7\frac{1}{4}$ m) and cross it acutely by a three-span, two-pier bridge of materials previously recorded. To the astonishment of strangers travelling, the train stops on top of the bridge for the engine to take water from the tank on its bank. This tank, on timber piling and replenished from the river, was installed to back-up the intermittent supply at Kilcoe station for the waterflow is seldom affected by drought.

There follows what can be a nightmare scenario in wet weather. The engine must pull its train up a ruinous incline entirely curved, from a standing start. With the skill born of years of experience, a good driver must call upon his fullest art to prevent the driving wheels from slipping and the fireman his expertise in actuating the sanding gear to allow the wheels to grip the rail-heads. Sheer cussedness would seem to cause the driving wheels to spin round helplessly as a contrary wind blows the sand off the rails before the wheels reach it. Many is the time when a train stalls and it is forced to drop

---

* This decline is noticeable as we go farther west but, here and there especially nearer the coast, are pockets of arable and pasture which make generalisation difficult. There are acres of low ground, waterlogged and marshy the whole year round, which cannot be brought into use. The higher ground is rough, thinly-soiled and strewn with bluffs and rock; it can support a limited number of livestock. These observations apply to the rest of terrain to be seen from the train, all the way to Schull.

No. 3s has plenty of steam while climbing up from Crooked Bridge. *Circa 1944.   A.P. Hughes*

Having climbed out of Ballydehob and crossed the road at Skeaghanore Cottage (Driscoll's), an Up train heads for the Crooked Bridge. 1936. *Gordon Tucker*

THE ROUTE - SKIBBEREEN TO SCHULL HARBOUR 139

back downhill to the far side of the river bridge and start again; here at least the gradient can be tackled on the move. An engine in difficulties here will advertise its problems by an enormous column of smoke, the clamour of wheels spinning aimlessly while the safety valves lift to reduce steam pressure raised by the un-necessary blast through the fire.

Like a snake, the line makes it way through cutting and over embankment to reach the road-side again at 7¾ mp, where is yet another BoW house for a lengthman. The final curve to bring the track to road-level enjoys a speed limit of a mere 5 mph, but the train is hardly likely to exceed this in the circumstances . . . In fact the road climbs even higher, but the railway cannot achieve this and avoids it by traversing a cutting on a left-hand curve. The climb eases at the level crossing beyond (175 ft asl), but the ascent still continues. The average grade since leaving Kilcoe is a nominal 1 in 30, but short sections are steeper than this. Complaints about shortcomings in the construction can be justified by the last mile alone.

In the excitement of the climb from the river, the one level crossing may have been missed; this is 'Ardura Cottage' 7 m. 810 yds, in Ardura More Townland; Newham refers to a Crooked Bridge Halt near here but does not identify the position. This seems the most likely: no other reference to it has been found. Throughout this tortuous length there are numerous speed limits which are observed in the breach, because the up-grade train seldom reaches them and the downhill working will be severely braked.

The worst is over: The Tram can trundle along the roadside for another 1¼ m. and then, after plunging down a fearful slope into Ballydehob, there will be an extended station stop with time to restore the *status quo* after the recent experience. Not yet though. The Tram has still to travel this more gentle rise to a lesser summit (186 ft), while some of its passengers may contemplate their surroundings. This a pleasant spot though to the south the view of coast and sea is blocked by high ground. To the north the rough foreground terrain stretches away to high ground in altitude somewhere between low foothills and young mountains. On the right day it holds for the viewer that elusive quality which symbolises the Irish landscape so beloved of painters such as Paul Henry. On a wet day the visitor wishes he had never trod foot here. The Tramway begins to fall, past the 8½ mp and sometimes on a low embankment to avoid dips in the road; now 120 ft asl at the turning for Skeaghanore Farm and for a short distance, the line falls out of sight below the road. At Skeaghanore Cottage (Driscoll's) (8 m. 1,440 yds) the old coast road comes in 'from behind' on the left side, thus combined, the 'Coach Road' drops steeply from here into Ballydehob, out of sight in the valley bottom ahead. The railway crosses the roads at the point where both enjoin (103 ft asl) and the once-gated crossing with cottage could have its dangers for both road and rail traffic, for there is reduced sighting due to the site being on the brow of the valley. This is Knockroe Townland.

Crawling along now, with brakes almost fully applied, the train slowly disappears from sight below the road, crossing an embankment (9 mp) and around a continuous curve taking it from a south-west to north-west direction, on the headland high above Ballydehob Bay. There opens out a fine view of Bay, river estuary, wooded islands and, if the tide has ebbed, a vast expanse of mud. As the train turns yet further, a panorama to the west is revealed with the huddled houses of Ballydehob on the hillside across the river and behind all, the summit of Mount Gabriel five miles away. The whole curve is check-railed and subjected to an 8 mph limit - not that the driver is willing to exceed this.

At 9 m., and with the precipitous descent to Ballydehob beginning, the westbound train passes Skeaghanore Crossing cottage (*left*). Speed is kept to a minimum as before the foot of the incline is reached, the brake-blocks will be almost red-hot. 1939.
W.A. Camwell

A Down working is standing at Ballydehob; it will not take water here as this has been done at Crooked Bridge. 1938.
H.C. Casserley

THE ROUTE - SKIBBEREEN TO SCHULL HARBOUR

As if to give full value for money, before the station is reached the track swings west again, past 9¼ mp, alternately occupying a shelf and then embankment. One is constantly in mind of d'Avigdor, the contractor and the howl of criticism at his shortcomings - given an honest builder and sufficient funds, how could this approach have been improved without earthworks on a prodigious scale?

The train runs off the descent in Ballydehob station, with now customary squeals and smells from the brakes and a re-assuring plume of steam from the safety valves - there was no risk of brake failure . . .* There is nothing to be gained by looking at one's watch and matching it to the advertised times; on average the train may have lost 30 minutes or more, but since it rarely leaves Skibbereen on time it is on a 'cannot win' schedule. The station is 9 m. 35 c. from Skibbereen and badly placed for the village, perched as it is on high ground above the opposite side of the Bawnaknockane River. A viaduct carries the line over this tidal inlet.

The station boasts the only intermediate passing loop on the system; an island platform lies between the tracks but when trains are not required to pass each other, the northern face is used. There have been modifications here since the line was opened, principally to the goods shed and the livestock pens on the northernmost siding. The building on the platform (now denuded of its awnings) is quite generous in size (48 ft x 12 ft 6 in.) and the Station Master has separate accommodation in a BoW-design house at the south-east corner of the site. A water tank for locomotives stands at the west end of the platform, which means that east-bound trains must stop outside the station limits for the engine to take water. It is fed from a spring on the hill half a mile away. All water tanks are supported in a similar way (see Skibbereen).

The access to the station comes in steeply on the north side from the main road; here a bridge crosses the river to reach the village. Along this road livestock are driven to or from trains to Fairs in the village; beasts sold for export entrain here *en route* to Cork (or) for shipment. The size of the station premises given over to livestock underlines the dominance of this traffic here.

Back at the train, all seems ready for departure on the remaining distance to Schull (*c.* 5 m.). For some miles back the engine does not seem to have been in the best of health; there is a gland leaking steam from some obscure place and other strange noises. Curly, the driver, does not seem unduly concerned, but he has added a spanner and hammer on his foray with the oil-can. Neither of the men on the engine bothers about the red glow which has given the lower part of the smokebox door the appearance of a lava flow . . .

---

* Sufficient steam must be held during descent to control downhill speed.

Ballydehob station. *Reproduced from the 25", 1901 Ordnance Survey Map*

THE ROUTE - SKIBBEREEN TO SCHULL HARBOUR

Ballydehob-Woodlands

On the departing whistle the train bundles onto the viaduct* with a gusto so far unseen; a short straight level run allows it to gather momentum before the most gruelling part of the run begins. It will lift the train from 30 ft to 123 ft in exactly two miles and contains fierce portions of 1 in 25 against the engine - these formidable figures undoubtedly disguise short lengths of 1 in 23-24 which are only acknowledged by the *cognoscenti*. First Class passengers, ladies and children may sit back in their seats but the young and virile may soon leap out and push to prevent the train from stalling and a run back to the station to try again. In emergency, men working in the fields nearby will be called to do their bit. (Revd Canon George A. Salter whose father farmed here, recalls his participation in these frivolities, especially on Fair Days and when Schull Regatta took place. Tradition is that trains were sometimes divided but unless a second engine was available, intermediate manoeuvres were confined to Ballydehob: problems were inevitable.)

There is a fiercesome pull from the viaduct made worse as the railway is obliged to turn left and try to adapt itself to the contours of the hill. Up on an embankment now, it crosses a single arch masonry bridge which takes it over a minor road which descends to the quay. Upwards still, it winds round the grounds and above the roof of the National School of 1892, threading 'the outer suburbs' of Ballydehob on a series of 3 chain curves limited at 8 mph (43 ft asl). This is now Shanvanagh Townland and the train has the Bay below on its left ; the course of the railway's steep descent into Ballydehob is clearly seen across the river.

Another reverse curve follows and the line crosses the old bridle road to Schull by a single-span overbridge having masonry abutments. Another reverse curve, a short cutting and then an extra-ordinary tangential level-crossing - one is left to speculate on the arrangement of gates needed here. The gate-house adjacent is to the customary BoW style and styled 'Shanvanagh No. 1 (Sullivan's)' (9 m. 1,340 yds, estimated height 70 ft asl).

The route bears southward and is obliged, now clear of the environs of Ballydehob, to enter a 30 ft deep cutting flanking Laurel Hill Farm. A lane is up above the cutting to the left but a branch leads off into this farm by means of a masonry arch; the track passes below it. Adjoining the bridge was a separate footbridge spanning the cutting and though the supporting walls remain, the span has gone; the legal necessity for this bridge would be interesting.

Up now on the side of Laurel Hill itself, and emerging from the cutting, (10 mp) on a downward grade the course becomes shelf-like and takes a sharp U-curve to the right having a 5 mph restriction. (This location is said to be 'Sweetman's' but these original terms have been difficult to confirm.) With more shelving and cutting, 'Shanvanagh No.

---

* *Ballydehob viaduct*. This major work deserves a description to itself. It was, and remains, the most outstanding monument to the undertaking and its excellence takes some of the heat out of the criticism of the contractor . . . allowing that construction was not sub-contracted. Coming down into Ballydehob from any direction, this fine 12-arch masonry structure catches the eye immediately. One writer says of it, 'The river is spanned by a twelve-arched bridge which has the stately proportions of a Roman aqueduct. When the tide is in, the Tourist might think that he has never seen a more beautiful place . . . low water is quite another matter . . .' The western-most arch contains the road leading from the village to the quay close by; it gives a clearance of 20 ft to the centre of the arch. The pillars are 4 ft wide. The three eastern-most arches span water as tide etc. allows. At track-level there is a clear width of 10 ft between the parapet walls and there is an inclination of the track-bed from east to west. The underside of the arches is concrete-reinforced.

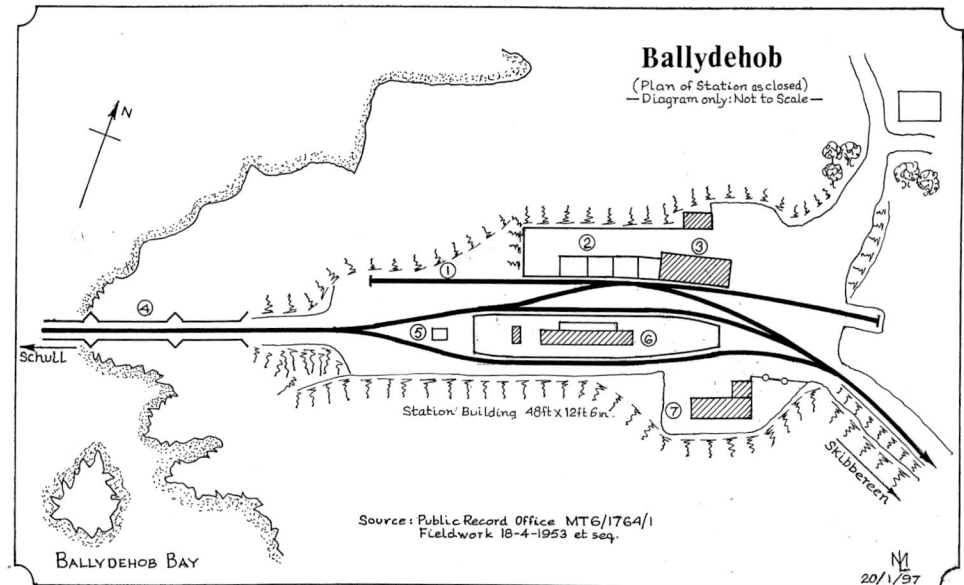

Ballydehob does not appear to have had any trackwork alterations throughout its life, though the buildings etc. were enlarged. *Key:* 1. Original site of small Cattle Dock, 2. Subsequent and enlarged Cattle Dock, 3. Goods Shed, 4. Viaduct, 5. Water Tank, 6. Station building with canopy on north side, 7. Station Master's House.

Down train with No. 3s takes water at Ballydehob. 1936. *Collection J.I.C. Boyd*

THE ROUTE - SKIBBEREEN TO SCHULL HARBOUR 145

The 1.45 pm from Schull stands at Ballydehob - waiting the photographer's pleasure. 1938.
H.C. Casserley

This bridge carried the railway over a bohreen to Ballydehob Quay; it was the only example.
Collection J.I.C. Boyd

A Schull-bound train has been stopped especially for the photographer; this is Ballydehob viaduct looking north. The train comprises GABRIEL, bogie coaches Nos. 5 and 7, brake van No. 54 and vans Nos. 31, 32 and 38.

Lawrence Collection

Schull-bound train crossing Ballydehob viaduct; the station is on the extreme right. 1936.

Collection J.I.C. Boyd

Above: Whilst at Ballydehob, the Down train had shed some vans so the slog up to Shanvanagh Crossing No. 3 was not so heavy. The train is coming to a summit here. The gateless road crossing itself is in the right distance, whilst in the right foreground, is the photographer's much-featured 'Morris 8' car.
W.A. Camwell

Right: The girder bridge carrying the track over the Ahboy River, Woodlands. A similar one was at Pig's Bridge. 1954. *J.I.C. Boyd*

2' (10 m. 620 yds) level-crossing is gained, the gate-house covering two crossings. Now travelling north-west, the main road is gained once more after traversing a high embankment and curving onto it at another acute crossing 'Shanvanagh No. 3 (Connor's)' (10 m. 800 yds, height 103 ft) and an 8 mph restriction.

Under any circumstances, the last two miles are a notable piece of railway, perhaps in view of what was expected of the original engines and men of the Tramway. Had it been built ten years later it would have been a location more akin to that traversed by the Manx Electric Railway and its curves and gradients less of an enemy. But to even contemplate an electrified line in a remote, poor and backward terrain is to indulge in fancy. To have expected the first design of tram engines - which were basically designed to work in town streets - to be appropriate motive power questions the contractor's knowledge or the advice given; perhaps it was simply a matter of conforming to character and buying the cheapest?

Undoubtedly winded, The Tram would come to a halt about the 10½ mp beyond the ledge high above the road at this point where the railway enters Clashmore Townland. Here a roadside Bench Mark witnesses it is 123 ft above sea level, and the appearance of the driver on the ground again confirms there are several minor adjustments to be made to the engine. Admitting delay is inevitable and without troubling to consult his Great Southern Railways' timepiece, the guard comes forward to him. Whether their talk is about the further delay to the train (which is obvious anyway) or about runners in the Punchestown Races today, one cannot say, but the chances are they are considering the opportunity open to The Tram of reaching Schull in time to listen to any of the race meeting on the Station Master's wireless.

For the next 1½ miles to Woodlands the journey is somewhat dreary - even on a fine day. Farmland to the left does not inspire and high ground blots out all view of the coast. Bog and marsh to the right provide all there is to see, backed by distant hills. Road and rail together press on with the tramway always side by side but frequently at different levels . . . was this a consequence of the several improvements to the alignment made down the years?

Now follows a slow fall but at 11 mp the road suddenly rises abruptly so the track takes to a deep cutting and rejoins it 133 ft asl. Another slow fall ensues and at 11¼ mp the lineside bog becomes a lake (Clashmore Lake) which in this treeless terrain, is hardly likely to hold the travellers' attention.* Just beyond the lake's termination, the course crosses a bridge spanning the Ahboy River which drains the area.† It is an inconsequential waterway despite its fine name. This is Cooragurteen Townland, and the gradients are very gentle.

At 12 mp comes Woodlands station; surely a misnomer if there ever was one, for apart from a few mangey trees which survive from a coppice planted about the turn of the century - Hicks' Plantation - across the road from the tramway, one looks in vain for a tree . . . or a 'Station', for that matter. True, there is a lane adjacent leading to the farm of that name and at one time occupied by John H. Kelly, a member of the Committee of Management, and a bi-lingual board on the fence proclaims 'Woodlands' in English and Irish. The name is taken from the Townland here, and a literal translation is 'The countryside of the woods' ('Dhu-ha-na-gweeltha').

That being said, the station is fractionally outside the Townland of that name, and just within Derreennatra - such are local anomalies . . .

---
* The badly-made retaining wall here had to be completely rebuilt.
† The bridge is of single span on masonry abutments as Pig's Bridge. It has an open iron railing on the off-road side.

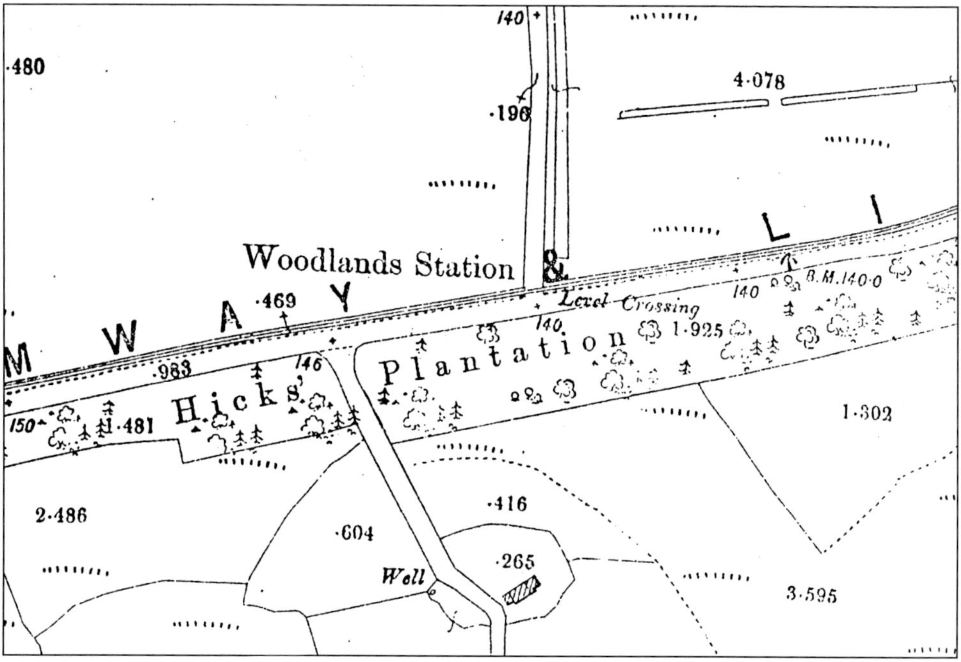

Woodlands station. *Reproduced from the 25", 1901 Ordnance Survey Map*

Woodlands Halt was set in bleak countryside; it possessed nothing but a nameboard. 1950.
Walter McGrath

THE ROUTE - SKIBBEREEN TO SCHULL HARBOUR

Woodlands-Schull

The Tram makes but an occasional stop at Woodlands, mainly for a handful of folk who patronise Schull for their needs (as they say in West Cork, 'to call in Schull for the messages') and for whom the usual farm transport is unavailable that day; an analysis of the halt's use would have made an interesting social study.

The westward continuation of the line makes it a gradual uphill task, but nowhere at more than 1 in 100, and at 12¼ mp an all-time summit is breasted at 168 ft. The rake can now begin its fall into Schull; steam will only be required occasionally and the fireman can let the fire die preparatory to cleaning it at the terminus.

At 'Woodlands Cottage; 12 m.1,000 yds' the road dives away suddenly to the left and descends, out of sight. The surroundings change but the tramway continues as before, passing a crossing-keeper's house on the right and on an embankment, traversing a sharp left-hand curve with 5 mph restriction ('Woodlands Curve': 131 ft asl) at 12¾ mp.* The railway's course now heads due south on embankment for quarter of a mile before meeting the road again. Both are now following the west side of the Ardmanagh River valley as it descends to the coast; high ground covered in gorse and bracken with rock here and there has small patches of pasture scattered between. Rathcool Townland is this west side.

The official inclination over the first of these curves down into Schull is 1 in 30 decreasing to 1 in 38, in that order, but enginemen know there are pitches considerably steeper than these figures, and make the descent with experienced caution.

Another severe curve with 8 mph limit comes at 13¼ mp and ends a gentler fall at 1 in 119 and heralds a short due-westerly run on embankment (53 ft asl), and over a stream which makes confluence with the river nearby. At 13½ mp the line turns at 3 chains radius due south on the 'Workhouse Curve' and resumes the fall at 1 in 76 - and then steeper.† The grim, ivy-covered stone walls of the derelict Workhouse and burial ground seen on the right, encapsulate all the poverty, suffering and death which West Carbery especially, has endured in the past two centuries . . . and in which the Tramway has featured at times.

Bounded by streams recently crossed, the railway now reaches Cooradarrigan Townland and at 13 m. 70 ch. emerges from the hinterland 55 ft asl; it takes a nasty 2½ ch. radius right-hand curve (8 mph restriction) involving an embankment to even the fall. The official figure of 1 in 30 here can be ignored, for any elderly resident remembers how a descending train, inefficiently braked, would leave the rails on the curve and at worst, end its journey on the road.

The Tram has at last reached the seaside and the vicissitudes of the journey are over. It may be minutes late (but probably much longer), and that clanking from some malfunction on the locomotive seems all the more demanding now that the 'puff' no

---

* The curves at the head of this valley are collectively designated, 'Woodlands Curves'. From Schull they are listed are: 1) 4 chain radius at 1 m. 26 ch; 2) 4 chain radius at 1 m. 32 ch; 3) 3½ chain radius at 1 m. 39 ch.

† Schull Workhouse (The Union Workhouse). Built to a standard design by British architect George Wilkinson in about 1850 to house 600 people; the perimeter wall, alongside of which the Tramway ran, was finished in 1852. Being among the last to be built, it was of a higher standard; it was described as a 'splendid and imposing building'. The ruins of the neighbouring hospital and of the enclosure walls still stand (1998). One account states it was burned down in 1917 to prevent the Black & Tans billeting there; others give the date as 1921. In any event, something of its grim past may be felt as the modern visitor rushes by in his car. [See also: MIZEN JOURNAL No. 4 (1996) p. 43.]

The 12.0 pm ex-Skibbereen approaches Woodlands Curve and bridge with No. 4s. 1938.
H.C. Casserley

A Down train drops down off Woodlands Curve nearing Schull Workhouse. 1938.
H.C. Casserley

THE ROUTE - SKIBBEREEN TO SCHULL HARBOUR 153

An Up train hustles up the steep climb from Schull, the Coosheen Mine chimney just visible on the hilltop. No. 3s is steaming well. 1944. *A.P. Hughes*

The line reaches Schull Bay following a long fall from Woodlands; here the line runs at the head of the Bay to the station (*off right*). 1953. *J.I.C. Boyd*

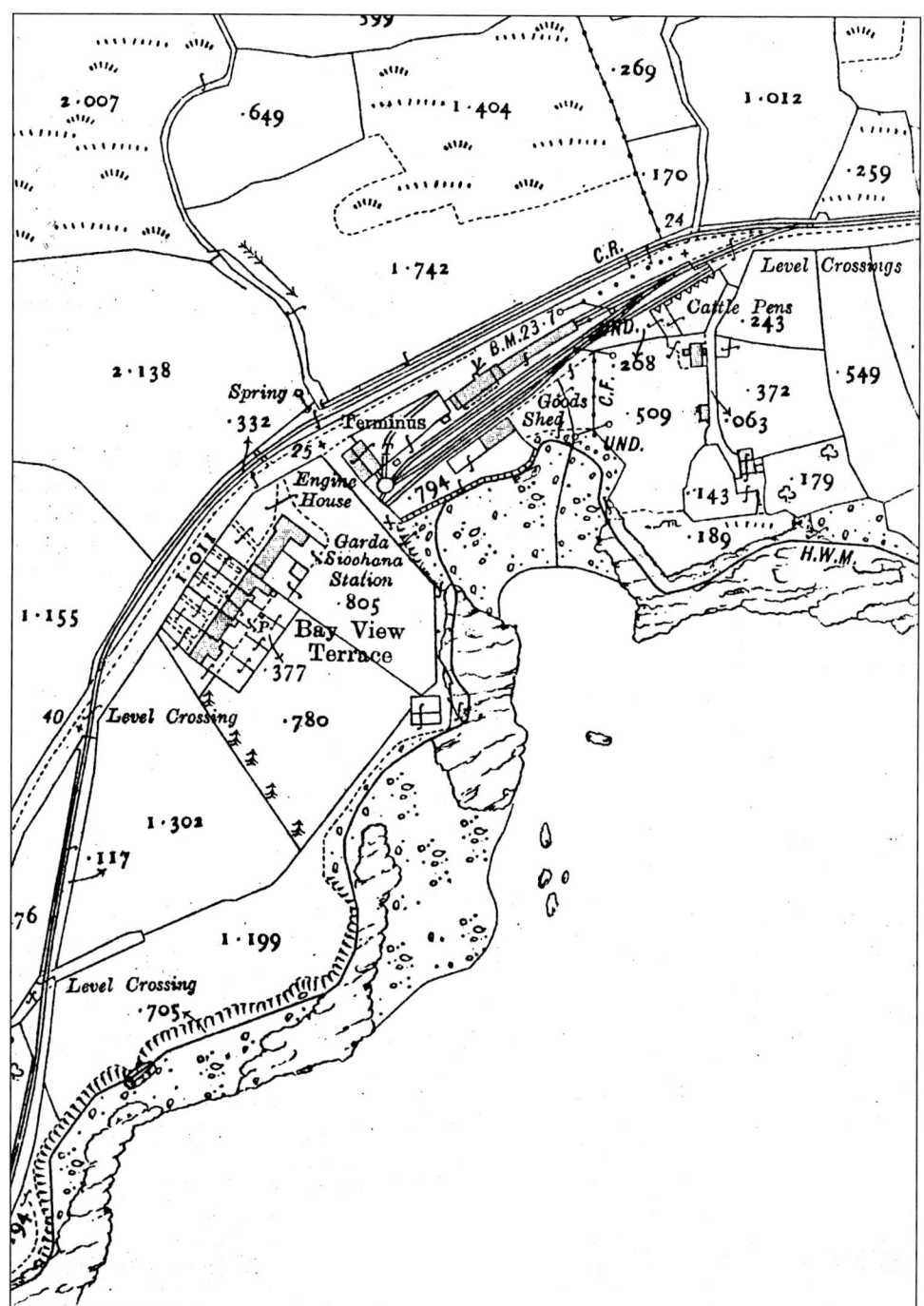

Schull station. *Reproduced from the 25", 1941 Ordnance Survey Map*

longer drowns the sound of it. The passengers have become used to the smell of hot brake blocks and the sound of their grinding on wheel-tyres as the long fall from Woodlands was made, but now there is the fresh smell of the sea as the shore of Schull Bay is traversed during the final quarter of a mile into the station. The line falls at an easy 1 in 82 above the shore-line, supported for some distance by a retaining wall above the road, so past the 14 mp. On a 2½ ch. curve it takes a sudden plunge across the road (23 ft asl) at 'Station Gates' level-crossing, 14 m. 500 yds from Skibbereen. So for the first time since leaving Ballydehob, (apart from diversions off the road to ensure an even grading) the train is on dedicated land again at the terminus. And it has passed under just one farm overbridge and one footbridge in the whole route, both at Laurel Hill.

Schull Station

As befits the first-named place in the title of the S&SR, Schull station mirrored its seniority in appearance and facilities . . . not that it had any real competitor, for Ballydehob was second-best, while, had he ever visited the place, E.L. Ahrons would have Skibbereen as an upgraded cow shed.

The substantial station building is of masonry with tiled roof. The raised platform is original and 50 yds-long, enjoying the benefit of a cantilevered awning on the station frontage. Added to the west end is a Parcels' Office and gents' urinal, with a portable building in timber beyond, to store various obsolete items of stationery, Rule Books, timetables which every station acquires. The non-railway face of the main building is very plain and has the main road alongside with (yet to be described), 'The Schull Extension Light Railway' running along the verge at its far side. There was a porched entrance to the Booking Hall. Enclosing the railway property at this end was a picket fence (later boarded) while alongside the road it was bounded by a stone wall.

At the extreme west end a narrow stone building with corrugated-iron roof *set at a right-angle to the site* serves as the Engine Shed and was capable of accommodating the three original tram engines; there are four large windows in the wall facing east - they were a unique feature but had been partly covered by corrugated-iron sheeting at the time of the original tram engines, probably for security. On the west side of the building a full-length 'lean-to' structure had been added *c.* 1900. It is windowless but borrowed light from the four windows and sky-lights in the inevitable corrugated-iron roof serves. Unusually, the running line and Engine Shed are accessed by a 22 ft 6 in. diameter turntable.

Although stripped of most equipment, this had been the place where miracles were wrought on the locomotives at all hours of the day and night to keep the train(s) running. The whole backs onto a wall skirting a bohreen which leads to the rocky foreshore. Lower down, there is a gate giving access to the goods shed.

Coming round to the south of the premises, old photographs show a simple, unconnected narrow gauge track opposite the original locomotive water tank. It has a small 'chaldron wagon' running on it and was possibly used for conveying ash and clinker. The present water tank is recent, but the old one was similar to others on the system except like that at Crooked Bridge, it had been boarded in around the timber uprights to make a small store. Originally the tank was fed from a mountain stream which comes down to the north of the station and passes under the road but the replacement installation uses mains water.*

---

* Perhaps a hydraulic ram was in use for every tank at first?

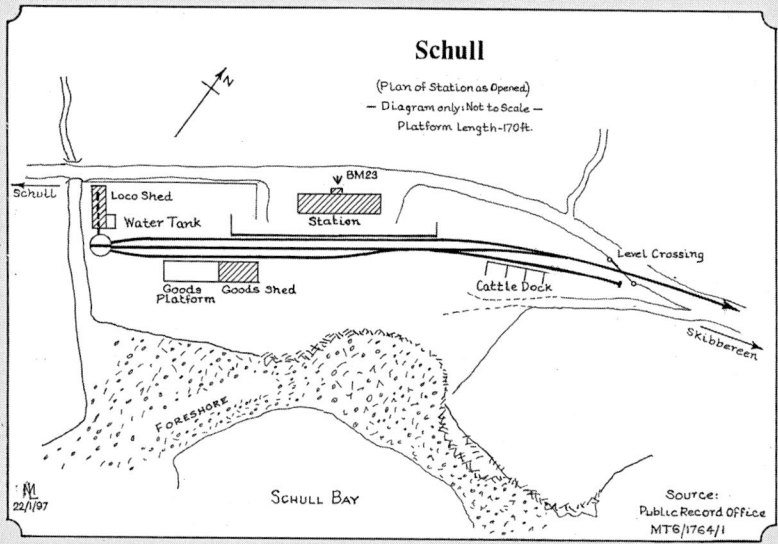

Schull in 1886 possessed a shed for the three tram engines whilst cover for any rolling stock was non-existent. Note the exposed position above the foreshore and how the roadside situation was adopted immediately the rails left the station.

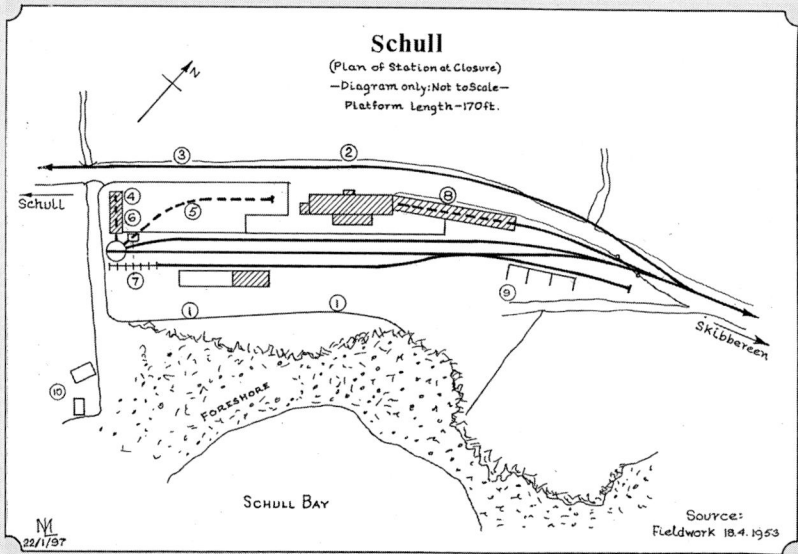

The ultimate form of Schull station, showing additions made since 1886 opening. These include the protective sea wall, Carriage Shed and Pier Extension. Note that the station building had been enlarged and fitted with a canopy on the south side. *Key:* 1. Sea Wall, 2. Starting point of Pier Extension, 3. Pier Extension - latterly disused and lifted west of 2, 4. Fitting Shop extension on west side of Engine Shed, 5. Temporary line into walled storage yard, 6. Latter day position of Water Tank, 7. Light tramway (latterly removed), 8. Carriage Shed, 9. Cattle Dock, 10. Coast Guard Station Rocket House (original function). (For identification of un-numbered features see plan of Schull as opened.)

Eastbound, the 1.45 pm train leaves Schull and towards the climb up the Workhouse curves. The Pier Extension disappears out of the scene, left foreground. 1939.   W.A. Camwell

On arrival at Schull, No. 3s shunts the train. The house behind the engine disappeared long ago. Circa 1920.   D.B. Bradshaw

Schull at last. KENT has run round its train and is about to make its second departure that day. In the brief time allowed the returning traveller has been able to catch brief glimpses of Schull Bay's proximity to the station. 1938.
W.A. Camwell

Journey's beginning; No. 4s (then the Schull engine), awaits the right away. 1936.
R.W. Kidner

THE ROUTE - SKIBBEREEN TO SCHULL HARBOUR

Schull, looking back towards Skibbereen. Locomotive No. 4s. 1938. *H.C. Casserley*

At Schull, No. 4s, turned ready for the next Up journey, shunts the mixed train. 1938.
H.C. Casserley

Schull. Mixed train on arrival; Carriage Shed right. *Circa* 1935. H. *Fayle*

Schull station, the Bay and Cape Clear Island seen from the north. *Circa* 1898.

Lawrence Collection

THE ROUTE - SKIBBEREEN TO SCHULL HARBOUR 161

Schull engine shed; KENT on turntable. 1938. *W.A. Camwell*

Schull terminus, Engine Shed and Goods Shed, showing the protective sea wall. 1953.
J.I.C. Boyd

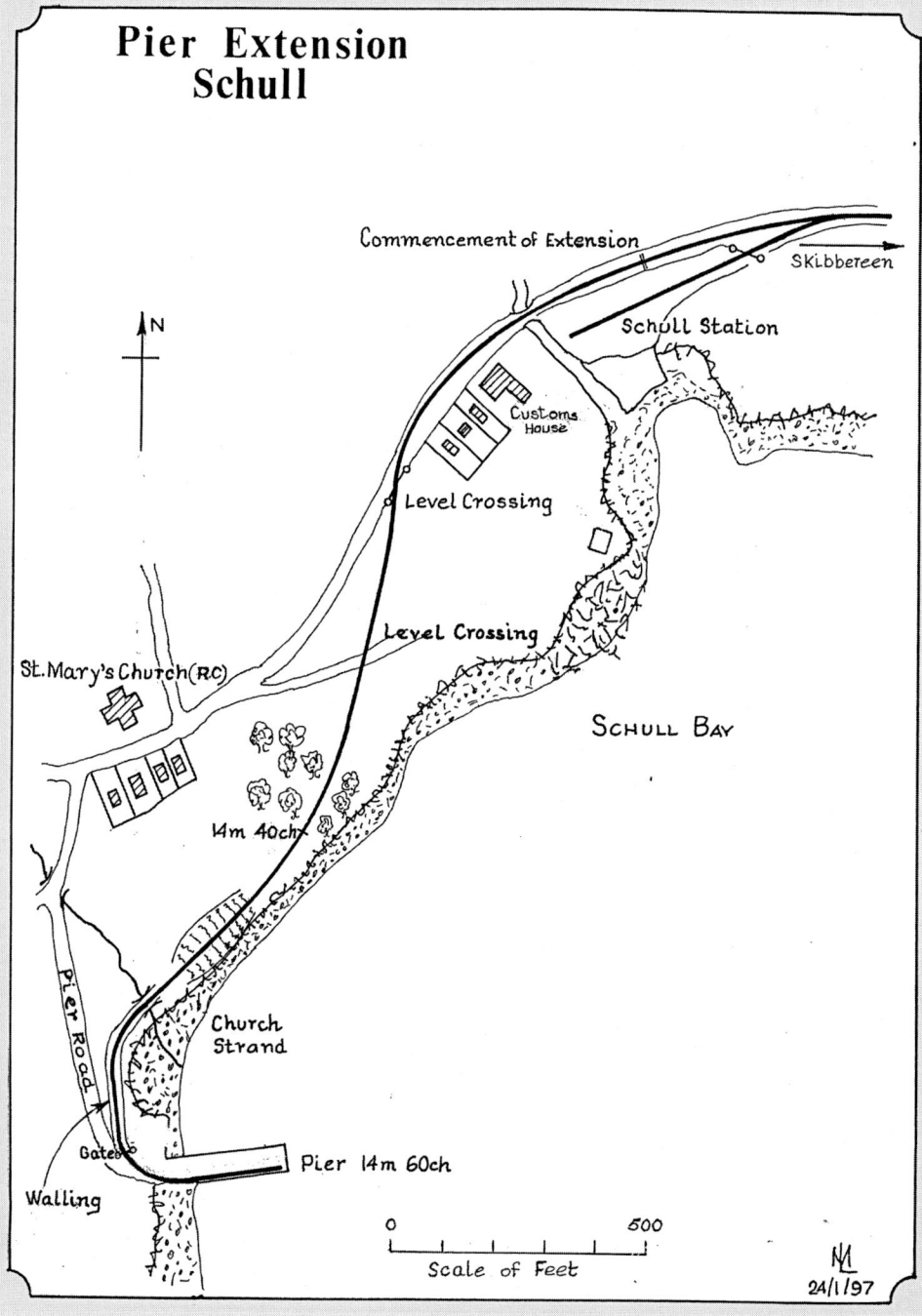

This Plan of the Pier Extension to Schull Harbour cannot disclose its steep fall to the shore and only suggests the severity of the curves at its west end. The site of the derailment of a locomotive during the Civil War is the small bridge over the stream at Church Strand (1922).

On the land opposite the main building is a plateau-like area on which a corrugated-iron Goods Shed and a goods platform stand. The plateau is protected from the sea by a substantial wall, for at high tide the water comes up to it. The building shows evidence of being enlarged in the past and itself is possibly a replacement of the original shed, being installed about the same time as goods facilities at Ballydehob were enlarged.

In the south-east corner of the layout is a Cattle Dock and loading platform served by a siding off the loop; its very size reflects the importance of livestock business to the concern.

Finally, a long, covered Carriage Shed of corrugated-iron projects from the east wall of the station building; it is much more convenient here than that at Skibbereen. The year of construction is not known but it was built after the tramway's opening. Like most similar sheds in the South of Ireland the side walls do not reach to the ground.

The most coveted feature in the whole station stood near the foot of the east wall, half-hidden under the Carriage Shed roof but accessible from the platform rear - a large water tap fitted with a long hose. Officially for washing down the carriage stock, sluicing-down the Cattle Dock and cleansing the platform, it was variously employed by the inhabitants of the premises for those myriad domestic jobs which need water. And in the terms of an obituary, it is 'sorely missed' (1999).

Schull Station-Schull Pier

The Extension westwards behind and beyond the station may have enjoyed its own grand title (The Schull & Skibbereen Extension Tramway and Light Railway) but The Pier Line, The Harbour Branch or The Extension were among the vernacular used to describe it, sometimes with a throw-away wave of the arm as if it was an un-necessary appendix. The GSR dubbed it 'The Pier Extension', which seems appropriate.

Although it continued on the north verge of the highway (as if it were a main line in its own right) from the place where The Tram crossed the road at Station Gates, the next few yards of railway were actually the property of the original promotion and would possibly have been once a siding. The commencement of the Extension was sited exactly opposite the north doorway of the station - and presumably there had once been a mandatory lineside marker to define the legal end-on junction of the two systems which would be the source of some local curiosity!

From here the line remains on the roadside and so past the Customs House, Coast Guard Station and Bay View Terrace, climbing to 40 ft asl before leaving the road at 'Pier Extension' level crossing (14 m. 810 yds) (gated but having no keeper's cottage), then running due south and traversing an un-gated crossing (no title): both these crossings are monitored from the station and operated by the train crew. From the second the line falls, dropping nearer to the rocky shore to reach the water's edge where it crosses a small river by a masonry arch; here was the scene of a runaway locomotive being sabotaged during The Troubles (see p. 93).

Beyond the bridge, the line curves south between the Pier Road and foreshore, contained by stone walling - the only instance of such protection on the whole system. Beyond, there was another sharp curve to the east and the track levels out along the pier. At the end the rails were given a sharp upward sweep to prevent railed vehicles over-running and landing on a ship's deck or into the sea . . . such mishaps did occur.

The Extension is a separate undertaking from the S&SR; roadside section apart, it runs on its own private right-of-way. The GSR includes it in the gross mileage from

Schull Pier showing stacked fish barrels beside the railway track. The Pier Extension followed the wall in the background. *Circa* 1898   *Lawrence Collection*

THE ROUTE - SKIBBEREEN TO SCHULL HARBOUR 165

The Pier Extension falls steeply to the foreshore. Schull station (*off; upper right*), St Mary's (RC) Church and Mount Gabriel in centre background. *Circa* 1898. *Lawrence Collection*

Schull Pier - the Pier Extension is behind the wall. *Circa* 1898. *Lawrence Collection*

Skibbereen, the first level crossing being 14 m. 37 ch., the point on the line exactly opposite St Mary's Church (RC) is 14¼ m. and the official distance at the pier end is 14 m. 65 ch. The curves from 14½ mp to the pier are subject to a 10 mph limit (which seems dangerously generous) and are styled 'Church Strand Curves'.

[To prevent trespassing, at the point where the line left the walled section to emerge on the pier, it is gated; all the same, the Extension is used by everyone as a footpath.]

* * * * * * *

The situations on the line where compulsory stops were made are listed on p. 50.) Heights above Sea Level are taken from soundings in Dublin Bay, April 1837.

Detail in this chapter is based on fieldwork and Ordnance Survey 25 inch/1 mile surveys of 1899 and 1912.

There are variations between detail shown on 25 inch Plans and the First Edition 1 inch/1 mile maps. The same stations vary in being shown as 'Stations' or 'Halts'; this particularly applies to New Court and Church Cross whilst the former is not shown on the 1889 25 inch Plan.

The GSR Gradient Section drawing gives no detail and omits figures. Gradients are calculated from the information on 25 inch Plans.

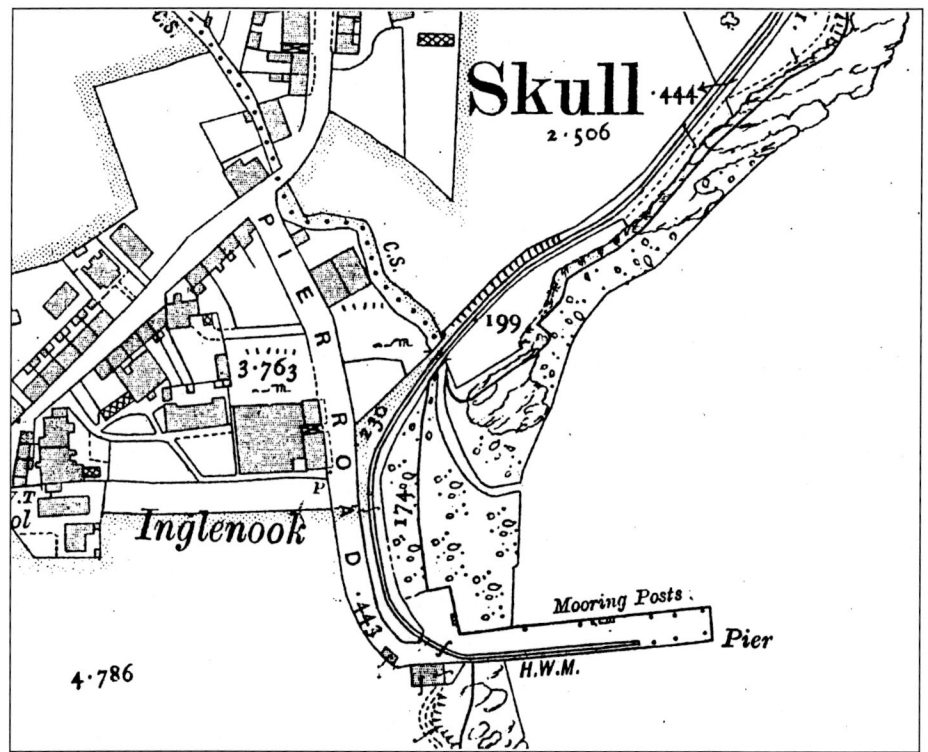

Schull Pier Extension.   *Reproduced from the 25", 1941 Ordnance Survey Map*

Chapter Fourteen

Locomotives

Early three-foot gauge tramways in Ireland using steam locomotives

To dispel any notion that the West Carbery was a pioneer steam tramway in Ireland, a short preface will suffice: it lists opening dates, length and supplier of tram engines and from this the dissimilarity of the WCT to its predecessors is obvious. It also makes the choice of a steam tramway system for West Cork the more incredible.

Title	Length	Opened	Engine builder
Dublin & Lucan Tramway	1¾ m.	6/1881	Kitson & Co., Leeds
Portstewart Tramway	1¾ m.	6/1882	Kitson & Co., Leeds
Giant's Causeway P&B Valley Railway & Tramway	*½ m.	1/1883	W. Wilkinson & Co. Ltd, Wigan
Castlederg & Victoria Bridge Tramway	7¼ m.	7/1884	Kitson & Co., Leeds

(Other three-foot gauge systems in Ireland which never used tram engines are not listed.)

It will be seen that none of the above four undertakings approached the WCT for length, that none used Dick, Kerr-built locomotives and that the operation, costs of each were available to the promoters of the WCT before construction started. In a period when steam tramway building was in vogue, perhaps established builders like Kitson and Wilkinson had full order books? Perhaps Dick, Kerr were anxious to break into the market and quoted a competitive price? These questions remain unanswered.

Tram Engines of 1888 (Builders: Dick, Kerr & Co. Ltd)

No.	Name	Wheel Arrangement	Cyls	Driving wheel diameter
	MARION	0-4-0 Tram Engine	9½ x 16 in.	2 ft 6 in.
	IDA	0-4-0 Tram Engine	9½ x 16 in.	2 ft 6 in.
	ILEN	0-4-0 Tram Engine	9½ x 16 in.	2 ft 6 in.

Dick, Kerr - formerly W.B. Dick & Co., of Britannia Engineering Works, Kilmarnock - built steam locomotives in the period 1883-1918 and developed a reputation for their street tramway engines which were widely used at home and overseas. The engines produced for the West Carbery Tramway were the fifth and seventh respectively made in the Works; they had been preceded by narrow gauge tram engines for the Alford & Sutton Tramway† in 1883 and the Penang Tramways in 1885 (one each). It might be remarked that their experience was then but slight. Incidentally they had an interest in the Alford & Sutton venture.

We can only conjecture the steps which led to the conception of the West Carbery in the form of a street tramway, though neither its length, gradients nor curves would be inadmissible as these features were frequently found in the towns of the West Riding (e.g. Huddersfield), but seldom of the severity and continuation of the WCT which soon proved the street tram principle unsuited to the terrain.

---

* Only this short distance from Portrush station was worked by steam.
† Opened in January 1883, it was the first municipal undertaking.

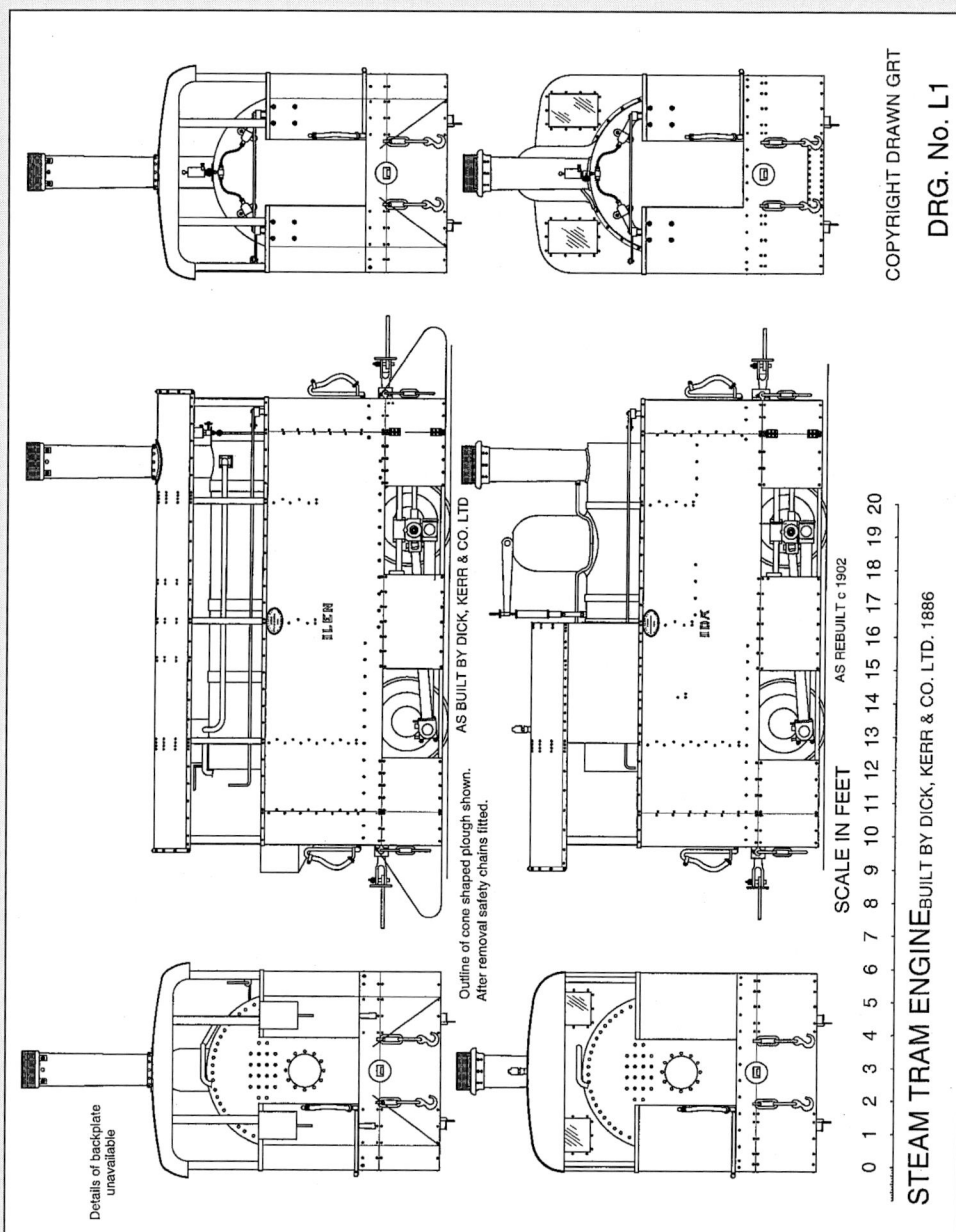

Earlier comments on these machines has been made elsewhere in this volume, so a summary will suffice; the boiler/firebox design and materials were unsuitable, the firebox brick-arches were faulty and all three were recommended for rebuilding with copper in place of steel where the latter had been used. The result of building in the wrong material led to weeping of the boiler/firebox due to unequal expansion of these materials. The weight in working order was 15 tons but they were unable to pull twice their weight on a gradient of 1 in 30.

Some of the blame was placed on the firemen who, it is imagined, were possibly inexperienced and found that simply piling coal into the box was no sinecure for falling steam pressure.

To comply with regulations sheet-steel skirting was taken down to a level approximately 3 in. above the rails; the rolling and pitching of the engine probably produced shrieks of protest as it scraped the rails. There was an entrance through the upper sheeting both front and rear; the former would allow the tubes to be cleaned. A narrow passage-way allowed the enginemen to pass along the side of the boiler and a suitable hand-rail for this purpose was more truly a rod to actuate the sanding-gear from either end.

So far as can be identified, driving could be done from either end though it was usual to have the firebox end leading. The skirting at the driving end (only) was fitted with a 'plough'; the couplings were of the 'hook-and-eye' type and did not couple on impact; at this period the mandatory side coupling chains had been omitted. The impressively tall chimney was surmounted by a 'chip-pan' spark-arrester.

The outside cylinders were 9½ in. diameter x 16 in. stroke; driving wheels 2 ft 6 in. diameter. With a coupled wheelbase of only 6 ft, the fore and aft pitching was considerable. Well tanks held 350 gallons, but of the inside valve gear, nothing is recorded. Condensing of the live steam was also a problem as the boilers were domeless. The firebox, tubeplates and tubes were specified to be ¾ in. thick but the maker's advised against this to no avail. They also felt that roof condensers would make the machines top-heavy and recommended a nest of tubes in the roof of the firebox instead. Exhaust steam would pass along the tubes, be reheated and be invisible on entering the atmosphere at the chimney top.

The Tramway Co. objected to this device but agreed to accept it if the maker's would hold themselves liable for defects; defects were immediately apparent. Dick, Kerr had called this a substitute for a real condenser; they conceived the idea of protecting it from the flames by fitting 'a very flat fire-brick arch'. This was found faulty within days of operation and leaking at the vertical seams of the firebox was attributed to it. The trouble was never eradicated though costly efforts were made; it simply became worse.

The engines were classed as Works' letters A, B & C and were delivered in a green livery. MARION and IDA were possibly named after Director's wives; ILEN is the river at Skibbereen.

As regards the conditions stipulated by the BoT in September 1886, conspicuous numbering of each locomotive was certainly not carried out; the name appeared in yellow characters c. 6 in. high below the maker's plate, on the centre of the side sheeting. Numbers, if they existed, had disappeared by the early years of the century. The bell and speed indicator are not evident on early illustrations.

These locomotives failed from the first; shortage of steam was countered by the early removal of the condensing gear, and the disconnection of the vacuum brake. Leakages of both boiler and firebox were put down to cost-cutting and the use of steel in

Tram engine ILEN as built, out of use at Skibbereen in 1906. *H. Fayle*

IDA out of use at Skibbereen; pulled from engine shed by KENT with long coupling bar (*off right*). 1924. *A.W. Croughton*

construction, the tubes were also of steel though no detail survives of what material was employed. Unequal expansion would cause leakage but such accounts of failure are only available as Director's or management submissions and not an Engineer's Report. The Company submitted, clearly with informed opinion, that the fireboxes were wrongly made and detailed leaking tubes, and cracks around the firehole door.

To remedy a dire situation, the cure was seen in fitting new fireboxes to the tram engines and then putting them on light duties; they would then be replaced by conventional engines of adequate power output. Though this objective was to be achieved over a number of years, the initial financial position forbade it.

'Make do and mend' had to suffice on a hand-to-mouth basis until replacements took over the working; in the interim the subsequent lives of the tram engines can be summarised:

MARION was in a dismantled state at Skibbereen in 1906.*

IDA when seen at Skibbereen on 29th May, 1924 was largely unused except in emergency. It had been heavily rebuilt in 1905 losing its tram-engine appearance together with ploughs from each end. With its overall roof removed, a more conventional cab was fitted having an open back; the side sheets were given a horizontal shutter which would close to keep out a little of the Atlantic gales. In May 1901 a new, bigger boiler was ordered from Nasmyth, Wilson & Co. costing £403; it was fitted and sported a huge dome on its first ring surmounted by Salter safety valves (the original engine had no dome, and this would make for wet steaming). A very tall chimney to aid combustion seemed inspired by Crewe practice and all controls were removed from this end. Sandboxes were retained. A large brass lubricator was mounted below the chimney and fed through the footplate into the valve chests below by means of heavily lagged feed-pipes which branched out below it. The larger boiler with Belpaire firebox transformed the engine but who by and where the work was done is not recorded; possibly the CB&SCR was involved. At this stage the engine could produce a tractive effort of 5,730 lbs. with 140 lbs./sq. inch boiler pressure.

In this form Harold Fayle found it in 1906; it seemed to have been taking its share of the traffic as the train behind it was a considerable one.

Further modification was done before 1924, when the locomotive had a smokebox extension necessitating a removal of the forward sandboxes so they were now outside the sheeting at both ends - as when new. The chimney was shortened too.

The machine lasted until the GSR take-over in 1925 but was not taken into stock; it was scrapped in 1926.

In its original form, this and its two sisters were planned to weigh 12 tons but the replacement roof condensers (or superheaters as they were termed) were made of two tubes through which the exhaust steam was directed; clumsy and apt to make for unsteadiness they increased the weight to 15 tons. As rebuilt, No. 2 scaled 16 tons (18 tons in working order).

ILEN was photographed by Fayle at Skibbereen in 1906 on the same occasion as IDA was seen. Nothing in the picture confirms the engine had been given a new boiler and

---

* Roycroft referred to this engine in evidence of November 1907. An equally 'decisive' observation was made to the writer during a long discussion about West Cork affairs in general on 19th April, 1953 with Paddy O'Keefe at Bantry: 'The old S&S engines were sold to an Englishman, Harry Jack, who cut them up on the spot'. Which may well have been true of the first two tram engines to be withdrawn from service.

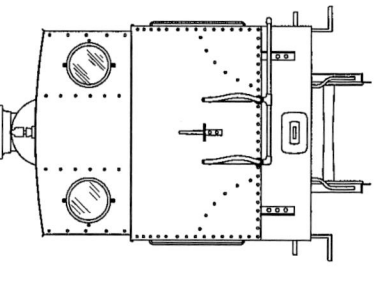
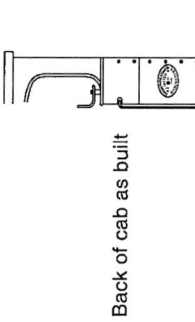

Back of cab as built

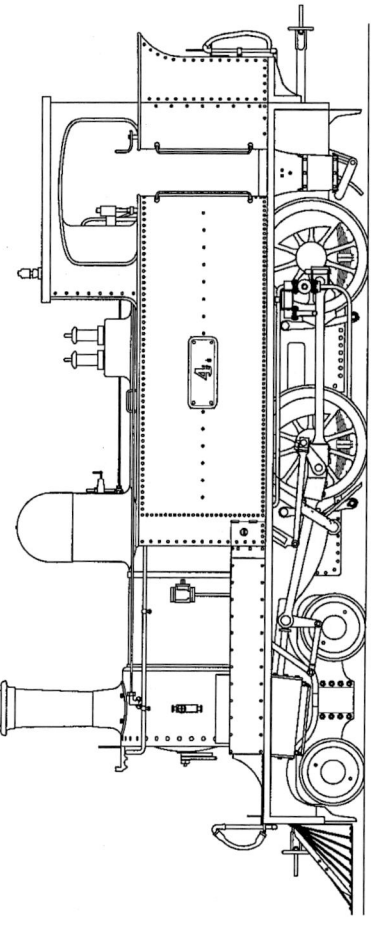
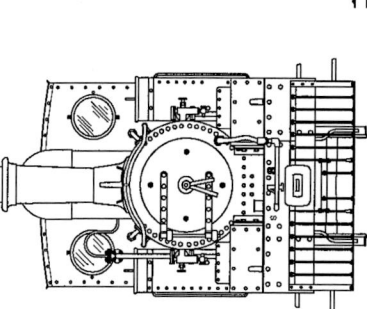

SCALE IN FEET
0 1 2 3 4 5 6 7 8 9 10 11 12 13 14 15 16 17 18 19 20

LOCOMOTIVE No. 4

BUILT IN 1888 BY NASMYTH WILSON & CO.

DRAWING SHOWS LOCOMOTIVE AS AT CLOSURE

COPYRIGHT DRAW GRT

DRG. No. L2

the external appearance is 'as built', but firebox replacement probably took place along with the other two tram engines in 1886/7. Fayle gives a scrap date of c. 1914.

Detail of Fayle's 1906 pictures reveal that MARION and IDA had been pulled out of the engine shed specially, and that ILEN was farthest inside and IDA nearer the door (suggesting ILEN was least in use?) had been dragged and separated for photography, using long iron 'tow bars' with eyelets each end to fit the coupler sockets, to separate the three engines; such was necessary to clear the ploughs at one end of the tram engines and the 'cow-catcher' on ERIN which provided the power.

1	GABRIEL	4-4-0T
3	KENT	4-4-0T
4	ERIN	4-4-0T
6	—	0-4-4T

ERIN. With the delivery of 4-4-0 tank engine, Works No. 342 in 1888 from Nasmyth, Wilson & Co. Ltd of Patricroft, Manchester, funded by a loan of £1,600,* the dire position of motive power was considerably eased. As delivered, vacuum brake was omitted, and the bogie had disc wheels with splashers on the rear set. The livery was green with white lining, and lettering on the side tank a little erroneously declared, 'WEST CARBERY TRAMWAY', with ERIN below but no number. It was a promising purchase and proved itself by outlasting the railway. Among its many miles of service it had received a replacement boiler from Peckett in March 1908 costing £428 and pressed at 150 lb., the work having been delayed pending the visit of the Vice-Regal Commission. It had 'pop' safety valves, and the dome had been heightened to accommodate a higher intake to the main steampipe and supply hotter steam to the injector. Replacement disc wheels were fitted and in 1909 an extended coal bunker was cantilevered out behind the cab as the capacity within was inadequate. The side opening to the cab was partly infilled with sheeting for evidently Patricroft did not realise that the rain for which Manchester is famous does not hold a candle to that experienced in West Cork..!

A Belpaire firebox was fitted from new and was reckoned to be first of its type in all Ireland, while the Walschaerts valve gear was a novel feature in that country.

Dimensions included:

Length over beams (excluding cattle guard)	22 ft	0 in.
Driving Wheel diameter	3 ft	4 in.
Bogie Wheel diameter	1 ft	10 in.
Coupled wheelbase	5 ft	6 in.
Total wheelbase	15 ft	1½ in.
Cylinders	12 in. bore x 18 in. stroke	
120 tubes	1¾ in. diameter	
Total heating surface	508 sq. ft	
Boiler pressure	140 lbs. (later 150 lbs.)	
Coal capacity (original)	½ ton	
Water capacity	500 gallons	
Tractive Effort @ 85% boiler pressure	7,720 lbs.	
Weight in working order	24 tons	

---

* The locomotive and bogie coach No. 5 were obtained by a hire-purchase arrangement at a combined cost of £1,818 9s. 6d.

THE SCHULL & SKIBBEREEN RAILWAY

ERIN, an official maker's photograph, showing engine in original condition.
Collection J.I.C. Boyd

No. 4s inside Skibbereen shed. 1929.
H.C. Casserley

ERIN as rebuilt, and now No. 4s, on the turntable at Skibbereen. *Circa* 1930.
Collection R.S. Carpenter

Between workings No. 4s stands at Schull. Driver Curly Hegarty on right. *Circa* 1936.
Collection J.I.C. Boyd

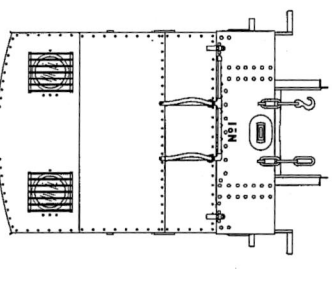
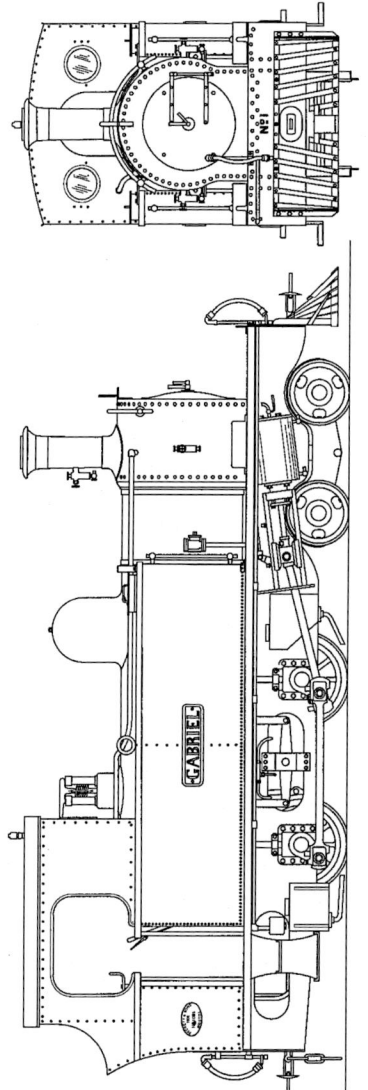

LOCOMOTIVE No. 1 BUILT IN 1906 BY PECKETT & SONS

DRIVING AXLES COMPENSATING GEAR REMOVED AFTER ARRIVAL AT SKIBBEREEN. REAR SAND BOXES ADDED. BOGIE WHEELS AS BUILT: LATTERLY FITTED WITH TYPE AS ON 'KENT'.

COPYRIGHT DRAWN GRT

DRG. No. L3

As built, only one injector was fitted, together with a crosshead-driven pump on the right-hand side. The evidence of the higher dome suggests that the steep gradients induced priming and modification was necessary to correct it; the original coal capacity was clearly too meagre for an engine required by the line's nature to consume more than average amounts of fuel.

A second injector was fitted later under the fireman's (left side) and fed a clack forward of the tank on that side. The dome-steam-supplied injector on the right-hand tank top fed a clack on that side and was unusual in being controlled from the driver's side. In view of what footplatemen recalled of conditions, this was a wise precaution as the fireman was so constantly feeding the fire and keeping a look-out that water-levels and injector controls could take second-place. Duplication was essential. (Injector controls on certain engines of the Festiniog Railway were placed on the driver's side only - for similar reasons.)

Except when in Skibbereen for repairs the engine was normally based at Schull and therefore became the regular duty engine; it was preferred to the Peckett-built engines which joined it later; the accessibility of the motion was a factor and the ride better with its longer driving wheelbase.

In 1925 it acquired tank-side number plates bearing the number 4s surmounted by small characters GSR; the suffix 's' to the number indicated S&SR section under the GSR. That concern classified it 'DN5', the only member of that class.

When services were withdrawn it was stored in Skibbereen shed, being drawn out again for the convenience of a visiting party in July 1950 and for a final time in April 1954 when it was taken to Inchicore for breaking up. By that time it had, like its stablemates Nos. 3s and 6s, acquired the double vacuum brake stand on the rear of the bunker.

(No. 1) GABRIEL. To replace MARION which lay in dismantled state at Skibbereen, a tender for £1,220 was accepted from Peckett & Sons Ltd, of Bristol* for a second 4-4-0 tank locomotive. Contrary to No. 4 with its inside frames, it was outside-framed and carried Works No. 1085; the shortcomings experienced with No. 4 were corrected, viz.: the driving wheels were reduced to 3 ft 0½ in. giving more tractive effort, the bogie wheels increased to 2 ft 0 in. diameter, the driving wheelbase brought down to 5 ft 0 in., bogie wheelbase 4 ft 0 in. (total wheelbase 15 ft). Boiler pressure was increased to 160 lbs and with cylinders the same size as No. 4 and smaller driving wheels, the tractive effort was enhanced to 9,650 lbs. Coal capacity was 1¼ tons and weight in working order 26½ tons which made for better adhesion. The grate area was 8 sq. ft and total heating surface 575 sq. ft. The men liked her and her oft times appearance in photos of the period are evidence of occasional preference; as with so many Irish narrow gauge lines, there was always a tendency for the newest engine, once proven, to be used to the displacement of others which being older, required more cost and time in maintenance! Eventually wear and tear would catch up with the preferred engine which might be

---

* Peckett & Sons Ltd. As Fox, Walker & Co., Atlas Engine Works, St George, Bristol, commenced building steam locomotives in 1864, mainly as four- or six-coupled tank engines for industry and later branched out into passenger engines and into overseas markets. They were taken over by Thomas Peckett in 1880 and traded as given. The building of GABRIEL was the forerunner of similar engines for narrow gauge for New Zealand and the Sarawak Railway. The last steam locomotive left the works in 1958. An engine built for New Zealand closely resembling GABRIEL still exists: built in 1923 for the Pukemiro Mine near Huntly it moved to the near-by Rotomaro Mine. It found a resting place at Motat in 1973 and is the responsibility of the Museum of Transport & Technology, Auckland.

GABRIEL's maker's photograph revealed its ultimate destination on the side tank. It was only for reference purposes.
Collection G.R. Thomson

GABRIEL featured propelling vans into the goods transfer platform, Skibbereen. 1929.
H.C. Casserley

consigned to the back of the shed requiring firebox or boiler work. So the old-stagers would re-emerge again, the best of them renovated to carry on as before . . . it is the pattern of human weakness and the S&SR was no exception.

The maker's were proud of their creation and their contemporary catalogue had an embossed representation of the engine on the cover; 'S. & S. RLY.' appears on the side tank. The frontispiece to the catalogue features 'An Opening Ceremony' to which reference follows. An official photograph shows the engine in works' grey and carrying the number 1085 on the tank side: the polished chimney cap, dome cover, safety-valve mounting and beading around tank and bunker top show the superb finish. Peckett was not usually an Irish supplier, and GABRIEL was a harbinger . . .

A second works' photograph was taken when the engine had received S&SR livery; on the right side 1085 had disappeared and in its place appeared in lettering about 5 in. high, 'SCHULL & SKIBBEREEN RAILWAY'; this too later disappeared and was replaced by a brass plate with raised rim and lettering, GABRIEL, the name being that of the mountain to the north of Schull.

In 1906 on the first arrival of the engine at Schull, it was turned and re-attached to the train. In an engaging little ceremony it was then blessed by Father John O'Connor, the Parish Priest of Schull who mounted the leading footplate, broke a bottle of champagne over the smokebox and duly named the engine. Witnessing this occasion were members of the Managing Committee, the Engineer Richard Evans and his son, John W. Loane the Skibbereen Station Master, Driver Jack Daly and his fireman James McCarthy, Guard Jim Stack and others.

It will be noted that on both this engine and its predecessor, ERIN, the cowcatcher was on the front end only. GABRIEL carried a wooden tool box and re-railing jack at the front end - or was the former for sand, as the front and rear sanding pipes so visible when new, are missing on later photographs? Furthermore, scrutiny of the maker's photograph shows only a leading sandbox below the footplate; the rear must be below the floor of the cab? Locally made rear sandboxes outside the frames appear more recently. Note too the usual Peckett displacement lubricator on the back of the chimney and the prominent compensating lever between the main driving springs. The weary-looking lamp which drooped at the foot of the chimney appears to be of carbide type; it would not give much illumination but would be a better warning than an oil one. It was carried on two brackets, shaped like a 'U'; the engine lamps were of conventional pattern.

The engine was classed 'DN4' by the GSR but exceptionally, the nameplates were not removed as was their custom, 'No. 1' being painted in small characters on the front beam instead, though the listed number was 1s. This, and the engines surviving to be absorbed in the GSR, were painted an un-lined black. The boiler, which had never received pop safety valves, was beyond repair in 1936 and the engine was scrapped in 1937. Its cylinders became a 'transplant' onto No. 3.

GABRIEL had proved itself to be prudent purchase. Its only major catastrophe occurred in Spring 1909 when the driving axle fractured; Peckett supplied a new one at half-price, having considered its age.

(No. 3) CONCILIATION (KENT). Purchased in 1914, this was another machine from Peckett which proved to be of equally good value. It was almost identical to GABRIEL, and under the GSR was given No. 3 to replace the tram engine ILEN scrapped at that time. The name KENT had been bestowed in place of the original by a nice piece of local patriotism. The Skibbereen fitter, Paddy Murphy, who had been moved by the

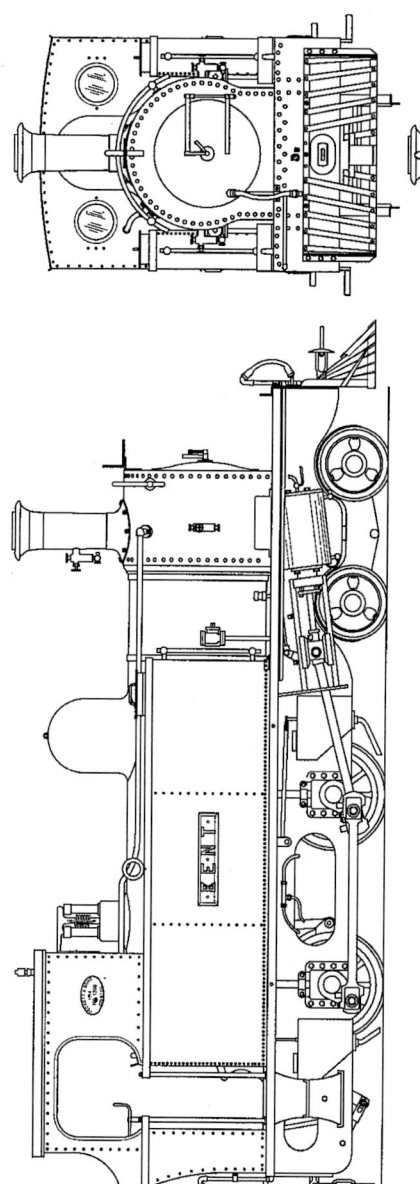

KENT outside the north end of the shed at Skibbereen, with turntable in the foreground. 1938.

H.C. Casserley

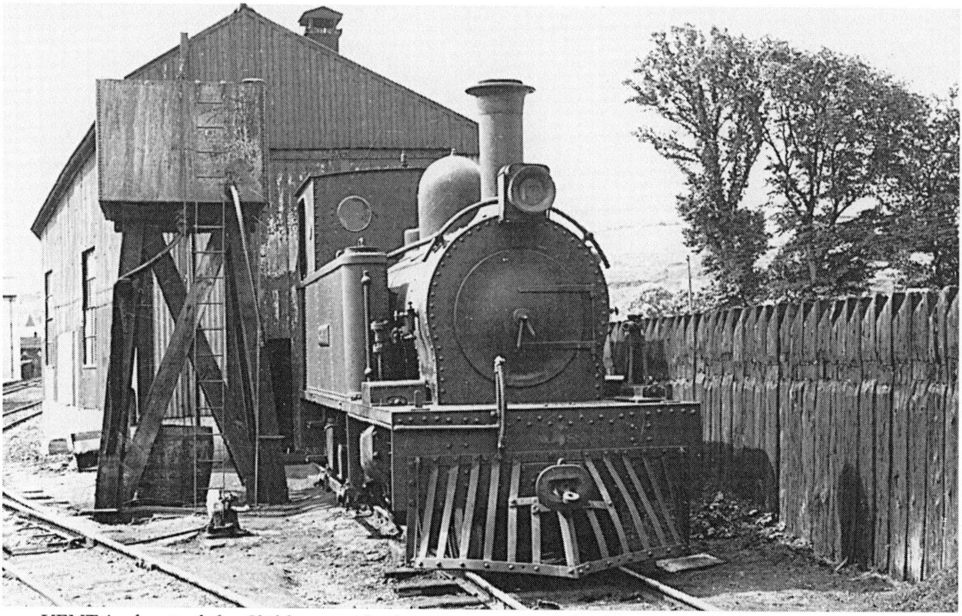

KENT in front of the Skibbereen shed, with water tank beside. Note the tapered end of the building. 1938. *H.C. Casserley*

Close-up of Hall cranks, wheels and motion. KENT inside Skibbereen shed. 1953. *J.I.C. Boyd*

execution of Thomas Kent in Cork gaol by the British in 1916,* contrived to make a new pair of plates from brass boiler tube and placed them before the Management Committee.†

This body, being sympathic to such a patriotic gesture, acceded to the request, and No. 3 was re-christened accordingly. So much for 'Conciliation' . . .

As this acquisition was a little shorter than GABRIEL (24 ft 11 in.), it had a reduced heating surface at 514 sq. ft, grate area of 7.58 sq. ft, a coal capacity of 18 cwt. and weight in working order of 25½ tons.# Painting, etc. was similar to 1s under the GSR and the engine outlasted the life of the railway.

The intrigue behind the name(s) is even more colourful than stated; Newham writes:

> When the new engine arrived at Skibbereen the question of a name arose. At the time the 'All for Ireland League' (O'Brien's party) had a majority on the Cork County Council, and was at loggerheads with the Redmond Party§ whom most of the townsfolk and tramway staff supported. It was decided therefore, that the engine be named CONCILIATION (after the party slogan, 'Conciliation, Conference, and Consent' - known as 'The Three C's'), and this was done.
>
> But within a short time the Redmondites secured the majority on the Council and the tramway staff, having objected to the name CONCILIATION, it was removed, it being intended to substitute HIBERNIA, after the Ancient Order of Hibernians . . .

However, the new name was never applied, events having overtaken things.

The engine was immediately distinguishable from GABRIEL as the maker's plate was on the cab sheet rather than the bunker. Beneath this plate was a small figure '3'; this disappeared during GSR days but the number was shown the leading buffer beam. Both engines were driven from the right-hand side (as was ERIN). Under the GSR, the engine was classed 'DN4'.

KENT was the second 'true' S&SR engine to be operable when the line closed, and stood in front of ERIN inside Skibbereen shed. Latterly neither of these engines had seen regular use, their duties having been usurped by incomer No. 6s.

[Intelligent observers maintain that No. 6s, transferred to the S&S section by the GSR in 1938, 'was used almost exclusively during the last years of operation'.] Under CIE which had taken over GSR interests on 1st January, 1945, and through the 1940s when the line closed, re-opened but only to close again, it seems doubtful if Nos. 3s & 4s had much use - if it all.

* The execution of Thomas Kent, who was seen as having died a patriot's death after the 'Easter Rising', in 1916 stirred the local imagination after the Sinn Fein party became very active after the 1914-18 War.

† The nameplate shows the neat workmanship but bears witness to the fitter who had not grasped the shape of an English K. It was suggested to the Writer by a former Chairman of Directors that the man had not memorised the difference between a letter B and a K so producing a hybrid. Another explanation was based on the idea that the man was unfamiliar with a K because there is no such letter in the Irish Gaelic alphabet.

Sometimes given as 24½ tons.

§ The brothers John Edward Redmond (1856-1918) and William Hoey Kearney Redmond (1861-1917) were Irish nationalist political leaders, and ardent Parnellites, the former becoming leader of the Parnellite Group in 1891, on Parnell's death. John stood for Cork but was heavily defeated; he captured Waterford - the only seat taken by the Parnellites. He gave 'tardy support' to the Irish volunteer movement in 1914 but he lost the confidence of many Irish when he deplored the 1916 rebellion. He aimed at a free Ireland within the British Empire. William suffered early imprisonment for being an 'Irish suspect', 1881. Served as an MP for various constituencies 1883-1917. He served in the Great War and was killed in France in 1917.

D.N.5.

(114)

CÓRAS IOMPAIR EIREANN
G. S. R^s.

CLASS. 4.5.
N°s. 4.

DATE BUILT———————————————
STEAM HEATING————————— NO
GENERAL DRAWING N^o———— 0325

WATER CAPACITY ———————— 600 GALS.
" COAL " ———————————— 2.0 CUB.FT
TOTAL WEIGHT ————————— 24 Tons 0 cwt..
" BRAKE POWER —————————

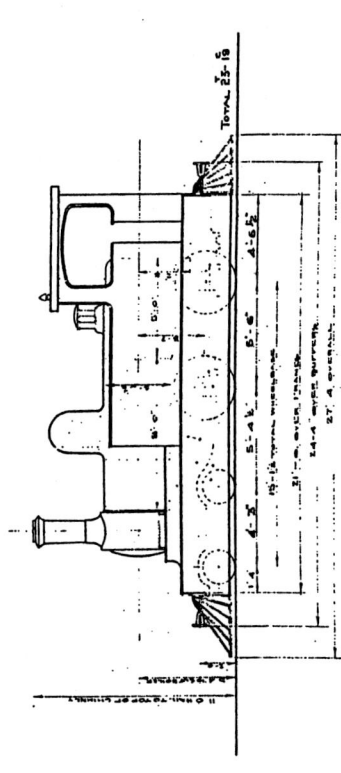

BOILER BARREL LENGTH ———————— 8.0
" DIAM. OUTSIDE ————————— 3-5½
FIREBOX CASING LENGTH ———————— 5-0
HEATING SURFACE FIREBOX ————— 54 SQ.FT.
" " TUBES ——————— 455
" " TOTAL ——————— 509
GRATE AREA —————————————— 9

CYLINDERS ———————————————— 12×16
WHEELS BOGIE ————————————— 1-10 DIA.
" COUPLED ——————————————— 3-4
CONNECTING ROD CENTRES ———————— 4-7½
WORKING PRESSURE ———————————— 150 LBS PER
TRACTIVE FORCE @ 85% BOILER PRESSURE ——— 8,260 LBS.
TUBES OUTSIDE DIAM. 1⅝ N^o ——————— 120

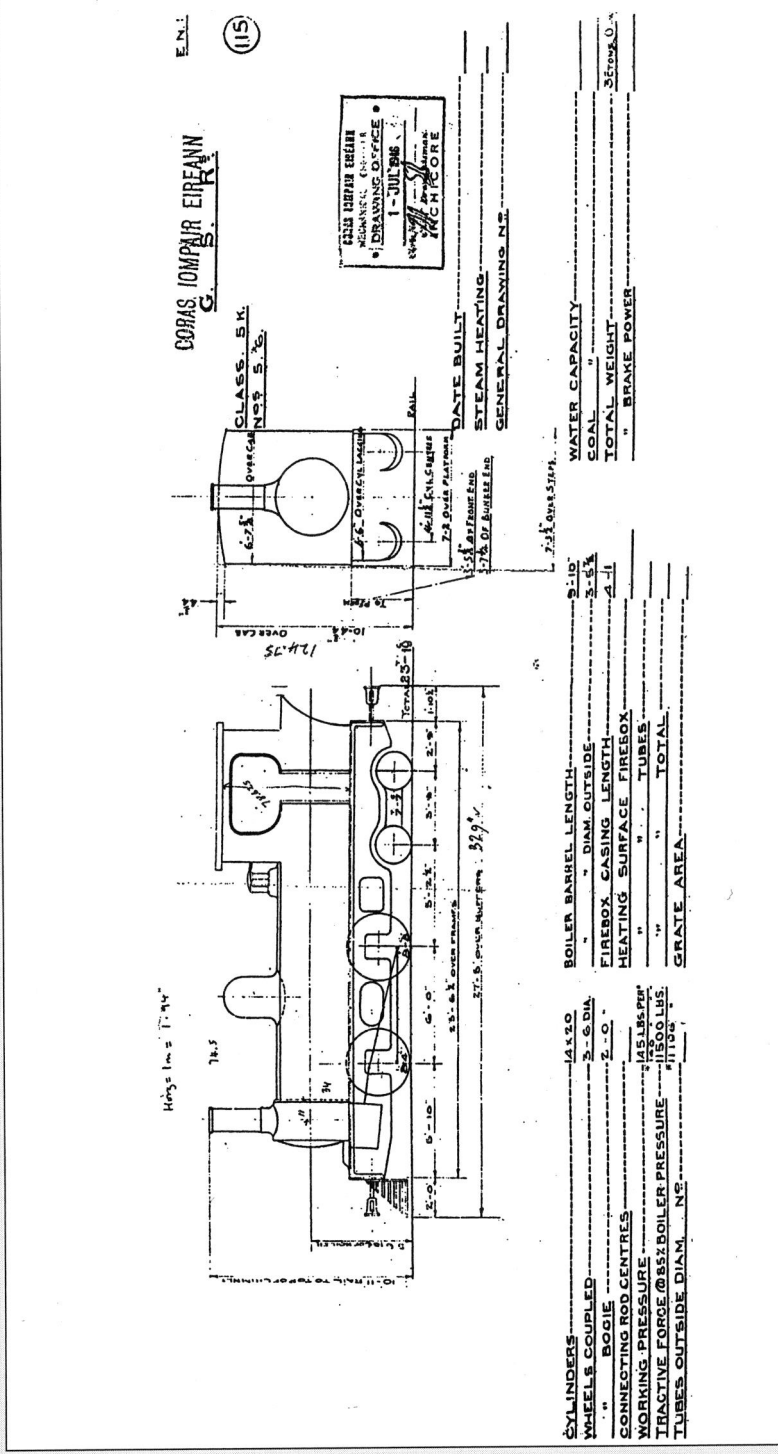

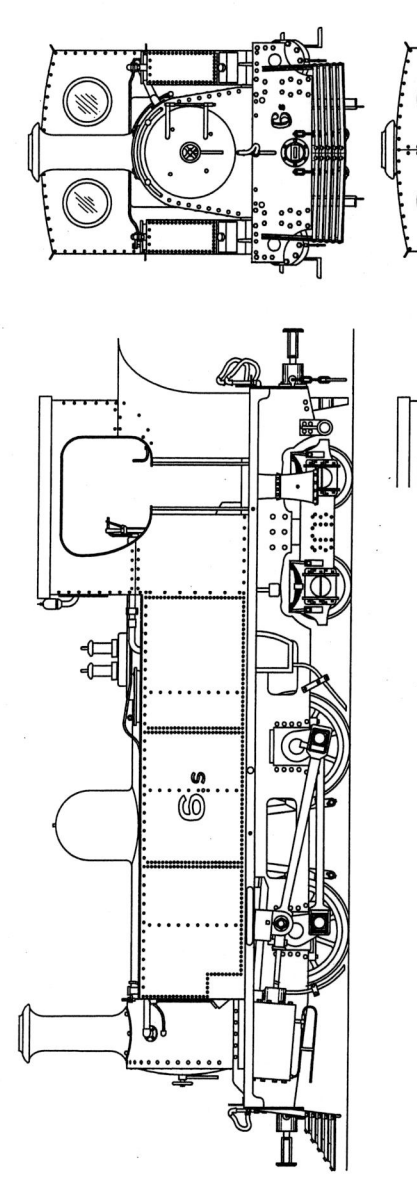
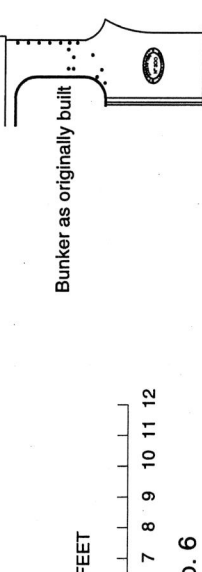

Bunker as originally built

SCALE IN FEET
0 1 2 3 4 5 6 7 8 9 10 11 12

LOCOMOTIVE No. 6
DRG. No. L5

BUILT IN 1893 BY THOMAS GREEN & SON FOR THE CORK & MUSKERRY LIGHT RAILWAY
DRAWING SHOWS LOCOMOTIVE AS AT CLOSURE OF S & S   COPYRIGHT DRAWN GRT

An unexpected excursion from storage saw Nos. 3s and 4s drawn out by No. 6s in July 1950 for Cyril Fry.

The final journey came in April 1954, when the three engines were taken on standard-gauge well wagons to Inchicore, Dublin for breaking up. (No. 4s had the chimney removed to clear the loading gauge as the well wagon did not give enough clearance.)

No. 6 (un-named). The origins of this machine are found in the Cork & Muskerry Light Railway ('The Old Hook & Eye') where it had operated as No. 6 (THE MUSKERRY later simply, MUSKERRY; No. 6k under the GSR) until 29th December, 1934 when that system was closed down completely by the GSR. It was one of the attractive narrow-gauge lines in the vicinity of Cork city, and had opened in August 1887. Its environs around the leafy lanes and pleasant valleys west of the city were in complete contrast to the S&SR (then the WCT) and its trains began their journey westwards from the city by passing along the street.

The fifth and sixth engines supplied to the C&MLR, were unusual in being of the 0-4-4 wheel arrangement - the only narrow-gauge examples in Ireland. They were bought to work the Donoughmore Extension Railway, opened on 6th May, 1893, a nominally independent section of the C&MLR which served a thinly-populated valley north-west of Cork. Delivered in 1892 and 1893 respectively from Thomas Green & Son of Leeds,* they were maker's No. 180 DONOUGHMORE No. 5 and maker's No. 200 THE MUSKERRY No. 6. As built, they had stove-pipe chimneys. In 1925 they became Nos. 5k and 6k (Class 'EN1') under the GSR who took them into Inchicore Works when the line closed. Here they were dismantled and stored.

Later No. 5 was re-assembled and numbered 9t for employment on the Tralee & Dingle section but was never transferred to Tralee.

No. 6 was similarly treated for service on the S&S section as 6s but it had to return to Inchicore again shortly afterward as the buffer beams fouled Ballydehob platform and the goods/cattle docks there and at the termini: also for alterations to the brake hose connection. After this it did sterling work.

Dimensions were: Cylinders 14 in. x 20 in., driving wheels 3 ft 6 in. diameter (somewhat large for the gradients of the S&S section), bogie wheel diameter 2 ft 0 in., coupled wheelbase 6 ft 0 in., total wheelbase 14 ft 10 in; 115 tubes 9 ft 8 in. long x 1¾ in. diameter, grate area 10.5 sq. ft, length firebox 3 ft 4½ in., total heating surface 600 sq. ft. Boiler pressure 140 lbs., water capacity 500 gallons, coal capacity 1 ton, weight in working order 25 tons; tractive effort at 85 per cent boiler pressure was 11,100 lbs.

It was the most powerful engine to work on the system so that at least those larger driving wheels would be offset on the steeper sections - the C&MLR had nothing of this nature to contend with. When working the Donoughmore line, Nos. 5 & 6 were usually turned at the end of each journey so that the cab was leading. The cowcatcher was at the front end for working the S&S section, whereas on the C&M Nos. 5 & 6 might sport the fitting at one end *or* the other!

When the S&S section closed No. 6s, for which there was no storage available under cover, stood outside Skibbereen shed door like a naughty child waiting to be let in.

---

* Thomas Green & Son Ltd. Thomas Green founded Smithfield Ironworks in Leeds in 1848; agricultural machinery was the main output. In the early 1880s they began locomotive building, principally allied to the steam tram boom then in vogue. Tram engine building ceased in 1898 but conventional locomotive construction continued until 1920; no tender engines were ever built. Green supplied engines for the Dublin & Blessington Tramway and their three machines built for the West Clare Railway (the heaviest in the firm's history) also went to Ireland.

Ex-Cork & Muskerry Light Railway No. 6 re-assembled and modified at Inchicore Works, Dublin in 1937-38 for use on the S&SR. Here in April 1938 it awaits transport to West Cork.
W.A. Camwell

Initially rejected by the S&SR section, No. 6s was dismissed to stand on Skibbereen's most northerly and distant siding and await return to Dublin. 1938.
R.W. Kidner

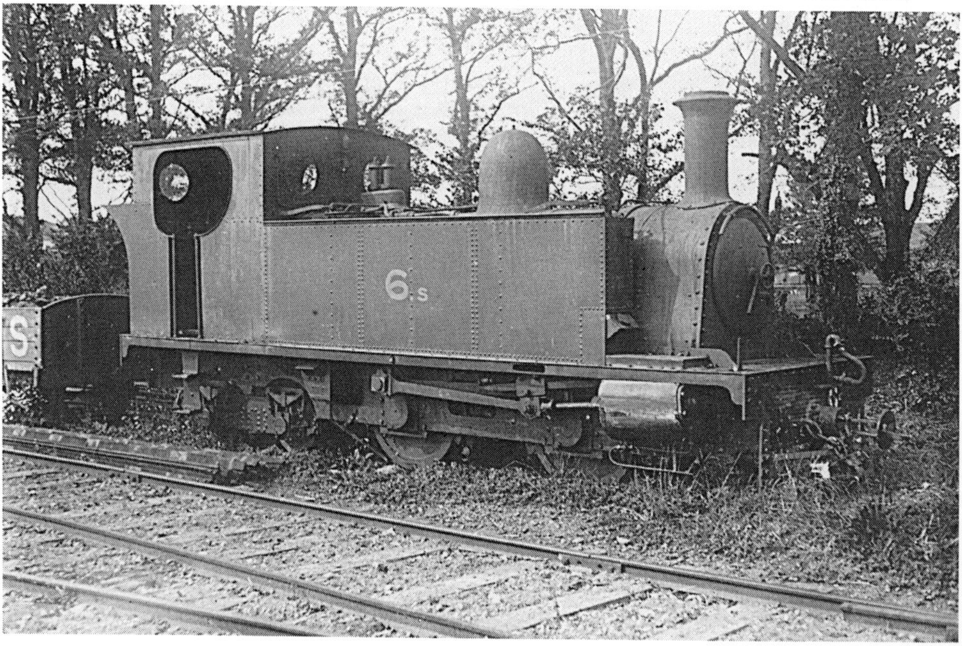

Unique for the S&S line, it was driven from the left side which was likely to have been unpopular with most firemen. The bunker itself was pathetically small as built but Inchicore provided a new one of greater capacity - the increased height was noticeable; the maker's plates were not replaced.

By coincidence, No. 6k hauled the last Up and Down trains on the Donoughmore line on the C&MLR's final day, and was the last engine in use on the S&S section too.

As regards the vacuum brake, it may be noticed that No. 6s had two brake hoses at the bunker end and a single hose at the front. The double hoses were found necessary because the original single hose would not reach the train hoses when traversing a sharp curve. To make matters worse, there was a swing at the bunker end, a drawback which the other locomotives did not have. On No. 6s the bunker was always next to the train with chimney leading.

To overcome this, when the engine returned to Inchicore to have the buffer beams 'trimmed', double hoses were fitted to the bunker.

A number of photographs were taken between July and September 1938 after the engine's unsuccessful debut on the S&S section; it stood on the siding at the northern extremity of Skibbereen and had clearly endured but the briefest of trials; the paintwork is hardly scratched or dirty. So back to Dublin.

Although the oval maker's plate (No. 200) survives no picture shows it attached to the engine when delivered to West Cork.

One further curiosity; the full-stop placed between '6' and 's' on the side tank.

Of the S&S section locomotives in general, William Lombard of Kinsale, who usually drove on the CB&SC section but worked down to Schull when required, said, 'The fireman was on his hands and knees all the way. They looked very pretty but they were hopelessly underpowered'.

Standing in the open as it had for much of its life on the S&SR section, No. 6s, the last engine at work would never be steamed again. Skibbereen. 1953. *J.I.C. Boyd*

No. 1s, an original vehicle, as heavily reconditioned in 1913. Note the curtains. The right-hand end compartment was used by Daniel Creedon. In Great Southern Railways livery. Skibbereen. 1938.
H.C. Casserley

No. 2 as first supplied to the WCT by Dick, Kerr but repainted as an S&S vehicle. Details of date, whereabouts and colours are not known; probably *c.* 1893.
Collection J.I.C. Boyd

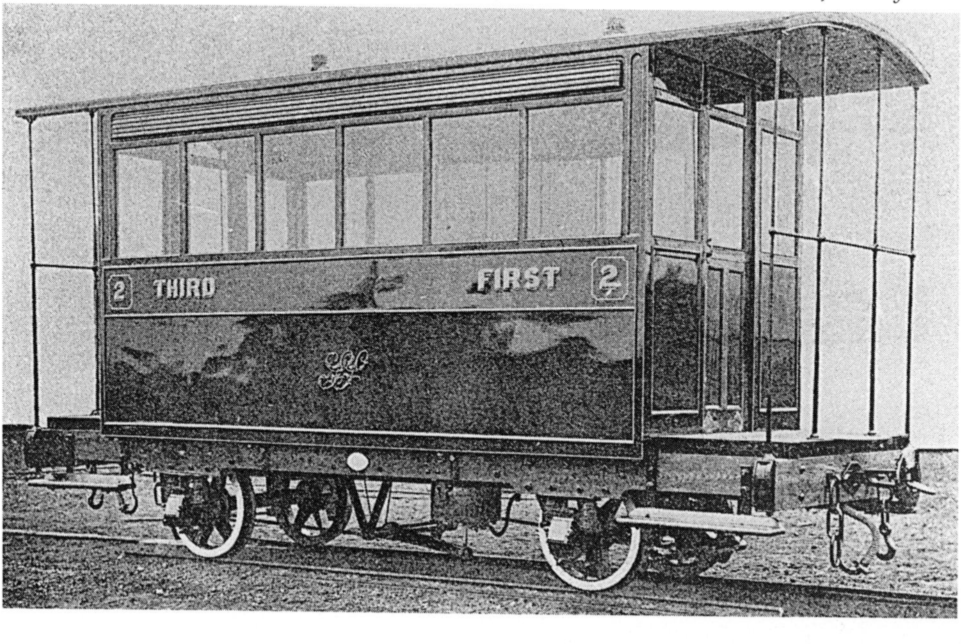

Chapter Fifteen
Carriages and Wagons

Passenger Carriages (condition Nos. 1-4 and 8 as found in 1953)

No. 1. Four-wheel; all 1st class. Dividing interior partition with door, ⅔ Smoking + ⅓ Non-smoking. GSR livery & 'No. 1s'. Open balcony platforms. Perimeter seats. Fitted electric light and vacuum brake. Glazed body ends with sliding doors. Steel underframe; 'Austens Patents' axleboxes. Coil springs. Disc wheels. Maker: Dick, Kerr, 1888. Heavily reconditioned, Spring 1913. (Daniel Creedon, the Manager, used the smoking section as his 'private saloon'.)

No. 2. Four-wheel; all 1st class. Dividing interior partition with door, half Smoking and half Non-smoking. Perimeter seats in red plush. CIE livery; paint date 8/1946. Fitted electric light and vacuum brake. Laminated springs. Steel underframe; solebars faced timber. Axleboxes read 'S & S T & L Ry. Co. 1914': 'Austens Patents'.* Disc wheels. Designed and rebuilt in 1910-12 from original WCT No. 2 by Mick Cottam the carpenter at Skibbereen ('. . . who has never worked for a day outside of Skibbereen'). THE SKIBBEREEN EAGLE & COUNTY ADVERTISER for 7th June, 1913 has one of several photographs taken on this occasion, the one in question being that including the workmen involved (another shows all Management Committee in celebration of the first carriage 'built' in the S&SR Works). Both pictures are taken with the personalities seated in front of the carriage, so obscuring it somewhat.†

Skibbereen was proud of the achievement, which was decorated inside with 'mahogany and bird's eye maple, and two powerful acetylene lamps . . . the cost was over £100 less than a similar carriage built in England . . . the Committee have in future, decided to build all their own rolling stock. This is an example of supporting Irish industry which might well be followed by others.' Seating capacity was 16.

When rebuilt, acetylene gas installed - electricity later.#

Length over body 17 ft; wheelbase 8 ft. Original open balcony ends closed in. Ends fitted with sliding doors and fall-plates. Note unusual fenestration and shape upper doors. [It should be stressed that a date on the axlebox covers is not a reliable date for construction.]

No. 3. Four-wheel; all 3rd class. Balcony ends; open interior with longitudinal lath seats. Gas, then electric lighting. GSR livery & 'No. 3'. Coil springs. Disc wheels (as all original WCT stock). Steel underframe faced timber solebars. Vacuum brake. Maker: Dick, Kerr, 1888. Received heavy repairs c. 1910.

No. 4. Four-wheel; all 3rd class. Similar, but having certain differences from No. 3s. GSR livery & 'No. 4s'. No interior partition. Electric lighting (formerly acetylene gas). Vacuum fitted. Unglazed at ends and in end-doors. Unlike Nos. 1s and 3s, has matchboard sides and laminated springs. Axleboxes read 'S & S T & L Ry. Co. 1911'.

Length of body section only 12 ft 6 in. Disc wheels 2 ft diameter as for Nos. 1 & 3. Maker said to have been Dick, Kerr in 1888; appears to have been fitted with replacement running gear.

In Creedon's note to James Gilhooly MP (undated, but c. 1906), he states ' in repair . . . new roof . . . new platforms'. Whilst the other four-wheelers had sliding end-doors, those on No. 4 hinged inwards.

---

* Austens Patents, some axleboxes marked 'WCT Co. 1888'.
† The necessary chairs are said to have been purloined from the West Cork Hotel!
# Electrically-lit coaches were supplied by batteries in the guard's van; there were no dynamos.

191

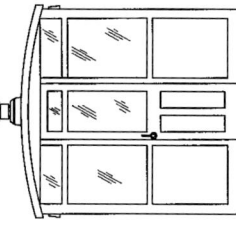

SCALE IN FEET
0 1 2 3 4 5 6 7 8 9 10 11 12 13 14 15 16 17 18 19 20

CARRIAGE No. 2
AS FOR OPENING OF TRAMWAY

COPYRIGHT DRAWN GRT
DRG. No. P1

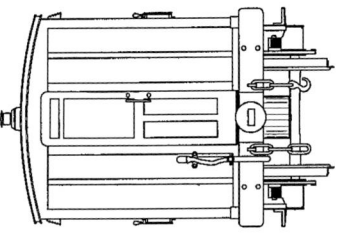

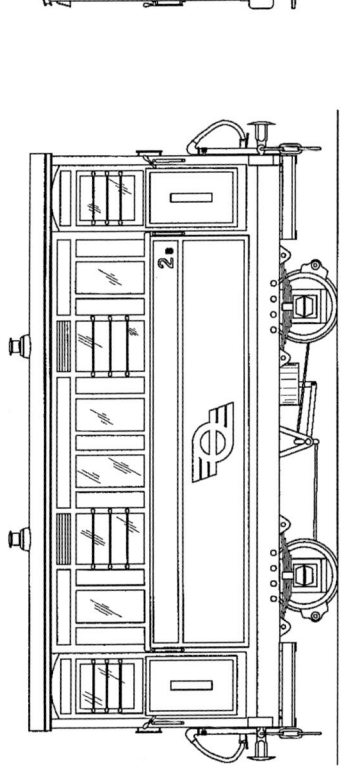

SCALE IN FEET
0 1 2 3 4 5 6 7 8 9 10 11 12 13 14 15 16 17 18 19 20

CARRIAGE No. 2
CIE LIVERY AS FROM AUGUST 1946 - ELECTRIC LIGHTING

COPYRIGHT DRAWN GRT
DRG. NO. P2

No. 2 after rebuilding at Skibbereen between 1910-13 with Directors, Management Committee and others present. Ned Roycroft (bearded) is seated centre, Daniel Creedon, Manager (*top left*), Michael Cottam, Carpenter (*top right*).
Southern Star

The evening sun at Schull highlights Nos. 2s and 8s after they were given CIE livery. *Circa* 1945.
Collection J.I.C. Boyd

CARRIAGES AND WAGONS 195

Nos. 3s and bogie carriage 6s in Schull loop in mid-1930s. The former received 'heavy repairs' in *c.* 1910. *Collection J.I.C. Boyd*

No. 4s was subtly different from other coaches with four wheels. Note the matchboarded sides, improved balconies and modernised running gear received pre-1914. GSR livery. *J.I.C. Boyd*

The spartan interior of No. 4s. It is not difficult to imagine it filled with the smoke of plug, the fug of crowded bodies and farmyard boots, plus the chatter of voices as it travels to Skibbereen Mart.
J.I.C. Boyd

Probably a heavy rebuild/rebody of the original No. 8, supplied by Dick, Kerr in 1912 and the last of the series. Note the later pattern of running gear and removal of end balconies. Little is known of the history of this vehicle. 1938.
H.C. Casserley

No. 8. Four-wheel; all 3rd class. Similar in style but with one central side door and rearrangement of lath side-seats in consequence. Matchboard sides. Electric lighting. Vacuum brake. Laminated springs. CIE livery. Maker probably Dick, Kerr, 1912, but rebuilt Skibbereen with enclosed body and new running gear. Note irregular fenestration.

In the heavy repairs or body rebuilding exercises, Cottam had established himself as something of an expert; '. . . Cottam is said to have taken the measurements and drilled the holes at the one time, the parts fitting perfectly on assembly - a real craftsman job'.*

The foregoing comprised carriages Nos. 1-4 & 8 which, without complete documentary evidence, appear to be the design as first delivered in 1888, with exception of No. 8 of the same design, 1912. Not one resembled another by the time the Author made a record in 1953, and such record seems to be the only one compiled. In general, the four-wheeled stock out-lived the bogie coaches in usefulness though this may be due to over-use by the bogie specimens to the point where they were too dilapidated to use: at the same time, the bogie variety seems to have become too big and heavy for the traffic offering in the latter days.

Passengers from off the CB&SCR trains who held 2nd Class (through) tickets were permitted to use 1st Class accommodation on the Tramway.

Perhaps the most difficult aspect of the system has been to unravel the ramifications of the carriages, and especially of the bogie stock. Without exception, written accounts of the railway during its operation gave scant attention to this aspect, and even less to its goods vehicles, and as these possessed such individual character, the subject is approached with mixed feelings.

It appears that on the evidence given at various enquiries the Company owned but three bogie coaches and that, despite its oft-expressed wish for more, this proved as useless as 'Whistling for the moon'. The three were based on the same design principle - a long body adaptable internally as required, accessed by end-doors served from open balconies. These balconies had steps each side and could be mounted from ground-level by all but the most disabled.

The passengers could thus be 'monitored' by the guard passing through the train, assisted by fall-plates on the balcony-ends which allowed passage between vehicles. This type of vehicle was popular with Irish narrow-gauge railway operators, and could be found on the Clogher Valley, Cavan & Leitrim and other systems. It was common overseas and originated in America on the standard-gauge about 1836.†

The three bogie coaches, all of the same character, carried Nos. 5, 6, 7 (with an 's' added in GSR days). No. 5 was quite individual but Nos. 6 & 7 were 'sisters', unalike to No. 5. Fortunately comparison is facilitated by a photograph taken *c.* 1907 showing Nos. 5 and 7, posed with a mixed train drawn by GABRIEL on Ballydehob viaduct - this picture has the bonus of showing four-wheel passenger brake van (number un-readable but probably No. 54), and covered vans Nos. 31, 32 and 38, proving that the vans were numbered differently from the latter-day system, possibly a legacy of GSR take-over.

Fortunately the bodies of Nos. 5 and 7 found their way into a pasture at Owynane Falls, north-west of Bantry, when the stock was auctioned, and though intended for

---

* Writes A.T. Newham.
† Carriages of this design were used on the Camden & Amboy RR; one remains restored in the Smithsonian. Windows were similar in style to those on the S&SR; the droplights fell into a space between the inner and outer shells. They were of light construction and featured peculiar wooden trusses hanging prominently below the sides. See also: AMERICAN RAILROAD PASSENGER CARS 1830-1977, (John H. White Junr.) pp. 59-63.

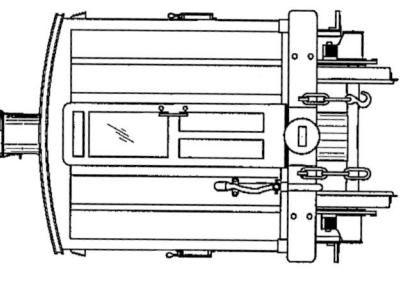

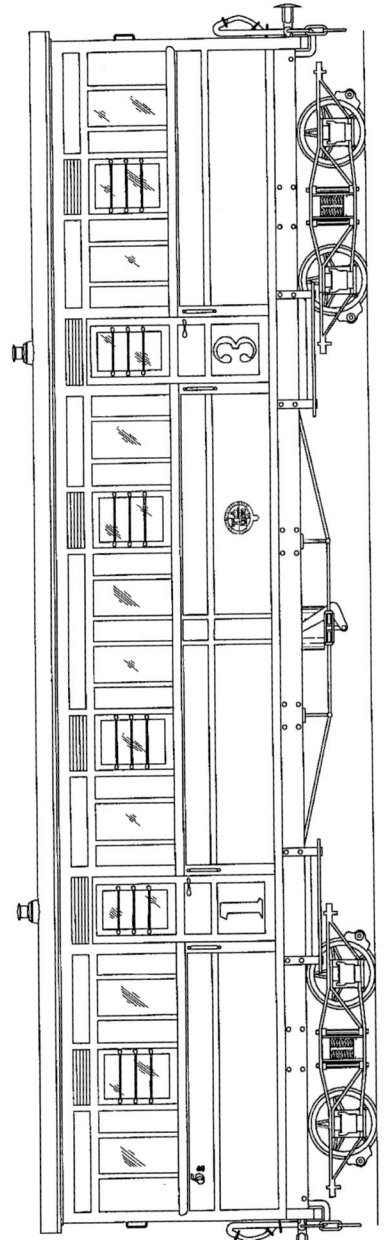
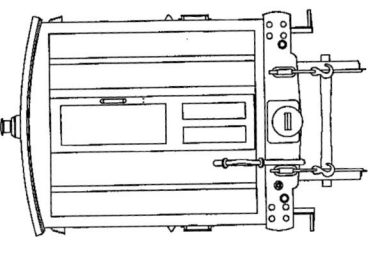

SCALE IN FEET
0 1 2 3 4 5 6 7 8 9 10 11 12 13 14 15 16 17 18 19 20

CARRIAGE NO. 5
AS REBUILT

COPYRIGHT DRAWN GRT
DRG. No. P3

No. 5s, the first bogie carriage bought in 1890, as rebuilt at Skibbereen before 1906. (See page 146 for the vehicle as purchased). Skibbereen. 1953.
J.I.C. Boyd

No. 6s in a remarkably good state after nearly a decade of disuse; it would be readily restored for further use if the circumstance obtained today. 1953.
J.I.C. Boyd

Nos. 6s and 7s languish in the forsaken Skibbereen station almost half a century since their first appearance. 1953.
J.I.C. Boyd

The bogie coach bodies were sold and endured fleetingly, one at farm near Skibbereen and the other two grounded near the Bantry-Glengariff road, whence the cognoscenti made pilgrimage. Here is one of the latter at its final resting place. Some seating survives at The Cross House Bar, Kilcoe.
J.I.C. Boyd

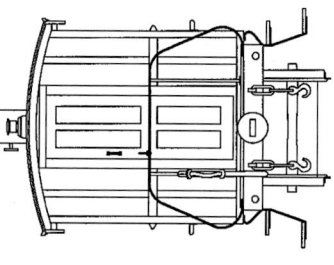
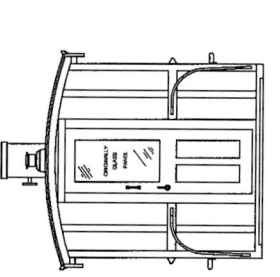

(When built lower steps ran length of carriage)

SCALE IN FEET
0 1 2 3 4 5 6 7 8 9 10 11 12 13 14 15 16 17 18 19 20

CARRIAGE NO. 7
AS AT CLOSURE

COPYRIGHT DRAWN GRT

DRG. No. P4

utilisation, there they remained. (Patrick O'Keefe, a well-respected resident of Bantry bought these vehicles many years ago; some of their seating can be found in The Cross House Bar, Meen Bridge, Kilcoe, today.)

No. 5. When Roycroft was interviewed in 1905 he said they bought a composite bogie coach in 1890 from Gloucester for £465 to carry 40 passengers. (On another occasion he said they purchased an all-3rd to carry 32 in 1896.) It is submitted that these were one and the same carriage - it is wiser to enquire of the Engineer than the Chairman about such things! (The earlier date is correct, using the loan of £1,600.)

When Creedon reviewed the stock in a Report to Gilhooly c. 1906 he confirms the extended and rough use this carriage had sustained (perhaps because of its light construction it was a bargain). It had received 'new bogies, sides and ends' and a 'new carriage to interchange No. 5 (was) needed'.

Newham writes that in '1908 bogie composite coach was completed at a cost of £70 17s. 11d. but it is likely this was the coach bought in 1888'. This is misleading; the reference is to No. 5's drastic rebuilding in which form it survived to the end. Roycroft's evidence of 1905 is more re-assuring: '. . . our composite coach of 1890 is badly worn . . .' A re-build would be logical.

In the rebuilding the balcony ends were closed in but the interior partition was retained to divide off the 1st class section. The bogies were noticeably different from those on Nos. 6 and 7; sliding doors had been fitted in the ends and there were perimeter seats. Vacuum brakes; electric lighting, and the solebars were faced in timber. The 1st class section had window blinds, floral moquette upholstery in a black/brown pattern and interior woodwork was stained darkly. There was a lincrusta ceiling and match-strikers on the window sills. The side doors opened inwards to prevent collision with lineside objects. The Patent axleboxes were marked 'S & S T & L Ry. Co. 1903'.

The interior doors had domestic door furniture but the end doors had only locking handles. The fall plates were rigid and the bogie pins set in 4 ft 11 in. from the ends.

No. 5 and the two sister bogie carriages were built by The Gloucester Railway Carriage & Wagon Co. Ltd.* Is it coincidence that this Carbery concern bought locomotives from a Bristol manufacturer - the two cities are only 33 miles apart? Was there a personal link here?

Nos. 6 & 7. These two 3rd class carriages are shown on the Works' photograph as being finished in April 1897 and April 1903 respectively. They appear identical. According to Roycroft, No. 6 was 'similar to that of 1896 . . . for £300'. (The date was actually 1890!)

They were solidly built and in the best traditions of the makers; even after they had stopped work and stood partly exposed to the weather for months on end, they were

---

* Gloucester RC&WCL. Started in January 1860 as The Gloucester Wagon Co. in Bristol Street, Gloucester the founders, apart from two who had railway associations, were a group of merchants, 'all substantial citizens'. Their original business was mainly the manufacture of open wagons which they hired out for the transport of coal and iron ore. The works was conveniently sited to serve South Wales and Staffordshire. In 1865 a large order for the Great Indian Peninsula Railway spread their business world-wide. Next it was Russia. They widened their products into carriages, street trams and horse-buses, etc. - the vehicles supplied to West Carbery had a strong likeness to those made for the Argentine a year later. On the walls of the Secretary's office in 1903 hung framed photographs of this archetypal carriage; only close inspection of the running gear revealed the variation in gauge on which they found an overseas home. In 1887 the firm faced great business difficulties when financial strain was felt by the whole nation; it is likely that the S&SR obtained the three bogie vehicles on advantageous terms.

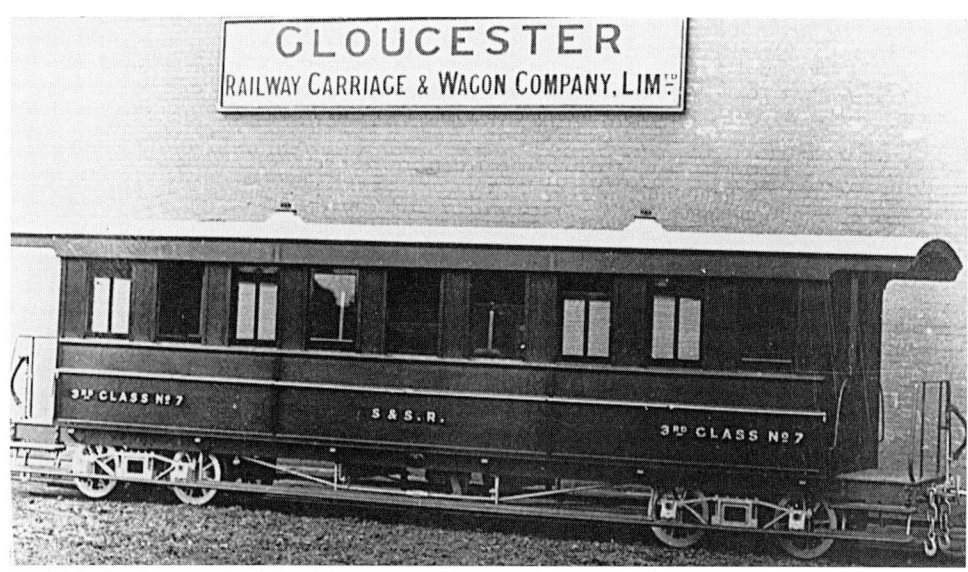

Maker's photograph of No. 7 built in 1903. (No. 6 of 1897 was similar.) It is uncertain if the lettering was that adopted by the S&SR, or merely applied to identify the product.

Gloucester RC&WCL

Interior of No. 7 before it was shipped to Ireland. We may imagine the reaction of this plain but highly-finished conveyance on a rural community more used to donkey carts etc.

Gloucester RC&WCL

CARRIAGES AND WAGONS 205

arguably the best vehicles the line ever had. As seen in 1953 they were in GSR livery and numbered 6s & 7s. Frames were of steel channel; there was vacuum brake and an obsolete gas generator on the roof and low voltage lighting did duty instead. The inside body was a single saloon. The side seats were of timber slats and Venetian Blinds could be drawn up inside the windows. There was continuous ventilator above windows 24 in. high x 18 in. wide. Sliding doors gave access from the balcony; the windows were barred on the north side only.

The bogies were subtly different from those on No. 5 and their box covers had a scroll device 'SSR' with the characters overlapping. The original gas lights were to the Ross Patent Acetylene System by J.T. Williams of Birmingham. The emphasis on ventilation and the Venetian Blinds which would act as dust screens, point to the carriages being suitable for tropical and rain-starved countries. For the S&SR the interior was finished in a buff stone colour with white ceiling. The slat seats were painted maroon.

Goods Vehicles

Vehicle numbers given below are those carried at closure. The original number series is not known.

Open Wagons ex-WCT Dick, Kerr. Nos. 1-5
Nos. 3, 4, 5 - 1x 1m = 5

Timber Bolster Wagons ex-WCT by Dick, Kerr. Nos. 6-9
Nos. 6, 8 - 2x = 4   (A)

Cattle Wagons ex-WCT by Dick, Kerr. Nos. 10-35
Nos. 10-31 inc., 34, 35 - 2x = 26   (B)
21 Numbered 11 on other side
23 Roofless type - solitary example.

Covered Wagons ex-WCT by Dick, Kerr. Nos. 36-45/47-49
Nos. 36-43 inc., 48-49 - 3m = 13   (C)
40 This number carried by two of the type.
43 Rebuilt as Cattle Wagon; original number retained.

Guard's Goods Brake Van ex-WCT by Dick, Kerr. No. 46
No. 46 = 1

Guard's Brake Vans ex-WCT by Dick, Kerr Nos. 47-49
3m = 3   (D)

(On 18th April, 1953: vehicles noted. x - number illegible; m - vehicles not traced.)

(A) Only 2 existed in 1906; 4 added under S&SR auspices.
(B) Only 22 existed in 1906; 4 added under S&SR auspices.
(C-D) Nos. 47-49 were ex-WCT Guard's Vans, but by 1906 Nos. 47 & 48 generally used as Goods Vans until completely rebuilt for the latter purpose. No. 49 was in very bad condition in 1906 and out of use; it was rebuilt also.

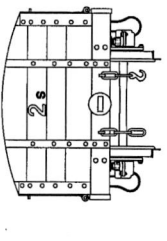

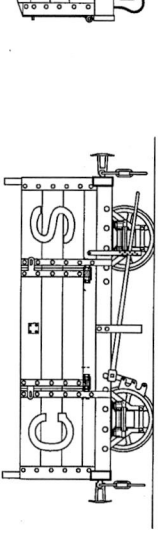
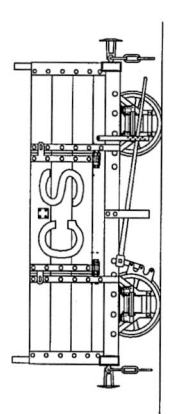

SCALE IN FEET
0 1 2 3 4 5 6 7 8 9 10 11 12 13 14 15 16 17 18 19 20

OPEN WAGON

Nos. 1-5

COPYRIGHT DRAWN GRT

DRG. NO. G9

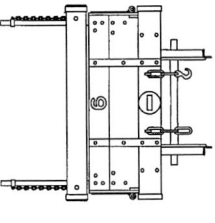

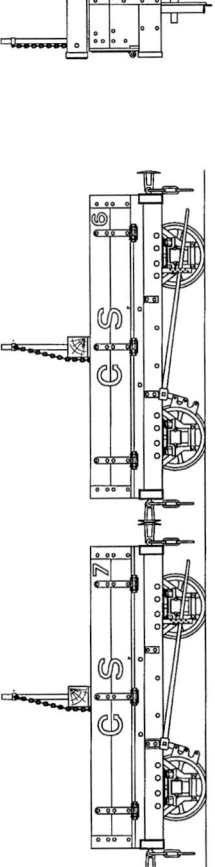

SCALE IN FEET
0 1 2 3 4 5 6 7 8 9 10 11 12 13 14 15 16 17 18 19 20

BOLSTER WAGONS
Nos. 6 - 9

COPYRIGHT DRAWN GRT

DRG. NO. G8

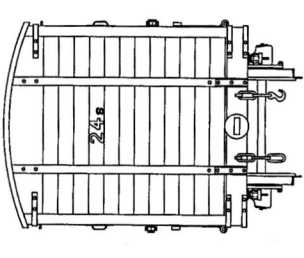

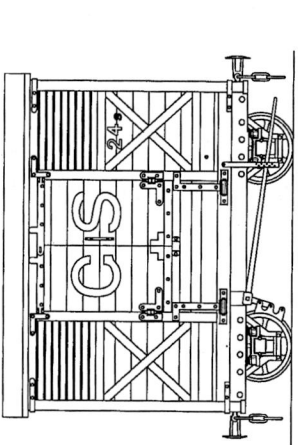

SCALE IN FEET

0 1 2 3 4 5 6 7 8 9 10 11 12 13 14 15 16 17 18 19 20

SMALL LIVESTOCK VENTILATED VAN
Nos. 10 - 35 (23 WITHOUT ROOF)

COPYRIGHT DRAWN GRT

DRG. NO. G6

CARRIAGES AND WAGONS

Cattle Wagon No. 12s and Open Wagon No. 4s. Skibbereen. Note the variation in style of axlebox. 1953.
J.I.C. Boyd

In the siding at Ballydehob are Nos. 28s and 35s, the former a Cattle Wagon of the original series. The latter has a Covered Wagon body, incorrectly numbered in the Cattle Wagon series. 1936.
Gordon Tucker

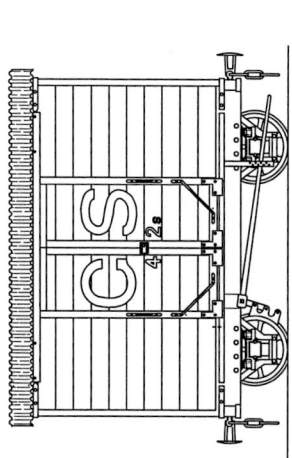
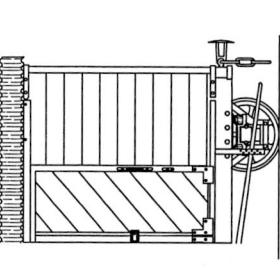

Some sliding doors repaired with diagonal planking

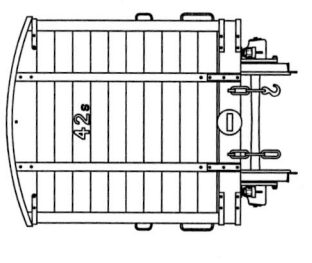

SCALE IN FEET

0 1 2 3 4 5 6 7 8 9 10 11 12 13 14 15 16 17 18 19 20

SMALL BOX VAN

Nos. 36 - 45 (43 REBUILT AS CATTLE VAN)

COPYRIGHT DRAWN GRT

DRG. NO. G5

CARRIAGES AND WAGONS 211

The derelict bolster wagons on the right are Nos. 6s and 8s. The long string of disused Cattle Wagons is headed by No. 28s. Skibbereen yard, north end. 1953. *J.I.C. Boyd*

No. 18s and No. 56s at Skibbereen, 1953, an original series Cattle Wagon and a Large Covered Wagon built *c.* 1910, surviving at Smithville, Castletownsend until *c.* 1990, respectively.
J.I.C. Boyd

Two varieties of van at Skibbereen: the left and right hand are Nos. 16s and 11s in the original Cattle Wagon series. No. 43s (*centre*) is the last of the original series of Covered Wagons - it lasted into the 1990s near the Castletownsend road. 1938.   H.C. *Casserley*

Abandoned in mid-repair, Nos. 48s, 39s and 37s stand in the silent Skibbereen workshops. No. 48s was a rebuilt WCT Guard's Brake Van. 1953.   J.I.C. *Boyd*

CARRIAGES AND WAGONS 213

No. 46s, sole survivor of four WCT Guard's Goods Brake Vans. Skibbereen. 1953. *J.I.C. Boyd*

Large Covered Wagon No. 49s rebuilt from original Goods Brake Van post-1906 and Covered Van No. 37s. Schull. 1938. *H.C. Casserley*

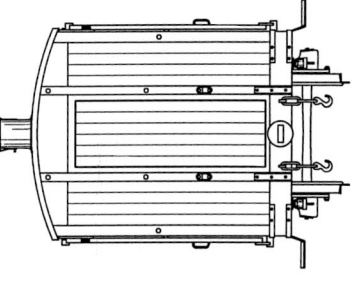
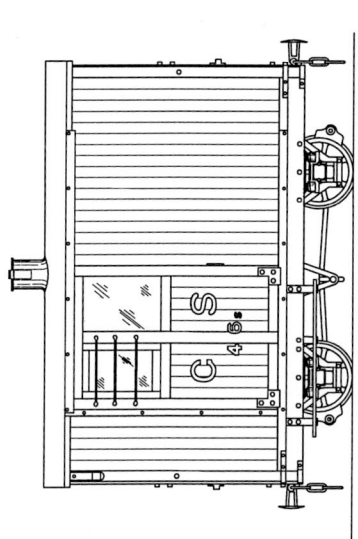

SCALE IN FEET
0 1 2 3 4 5 6 7 8 9 10 11 12 13 14 15 16 17 18 19 20

GOODS BRAKE VAN No. 46

COPYRIGHT DRAWN GRT

DRG. NO. G1

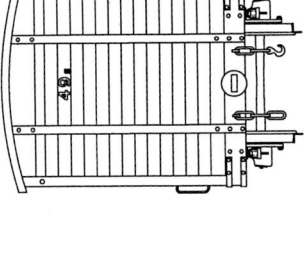
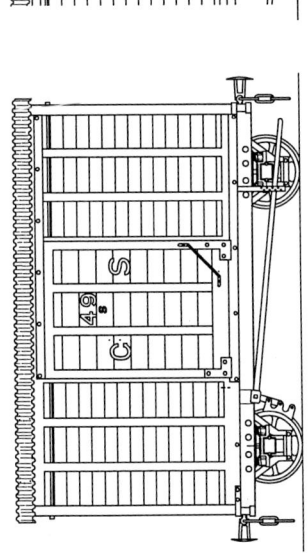

SCALE IN FEET
0 1 2 3 4 5 6 7 8 9 10 11 12 13 14 15 16 17 18 19 20

12 FOOT BOX VAN
Nos. 47 - 49

COPYRIGHT DRAWN GRT
DRG. NO. G4

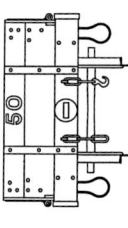
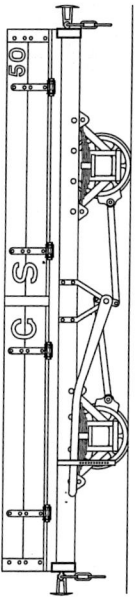 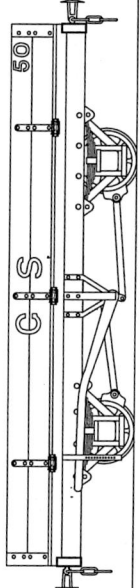

ALTERNATIVE

SCALE IN FEET
0 1 2 3 4 5 6 7 8 9 10 11 12 13 14 15 16 17 18 19 20

BALLAST WAGON - ASSUMED DESIGN
No. 50 - 51   NO ILLUSTRATION AVAILABLE

Copyright Drawn GRT
DRG. No. G7

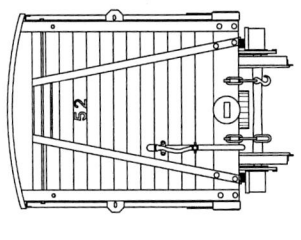

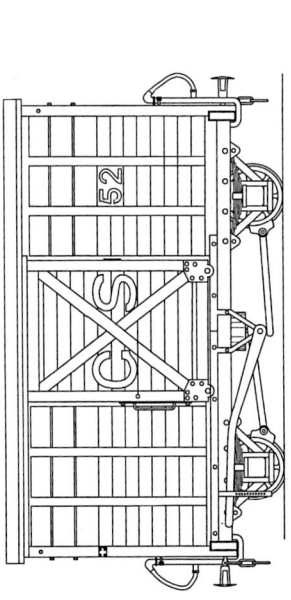

SCALE IN FEET
0 1 2 3 4 5 6 7 8 9 10 11 12 13 14 15 16 17 18 19 20

LARGE CATTLE VAN
No. 52 BUILT c1909

COPYRIGHT DRAWN GRT

DRG. NO. G3

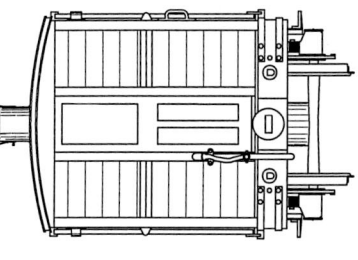
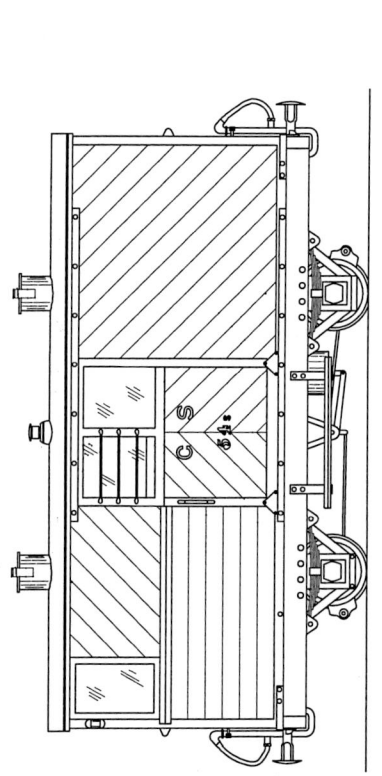

SCALE IN FEET
0 1 2 3 4 5 6 7 8 9 10 11 12 13 14 15 16 17 18 19 20

PASSENGER BRAKE VAN
Nos. 53 & 54

COPYRIGHT DRAWN GRT
DRG. NO. P6

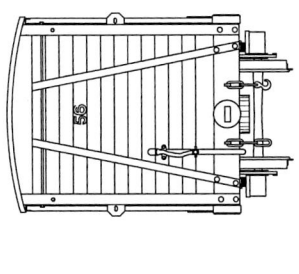
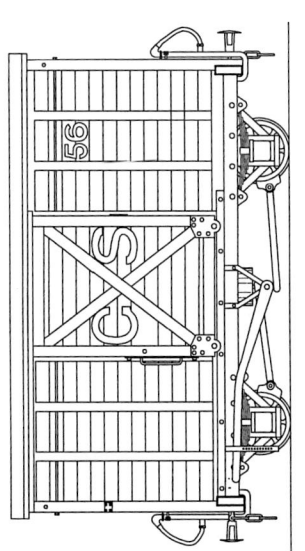

SCALE IN FEET
0 1 2 3 4 5 6 7 8 9 10 11 12 13 14 15 16 17 18 19 20

LARGE FITTED BOX VAN

Nos. 55 - 60 BUILT 1909 - ONWARDS

COPYRIGHT DRAWN GRT
DRG. NO. G2

A long string of semi-derelict goods stock at Skibbereen platform in August 1950; the unroofed Cattle Wagon peeps shyly between. *D.L.G. Hunter*

Ballast Wagons ex-WCT by Dick, Kerr. Nos. not known
The Creedon Report makes reference to four Ballast Wagons in 1906 'each of which requires a thorough overhaul'. No trace existed in 1953.
Additional vehicles carrying Nos. 50-60 were built following the recommendations of the Creedon Report (1906). Running gear etc. was probably obtained from an outside contractor (e.g. Pickering or Gloucester RC&WCL) but the bodies appear to have been built at Skibbereen. Though of the same width as the WCT vehicles, they are of greater length/height and carried on leaf springs etc.

Open full-drop-side Ballast Wagons (12 ft long) Nos. 50-51
2x = 2

Cattle Wagon (Size as Nos. 55-60) No. 52
52 = 1

Guard's Brake Vans Nos. 53-54 (Built c. 1909)
53, 54 = 2   (E)

Covered Wagons Nos. 55 - 60 (Built 1909, 1910, 1912 etc.)
56, 58, 59, 60 - 2x = 6   (F)

(On 18th April, 1953: vehicles noted. x - number illegible.)

(E)   Fitted seats inside (for drovers (?) etc.) No. 53 carried No. 54 on other side.
(F)   Axlebox covers read '6x8 1900'

A copy-letter which survived until the run-down period indicates the Weekly Wagon Returns were sent to the Locomotive Foreman (R. Savage) at Glanmire, Cork. One imagines that by this date Skibbereen yard was full of stock which was past repair.
C. Murphy the carpenter had five vehicles in hand on 12th August, 1944:

Under repair
40s   Covered goods wagon. Requires new headstocks and corner pillars.
23s   Cattle wagon. Repairs to flooring and pillar.

Awaiting repairs
11s. 22s.   Cattle Wagons. Awaiting brake gear and axleguards.*
58s   Covered goods.

(The above is copied verbatim. It reveals that Livestock Wagons Nos. 10-35 were known as 'Cattle Wagons' although they carried other animals. Also, that Box Vans Nos. 36-43/55-60 were 'Covered Goods'.)

Author's note. In the foregoing, any reference to the makers of the Tramway etc. stock being built by Dick, Kerr is based on informed assumption. There is no confirming evidence and Dick, Kerr may have put out coach and wagon building to another manufacturer.
* ironwork probably in short supply owing to World War II.

Another note (probably c. 1906):

47 In use as Goods Van
48 In use as Goods Van
49 Guard's Van to overhaul. Crumbling - Three new Guard's Vans for passenger trains as existing ones are worn out! There is now an extra van on every train. [These would become 53, 54 , ?. Evidence suggests 54 (see list) rebuilt c. 1909 with some seating inside].

Had the Railway been better known and more frequently visited in the past by those who put their findings on record, occasional references to certain 'mysteries' would not be necessary; even when such findings came about, the primary object of interest was the steam locomotive while the humble goods wagon was almost ignored.

So it is impossible to conclude this chapter with satisfaction; for instance, in 1938 an unidentified flat wagon with side rails similar to those used in early times to carry horse-drawn road vehicles, was in use - a curious vehicle about which nothing is yet known. The S&S is the more interesting for such!

Guard's Brake Van No. 54s, built c. 1909, outside carriage shed, Skibbereen. (This vehicle may carry number 53s on the other side; see text p. 221). No. 42s attached. 1938.   H.C. *Casserley*

Chapter Sixteen

Operating

While one can understand the farmers who deliberately drove their beasts onto the railway track each night to graze where 'the grass was greener', this placed an added burden on the train crew who were bound to stop and clear them off, so avoiding a claim from the owner. The Company became well used to false claims being made, the commonest being for 'Prize Cattle' whereas some wretched beast had probably been left deliberately to meet its end on the line.

If recollections are valid, despite the absence of fencing between road and tramway track, the sight and sound of an approaching train was a distant warning to keep clear. Where it was desirable to raise the tramway by a modest amount above the road, a high curbstone paving would afford some protection to road users. An exception to this was the Lancia car used by the Directors to attend meetings; the railway often 'retaliated' to this shameful use of competitive transport which often ended its journey, abandoned, on that same curb, with a broken front axle. Witnesses would assume that the meeting had been a trifle exuberant, and that some of those in attendance had been obliged to walk home. (Such Lancia cars were a legacy of the Civil War; some were armoured.)

Alarming and noisy The Tram may have been, its approach was not heeded by a woman who, hidden by the Schull Workhouse wall and thus unseen by the train crew, stepped into the path of the engine from a field at the end of the wall.

From occasional mention in the Minutes we have a flavour of incidents at Kilcoe, the former affair confirming that the crossing gates and gatehouses were still in use during World War I. In 1916 a Special working was returning to Schull but the gatekeeper, thinking the train would not be returning, omitted to open the Kilcoe gates for it. He was arraigned before the Committee who ordered him to pay 3s. 6d. a week for a month; furthermore, he was warned he would lose his gatehouse if it occurred again.

With the new Board being formed to administer the system through its monthly meetings at Schull - no doubt chosen in preference to the office at Skibbereen because of its convenient location for the members - a close eye could be kept on parochial happenings. Thus, it was reported that a small barrel of porter had been taken from the waiting room at Kilcoe, the door having been forced on 23rd December, 1918. It was subsequently found, empty, in a nearby dyke.

Continuing its new-found mention of local affairs, the 1919 Minutes record the suspension of all trains from 6th February when a landslide blocked the line at Roosnagoose Townland near Skibbereen. Then on 25th October, firewood drying in the smokebox of a locomotive in Schull engine shed, burst into flames in the absence of the cleaner responsible. Luckily, the blaze and smoke were spotted from the Coastguard Station next door, and its men put out the fire. The Station received a vote of thanks, and the cleaner a reproof . . .

The local reporter for the CORK EXAMINER kept a sharp eye on the line too; on 18th December, 1907 the paper referred to a 'near accident'. The article was spotted by the Vice-Regal Commission who quoted it in their letter of 20th December to the BoT as '. . . an everyday occurrence, not often reported'.

Note: During certain periods of Civil Unrest, War of Independence, Government Control, Fuel Shortages and The Emergency, train services were suspended.

Extract from Bradshaw's Timetable, May 1898

Weekdays

Down

	CFD	ThO	ES	SO	
	am	am	pm	pm	pm
Skibbereen	6.00	10.30	12.30	12.30	6.30
Schull	..	..	1.40	1.50	7.50

Up

	CFD	ThO	ThO	ETh	
	am	am	am	am	pm
Schull	6.00	6.30	8.30	9.15	4.00
Skibbereen	..	7.50	..	10.35	5.20

Sundays

Down

	pm
Skibbereen	5.20
Schull	..

Up

	am
Schull	11.20
Skibbereen	..

Notes
ES - Except Saturdays, SO - Sats only, ThO - Thursday only, ETh - Except Thursday.
CFD - Cattle Fair Days (place not specified), .. - Arrival time not given.

Schull & Skibbereen Tramway & Light Railway.

ALL TRAINS 1st and 3rd CLASS.
TIME AND FARE TABLE, MAY, 1900, and until further notice.

Miles from Skibbereen	STATIONS.	DOWN TRAINS.		Fares from Skibbereen.		Miles from Schull.	STATIONS.	UP TRAINS.		Fares from Schull.	
		1	2	Single.	Return.			1	2	Single.	Return.
		P.M.	P.M.	1st 3rd	1st 3rd			A.M.	P.M.	1st 3rd	1st 3rd
				s. d. s. d.	s. d. s. d.					s. d. s. d.	s. d. s. d.
	Skibbereen dep.	12 20	6 30				Schull dep.	9 15	4 0		
4	Newcourt	12 33	6 43	0 6 0	3 —	2	Woodlands	9 25	4 10	0 4 0 2	— —
4	Church Cross	12 40	6 50	0 8 0	4 —	5	Ballydehob arr.	9 40	4 25	0 10 0	5 1 4 0 8
6	Holyhill	12 50	7 0	1 0 0	6 —		Do. dep.	9 45	4 30		
7	Kilcoe	12 55	7 5	1 2 0	7 —	8	Kilcoe	10 0	4 45	1 4 0 8	— —
	Ballydehob arr.	1 10	7 20	— —	— —	9	Hollyhill	10 5	4 50	1 6 0 9	— —
10	Do. dep.	1 15	7 25	1 8 0	10 2 3 1 4	11	Church Cross	10 15	5 0	1 10 0 11	— —
13	Woodlands	1 30	7 40	2 2 1	1 — —	12	Newcourt	10 22	5 7	2 0 1 0	— —
15	Schull	1 40	7 50	2 6 1	3 3 6 2 0	15	Skibbereen	10 35	5 20	2 6 1 3	3 6 2 0

Return Tickets are issued between Skibbereen, Schull, and Ballydehob only. They are available for one week

On every Thursday a Special Train will leave Skibbereen at 8.30 a.m. for Ballydehob and Schull, returning at 10.30 a.m. from Schull, and arriving in Skibbereen at 11.50 a.m.

A Special Train will leave Schull at 6.30 a.m. on Skibbereen Cattle Fair Days, arriving in Skibbereen at 7.50 a.m.

On every Thursday the 9.15 a.m. Train from Schull will not run; a Train leaves instead at 6.30 a.m., arriving in Skibbereen at 7.50 a.m.

On Schull and Ballydehob Cattle Fair Days a Train leaves Skibbereen at 7 a.m. arriving in Ballydehob at 7.50 a.m., and Schull at 8.20 a.m. Market Tickets are issued at reduced fares. Particulars at Stations.

a Starts at 1.0 every Saturday.

Schull & Skibbereen Time and Fare Table, May 1900.

OPERATING

Extract from Bradshaw's Timetable, May 1909

Down	Weekdays				Sundays*
	ThO	ETh			
	am	am	pm	pm	pm
Skibbereen	9.30	11.30	3.35	6.50	2.45
Newcourt	9.43	11.43	2.48	7.03	2.58
Church Cross	9.48	11.48	2.53	7.08	3.03
Hollyhill	9.57	11.57	3.02	7.17	3.12
Kilcoe	10.03	12.03	3.08	7.23	3.18
Ballydehob	10.25	12.25	3.30	7.45	3.40
Woodlands	10.40	12.40	3.45	8.00	3.55
Schull	10.50	12.50	3.55	8.10	4.05

Up	Weekdays				Sundays
	ThO	ETh			
	am	am	pm	pm	pm
Schull	7.00	9.30	1.10	5.30	7.15
Woodlands	7.10	9.40	1.20	5.40	7.25
Ballydehob	7.30	10.00	1.40	5.50	7.45
Kilcoe	7.47	10.17	1.57	6.07	8.02
Hollyhill	7.53	10.23	2.03	6.13	8.08
Church Cross	8.02	10.32	2.12	6.22	8.17
Newcourt	8.07	10.37	2.17	6.27	8.22
Skibbereen	8.20	10.50	2.30	6.40	8.35

Notes
ThO - Thursday only, ETh - Except Thursday.

Extra - Schull to Skibbereen, on Skibbereen Cattle Fair Days at 6.00 am arriving 7.20.
Skibbereen to Ballydehob and Schull on Cattle Fair Days at 6.00 am arriving at Ballydehob at 6.50 and Schull at 7.20.

* Note that Sunday's workings emanates from Skibbereen.

Schull & Skibbereeen Timetable taken from the ABC Timetable for December 1914.

Schull & Skibbereen Tramway & Light Railway.
TIME & FARE TABLE from 1st October, 1915, and until further notice.
ALL TRAINS 1st and 3rd CLASS.

Miles from Skibbereen	STATIONS		DOWN TRAINS					Fares from Skibbereen			
			1	2	3	4	Sun.	Single		Return	
			P.M.	P.M.	P.M.	P.M.	P.M.	1st s. d.	3rd s. d.	1st s. d.	3rd s. d.
	Skibbereen ... dep.		1A 0	6 50	—	—	—	0 6	0 3	—	—
3	Newcourt		1 13	7 3	—	—	—	0 6	0 3	—	—
4	Church Cross		1 18	7 8	—	—	—	0 8	0 4	—	—
6	Hollyhill		1 27	7 17	—	—	—	1 0	0 6	—	—
7	Kilcoe...		1 33	7 23	—	—	—	1 2	0 7	—	—
10	Ballydehob ... arr.		1 50	7 40	—	—	—	1 8	0 10	2 3	1 4
	Do. ... dep.		1 55	7 45	. —	—	—	—	—	—	—
13	Woodlands		2 10	8 0	—	—	—	2 2	1 1	—	—
15	Schull ... ... arr.		2 20	8 10	—	—	—	2 6	1 3	3 6	2 0

Miles from Schull	STATIONS		UP TRAINS					Fares from Schull			
			1	2	3	4	Sun.	Single		Return	
			A.M.	P.M.	P.M.	P.M.	P.M.	1st s. d.	3rd s. d.	1st s. d.	3rd s. d.
	Schull ... dep		9 30	4 20	—	—	—	0 4	0 2	—	—
2	Woodlands		9 40	4 30	—	—	—	0 4	0 2	—	—
5	Ballydehob ... arr.		9 55	4 45	—	—	—	0 10	0 5	1 4	0 8
	Do. ... dep.		10 0	4 50	—	—	—	—	—	—	—
8	Kilcoe		10 17	5 7	—	—	—	1 4	0 8	—	—
9	Hollyhill		10 23	5 13	—	—	—	1 6	0 9	—	—
11	Church Cross		10 32	5 22	—	—	—	1 10	0 11	—	—
12	Newcourt		10 37	5 27	—	—	—	2 0	1 0	—	—
15	Skibbereen ... arr.		10 50	5 40	—	—	—	2 6	1 3	3 6	2 0

A Starts at 1.30 p.m. on Saturdays and Skibbereen Cattle Fair Days.

Return Tickets are issued between Skibbereen, Ballydehob, and Schull, and from Kilcoe, Hollyhill, and Church Cross to Skibbereen. They are available for one week.

Market Tickets at reduced fares. Particulars to be had at Stations.

On every Thursday a Special Train will leave Skibbereen at 9.30 a.m. for Ballydehob and Schull, returning at 12.45 p.m. from Schull.

A Special Train will leave Schull at 6 a.m. on Skibbereen Cattle Fair Days, arriving in Skibbereen at 7.20 a.m.

The 9.30 a.m. from Schull will not run on Thursdays. A train leaves instead at 7.0 a.m., arriving in Skibbereen at 8.20 a.m.

On Schull and Ballydehob Cattle Fair Days a Train leaves Skibbereen at 6 a.m., arriving in Ballydehob at 6.50 a.m., and Schull at 7.20 a.m.

Through Passenger Fares, Cork and Schull.—SINGLE— 1st Class 9s. 9d.; 3rd Class, 5s. 2d RETURN— 1st Class, 14s. 7d.; 3rd Class, 9s. 4d. Week-end—1st Class 12s. 2d.; 3rd Class, 6s. 6d.

Schull & Skibbereen Time and Fare table, 1st October, 1915.

Timetable for Great Southern Railways (Schull & Skibbereen) July 1925

Weekdays Only

Down				Up			
		pm	pm			am	pm
Skibbereen		12.20	7.55	Schull		10.30	3.30
Newcourt		12.33	8.08	Woodlands		10.40	3.40
Church Cross		12.38	8.13	Ballydehob		10.55	3.55
Hollyhill		12.47	8.22	Ballydehob		11.00	4.00
Kilcoe		12.53	8.28	Kilcoe		11.17	4.17
Ballydehob		1.10	8.45	Hollyhill		11.23	4.23
Ballydehob		1.15	8.50	Church Cross		11.32	4.32
Woodlands		1.30	9.05	Newcourt		11.37	4.37
Schull		1.40	9.15	Skibbereen		11.50	4.50

On Cattle Fair Days at Schull and Ballydehob, a train leaves Skibbereen at 6.00 am.

Extract from Bradshaw's Timetable, March 1928

Weekday Onlys

Up

	am	pm
Schull	10.00	2.10
Skibbereen	11.20	3.20

Down

	pm	pm
Skibbereen	1.20	3.45
Schull	2.40	5.05

Timetable for Great Southern Railways (late Schull & Skibbereen)
September 1932
From Bradshaw's Guide

Weekdays Only

Up	am	pm	Down	pm	pm
Schull	10.00	2.00	Skibbereen	12.00	3.45
Woodlands	10.10	2.10	Newcourt	12.13	3.58
Ballydehob	10.30	2.30	Church Cross	12.18	4.03
Kilcoe	10.47	2.47	Hollyhill	12.27	4.12
Hollyhill	10.53	2.53	Kilcoe	12.33	4.18
Church Cross	11.02	3.02	Ballydehob	12.55	4.40
Newcourt	11.07	3.07	Woodlands	1.10	4.55
Skibbereen	11.20	3.20	Schull	1.20	5.05

On Cattle Fair Days at Schull and Ballydehob, a train leaves Skibbereen at 6.00 am.

Notes

The above is the public timetable; on the Working Timetable (Tables Nos. 76 and 77), each worling is shown as 'PAS' though in practice it would be Mixed.
A footnote to the DOWN table has: 'On Schull & Ballydehob Cattle Fair Days a Train leaves Skibbereen at 6.00 am'.

The Great Southern Railways Timetable for 1st July, 1933 was identical to the foregoing. Trains Cork-Skibbereen-Cork were:

	am	pm	pm
Cork	9.15	12.55	5.30
Skibbereen	11.27	3.12	7.39

	am	pm	pm
Skibbereen	8.45	12.30	5.14
Cork	11.10	2.45	7.20

Great Southern Railways Working Timetable, September 1937

Down	Pass. pm	Pass. pm	Up	Pass. am	Pass. pm
Skibbereen	12.00	3.45	Schull	10.00	1.45
Newcourt Halt	12.16	4.01	Woodlands Halt	10.11	1.56
Church Cross	12.22	4.07	Ballydehob	10.27	2.12
Hollyhill	12.33	4.18	Ballydehob	10.32	2.17
Kilcoe Halt	12.39	4.24	Kilcoe Halt	10.49	2.34
Ballydehob	12.56	4.41	Hollyhill	10.55	2.40
Ballydehob	1.00	4.45	Church Cross	11.06	2.51
Woodlands Halt	1.16	5.01	Newcourt Halt	11.12	2.57
Schull	1.27	5.12	Skibbereen	11.28	3.13

On Schull and Ballydehob Cattle Fair Days a Train leaves Skibbereen at 6.00 am.
Note that three stopping places are now 'Halts'.
Though listed as Passenger trains, all workings ran Mixed.

****

	am	pm
Cork	9.00	1.10
Skibbereen	11.20	3.33

	pm	pm
Skibbereen	12.30	5.15
Cork	2.52	7.42

Great Southern Railways Public Timetable, July 1941

Down	pm	Up	am
Skibbereen	*4.30	Schull	11.45
Newcourt Halt	4.46	Woodlands Halt	11.56
Church Cross	4.52	Ballydehob	12.12
Hollyhill	5.03	Ballydehob	12.17
Kilcoe Halt	5.09	Kilcoe Halt	12.34
Ballydehob	5.26	Hollyhill	12.40
Ballydehob	5.30	Church Cross	12.51
Woodlands Halt	5.46	Newcourt Halt	12.57
Schull	5.57	Skibbereen	†1.13

Notes

* Connection from Cork leaves 1.55 pm arrives at Skibbereen at 4.20.
† Connection to Cork leaves 5.10 pm arrives Cork at 7.41.

There was only one daily connection with CB&SC section of GSRlys.

During its sixty-one years of operations, the Railway experienced six fatal accidents, a remarkably low figure considering its hazardous nature and a tribute to its careful operators.

In late July 1892 it was revealed that a considerable tonnage of goods was being imported through Schull - 60 tons or so a week - and questions were asked about the feasibility of moving increased tonnages by the Tramway, instead of by coastal vessel, 'so raising the revenue of the line and reducing the guarantee?' Schull was referred to as 'a rising place' but it was pointed out that sea freightage was considerably cheaper than by railway; it would only bear fruit if rail charges between Cork and Schull were reduced to sea rates. At the time ships claimed twice the tonnage of the railway . . . but it hoped that the proposed line to Schull Pier would bring benefit to the Tram.

The Tramway had run a special train in that same July, to accommodate those wishing to observe a Cycle Race from Schull to Skibbereen; the Tram would make an unusual viewpoint as it ran alongside the contestants. The Down run to Schull was uneventful but when the Up return journey was about 150 yards out of Schull station a male passenger fell from a carriage balcony, was run over and died from his injuries. The cause is a mystery to this day.

The man was a well-known farmer, Denis W. O'Regan, a member of the Board of Guardians of Schull Union and enthusiast for the activities of the Bicycle Club; he fell from the carriage head first and the vehicles following ran over his leg below the knee. At the inquest held in Schull Courthouse, the deceased was said 'to be sober, but may have the drink taken'. Although some had seen O'Regan fall off, the train did not stop although the guard had been told about the incident - but only when he came round to collect the tickets. It all seemed very casual. Apparently there was a 'bell' in the carriage to ring in emergency but no one understood it and it was not used. Someone had felt a bump, 'as if going over a stone'. A witness said the carriage 'was shaking so hard that he had to hold on to his seat' (laughter).

For the Company it was said the deceased was a trespasser as he had no ticket and they could show he was drunk. (Later in the Hearing, the remark about drunkenness was withdrawn on advice.)

Patrick Barrington confirmed he had been employed as a guard since the opening and was on the train; the train consisted of five carriages and two vans. He agreed they often stopped when there were animals on the track (but what had this to do with it?). There was plenty of room in the train and no necessity for standing on the balcony. When told about the accident he did not think the informant was serious. He told the Railway Manager (Creedon), who was travelling on the engine, what had been said but Creedon felt as they were already 1½ miles from the spot, that it was only a joke - had he known it was serious, they would have stopped.

An extremely unfortunate affair resulted in the death of McDonagh, the man employed in Schull engine shed to clean the locomotives and raise steam early in the day for the morning train, etc.

Apparently it was the practice to allow the cleaner to stable the engine overnight inside the building by running it onto the turntable from off the last train; the engine would then be turned to enter the shed smoke-box first (see layout diagram p. 156). This allowed the engine to leave the shed cab-first and made it easier to position the engine exactly on the turntable again.

The shed doors were not over-large and gave scant clearance as the cab passed through them; worse, on windless days, even when the doors were opened, the engine obstructed the opening to such extent that a through-draught sufficient to encourage quick steam-raising was impossible. On mornings when the steam pressure had

Skibbereen to Schull.   Schull to Skibbereen.

Down Trains.				Week Days.		Distance from Schull.	Up Trains.			Week Days.	
				1. Mixed.	2.					3. Mixed.	4.
				p.m.		Miles.				a.m.	
SKIBBEREEN	...	W ●N	dep.	3 45	...	—	SCHULL	...	...●N dep.	10 0	...
NEWCOURT HALT	...	... N	,,	4 2	...	2	WOODLANDS HALT	...	N ,,	10 14	...
CHURCH CROSS HALT	...	N	,,	4 9	...	5	BALLYDEHOB	...	N arr.	10 32	...
HOLLYHILL	...	... N	,,	4 20	...	—	,,	...	... dep.	10 35	...
KILCOE HALT	...	... N	,,	4 27	...	8	KILCOE HALT	...	N ,,	10 54	...
BALLYDEHOB	...	... N	arr.	4 46	...	9	HOLLYHILL	...	N ,,	11 1	...
,,	...	...	dop.	4 50	...	11	CHURCH CROSS HALT	...	N ,,	11 11	...
WOODLANDS HALT	...	... N	,,	5 7	...	12	NEWCOURT HALT	...	N ,,	11 16	...
SCHULL	...	...●N	arr.	5 20	...	15	SKIBBEREEN	...	...●N arr.	11 33	...

●—Engine Turntable.   N—No Telephone Communication.   W—Water Column.

CIE Working Timetable for 1946. This was the last full year of working. The running time over the whole section has been slightly increased. No recognition is given to water tanks at Schull, Ballydehob and Leemawaddra River bridge (Kilcoe).

TABLE No. 46.

SCHULL AND SKIBBEREEN.

	Arr. p.m.	Dep. p.m.		Arr. a.m.	Dep. a.m.
SKIBBEREEN ...	—	3 45	SCHULL	—	10 00
Newcourt	4 01	4 02	Woodlands ...	10 13	10 14
Church Cross ...	4 08	4 09	Ballydehob ...	10 32	10 35
Hollyhill	4 19	4 20	Kilcoe	10 53	10 54
Kilcoe	4 26	4 27	Hollyhill	11 00	11 01
Ballydehob ...	4 46	4 50	Church Cross ...	11 10	11 11
Woodlands ...	5 06	5 07	Newcourt	11 15	11 16
SCHULL	5 20	—	SKIBBEREEN ...	11 33	—

The above service will cease to operate on and from Monday, 27th January, 1947.

Timetable for services up to 27th January, 1947.

dropped markedly and the engine would not move, the practice (the world-over) was to move the engine into the open by means of inserting a pinch-bar at the point where a wheel made contact with the rail, and to lever the locomotive to the desired spot.

A common happening was for an engine, as soon as the initial movement was imparted, to set off on its own if the regulator had been left open in an attempt to move it without a bar. It was then necessary to jump up and into cab, close the regulator and apply the hand brake. Runaways were frequent.

It seems McDonagh had, through a similar happening or some other, been trapped between the door-jamb and the moving engine. Perhaps the engine 'had got away', as had happened more than once for derailments on, or due to over-running the turntable, are often recalled; part of the engine might be down in the turntable well! Truly, the Schull turntable was the Achilles' Heel of the whole undertaking.

Up until 1925 the responsibility for the Railway rested upon the Board (as it was termed latterly). According to the temperament of each member, this must have given some sleepless nights. For instance, the everyday running gave William O'Regan constant worry outside his own business in Aughadown.

The Board was greatly concerned with the excessive tyre and flange wear caused by the curves. We were aware of it as a daily happening [implying that the Engineer was in far-off Cork city]. Because of it, far too many vehicles were laid off in Skibbereen awaiting repair and we could not carry the business offering. The noise of the pounding engine was mixed with the squeal of the wheels. In Summer there was dust flying everywhere and the sparks from the chimney left lineside fires, some of them leading to Claims from landowners. They used more coal than between Skibbereen and Cork . . .

The Revd Canon George Salter's father farmed at Ballydehob and he had clear recollections of the confusion which reigned there as crowds of race-goers tried to board the train at the conclusion of the Ballydehob Horse Races. Men clung to the outside of the carriages and dropped off, then on again, when the train needed a push; some tried to reach the roof and the guard was unable to control the situation. Many were without tickets while others were sober. Possibly the train was left unattended as the crew was as eager as the passengers to witness the proceedings.*

Latter day Operation of Fair Specials

Before World War II it was customary to work an empty livestock special from Skibbereen at 8.10 pm on the evening previous to a Fair. This comprised up to 20 wagons with a carriage added for buyers; it is possible that the train was double-headed if the occasion demanded. It is assumed the engine returned light to Skibbereen that evening.

On the day of the Fair a light engine(s) left Skibbereen at 9 am and worked to Schull, to return with stock already loaded. The possibility of double-heading - which would have meant three engines and crews being needed on one day - is thought to have been remote as the GSR only aimed to keep two engines in service and only two crews were available. It is known that main line drivers were called in when necessary and their opinions of working conditions made a deep impression on the Author!

* At the conclusion of the Listowel Races in the 1950s, the writer and his wife, who were on their way to Tralee, were advised to remain on the engine footplate until they reached Tralee, such was the boisterous crowd.

The ultimate death-knell of Fairs was sounded after the S&S section closed; the advent of the Co-operative Marts and the road lorry usurped them.

Peculiar to the way of life in West Cork was the incessant carnage among pigs, cattle, horses, donkeys, etc. struck by these early morning Fair Specials. Farmers would turn out their stock to graze on the line at night, thinking the last train had gone. They would overlook the time of the month and the day, and in the morning darkness the crew might be unaware of a larger beast until it was under the wheels . . . This stretch of grass alongside the line was known as 'The Long Meadow'!

The Weekly Circulars of the 1930s and 1940s contained:*

Special Trains

Second Friday each month: Schull Cattle Fair
Dep. Skibb. 6 am. Loading 8 cattle wagons + carriage for buyers. Return Dep. Schull 10.30 am. (By previous day at least, 10 wagons would already be at Schull.)

Third Thursday each month: Ballydehob Cattle Fair
Dep. Skibb. 7 am. Return Dep. Ballydehob 11.15 am.

*First Monday each month: Goleen Cattle Sales**
Additional cattle wagons worked to Schull; Goleen sales held first Tuesday in month.

Special trains resumed after withdrawal of all services 24th April, 1944, viz.:
Schull Fair: from Friday 14th December, 1945: Down 7 am. Up 1 pm.
Ballydehob Fair: from Thursday 20th December, 1945: Down 7 am. Up 11.30 am.

Workings which required Cattle Van Specials once a month.†

Market & Fair Days requiring special trains worked *from Skibbereen* Down empty stock, and Up loaded at:

Day of Month	Tuesday	Wednesday	Thursday	Friday
SKIBBEREEN#	-	-	-	First A
BALLYDEHOB	-	Third P	Third C	-
SCHULL	-	-	Second P	Second C
GOLEEN	First CPS	-	-	-

Workings		
First Tuesday to Schull for Goleen†		Week 1
First Friday into Skibbereen		
Second Thursday to Schull		Week 2
Second Friday to Schull		
Third Wednesday to Ballydehob		Week 3
Third Thursday to Ballydehob		

| A | All beasts | C | Cattle | P | Pigs | S | Sheep |

This Calendar has been compiled from local sources.
* This traffic appears to have ceased *c.* 1940 when the two-train service was withdrawn.
† Extra vehicles may be run the previous day.
# With the exception of Skibbereen (and Goleen for which Schull was used), all Down trains terminate at the place of Market, and return to Skibbereen when loaded.

---

* The Author is indebted to A.M. Davies for extracts from the Weekly Circulars held in the IRRS Library; to Mrs Etta McCarthy of Schull for local affairs and Patrick Cleary of Skibbereen for details of an agricultural nature.

OPERATING   233

So far is known, no loaded train was run into Skibbereen for the Market; there may have been instances of running a Down loaded train *after* a Skibbereen Market, but confirmation is lacking.

Schull Regatta Services (15th August, 1946)

Regular services were suspended on this Thursday and a special timetable obtained:

Skibbereen	7.00	1.00	Schull	-	7.00
Ballydehob	8.00	1.55	Ballydehob	11.15	7.25
Schull	-	2.50	Skibbereen	12.15	8.20

It is suggested that the first and usual working on this day to Ballydehob Cattle Fair was worked with Skibbereen men (Jack Daly: driver), and that the same crew manned all trains. A second engine with Schull crew (Curly Hegarty: driver) would be available to provide a second engine which would be necessary for the 7.00 pm departure from Schull which was traditionally the heaviest working of the *year*. This engine and crew would return light to Schull so as to work the regular train out of there next morning.

It was the last occasion of the annual Schull Regatta Special which became the hallmark of train working on the S&SR, and loadings reached unbelievable numbers. In the early 1930s the record number ever carried in one such day reached 752, many folk travelling in open wagons ... it may be assumed the GSR authorities in Dublin and Cork turned their backs on events and kept their fingers crossed ... The sight of passengers pushing the train out of Ballydehob remains a stirring memory: GABRIEL is given the credit for this feat.

In general rather than in a particular year, the Regatta took place on each 15th August, which being the Feast of the Assumption of the Blessed Virgin Mary, is treated as a Church Holiday; if for any reason it was necessary to hold it on another day, a Public Notice in the newspapers would appear to state the altered date.

Appreciating the importance of this annual event, it came as no surprise to learn that a Special Train for the 1947 Regatta was to run as usual, although the line was closed! The Schull Parish Priest had phoned CIE in Dublin and Cork to confirm it, but the Area Manager in Cork is reputed to have forbidden it.

Having hinted at the number of passengers carried on Schull Regatta days the question may arise as to the passenger loading of a typical mid-winter train on a day when no Market or Fair was operating? Was it a characteristic of the local people only to use the Railway for a fair or market (for instance) or when some recreational event was held, i.e. the local horseraces? Undoubtedly the foregoing would form the basic traffic.

Among the people of the Irish countryside the late Victorian and Edwardian lifestyle of English railway travellers was absent; the countryman did not move into town to 'go shopping', commuting was almost unknown and a day at the seaside for folk who lived beside it was unattractive. Having considered all the factors, and taking in the figures which the Annual Returns reveal, daily passenger takings would be relatively small, leaving the Railway to depend on livestock traffic for the largest income. Taking 1902 as one of the best years in the statistics, in a week of four workings on a week-day plus two on Sundays, an average of 34 passengers *per train* would be carried but in the years 1890-96 an average of 26 per train would be normal.

Newham quotes average passenger figures for Saturdays in the mid-1930s as 250, but the figure is more likely to apply to Sundays as Saturdays are not a holiday in rural Ireland. (This figure was given in the CORK EXAMINER for 24th August, 1956 in connection with the official abandonment, but simply repeats the error.)

School Children

The older children who lived along the line came into Skibbereen for school; there were two well-patronised establishments in the town, Hosford's Academy and St Fachtna's School.

It was the former which claimed to have performed the most outrageous deed on The Tram; the children were returning home on a Down train when it stopped at Hollyhill. While the crew was attending to the engine and the guard had left the van, some boys uncoupled the last few vehicles ... and the van. 'Right away' waved the guard, so Curly started the engine and near-coasted downgrade to Meen Bridge. He was not aware that the load seemed lighter as they climbed up past The Cross House Bar, and only when he came to pull up at Kilcoe platform did he notice a change in the braking characteristics ... meanwhile, half the train and the guard was marooned at Hollyhill.

It seems that St Fachtna's could not match this and if they did, the escapade has not become local lore. On one count the schools were equal - the excuse for being late in the morning was identical for both, 'The train was late'. It was seldom on time but not too bad considering - the school never rang up to check. What still remains unclear is how a special school timetable was provided for pupils who travelled on the train - the schools must have had to compensate for the shorter hours of attendance? Did standards improve when 'bus travel took over?

Problems with Turf

From a letter found in Accounts Ledger 1903-on.

Skibbereen
26th November, 1942

District Locomotive Superintendent
Cork.

TURF SUPPLIES - SCHULL

In reply to yours of 25 inst. I beg to state with regard to the turf purchased at Schull on 10th October; on this date I received a wire from Driver Hegarty, Schull that he was unable to raise steam with the turf owing to its been wet, as the date in question was Market Day in Skibbereen and a number of passengers would be travelling to attend it, and as there was no possibility of supplying turf otherwise, I wired Driver Hegarty to purchase a supply locally to enable him to work the train to Skibbereen. I at the same time wired Loco Foreman R. Lanages [name almost illegible] of the position and what I had done; so as regards sleepers I on one occasion wrote Station Master Schull asking him to supply four sleepers to light engine, and that I would replace same when I would get sleepers, which I did not get.

C. Murphy.

Single Line Operating and Signalling

Throughout the life of the system the basic timetable was founded on Schull, the springboard for operation. At its best, two trains in each direction were worked to Skibbereen and back on weekdays, though in earlier times similar workings appeared on Sundays.

It was usual to append somewhat lengthy footnotes about extra workings on certain days or the cancellation of normal runs. Such special workings ran on certain days of the week/month/year in connection with Fairs, Cattle Markets, Cycle Races, Gaelic Sporting Fixtures, Schull Regatta and the like, emphasising that the system was operated mainly for local convenience; such was confirmed in that for most of its early life, no attempt was made to connect with main line trains at Skibbereen - it was as if the world beyond its own metals was of little consequence.

A stranger attempting to digest the footnotes of the timetable was assumed to have ascertained on what days Markets, Fairs etc. were held before he consulted it . . . he might be found waiting helplessly at Church Cross on a Thursday for a train which had already been and gone.

On paper at least, the usual daily service could be worked by one engine and available coaches. The coaches were marshalled behind the engine and any goods stock and brake van behind them. This arrangement met with the Board of Trade's approval and was most economical in staff; furthermore, the rake returned to its starting point each night. In practice, this method (should any delay occur) had a knock-on effect as the day wore on unless the time available at termini was sufficient to shunt wagons, coal and water the engine. In later days when connecting trains from Cork *were* advertised, a Schull departure from Skibbereen would be held to await it; in such circumstances the Schull crew might deem it opportune to seek refreshment in the town . . .

On occasions of dire need at Skibbereen, the S&S staff concentrated on preparing the engine for the return journey; the main line station staff might be called from goods shed or station office to give a helping add to assemble the Down S&S train by shunting the stock by hand, be it of either gauge. Thus on the arrival of a late working from Cork (usually this had the branch engine to haul the through coaches for Skibbereen and Baltimore from Drimoleague Junction), interchange of passengers, parcels, etc. would incur minimum delay.

The need to steam a second engine or run an additional train was given extra flexibility by the passing loop at Ballydehob; this was not strictly laid out for through running but could stable a train if required. The only other siding was at Hollyhill, and was unsuitable. To meet such a need, the line was divided into two sections on the Staff-and-Ticket method; the wooden Staff Tokens were coloured and had the stations' names painted thereon. When these Tokens became battered through mis-use, steel tubes with raised lettering took their place. To these tubes a heavy chain was attached and had an enormous key on the other end. This fitted a Ticket Box painted the same colour as the Token - red Skibbereen-Ballydehob and green Ballydehob-Schull. The boxes had white lettering and were kept in the Skibbereen Company Office, and the Station Master's offices at Ballydehob and Schull respectively. The Ticket Boxes were strongly made and possessed a home-spun appearance, clearly being a product of the Skibbereen workshops. A heavy mechanism prevented the key being withdrawn from the Box unless the lid was closed.

Authority to enter a single line section was possession of the appropriate Token. If

1200-7-'14.

The Eagle Limited, Skibbereen.

The Schull and Skibbereen Tramway and Light Railway.

Train Ticket No. 2339   [DOWN]

To Guard_____

and

Engineman_____

You are authorized, after seeing the Train Staff for the Section, to proceed from **BALLYDEHOB** to **SCHULL**. The Train Staff will follow.

Signature,_____

Skibbereen,_____o'clock.

_____day of_____191   [OVER.

Two examples of Train Tickets.

15-11-'20. (48).

Schull & Skibbereen Tramway & Light Railway

TRAIN TICKET NO. 2993   [UP]

To Guard_____

and

Engineman_____

You are authorized, after seeing the Train Staff for the Section, to proceed from **SCHULL TO BALLYDEHOB.** The Train Staff will follow.

Signature,_____

Schull,_____o'clock

_____day of_____192   (OVER

"STAR" SKIBBEREEN.

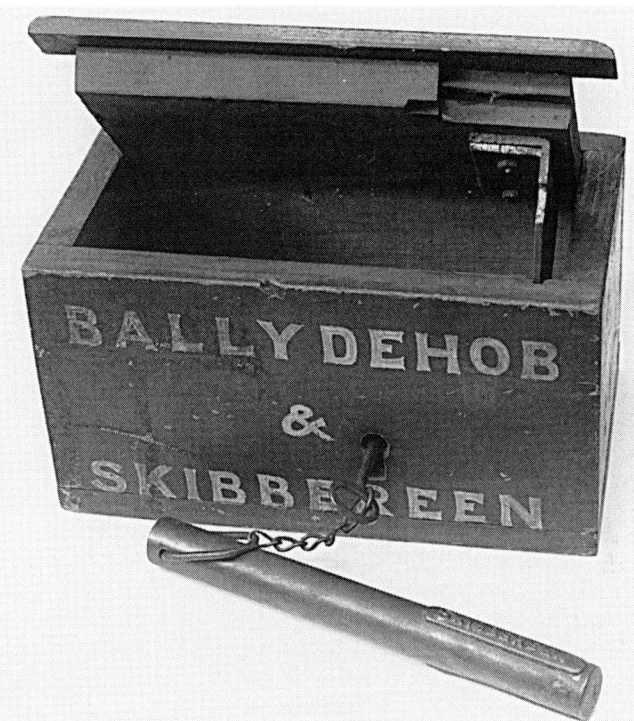

Two photographs of the Skibbereen-Ballydehob Staff Ticket Box with Single Line Token having key to Ticket Box attached.

one or more trains ran in the same direction, following one another, authority was the possession of a cardboard Ticket suitably made out for the journey, the Ticket holder being assured that the Token itself was in the issuer's possession. The Token would be carried on the last train running in that direction.

(There is an interesting sequel to this. When services closed and everything stood in limbo, but with the main line still being operated, the Skibbereen Station Master presented the Skibbereen-Ballydehob Token to the Author. Over a decade later the Company Offices in Skibbereen station yard were put up for Auction and the day previous to this event the Author investigated their interior. Besides many other items in neglect and disarray, was the Ticket Box (Skibbereen-Ballydehob) the key for which had been in the writer's keeping for many years. Someone had jammed a foreign key into the hole in an effort to force the lid open but it was too well-made to succumb.

It was time for the Box and Key to be re-united, but the Author was obliged to await his return home before the correct key might be inserted and 'marriage' could be consummated. It did not disappoint . . .)

Apart from the afore-mentioned description of protecting single line working, the system luxuriated in no further sophistication. Points were worked by local ground levers and padlocks to prevent unauthorised movement were absent, truly akin to the policies regarding an urban street tramway; as is the case elsewhere, communities known for their civil disobedience do not usually inflict on their own kind. There was no necessity for lever ground frames nor was there any form of semaphore signalling. With the stringent speed restrictions imposed where road crossings, sharp curves and severe gradients arose, the Board of Trade was satisfied that its regulations were adequate and paramount among these was the efficiency of the automatic vacuum brake.

At no time was there any serious mishap due to operating deficiencies; rather most incidents were caused by road users and wandering livestock. The railway staff must claim the honours for professional skill.

Rule Book

The Company used the 'model' Rule Book produced through the Board of Trade, and there was correspondence between the Company's Secretary and the Board at the time. It is likely that most of the stipulations laid down were quite irrelevant to the system's operators and may have been more a confusion than a guide.

On 31st August, 1920 the Board of Management produced its own Book, much trimmed down to 86 injunctions but still adhering to the somewhat pompous vocabulary of its originator. Many of the conditions about signalling were still superfluous and the usual cautions about staff entering Refreshment Rooms (of which there were none) during the hours of duty was easily honoured, the nearest being in Cork city.

Among Rules which were somewhat different and individual were:

a) Guards started their trains in daylight by whistle, after dark by green lamp. (There is no mention of flags). They also had to satisfy themselves 'that the train is . . . properly oiled'.
b) Engine-drivers must have with them on the engine: one draw bar (i.e. coupling - Author), one link, a set of lamps, a bar, a set of fire irons, a screw jack . . .

'He must drive from the leading end of his engine . . .' This injunction possibly stems from the cab-first working of the original tram engines: all the later locomotives - including that from the Cork & Muskerry section - were driven chimney-leading.

'He must stand up and keep a good look-out . . .'

'He must pass along the proper line, which is the left-hand side of the platform, in the direction in which the engine is travelling'. This Rule was unattainable.

'The Engine Bell' was to be sounded on entering or leaving all sidings or crossing places, upon starting, on all curves and whenever the driver considered it necessary. Another uncorrected Rule taken from the Tramway period: the whistle should have been stated.

Trains were not allowed to follow one another at intervals of less than twenty minutes.

There were minor rules of interest; drovers travelling with stock on cattle trains had to produce 'Cattle Tickets' before they were issued with train tickets. Use of flags follows the provision of sets to Gate Keepers, Gangers and Milesmen. Permanent Way men were given instructions about the use of their 'lorries', an old term for Gangers' Trollies, which were not permitted 'to be attached to a train'. While there are instructions regarding the Train Staff and its use (the term 'Token' is not used), there are none regarding the use of 'Tickets'.

An impression given on reading the Rule Book is that it contained a number of curious stipulations and omissions, and that any one closer to the 'Hands-on' daily work of the system would have noticed them. The fact that they were approved by the Board of Directors who, in their own admission to the Author, were not fully informed, can be ignored.

The Book was printed by SOUTHERN STAR LTD, Skibbereen, the premises of the local newspaper.

Speed Restrictions (Great Southern Rlys. 1935)

Location	Max. speed (mph)
Skibbereen-Schull	12
Crooked Bridge Curves	10
Church Strand Curves	10
Sweetman's Curve	5
Woodland's Bridge	5
West of Newcourt, around Young's House	8
Church Gate, at Church Cross	8
West of Hollyhill, below Allen's House	8
Meen Bridge	8
Both sides of Crooked Bridge	8
Check-rail Curves, East of Ballydehob	8
Curves, West of Ballydehob Bridge	8
Curves, West of Woodland's Bridge	8
Curves, West of O'Connor's Gatehouse	8
Wheelahan's Curve	8
Workhouse Curve	8
Weaver's Curve (& all other curves under 10 chains radius)	10

Note the variations in spelling in various official Railway publications, and with the Ordnance Survey, Dublin.

Identification of all the above locations has not been possible.

Gatehouses ('cottages') and Level Crossings

The earliest contemporary maps confirm the existence of crossing gates and accompanying accommodation; the latter was based on the basic Board of Works' cottage which was found throughout Ireland. A handful still stand beside the S&SR route, and might be occupied by a permanent way employee and his wife. No surviving list of the original arrangement exists, but the Great Southern Railways APPENDIX TO THE WORKING TIMETABLE, March 1936 gives (all locations were unsignalled and had attached cottages):*

Name of Crossing	Station to which attached	Distance from Skibbereen
Newcourt	Skibbereen	2 m. 1,470 yds
Hollyhill	Hollyhill	5 m. 860 yds
Kilcoe No. 1	Kilcoe	5 m. 1,650 yds
Kilcoe No. 2	Kilcoe	6 m. 1,015 yds
Ardura	Ballydehob	7 m. 810 yds
Skeaghanore (Driscoll's)	Ballydehob	8 m. 1,440 yds
Shanvanagh No. 1 (Sullivan's)	Ballydehob	9 m. 1,340 yds
Shanvanagh No. 2 (Connor's)	Ballydehob	10 m. 620 yds
Shanvanagh No. 3 (Connor's)	Ballydehob	10 m. 800 yds
Woodlands	Schull	12 m. 1,000 yds
Station Gates	Schull	14 m. 500 yds
Pier Extension	Schull	14 m. 810 yds

* Schull Station Gates and Pier Extension crossings did not have attached cottages.

Water Columns (Great Southern Railways 1935)

Station	No. of	Where situated	Capacity Galls	Remarks
Ballydehob	1	Down road	1,030	
Schull	1	Down platform	1,025	
Skibbereen	1	Loco. Yard	8,412	Combined total with main line Engine Shed tank.

Propelling of Ballast Trains

This was prohibited in both directions.

Brake Power on trains

Owing to the steep gradients on this Section, Guards must be prepared to give Drivers every assistance, by using the handbrake.
Drivers will be held responsible for their brakes being kept in perfect order.

OPERATING   241

Dimensions of Loads

Width of load	Height in Centre from Rail	Height at Side from Rail
6 ft. 0 in.	12 ft 6 in.	9 ft 6 in.

Station Clocks etc.

All station clocks, guard's timepieces etc. for the Section to be taken daily at Skibbereen.

'Engine head-lights' (Great Southern Railways 1935)

One Acetylene Lamp on Engine Funnel.
(*Two White Lights* - one on right and one on left in front of Smoke Box of engine - *used only on Special Trains.*)

Fares

The interesting feature of the 1898 and 1915 fare tables reproduced (p. 242) is that over a period of seventeen years the value of money, so far as it concerned the Railway, had not changed. Such stability is rare nowadays.

A second feature is that the fare structure appears to be based on 'One Penny per Mile' (lower class) which is rather more than the 'going rate' for the late 19th Century but fair value at the start of World War I. How fascinating it would be to have overheard a conversation regarding fares in a pre-1900 train, and to witness the social structure of those travelling!

When the Board of Works examined the Committee of Management's accounts in 1901 they were critical of short-sighted policies which reduced the Railway's income. By the time of the first Vice-Regal Commission in 1907 the Railway Board had asserted its policies for instigating improvements; these included:

1) A third working on weekdays during the Summer months to cater for tourists. (This was a time when both royalty and nobility were recognising the beauties of Cork and Kerry).*

*Although the S&SR was not noted for its publicity (none has come to notice) two Co. Cork railways lost no time in taking up the opportunity.

In 1899 the *Cork Bandon & South Coast Railway* published a considerable booklet to extol their connecting four-horse coach link from Bantry to Killarney via Glengariff over which the Prince of Wales had travelled in 1858. It was dubbed, THE PRINCE OF WALES ROUTE and the accompanying map took in the whole of Cork and Kerry and included the S&SR. The text, though flowery, is as true of the landscape today as then. In 1899, a Parliamentary Party of the Lords and Commons visited Killarney by this route. There is fleeting mention of the S&SR as the means to visit 'The West Cork Mining District'.

Using the same publisher, format and similar cover illustrations, the *Cork & Macroom Direct Railway* publicised their cars and waggonettes which reached Killarney from Macroom station via Inchigeela, Gougane Barra and the Pass of Keim-an-eigh, entitled THE TOURISTS' ROUTE. The map showed the road connections to be far more extensive than the mileage of the modest C&MDR. Publication date was *c.* 1903.

2) A revised timetable which gave mainline connections at Skibbereen.
3) A revised classification of goods rates.

There remained however, a stubborn refusal to quote for through-booking, and the reason is still unclear - a clash of personalities could be the cause. A significant step was the introduction of Cheap Day Returns on Saturdays only; these were available on the Up train leaving at 7.15 am to passengers joining at Schull, Woodlands and Ballydehob only. Those joining a train east of Ballydehob had to use the 10.20 am Up train. Presumably this was to avoid overloading on the early working, and a special timetable for that day applied?

*Fares from Bradshaw's Railway Guide May 1898**

Station	First Class		Second Class	
	s.	d.	s.	d.
Skibbereen				
New Court	0	6	0	3
Church Cross	0	8	0	4
Hollyhill	1	0	0	6
Kilcoe	1	2	0	7
Ballydehob	1	8	0	10
Woodlands	2	2	1	1
Schull	2	6	1	3
Schull				
Woodlands	0	4	0	2
Ballydehob	0	10	0	5
Kilcoe	1	4	0	8
Hollyhill	1	6	0	9
Church Cross	1	10	0	11
New Court	2	0	1	0
Skibbereen	2	6	1	3

Fares from Timetable Bill; October 1915†

			Fares from Skibbereen					
Station	First Class		Third Class		First Class		Third Class	
			Single				Return	
	s.	d.	s.	d.	s.	d.	s.	d.
Skibbereen								
New Court	0	6	0	3				
Church Cross	0	8	0	4				
Hollyhill	1	0	0	6				
Kilcoe	1	2	0	7				
Ballydehob	1	8	0	10	2	3	1	4
Woodlands	2	1	1	1				
Schull	2	6	1	3	3	6	2	0

* From Roger Heywood-Waddington collection.
† Source: IRRS Library, Dublin.

Station	First Class Single		Third Class Single		First Class Return		Third Class Return	
	s.	d.	s.	d.	s.	d.	s.	d.
Schull								
Woodlands	0	4	0	2				
Ballydehob	0	10	0	5	1	4	0	8
Kilcoe	1	4	0	8				
Hollyhill	1	6	0	9				
Church Cross	1	10	0	11				
New Court	2	0	1	0				
Skibbereen	2	6	1	3	3	6	2	0

RETURN TICKETS issued between Skibbereen, Ballydehob & Schull: Return tickets are issued from Kilcoe, Hollyhill and Church Cross to Skibbereen. They are available for one week.

MARKET TICKETS at reduced fares - particulars may be had at stations.

Fares and Classes

The earliest reference comes in the Vice-Regal Commission of 1906-7. The Commission was told fares were 'about the same' for Third Class at $1d.$ per mile. This formed the bulk of the traffic. There was no Second Class by then and First Class fares were based on $1.66d.$ per mile which it was hinted at were slightly above other railways' Second Class.*

Rates for goods were similar to other Irish lines.

---

* The average national fare between 1897 and 1917 was about $0.9d.$ per mile; in 1917 the Government directed an increase of 50 per cent to discourage people from travelling. [On p. 247 HISTORY OF THE GREAT WESTERN RAILWAY VOL. II (MacDermot, revised Clinker) publ. 1964.; there is useful information on GWR fares at this period].

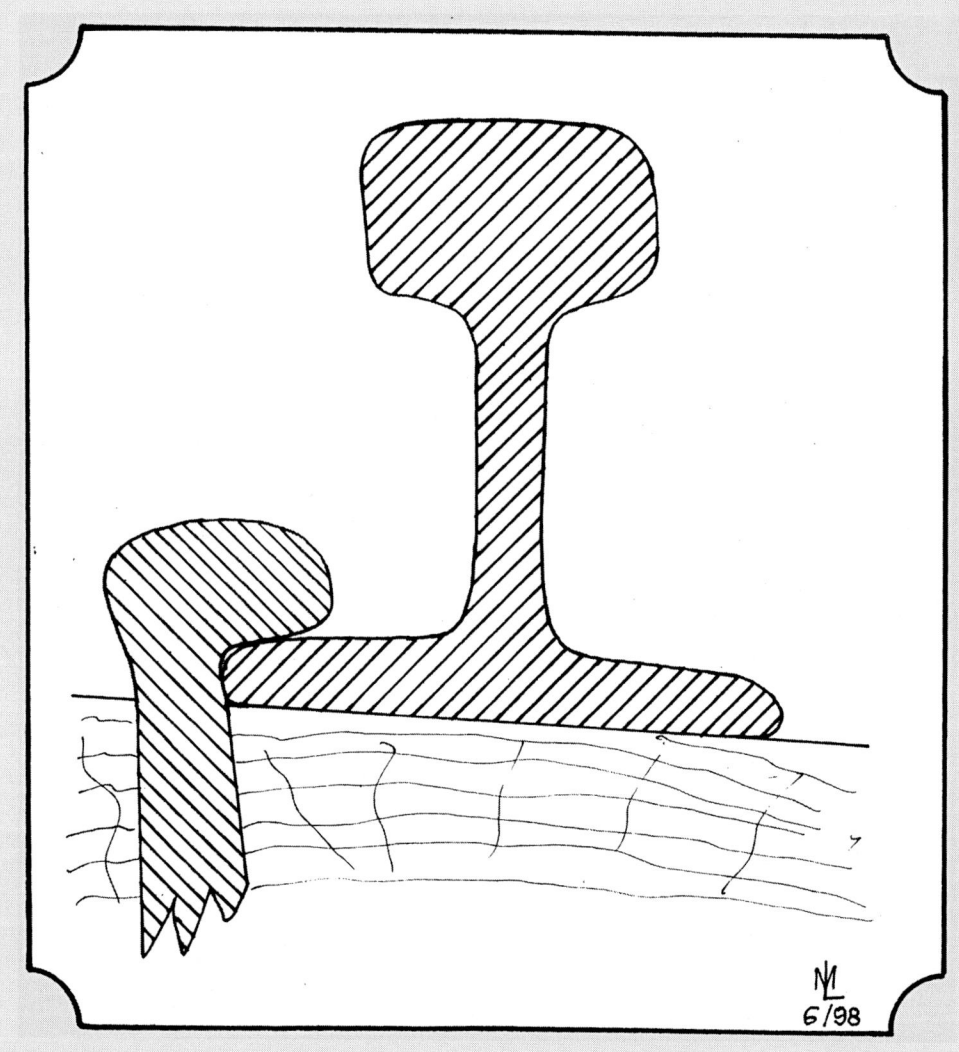

Chapter Seventeen

Permanent Way

It has already been noted that the Commissioners of Public Works in Ireland had appointed H.U. Townsend to hold an Enquiry as to the original intentions of the promoters and to make a Report thereon; this duly appeared dated 29th January, 1884.
The Promoter's intention was to use:

Steel rails - Flat-bottomed, weight 45 lbs. per yard, 30 ft length. [Later amended to 60 lbs.]
Sleepers - Baltic red-wood, creosoted; 6 ft length, 8 in. wide, 4 in. deep.
Fastenings - One ⅝th in. fangbolt at each end + eighteen dog-spikes per rail except on steep gradients.

The Contractor had actually installed:

Rails - Flat-bottomed, 30 ft length, 45 lbs. per yard (much second-hand from C&BR).
Sleepers - Mainly untreated Larch: 10 per rail.
Fastenings - Dog and Fang spikes.
Ballast was glacial gravel.

The Light Railway Investigation Committee of 1921 produced its findings, they were:

Ballast - gravel: Sleepers - 6 ft x 9 in. x 4½ ins., laid at 1,760 per mile. Much of the foregoing were replacements and some of the rail was now 55 lbs. per yd. The Committee accepted a maximum grade of 1 in 30 [obviously their figures were taken from the questionnaire they had circulated, and no personal visit had been made]. Minimum curves were said to be 2 chains radius; permitted and actual axle loading was 5 tons. Whilst the authorised maximum speed was 12 mph, in practice this was 10.7 mph.

[It is interesting to compare these standards with those adopted by CIE since 1945 as the recommended for Irish 3 ft gauge lines; these became 60 lbs./yd rail for an axle loading of 10 tons on which the permitted maximum speed was 25 mph: 50 lbs. was the previous figure].
The LRIC of 1921 recommended a 65 lbs. rail in future, but where axle weights were less than 10 tons, they accepted 50 lbs. Based on these findings, and even in view of the curves and gradients, the original track to carry an axle load of 5 tons, would have required 25 lbs rails. In the event, the materials laid down were heavier than this basic minimum . . ! [The calculations were based on Indian metre-gauge practice.]
Although there was persistent criticism of the sharp curves, the design and the construction of which was not to blame, the curves had been laid correctly but on a downhill run followed by a curve, the train would push the rails forwards and so sharpen the bend in front. A train in the reverse direction would not correct this, as its speed uphill would be insufficient.
Dorman's opinion was that untreated larch - if cut at the right season - was eminently suitable for sleepers, having three times the life (16 years) of Baltic red-wood; in any case he defended their creosote treatment, and said he was following Cork & Bandon Railway practice.

Occasionally, the subject merited recording in the Minute Book; in 1909 a portion of the line on curves at New Court was relaid in 55 lbs. rail and in January-June 1912 sixty-eight lengths of this rail were laid at undisclosed locations, probably on curves.

Possibly with the benefit of appeals to the Government for finance to renew some of the track, it was possible to purchase and relay with 260 tons of new rail (weight not given) in the period 1910-15. In 1916 120 yds of track was renewed at Hollyhill, again, over a curvaceous stretch.

To improve efficiency at a time when all the railways were under Government control, the Committee of Management enjoyed a change of structure and a new body, the Board of Management was set up, having its monthly meetings in Schull so recognising the primacy of location so far as Railway administration was concerned.

With a new broom sweeping clean, it was not long before the Board maintained that permanent way stocks had been allowed to fall to a dangerous level; 3,408 sleepers were required but only 11 were on hand. (This may have been due to wartime conditions.) One hundred tons of rail were now ordered, to cost £11 0s. 0d. per ton.

Under the GSR from 1925 and CIE from 1945, independence ceased and the Ballineen (exc.)-Baltimore and Bantry lines (5 ft 3 in. gauge) together with the S&SR were taken as one Division under Drimoleague of the Cork District Permanent Way Department.

All the foregoing comments applied to the S&S section 'main line' but not the Pier Extension which remained unaltered as first laid in 45 lbs. rails, with 3 ft sleeper centres, reduced to 2 ft 6 in. at joints. The formation width at track level was 9 ft with 10 ft in cuttings, on bridges etc.

In more recent times there was much upgrading of the track. All curves were check-railed; the rails were held down with coach-screws, dog-spikes being used in minor locations. Latterly base-plates had been inserted between rail and sleeper and to avoid widening of the gauge, a special base-plate incorporating a single raised 'clip' was used where advisable; the 'clip' secured the outer base flange of the rail.

A feature of the climate was the blanching of the sleepers which appeared like rows of the Biblical 'dry bones', having a ghostly white appearance; they had lost the benefit of their creosote treatment aeons ago.

On the roadside sections the rail-joints were staggered; it is said that this improved the riding of rolling stock. It certainly made the train *sound* as if it was travelling faster!

At some period the crossing-frogs (the originals must have been worn and unsafe) had been replaced with a one-piece casting. This was probably a GSR feature as the same type was also used on the Tralee & Dingle line.

In the last years ballasting might be described as 'little but good'. It was mainly of local river gravel (which lacked adequate binding properties), or poor slatey rubbish. In a few places good, broken stone was applied.

Drainage was done in the familiar Irish pattern, having a central open drain running along a depression between the rails, under the sleepers. This was quite effective. On other Irish railways this type of drain was self-creative; the sleepers were given ballast packing each end and the middle left hollow with the sleepers unsupported in the centre.

In a conversation with Mick McCarthy ('Mick the Fox'), the Foreman Ganger on the line, the Author learned that the track was weak because of the light rail and poor sleepering:

> It was much worse on curves. It was only recently we were allowed to add an extra ⅜in. to the gauge on curves, although we had been always asking for it. On curves, the outer rails became very worn and it was a heavy job to replace them.

I managed to have some sleepers sent - I think they came from the North - but they had been well used. We cut them to make two sleepers out of them but they were too short in this way. We tried double-spiking them but the cut sleepers were too light.

It was difficult to take out old sleepers; the hedge was too close at one end and the hard surface of the road at the other. So we left them there and just slipped in extra sleepers where we had to. So the track gradually became bad.

My father Denis was Foreman Platelayer for nearly all his life; he and his brothers were there for the building of the line. We got other jobs as well - occasionally we was put to firing. My father was living in Skibbereen in February 1950.

The old track had no plates under the rails and they dug into the wood; we got a lot from the Cork & Bandon Railway which made the track better but the plates were different sizes and we had difficulty in keeping them apart . . .

When we took out the old rails we sold them for 4s. 3d. a foot. When the Railway was taken up in 1953-54, some rails went to Bord na Mona. Of course by then, I was sent to work on the main line.

My father said the line cost £57,000 to build. They cut the ground first at Ballydehob and started on the viaduct there, and at Skibbereen the same moment. It was two years building. At one time there were forty men on the Railway.

This conversation took place in Mick's favourite Bar in Upper Bridge Street forty years ago. The Irish are compelling conversationalists and Mick's entertaining comment may be compared with Evans' Report of 15th May, 1906; things had not changed very much in fifty years: 'Under the circumstances it is a mystery how the (BoT) Inspector passed the line for the Contractor . . .' [He goes on to suggest the BoT failed in its duty in allowing an inefficient line to be passed fit for traffic.]

At the risk of repetition, Evans' Report of 2nd March, 1907 contained this paragraph :

Rails: Length 30 ft - Weight 46 lbs./yd
Sleepers: 10 per rail
Gradients: 1 in 25 and 1 in 30
Curves: 2-3 chains radius
Haulage limits: Small locomotives 40 tons - Large locomotives 60 tons
Quick curves are generally situated at the end of steep inclines.

Evans confirmed that it would not be possible to reduce the permanent way annual maintenance costs, then running at £70 per mile per year, so long as they were obliged to replace the original light rails and fit check rails on every curve. Thus the system was caught between the expense of working, the cost of maintenance and the limited capacity to convey more traffic, if such offered.

With the back-up of Evans' figures, the Committee of Management's submission to the Chief Secretary for Ireland on 15th May, 1906 stated: 'Our loss for the last twenty years is £23,329 11s. 4d. plus £56,814 18s. 10d. interest on capital - a total of £80,144 10d. 2d. We have spent £600 per year for maintenance purposes . . .'

It was in that same year (1906) that Harold Fayle, undoubtedly the doyen of Irish railways, made his first visit to West Cork.* He travelled in a four-wheeled carriage and noticed (possibly with envy) the newly-delivered bogie vehicle. He wrote, '. . . the movement of the coach was equal to a sea trip . . . and by no means smooth . . .' nevertheless, on looking back after his return, his verdict on the journey was, 'Recommended'.

---

* Fayle's Father was employed by the Irish Board of Works in Clonmel. He himself was then a student at Owen's College, Manchester (now Manchester University).

Mileposts

There was a post every quarter mile, situated on the right of the line proceeding from Skibbereen. The latter-day zero point was the buffer stop marking the end of the reversing neck there. The posts were of redundant lengths of rail.

Numerals were painted black on a yellow-painted metal sheet fixed to the post; each was shaped according to value. The full miles were square; the quarters were square but mounted in diamond fashion. At half and three-quarter miles a triangular shape was used, pointing upwards for the former and downwards for the latter.

This system was found on several Irish minor railways and was economical in that in the ultimate, only the numerals of the full miles required stating.

Permanent Way - Stock-taking 20th February, 1946 (verbatim)

New materials
Skibbereen
150 plain fishplates

200 sleepers

38 spikes
4 fishbolts
88 fangbolts

Old materials

110 plain 55lb. fishplates
120 angle 50lb. fishplates
24 plain 45lb. fishplates

83 washers
247 hookhead spikes

14 soleplates
(No sleepers)

Schull
800 hookhead spikes
200 nib-neck 5 in. fishplates
10 2-hole 75lb. fishplates
6 C&BR soleplates
7 crossing bolts
(No sleepers)

Formation
Width on open line 9 ft 0 in.
Width in cuttings 10 ft 0 in.

Chapter Eighteen

Miscellanea

Over the half century during which I have formed close associations with West Cork, there have been many reminiscences, conversations and situations surrounding this subject which were noted down at the time in the hope of further attention. Some were legendary, others biased, a valuable few were personal but all gave me an insight as the ethos of the local people in relation to their railway.

Bearing in mind that during those fifty years the line has closed completely and many of my informants have passed away, their memories have been set down here as a worthy of record. Such recollections do not fall neatly into the pattern of the previous pages, so form a chapter entitled Miscellanea.

****

You were asking me about the men who worked on the track, and who lived in the crossing houses?*
There were two sets of men: one between Skibbereen and Ballydehob and the other went from Ballydehob to here. Denis McCarthy (or 'Foxey Din' as we called him on account of his red hair), his son Mick (he went on the broad gauge when the S&S closed), and Batty Harrington. Sometimes Paddy O'Donovan would help them.
From Ballydehob we had Connie O'Sullivan, Jackie Daly (who was the Foreman for the whole line) and Gerry McCarthy, who was known as 'Vanderbilt' from the careful way he had with money.
Then at the Skibbereen workshops there was Charlie Murphy the chargehand/fitter and Willie Cottam, the carpenter.
I don't remember about all the gatehouses - Mrs Connor was in Kilcoe and Hollyhill was occupied by two men; they may have been gangers. When the railway closed, the occupants were given the first opportunity to buy.

Timothy O'Donovan was the last man at Skibbereen to be involved with the loading of the S&S goods train. The vans were not marked in any way (with the customary method of writing messages, dates, destinations, etc. in chalk on the outside, as used elsewhere) but were loaded in relation to their position *vis-a-vis* the locomotive. 'Sundries' were put in the first van i.e. flour bags, hen meal, cattle feed: a van was kept for beer, etc. barrels, and the empty casks in return. Awkward loads such as farm machinery had to go in a separate vehicle, as did barrels or boxes of fish in ice. Packages, parcels and perishable foods travelled in the van under the eye of the guard.
Timothy recalled that during The Emergency coal was not shipped into Schull, it came in main line wagons from Cork; with it many old sleepers went to Schull for lighting up the locomotive.

In the long school holidays, mother used to send us children out with a large tin bath of the sort we used in front of the open fire in winter. On reaching Schull station we, and the bath, would ride the first train, to drop off at the best places and comb the fields for mushrooms, only stopping when the bath was full.
Then, dragging the unwilling receptacle behind us, we would bring it to the road alongside the railway, and so back to Schull again on the returning train . . .

Some of the stations were little more than open shelters. They were popular places for the local urchins to scrawl graffiti in either whitewash or paint, and for the politically

---
* Reminiscences of Mrs P. McCarthy of Schull.

motivated to vent their opinions of the Government; the latter usually contained condemnation of the ruling party's policies on the railways of West Cork. The walls were used as bill-boards, advertising a forthcoming auction, the visit of a circus or a portrait of a candidate for local election. It was fruitless to look for a timetable of trains . . !

Following the closure, reliable witnesses of the Railway's operations became scarce. Tales of the line survived though, often growing with the telling; such tales tended to contradict one another.

John Browne of Creagh and his wife, the local school-mistress, had many personal links with the S&SR as John's sister Eileen was married to Daniel Creedon, then Manager, at Shandon Church, Cork on 10th September, 1908. (Daniel was previously with the Cork & Macroom Direct Railway, becoming S&SR Manager in 1904. His father Timothy was Manager before him; Daniel died in 1924.)

Daniel Creedon appropriated part of carriage No. 1 for his own use so that it was widely known as 'The Manager's Saloon'; his young brother-in-law often travelled with him. If it happened that the Manager wished to travel, the mixed train would be made up accordingly and 'his' carriage marshalled at the end. If, on the return from Schull, the train was too long for the reversing neck at Skibbereen, the guard would divide it behind the passenger coaches; this section went ahead into the neck while Creedon in his coach and a string of vans would left at the roadside until it was convenient for the engine to collect them. Browne continues:

> The Secretary of the Company [William Goggin] owned a bar at the corner of the main street [of Skibbereen] and that to the station . . . it was very convenient for those going by train.
> When the Directors wished to visit Skibbereen they ignored the Railway and used a converted Lancia armoured car, the property of one of their number. On alighting at the Skibbereen office, there would be fussing and genuflexion akin to a royal visit.
> The curb-stone margin which divided the Railway from the highway in numerous places, was a considerable barrier. A party of my friends attended the Ballydehob Fair in an open car. On the return journey the driver was 'very happy', misjudged a bend and struck the curb. The damaged vehicle had to be abandoned. The revellers walked back to Skibbereen, leaving the car to block the passage of the first Up train from Schull. However, the combined efforts of all the passengers and crew were needed to drag the wreck back to the road.
> It was the fish traffic which was second only to the carriage of livestock. I remember the different speech of girls from Donegal, Isle of Man, Scotland and Cornwall who came on to us at Baltimore from Schull to gut and pack the fish in ice or salt. A speciality was the 'Corned Mackerel' which was sent to the USA. All the work was done in the open on Schull Pier and the barrels put into vans on the Extension there.
> There were certain days which I remember especially because like all my school friends, a ride on The Tram was a very special treat - there was nothing to equal it in those times. Sometimes there would be as many as 25 trucks of cattle on the back of the train. Before the train could go into Skibbereen, it had to divide in the roadway. On the day of Schull Regatta it was worst of all, with utter confusion on the roadway at Skibbereen station and people jumping off the train before it stopped, falling down on the muddy road . . . there would be horses and carts too, all in a jumble.
> There was some shunting to do at Hollyhill and for a prank someone unhooked the Guard's Van; it was left behind with the guard shouting after the engine.
> About the water tank at Kilcoe station; they had it moved down to the river at the Crooked Bridge where they could get more water. They had to go slowly down from Kilcoe station anyway, so it was no bother to stop at the tank at the bottom . . . they would get up the other side all right.
> Tom Kelly, had the pumps in Ballydehob.* His father was a Director and his father's brother was the Station Master at Ballydehob. If the Directors had a meeting in Cork, on return they would go straight off the CB&SC train and into the West Cork Hotel, even if The Tram was waiting. The Tram was not allowed to leave until they had finished.

* He meant that the petrol pumps were outside Kelly's stores in the main street.

Willie Salter of Castletownsend said that a pony and trap from Skibbereen often reached Ballydehob before the train; it was better that way if you were in a hurry. He would see passengers getting out near Crooked Bridge or Church Cross to give the train a push.

Regular supplies would travel in the little van No. 5 attached to the end of the mixed train. These included large wicker hampers of bread from Thompson's of Cork, long cardboard boxes of sausages from Dennys and similar suppliers in that city. In the days before road transport and freezers, regular and daily delivery was essential. On certain photographs of Schull station, Thompson's empty hamper may be seen, awaiting return.

Bread and sausages shared the van with the occasional passengers for whom there was limited 'overflow' accommodation. The van also contained the wet batteries for the lighting, as the oil lamps and later gas system had been abandoned. Some vehicles were fitted with electric lights, and these received power from the van via jumper cables between vehicles. In the Autumn of the year there was a minor panic to make the lights function.

In its day the Railway was a source of wonder to the children of Ballydehob. Living in a rural area without such benefits of life-style as were common-place in England, the children used to gather eagerly in the school playground as the train made its noisy and slow progress up the gradient from the viaduct, so close that they could almost touch it. In dark evenings fire and smoke would issue from the chimney and the outline of the footplate crew was silhouetted against the darkness by the glow from the firebox. It was magic, and the teacher could not prevent attention wandering outside the class-room windows.

In holiday-time the children would take half-pennies and lay them out on top of the rails for the wheels of the train to squash and enlarge them to penny size. Then, at twilight they would hasten to Martha Roycroft's small shop at the end of Staball Hill hoping they might buy a pennyworth of sweets with their amended coinage. The proprietor did not light her oil lamp until it was almost completely dark and in the dim light which preceded, many a penny's-worth of sweets was obtained for half that sum.

Most of the older boys in the district had taken illicit rides on the train by hanging on as it left Skibbereen and then dropping off onto the adjacent road. It was easier still at Schull where the train's slow pace allowed one to hang much further. Ballydehob, which had no roadside, had its dangers as to drop off into the boscage meant cuts and bruises.

The excitement of taking a legitimate journey in The Tram was often so intense that children could not go to sleep on the night previous to travelling. We may imagine the feelings of whole families on their way to emigrate from Queenstown (Cobh), making perhaps the first - and last - journey by train; they might be counted in dozens.

> I remember on one occasion I was on The Tram and a donkey had got onto the line. We must have chased it for at least a couple of miles, with the driver shouting and throwing lumps of coal at it. All to no purpose and it eventually went off itself, unharmed.
>
> I can also remember running beside The Tram, holding onto the hand-rail at the end and being rebuked by my mother.

These two brief reminiscences of a Naval Captain and an Army Colonel of their boy-hood demonstrate the lasting child-time impressions The Tram left with them . . . and to many others.

Like all children, the boys of Ballydehob found the platelayers' trollies irresistible. A lady in Cambridge, Massachusetts wrote about her father (born in The Skames in 1900). Her father and some small boys recalled a 'small hand-cart' [sic] which was kept near the station and used by the platelayers. 'When Mr Crocker, the station master, was not alert the small boys, led by Connie Sullivan, the acknowledged leader of the group because his father, Jack, worked on the railway, were able to steal off the cart. They would push it by hand towards Schull, getting the cart about one mile above the station. Then the boys would pile on and off they'd go down the hill past the station and up the hill on the far side until, caught by gravity, back would come the cart again at such breath-taking speed that it would rocket across the viaduct, then run back through the station.

Mr Crocker would come out to see the speeding cart and sometimes shoot with a gun, always in the air and never to do any harm. He was a good chap, and we took advantage of him at the time . . .'

Timothy O'Donovan's recollections of former days at Schull station re-live the life and times of the line:

> We would load large wooden crates, painted green, of butter into the vans; at that time butter was the county's biggest export. Then there was the cattle, herded into vans here with great commotion by the drovers. Most had been here all the previous night, and not all the cattle could be fenced so they roamed everywhere and had to be coaxed back to the station by men with heavy sticks. Most of the beasts were put on ship at Cork, bound for the English markets, the West Country in particular.
>
> The engine would go down to the pier when a coal boat came in from South Wales, and drag the loaded coal wagons up to the station. They started buying coal from Holland and when the last war started and they could not buy coal from places then occupied by Germany, and Welsh coal could easily be sold without bringing it here, it left us very short. The engine driver had to go round begging for old sleepers, turf - anything that would burn. The train frequently stopped for want of steam.

The landing of household and railway coal by ship was a cross-channel not a coastwise competing trade. Smaller tonnages in small sailing vessels would land at ports at along the south Irish coast. Frequently the skipper bought the cargo from the owner at the port where loaded, and where no buyer was specified, on landing at Schull (for example), he would go into town to sell his cargo to persons with whom he did the business regularly. Meanwhile the crew made re-acquaintance with the young ladies of the place, and marriages often resulted.

At ports ample warehouse accommodation was made for storing the coal and where difficulties existed, the coal was loaded into lighters to be towed to a discharge point (Skibbereen quays, for instance after haulage up the Ilen or, as at Castletownsend, for haulage up Castle Haven where the lighter was beached and unloaded into carts. Hulks of old lighters littered certain Co. Cork anchorages).

A typical instance on record is of the discharge of skipper-owned Forest of Dean coal boat from Lydney at Castletownsend Pier in 1923; the selling price was £2 2s. 0d. per ton ex-ship).

> The men preferred the Welsh coal; it was hot and not so smoky.
>
> Schull Regatta was our busiest day; I believe it started around 1884 as part of the Gaelic Athletic Association activities. It attracted people who were not seen at any other time. For instance, we had to lock the ne'r - do - well vagrants and their 'hurdy-gurdies' (only one instrument could fit in each vehicle) in the van to prevent trouble. Drink was especially plentiful and barrels of it would be rolled off the train at any desired point on the line - the train crew joined in the sprit of the occasion. (The founding of the GAA in 1884 had the effect of creating a nationalistic movement. The S&SR felt a fortunate repercussion in the need for better transport for teams and their supporters, and the then infant Tramway benefited accordingly. Local clubs quickly sprang up in the district but perverse as it was, to some extent it died just as quickly around Schull. The West Cork Railway was imaginative and promoted the GAA football game, offering a competitive Shield. It still exists as The Railway Shield.)

MISCELLANEA

The mention of drink reminds me that although there was a station house at Schull, the Station Master, both here and in Ballydehob, lived at pubs in the town. The guard lived in the Schull house. The engine got into the pit several times when the Cleaner forgot to turn the table ready for it to come out of the shed. The wheels would hang off the end and they would have to build up with wood to put them on again [using a sleeper crib and the jack off the engine - Author].

Denis Sheehan was our last porter in Schull.

They say that the copper went to Swansea without coming on the railway; there was an overhead cable-way from the mine to landing place. Some of the new houses have been built over the shafts which seems a bit risky. J.F. Sullivan was once the Payclerk at the Dreelamone Copper Mine.

In the 1930s I replaced the steam-raiser at Schull who had been sacked. The reason for his dismissal was his inventiveness; the Schull engine water tank was filled by hand-pump and in dry summers there was always a shortage of water. Being something of a handyman, he contrived a tank connection with the town mains supply so saving himself much pumping.

Some time later the GSR received an unexpected bill for water at Schull at a time when there was severe rationing. The ruse was detected and the man sacked there and then.

The man who told me this story was an engine fireman during The Emergency;* one day he was rostered to fire on an empty Ballydehob Fair Day Cattle Special. It was a time when the shortage of coal was most serious, and the engine was piled high with hard-won turf on every convenient place. As was the usual experience, most of the turf had been consumed ('burned' is not an appropriate word) by the time they reached Ballydehob. They contacted the Skibbereen foreman-cum-fitter Charlie Murphy who arrived in Ballydehob much later with a road-truck piled up with further turf.

Charlie returned with them on the footplate and they took the opportunity to refresh themselves at each convenient rail-side bar. They reached Skibbereen again just twelve hours after they left it.

As a post-script to this last cameo, we learn that it took place in 1943 with loco No. 4. Jack Murphy was the driver. (Jack was nick-named 'Sergeant' after driving with the Railway Protection Brigade during The Civil War.) His fireman was John V. Ryan. They were sent to Skibbereen for this one turn.

Charlie Murphy had been adjusting the brakes on No. 4 and one cause of all the turf being used up was that the brakes were still tight when they left Skibbereen. Turf consumption was far worse than usual, for the engine had an open wagon attached to it, also piled high with turf. Much of this went up the engine's chimney, unburned . . .

John V. Ryan, a fireman from off the CB&SC section who would be sent to work on the S&S section from time to time, complained to Charlie Murphy the fitter that the wheel flanges were covered in grease on his engine, (making it liable to wheel-slip in the most unsuitable situations).† Charlie, being a man of means and a fitter quite used to meeting any problem, made John a makeshift scraper and sent it along to John with this message: 'Don't think this is a silver spoon for your soup - use it to scrape grease off wheel flanges'.

When electricity came to West Cork, gangs of men could be seen digging the holes for the posts which were to carry the wires. Some of these were alongside the Railway where it ran along the roadside. A 'busy-body' of the Gentry class was riding by and reined-in her horse; at that moment the men were digging a hole in which to bury a donkey, killed by a train that same morning.

Rider: 'Young man, just what are you doing?'

---

* The Irish term for the period of World War II.
† It is not clear whether this grease was the customary product of engine oil and grit from the trackside forming a 'gooey' compound, or whether the practice of greasing the rails on the sharpest curves was still in vogue!

Young man (imitating her style of enunciation): 'We're digging an ass-hole, ma'am.'
[A story which in fact, might have come from an old copy of PUNCH.]

Elsewhere it is explained that a second engine was steamed at Schull for Market, Fair Days, etc. when the early morning special train ran for livestock purposes and carry their drovers. This train slaughtered many an animal left to graze overnight on the roadside. It appears that on the afternoon before the special was due to run the next day, Curly Hegarty the Schull driver would have raised steam in the second engine shedded there and driven it to Skibbereen; it would then require little attention when it left Skibbereen in the early hours of the following day, hauling the empty cattle train.

****

Coming off the main line train from Cork, ladies travelling alone were obliged to sit in the empty, non-heated carriages of 'The Tramway Train' - often in the dark - knowing that the train crew and other passengers were enjoying the light and warmth of some Skibbereen hostelry. Summing up courage, they might enquire of (say) the signalman as to when The Tram might be going. The reply was always the same: 'They'll be off whenever they're ready. The Station Master would be sent up the street to hurry them up; it was more than time to start. There would follow a mad scramble to start the train with men who had refreshed themselves well trying to climb onto the carriage platform while the train was moving. The driver would stop the train anywhere, especially for his friends and the Directors; often the Directors would all travel together in a saloon carriage.'

****

'During 'The Emergency' and I was a young teacher alone on The Tram, it never left to time and so it was often dusk when we set out from Skibbereen. The lights in the carriages would not work. They had little coal in those days and the engine would be packed with turf to dry it before it went on the fire. The hill at Church Cross was always too much for the engine and we would stop there in complete darkness as the men threw old sleepers and turf in to make extra steam. We would then move, but after a few yards we would stop again. It was all rather frightening.'

****

'The Tram always went very slowly and never fell off the rails at the points. The trains on the Cork line fell off frequently.'

****

'The Tram got a new lease of life when the Irish Government introduced petrol rationing in 1944.'

****

Overheard from breathless lady arriving at Schull station some time after the train should have left, on seeing it was still at the platform: 'Better to know ye're there, than "Where are ye?"'

Chapter Nineteen
Personalities

Like most of Man's achievements, a subject is recalled and judged by the people connected with it. A school's merit can be exaggerated by the good friends made in childhood; a business condemned by the reputation of its Directors; a Football Club made suspect by a rapid change of Managers . . . and so on.

The S&SR was no different. It is remembered not so much for its technicalities - adequately covered herein - but by the characters of the men who served it. Would that we knew more about them.

Augustine Francis Cruise [Cruize] (1855-1945)

Probably the best-known and longest-serving employee, he was born to John and Helena (Ellen) Cruise (née Robinson) on 1st June, 1855 at 66, Gas Street, Rugby, Warwickshire and was one of triplets. On his Birth Certificate his Father is described as 'Engine Driver'. The family address was 3, Railway Terrace, Rugby, a property still extant: Helena was the first trained Catholic school teacher in Rugby following the Catholic Emancipation Act 1829.

He is likely to have joined the LNWR at Rugby; as his father he became an engineman, but is unlikely to have progressed further than fireman in the slow promotion of those days. Next he is found to be an engine driver on the Severn Tunnel construction* where he met and married Sarah Ann Jackson, daughter of one of the sub-contractors and born in Bideford 1856. It was she who scotched his idea of going to Turkey; instead they moved to Ireland in 1882; a son, John, was born in 1882 in Co. Clare, and another, Augustine II, in Monnypenny, Co. Wexford in 1884. Augustine was probably a driver at each place.

In 1885 he moved to Schull as first driver on the Tramway; he served for over forty years and retired to Cardiff about 1930. He died, aged 89, at 25, Ferndale Street, Cardiff on 24th January, 1945.

Augustine Francis Cruise II (1882-1938)

Augustine's second son carried his father's name and was apprenticed on the Railway from 1897, becoming an Engine Fireman. In Autumn 1904 he decided to better himself and obtained a good testimonial from his employers in October 1904; from September 1904 to February 1905 he became 'Mechanic and Engineman' to The Simplex Copper Extraction Co. Ltd (Ireland), of Schull but lost that post when that employer closed down. The mine re-opened and between February 1906 and June 1907 he worked for the successors, Coosheen Minerals Ltd of Schull, in charge of 'Winding Engines, Suction Gas Engines and Plant, also as a practical Fitter'. The mine then closed again, and he left Ireland to work with brother John in Grangetown Gasworks, Cardiff but emigrated to the USA in 1912. Married, he returned to Schull but finding circumstances unsuitable, a return to Cardiff and the Gasworks was made. He died in 1938.

---
* Severn Tunnel. At the time of the WCT opening it was incomplete; it first opened for goods traffic on 1st September, 1886.

Railway employees on Schull station c.1899. (left to right) Augustine Francis Cruise II (fireman), ? (probably porter), Patrick Barrington (Guard), Daniel O'Donovan (Station Master - seated), Augustine Francis Cruise I (Senior driver), ? (probably porter), ? (engine cleaner etc.), Locomotive No. 4; note absence of platform roof and carriage shed.   *Collection James Cruise/JICB*

Francis Cruise ['Frank'] (1900- ?)

The youngest son of Augustine II, and born in Schull, he joined the Great Southern Railways and eventually became a driver on the former CB&SC section, firing and then driving over the S&S section from time to time, the third family member to do so. He had also worked on the Cork & Muskerry and Cork, Blackrock & Passage sections until they closed in the 1930s. He retired about 1960.

The Cruise Family still retains its links with Schull.

Personnel

At the outset it is admitted that it has been impossible to confirm the accuracy of the following lists. There are differences between the verbal and printed sources used by the Author who nonetheless hopes it will go some way to satisfying the obvious interest of local people in the activities of their forebears.

As examples of the difficulty, the first train's crew is recorded as Augustine Cruise (driver), Denny O'Brien (fireman) and James Copithorne (guard) but neither fireman nor guard with these names is recalled elsewhere. Was once enough?

Incidentally, Copithorne 'had been rewarded with the job because of his partially successful efforts in placating the Skibbereen jarveys, who looked upon the project with suspicion and not a little hostility' (CORK EXAMINER).

PERSONALITIES

West Carbery Tramways Directors 1883-1892

Thomas H. Somerville
Richard Carey   Manager, Munster Bank, Skibbereen. Pioneered the Baltimore fishery. The only Director to serve continuously.
John J. Johnstone   Engineer, West Cork Railway.
John Limrick JP   Union Hall.
Capt. A. Morgan
Dean Reeves   Dean of Ross.
John S. Levis TCD   Doctor, Glenview, Skibbereen. Member of Skibbereen Union. Pioneered the Baltimore fishery.
J. Ralph H. Becher JP   Lough Ine. Member of Skibbereen Union.
G.H. Swanton

Secretaries
Edward H.Dorman   Secretary to Cork & Bandon Railway. Secretary of Ilen Valley Railway. Brother of J.W. Dorman, Civil Engineer to Cork & Bandon Railway.

C.T. Oliffe
C. Macdonald

Solicitor
Thomas Downes   Offices in Skibbereen and Dublin.

Registered Office
1886:   60 North Street, Skibbereen.
1887:   54 South Mall, Cork.

Schull & Skibbereen Railway - Committee of Management 1892

Patrick Hegarty, Schull	1913-1914. Schull RDC.
John O'Driscoll, Schull	1914. Schull RDC, Chairman.
Jasper Travers Wolfe, Skibbereen	1914. Crown Solicitor, Skibbereen.
Edward 'Ned' Roycroft, Mt Gabriel, Schull	1900-1914. Cork C.C., Chairman, Committee of Management, Chairman.
John H.Kelly, Skeaghanore, Ballydehob	1900-1914. Cork C.C. Chairman, Schull RDC.
William O'Regan,* Aughadown	Not before 1913. Schull RDC.
W. Wood Wolfe, Skibbereen	Not before 1913. Confectioner, Skibbereen.
Patrick Collins, Skibbereen	Not before 1914. Draper, Skibbereen.
Henry Cullinane†	1900 (Chairman) -1901. Skibbereen.
Daniel Burke, Skibbereen†	1899-1909. Chairman, Skibbereen RDC.
Timothy Hayes†	1900 (only).
Peter O'Driscoll†	1903-1904; 1906-1907; 1909.
John Sheehy†	1903-1904; 1907; 1909.
Florence McCarthy, Crookhaven†	1901 (Chairman) Ballydehob. Cork CC from 1899.

* Father of Bernard O'Regan, Aughadown.   † Appointed by Cork County Council.

Cork CC Minute Books for 1899-1905 show appointments made to Committee of Management 9th August, 1900, viz: Florence McCarthy, Henry Cullinane, Edward Roycroft, Daniel Burke, John H.Kelly, Timothy Hayes.

Secretaries
W.L. Carey
William Goggin, Skibbereen

Solicitor
J.J.Healey, Skibbereen

Manager
Timothy Creedon (until 1904)
Daniel Creedon (latterly with SKIBBEREEN STAR newspaper)
W.H. Loane

Engineer (from 3rd December, 1901)
Richard Evans (not a residential appointment); previously Armstrong.

Universal Directory of Railway Officials

Committee Of Management, 1922

Wm. J. Roycroft	Clerk Of Union	Schull
P. Hegarty		Lawerton
Tim O'Mahoney		Goleen
James Duggan		Skibbereen
Patrick Walsh		Skibbereen
Patrick O'Driscoll		Caheragh
Secretary: W.Goggin	Bridge St	Skibbereen
Solicitors: Jos. J. Healy & Co.		Skibbereen
Gen. Manager: Daniel Creedon		Skibbereen
Tel. Address: The Terminus		Skibbereen
Engineer: Richard Evans	53 South Mall	Cork
Traffic Auditor: W.H. Loane*		Skibbereen

* Later General Manager

Employees

Drivers

Augustine Cruise, Schull	
Cornelius Hegarty ('Curly'), Schull	Ex-Fireman.
Jack Daly, Skibbereen	Main line driver frequently rostered to S&S section. Often drove Fair Specials from Skibbereen.
Dan Hallihane, Bandon	Main line driver frequently rostered to S&S section.
Frank Cruise, Cork (?)	Main line driver frequently rostered to S&S section.
Jack McCarthy, Tralee	Main line driver frequently rostered to S&S section. Drove last train on S&S section.
Dave Higgins	Main line driver frequently rostered to S&S section.
William Lombard, Kinsale	Main line driver frequently rostered to S&S section.

Other loco men included: Michael Cronin, Dave McCartney, Dick Nagle.

Firemen

Danny O'Brien, Skibbereen	Fireman on first train.
Amos O'Reilly, Schull	
Augustine Francis Cruise, Schull	
Cornelius Hegarty, Schull	
James McCarthy, Skibbereen	Jack Daly's fireman.
Charles O'Donovan, Creagh	
Thomas Devane	
John V. Ryan	

PERSONALITIES

*Guards**
James Copithorne, Ballydehob	Son of Hackney driver. Guard of first train.
Patrick Barrington, Skibbereen (?)	
James Florence O'Sullivan, Schull	Known as 'Jimmy the Guard'; later Station Master at Schull.
Jack Con O'Driscoll, Schull (?)	
James Stack	
Daniel McCarthy, Skibbereen	Known as 'Big Dan'
Denis Sheehan, Schull	Porter at Schull; last guard.

Station Masters - Schull
Michael O'Sullivan	
James Daly	
Daniel O'Donovan	Became General Manager in 1924.
James Florence O'Sullivan	See also under Guards.

Station Masters - Ballydehob
James Daly	Later at Schull.
James P. Swanton	
Cornelius Kelly	
Daniel Ducey	
Daniel Bradley	

Station Masters - Skibbereeen†
James Neale
Patrick Slattery
William Whalley
John W. Loane
Thomas Barry

Landowners - Intermediate Stations ('Haltkeepers')
William Trinder, Church Cross
Jeremiah O'Driscoll, Hollyhill
William Nolan, Kilcoe

Skibbereen Workshops
Patrick Murphy	Fitter
Charles Murphy	Foreman Fitter
Michael Cottam	Joiner/Carpenter

Permanent Way
Denis McCarthy	Foreman Platelayer
Michael McCarthy	Foreman Platelayer

† Shared with main line station.

Many of the foregoing are mentioned in more detail in the text.
These lists have been compiled from personal contact and are known to be incomplete. Amplification/correction would be welcomed by the Author c/o The Oakwood Press.

* Initially 'conductors'.

Appendix One
Waterborne Competition and Coastal Shipping

There were a number landing places on the West Carbery coast at which a coastal shipping trade could be found. Roaring Water Bay was once dotted with vessels of all kinds, some on inter-island voyages and others making passage from such islands - or the seas beyond them to the principal anchorages in the district served by the S&SR; these would naturally include Skibbereen, Ballydehob and Schull but also a host of smaller quays which are largely deserted today save by small or pleasure craft.

Communication by sea was the backbone of transport long before the roads were tolerable and the railway envisaged. The difficulty now is to assess the volume of this well-established waterborne pattern and judge whether the S&SR would (and did) make any inroads into it. It must be concluded that a trifling amount of business by water was 'taken onwards' from small craft, mainly at Schull. Only Schull pier could accommodate larger coastal ships (sail or steam). Baltimore had facilities akin to Schull and both sent cargoes onward by rail. But ultimately, most of the coastal shipping business faded as the railway was more suited to smaller cargoes - a notable exception being coal.

Sand for fertiliser won from off-shore island beaches came up the Ilen on the flood tide, assisted by oar or pole, and by lug-sail when favourable. In the 1920s the business had become so small that none were employed full-time. There was revival in the 1930s and during The Emergency of the 1940s. An account of this shipping mentions the quays in Skibbereen in use then:*

Steam Mill Quay	(adjacent to the Ilen Street bridge)
Burke's Quay	(now part of the West Cork Hotel, car park)
Levis's Quay	(owner J.F. Wolfe)
Fuller's Quay or Long Quay	(adjacent to their merchant's yard)
Nagle's Quay	(off North Street)
Minihane's Quay	(off North Street)
Chapel Quay - site of	(now the site of the Public Library etc.)

Certain boats would carry gravel for building, and seaweed. Skibbereen quays were also the berths for ships which supplied the islands with domestic needs.

Coal boats could not reach Skibbereen and their cargoes were transhipped into lighters or carts at Old Court Quay; O'Regan of Aughadown and O'Neill of Church Cross imported coal but in these cases the coaster moored off Aughadown graveyard and coal was lightered into Reenaduna Quay for O'Regan, and Marsh Quay for O'Neill. So the tramway had nothing of the business. Steamer SS JANE anchored off Reenaduna in 1934 brought 214 tons coal; it was distributed by horse cart to Skibbereen, Aughadown and Kilcoe, and so the old methods prevailed.

Coal imports ceased with World War II and Fuller & Co.'s lighter which was 60-70 ft long and carried up to 70 tons, was the last to survive on the Ilen. O'Regan's last importation was 220 tons of coal into Reenaduna by the schooner INVERMORE, in July 1940.

The established coastal trade was badly hit in periods when the fishing industry was facing hard times. Fishing boats would then load cargoes in Cork and bring general merchandise into Old Court landing it at rates which undercut the established sea traders and naturally, competing railway services. This state of affairs reached a peak during the War of Independence (1916-21) and the Civil War (1922-23) when small ships came into their own, often manned by one or two men and making passages to which they were unaccustomed - and sometimes quite unfitted - in order to exploit the situation. They pirated the seas without the use of firearms. The closure of the CB&SCR and S&SR by Government Order and the intervention of the military brought an unexpected bonanza to these small ships, but their influence did not have much lasting effect on the railways as shipping was also prey to the road lorry.

---

* For much of the background information given here I am indebted to the MIZEN JOURNAL No. 5 1997 (p. 8 'Sands of Time': Cormac Levis), the Harbour Master at Schull, Kenneth Austin and Roy S. Fenton.

APPENDIX

The influence of shipping had little effect on the S&SR and the larger vessels had been withdrawn by their operators; the most important of these was the Clyde Shipping Co. of Glasgow who used the VALENTIA between 1890-1905 out of Cork city to serve the coastal fringe of Munster. Built in Dundee in 1890, it was sold in 1905, having several owners thereafter to be finally sold as a wreck in 1923. It was not replaced by the Clyde Shipping Co.* The VALENTIA made a weekly sailing, and its arrivals in Schull were most reliable. In consequence it had become the custom for Cork city merchants to load onto the VALENTIA at city quays; even goods for Skibbereen and around were sent this way, travelling the last 15 miles by S&SR. Non-perishable consignments which did not require speedy travel were very suited to this mode; it was dependable and inexpensive.

In the sea-girt land of West Carbery transport by sea enjoyed pre-eminence. Steam-driven coasters were more economical than a railway train; they spent a minimum of time lying idle and required a lesser number of men in relation to the tonnage carried. They could sail at all hours of the day and night and might load and discharge on a quay with the ship's own crane. Around the Cork coast the loads were similar all year round; such required predictable delivery but not necessarily, rapidity.†

At the period when the WCT opened, a sailing ship carrying 150-200 tons and manned by two men and a boy could cut costs by running onto a beach to avoid harbour dues. The Carbery coast boats carried sand, gravel, ballast, bricks, slate, bulk lime, or coal primarily; livestock was frequently shipped but might swim smaller distances.

Schull Pier was adapted more than once during the life of the S&SR. In 1899 the Clyde Shipping Co. complained that 'the piling on the new portion of Schull Pier will damage the plates of the VALENTIA'.#

As noted, Ballydehob was unsuited to larger vessels but there was a West Store and an East Store on the quay - the East long gone; both were built for storing corn during The Famine.

The most regular users of Schull and the Pier were the boats of the fishing fleet. The catch was mainly of herring which were salted and packed on the Pier by local girls and others from Donegal or Scotland who followed the fleet round the coast. The barrels were loaded on S&SR vehicles at the Pier and their loads dispatched to Cork and Dublin.

The pattern of fishing was: Monday - sail out. Tuesday - fishing. Wednesday - return. Thursday - unload; fish barrelled and put on rail. On Friday the fish would be sold still fresh, for eating on the Fast Day.

A business which was won from the sea traders was the carriage of potatoes to Cork and Dublin etc. for export. Potatoes had formerly been carried in 40-80 ton sloops; it was a trade peculiar to Co. Cork and Co. Waterford. A legacy of the Famine had been the shortage of cattle and therefore of manure; a substitute known as 'seawool' derived from seaweed was used instead. In season, the S&S carried potatoes for transhipment at Skibbereen; the trade was so demanding of field labourers at this season that the fishing fleet was reduced (most fishermen were small-time farmers themselves).

Among other shipping concerns active in the area:

WEST COAST STEAM SHIPPING CO. operated the SS ILEN which called at Cork, Oldcourt, Berehaven and Caherciveen. They also used the lighter THE PETRO between Oldcourt and Skibbereen.§

THE ILEN LIGHTER & TOWING CO. (1874) using the 1874 Skibbereen-built ANNIE S. Len. 50 ft x Beam 10 ft.§

SKIBBEREEN & WEST COAST STEAMSHIP CO. LTD. Inc. Dublin 11th November, 1871 to ply between Skibbereen and various (un-named) places on the West Coast of Ireland. (Did Company actually operate?)

BANTRY BAY STEAMSHIP CO. LTD. A subsidiary of the Cork, Bandon & South Coast Railway with railway association from 1881 when the Bantry Extension Railway was opened (authorised 1880). Operated mainly in and around Bantry Bay. In 1906 the Congested Districts Board built a pier at Glengariff, paying a subsidy to the BBSCo to run a steamer service. Ships: SS COUNTESS OF BANTRY: SS PRINCESS BEARA: LADY ELSIE. [A daily service - Sundays excepted - plied between Bantry & Castletownbere.]

* Built W.B. Thompson of Dundee; 3-cylinder steam turbine. 420 gross Tons. 165 net Tons. 156 ft len. x 24.6 ft beam x 11.2 ft depth. Became CORNUBIA 1906 (see CAMBRIAN COASTERS; R.S. Fenton).

† Ref: JOURNAL of the RAILWAY, CANAL & HISTORICAL SOCIETY Vol. 32 No. 166 March 1997 p. 245 for consideration of coasters and railways, (John Armstrong).

Ref: Minutes of Cork County Council October 1899, and Minutes of its Law & Finance Committee August 1899 re 'the old part of Schull Pier'.

§ A limited source of reference is in the Skibbereen Public Library.

The dominance of the fishing trade; the Manx fleet in Irish waters at Kinsale. 1898.
Collection J.I.C. Boyd

CLYDE SHIPPING CO. Operated a local steamer service between Cork and Dingle from 1876-1905; from 1890s one round trip each week calling Schull, Castletownbere, Bantry, Kenmare, Sneem, Castletownbere and Dingle, when and if cargo demanded. Subsidy paid by Congested Districts Board annually, 1901-1904; when ceased, steamer service withdrawn.
Ships included: RIO FORMOSA: FASTNET: ROCKABIL: SKELLIGS: VALENTIA. In 1878, a few trips were made by chartered vessels: VIKING: AGATE.

Sea communications during the Civil War (1922-1923)

In 1922 during August and September rail services in Co. Cork were affected by the fighting between Irish Free State and Irregular Army forces (see p. 92-95). Fishing prospects were unfavourable too and encouraged by the excitement and success of nocturnal gun-running, etc. some trawler owners turned to more peaceful cargoes in the mid-1920s. Among others CARBERY KING, CARBERY QUEEN and CHEERFUL MAID could be found alongside Cork city quays, loading for Castletownshend, Baltimore, Schull, Castletownbere, Adrigole and Kenmare and with their very low charges they could undercut the Railways. [A typical Schull boat was the HIBERNIA (Len. 60 ft; 46 gross tons, 29 net) built Arklow 1917, loading for West Cork at Union Quay c. 1926.]*
Also recalled, is '. . . the number of tiny steamers coming into Bantry, Castletownbere and other western piers from Russells, the Limerick millers. Their business was lost to Furlongs of Cork, who had large warehouses on Schull quay (managed by the O'Sullivans) and in Kenmare.'*
In short, the coastal railways of Co. Cork remained a one-time prey to maritime opportunists who, like a terrier dog nipping their ankles, could snatch cargoes as they appeared and transport and off-load them at minimal cost. But, like the railways, they were unequal to road competition.
In the early days of absorption by the GSR when drastic renewals to the S&S section track were needed, a ship berthed at Schull Pier bringing 400 tons of rails and fishplates for general relaying. These were brought up the Extension and given temporary storage space on the land between Schull station house and the Engine Shed. Harbour dues were paid at 1s. per ton. Sleepers arrived by the same ship [presumed to have come from a South Wales port - Author].
Bristol Channel schooners brought in South Wales railway coal at 100-150 tons per ship; harbour dues were paid at 1d. per ton.
Of the importation of coal on the Carbery coast there was general agreement that Lydney (Forest of Dean) shipments were preferred. Compared with 'the present foreign lignite rubbish, it has gold-yellow streak in it'. At Castletownsend (one of the harbours served) Mrs Kelly recalled the three regular schooners in the coal trade: KATHERINE & MAY (Capt. Stoneham: Master), ISALLT and EUGENE.

* Sources: IRISH PASSENGER STEAMSHIP SERVICES Vol. 2 p. 118 & 137 Reminiscences Barney Bennett. References: per Roy Fenton.

Appendix Two
West Carbery Mining and the Railways

An appropriate summary of the district around Schull was written by the Mines Inspector in 1841:

It is the wildest, poorest country I have ever met with . . . hardly anything but mountains and rocks and not even a blade of grass . . . no roads, no market nearer than Skibbereen, no employment for the people and their condition living in hovels amongst the rocks, cultivating little patches of land, indescribably wretched. At Coosheen Mine, 120 are employed, 40 of them young women . . . we have a lazy and good-for-nothing population . . . at times men are too weak to work through lack of food . . .

There was worse to come. An account of 1847 (a year of the Famine) says:

The people are living in filthy hovels not fit for pigs . . . of 26 families visited . . . seven are without any means on earth of subsidence . . . the remaining nine are all but starved . . .

These references throw a clear light on the appalling state of people in the mining district both before and after the Famine; during the Famine all mines seemed to have ceased work though many had re-opened in the early 1850s. Even when the prospect of a railway link to Cork became known there was little interest, and mining had entirely ceased by the time the S&S was conceived. Mine owners turned to the sea rather than the land for their transport needs, linking the workings by aerial ropeways to the coast. Copper, being the most important of the ores extracted, was shipped to Swansea but a decade before the S&S was completed, copper mining had finished (as it did in Cornwall about the same time). Barytes, lead, silver, and manganese were also found in small quantities.

Copper mining on Mount Gabriel can be traced back many hundreds of years. In the 19th century most of the miners, expertise and Captains came from Cornwall, local labour being confined to 'strong stout girls' who were employed on 'cobbing', knocking off the waste on small pieces of ore with a light hammer.

In an open quarry on the west side of Audley Cove, slate was obtained and in connection with it, a short, light tramway ran down to a pier. In 1837 Lord Audley, the local mines, etc. owner, employed 500 men in two slate quarries hereabouts; he sold out in 1852 but not before acquiring an evil reputation.

There are many promotional accounts in favour of building a railway to Schull and, in other references to the completed Tramway, where the potential of a railway to the mining industry is glowingly presented. Such bear remarkable similarity to the publications which stated the bright prospects for such-and-such a mine in order to attract venture-capital.

Many of the workings had short-lived spasms of activity and in account of IRISH MINERAL RESOURCES in the IRISH DAILY TELEGRAPH in 1873 there is strong criticism not only of the way finance was raised, but management at the site itself.

The mines themselves were often of the 'Jam tomorrow' category, whilst the potential of the West Carbery Tramway to serve them was simply notional.

Further reference: MINING JOURNAL 1856 p. 289 Mines of West Carbery.
MINING JOURNAL 1875 p. 551 Mining & resources of S.W. Ireland.

Cappaghglass Copper & Lead Mine site, Ballydehob. Looking south to Audley Cove and Roaring Water Bay.
J.I.C. Boyd

West Carbery Mines*

1.	Ballycummisk	Copper, open pre-1857; Ballycummisk Copper Mining Co. Ltd 1872: aban. 1878 at 1368 ft deep. Not worked again. (a)
2.	Cappagh†	Copper, open by 1827, Mining Co. of Ireland#. Great Cappagh Copper Mining Co. Ltd 1857, Cappagh Mining Co. Ltd 1869. aban. 1873. (b)
3.	Long Island	Copper.
4.	Audley Cove	Copper. (e)
5.	Audley Cove	Slate.
6.	Horse Island	Copper; open pre-1835. (d)
7.	Coosheen	Copper, Coosheen Copper Mining Co. 1852-57; Schull Bay Mining Co. 1858. aban. 1877. (c)
8-10.		Barytes workings.
11.	Scart	Barytes 1876-1908.
12.	Derreenatra	Copper open by 1843.
13	Coney Island	Copper.
14.	Gortnamara	Copper.
15.	(see 1.)	
16.	Ballydehob	Lead, Copper; South Cork Mining Co. 1852-6, open pre-1843; aban. 1864.
17.	Kilcoe	Copper; Mining Co. of Ireland in 1856; aban. 1864.
18.	Roaring Water	Copper, open pre-1844, Roaring Water Mining Co. etc. 1852, aban. 1871.
19.	Castle Island	Copper.

(a) Mine Engine & Chimney, engine built 18??
(b) Mine Engine & Chimney, first engine and chimney, 1826.
(c) Mine Engine & Chimney engine built 7/1860. 'railroad'. Started 1839.
(d) Mine Engine & Chimney by 1857.
(e) Mine Engine & Chimney by ?

* (Source; THE ABANDONED MINES OF WEST CARBERY: Cowman & Reilly (1988) Geol. Survey of Ireland).
† Listed occasionally as Ross Brin (under Welsh mines!)
# Later West Cork Mining Co. - also on Horse Island. Ballycummisk, Cappagh and Coosheen linked in the latter period.

Appendix Three

Tickets

Tickets were issued from the Booking Office at Skibbereen, Ballydehob and Schull, the foremost office being shared with the main line. At unstaffed stations and halts tickets were available from a rack in the guard's van. Colours of ticket varied according to the issuing point. Some public timetables included a footnote as to where tickets were available e.g. ABC RAILWAY GUIDE 1912.

The tickets were cancelled *en route* by the guard using the traditional 'hand nipper' from his pocket: the portion removed by the 'nipper' on the S&S section was rectangular with a semi-circular addition on one long side.

The 'Mystery Station' at Crooked Bridge mentioned by Newham, does not appear on any surviving ticket ... nor in any timetable.

A retired naval captain and friend of the Author wrote: 'When I was a small boy my mother and I with Sealyham dog travelled to Ballydehob on the tram, with the object of putting the dog to stud. At Skibbereen no dog ticket could be found but eventually she was given a bicycle ticket and the Booking Clerk said he was sure that it would do. It did'.

Charles Gordon Stuart was an authority on tickets; his findings were that the earliest were headed 'West Carbery Trams'. With change of title this became 'Schull & Skibbereen Tramway' and for stations off the system e.g. 'S&SLRY & CB&SCRY'. Colour distinction was applied from the beginning.

Stuart wrote that First Class tickets were:

White - issued at Skibbereen
White upper and Green lower - issued at Schull
Mauve and White - issued at Ballydehob

Third Class tickets employed an entirely different colour scheme.*

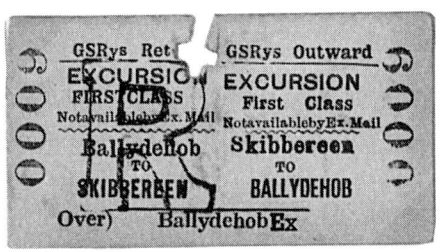 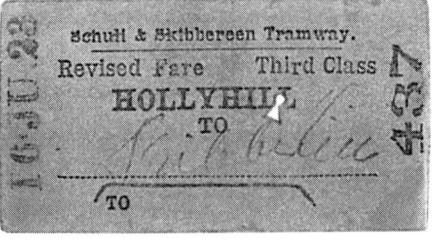

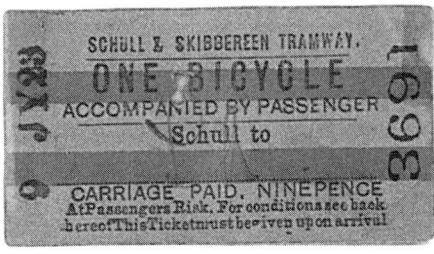 

* For a fuller account of the complexity of the tickets, see NARROW GAUGE RAILWAYS OF IRELAND, (H. Fayle), Greenlake Publications, [1946], p. 198.

Appendix Four

Accounts

Over forty years ago the former S&SR (office) premises were a sorry sight. They had been vandalised for every useful content, even including the floorboards; an auction of the site was pending. Evidently someone responsible had carefully kept the doors and windows locked of the Company's office and none of the window glass was broken.

The writer took the last opportunity to explore the almost lightless building and among the debris found a large discarded tome, entitled in full in gold leaf. Like all similar objects in a Counting House, whilst its owners might have been forced to indulge in penny-pinching tactics, nothing but the best would satisfy the Accountant. It was (and is) a substantial volume and it is curious that the Great Southern Railways did not claim it when they absorbed the system in 1925.

Any optimism felt by the writer as to how much the contents would reveal was quickly curtailed when the pages were found to be so torn that few were complete - decades of using the book as a source to light the office stove, re-light a 'dimp' or ignite a pipeful of shag, had taken their toll. Worse, the pages were obliterated by ink splodges and flattened bodies - a graveyard which entomologists and arachnidites might find valuable .

Despite the incomplete pages, it is possible to deduce that in the early 1900s:

Blacksmiths employed on permanent way repairs (Skibbereen blacksmith excepted) were paid through the local stationmaster. The Skibbereen blacksmith would be called upon to effect loco repairs, make ironwork for wagons, and pointwork, etc. It is likely that Schull engine shed had its own blacksmith.

Brakes equipment was supplied by the Vacuum Brake Co.

Locomotive Coal came from the Ebbw Vale Coal Co., South Wales. It would be shipped from Cardiff. A typical shipping charge would be £69 2s. 0d.

Thomas Fuller (later Fuller & Co, Skibbereen) sent men to perform various tasks including - wagon repairs, permanent way repairs, carriage upholstery repairs . . .

The Engineer and Secretary were paid monthly.

The Railway Timetable appeared in the *ABC Guide*, this cost the Company 5s. annually.

The Manager benefited from a bonus scheme linked to Traffic Returns.

Tangyes Ltd. of Hayle, Cornwall supplied pumps for the Company's own water system, and locomotive needs.

Office Rent (presumably 60, North Street, Skibbereen) £10 per annum.

Traffic Auditor was paid £10 year. (His duties are unclear.)

Rent for share of CB&SCR Station £31 5s. 0d. quarterly.

There are various payments to *Nasmyth, Wilson & Co., Dick, Kerr & Co., Gloucester Wagon Co.* which give no detail but show which suppliers have a current account.

Oil was bought in barrels from G.F. Vickery; when empty the barrels were sold for 2s. 3d. each.

Worn-out rails were sold locally in 2/3 lots; they raised £15 in six months.

Locomotive coal per Skibbereen. Captain Nolan was paid £39 10s. 1d. for a shipment (? landed at Old Court). The Company paid £3 19s. 4d. for cartage to Skibbereen station. Coal was bought at low summer prices; a shipment would last six months.

R. Perrott & Sons of Cork Iron Works contracted to repair locomotives on site.

Gloucester Carriage Co. New carriage, carriage of same December 1903. (The page is torn out.)

In 1907 the Manager received a bonus of 5 per cent due to traffic increase; the Engineer was paid £12 for inspecting sleepers; £531 3s. 1d. was spent with Dick, Kerr in keeping the tram engines operable; coal was bought from Powell Dyffryn Colliery Co. for £136. 2s. 0d. (sea freight £38 10s. 7d.)

Directors Messrs Roycroft, Kelly, O'Driscoll, Sheehy, Healey and Burke received £6 16s. 6d. each for January-June 1907.

In 1908 the following firms sent their employees to Skibbereen:

Nasmyth, Wilson	Patricroft	Locomotive repairs
Peckett & Sons	Bristol	Locomotive repairs
Bristol Wagon Co.	Bristol	Wagon repairs
Pickering & Co.	Wishaw	Wagon repairs
Metropolitan Wagon Co.	Saltley	Small carriage repairs

which reflects a desperate situation with which the Skibbereen workshops could not cope.

Isca Foundry, Newport sent a quantity of track materials; to save sea freight they were combined with a shipment of coal to Schull.

The EAGLE sent an account for printing excursion bills. 'The excursion produced no receipts' (this in red ink).

Permanent Way 1909. Heavy expense on rails (Isca) and English sleepers (Burt, Boulton & Heywood); eight men employed on relaying. Large amounts of old rail being sold. (Pencilled note states 'new locomotives need new rails'). Pointwork bought from Thomas Ward Ltd., Sheffield.

Pickering of Wishaw. A large sum (largely illegible) spent 1910. (Possibly new chassis/running gear for wagon rebuilding/building etc. of 1909-1912 period?)

Permanent Way 1911. Considerable relaying taking place. Burt, Bolton & Heywood supply quantities of sleepers. (They were shipping to the Isle of Man Railway also at this time.) Wards and Burkes were making new pointwork for local labour to lay.

In 1912 Captain Nolan continues to ship *coal* into Old Court for the railway; there may have been a crisis for £36 15s. 4d. was spent with the 'Timoleague Railway' in acquiring coal.

By 1913 the *Directors* still received £6 16s. 6d. for the half year. The Board comprised Messrs Roycroft, Kelly, Hegarty, Wolfe, Healey, O'Regan.

It has been possible to quote but a few of the entries from this much-damaged source. They provide a reflection of the people and businesses connected with this small railway, its Directors and employees in Cork city and county and its cross-channel links with South Wales, Gloucester, Bristol, Kilmarnock, Renfrewshire and Manchester which continued unbroken from the mid-1880s to the mid-1920s. Readers less interested in the technical background of the railway will find the foregoing a useful insight into the ecological and commercial benefits which the S&SR brought to West Carbery.

A yardstick to costs in the period is that new locomotive prices were often quoted on the basis of £100 per ton (e.g. S&SR locomotive ERIN might cost c. £2,300 ex-Works). The 22s. per week paid to the first driver was equivalent to wages paid in England, and a ten-hour working day was normal; only the Manager received a salary increase based on Traffic Returns. There was no such thing as wage-increases to meet the rising cost of living as in those times, inflation was almost unheard-of and deflation was not unknown.

S&SR Breakdown of Income *(All figures are £)*

July-December 1904

	Pass	Parcel	Goods	Cattle	Horse	Fish	ex-Line	Total
July	124	15	66	30	2	-	1	238
August	131	14	76	32	2	-	1	256
September	127	12	74	33	2	-	1	249
October	135	15	94	47	2	-	2	294
November	85	11	75	42	1	-	1	215
December	133	12	72	45	1	-	1	264
								£1,516

There is a heading 'Fish' but no entries.

The Schull & Skibbereen Tramway & Light Railway.

Abstract showing Receipts, Working Expenses, and Interest on Capital, since the Line opened for Traffic, September, 1886.

Half-year ending		£ s. d.	Loss to Baronies. £ s. d.	Half-year ending		£ s. d.	Loss to Baronies. £ s. d.
31st Dec., 1885 30th June, 1886 31st Dec., 1886	Interest on Capital Interest on Capital Receipts Expenditure	632 11 7 1,394 14 11	365 8 8 658 19 8	30th June, 1896	Receipts Expenditure Interest on Capital Loss on Working	1,081 1 0 1,613 16 0 682 15 0 1,425 0 0	2,007 15 0
30th June, 1887	Receipts Expenditure Interest on Capital Loss on Working	662 3 4 2,340 18 0	2,033 1 4	31st Dec., 1896	Receipts Expenditure Interest on Capital Loss on Working	1,246 1 6 1,724 6 3 479 3 9 1,425 0 0	1,904 3 9
31st Dec., 1887	Receipts—(not working from March to December, 1887 Expenditure Loss on Working	435 11 10 1,041 13 0 603 1 2 1,494 17 6	2,030 18 8	30th June, 1897	Receipts Expenditure Interest on Capital Loss on Working	1,046 9 8 1,532 5 9 485 16 1 1,425 0 0	1,910 16 1
30th June, 1888	Receipts Expenditure Interest on Capital Loss on Working	nil 443 14 6 442 14 6 1,424 17 8	1,867 12 0	31st Dec., 1897	Receipts Expenditure Interest on Capital Loss on Working	1,232 15 5 1,944 18 10 612 3 5 1,425 0 0	2,037 3 5
31st Dec., 1888	Receipts Expenditure Interest on Capital Loss on Working	736 16 3 1,176 1 9 439 5 6 1,424 17 6	1,864 3 0	30th June, 1898	Receipts Expenditure Interest on Capital Loss on Working	1,043 19 3 1,809 13 10 765 14 7 1,425 0 0	2,190 14 7
30th June, 1889	Receipts Expenditure Interest on Capital Loss on Working	977 3 8 1,034 8 8 157 5 0 1,425 0 0	1,582 5 0	31st Dec., 1898	Receipts Expenditure Interest on Capital Loss on Working	1,389 8 5 2,276 6 9 1,037 2 4 1,425 0 0	2,462 2 4
31st Dec., 1889	Receipts Expenditure Interest on Capital Loss on Working	489 19 4 1,425 0 0 995 10 4 1,591 16 4	1,914 19 4	30th June, 1899	Receipts Expenditure Interest on Capital Loss on Working	1,003 15 10 2,360 16 3 1,166 19 5 1,425 0 0	2,591 19 5
30th June, 1890	Receipts Expenditure Interest on Capital Loss on Working	598 6 0 1,425 0 0 1,178 19 5 1,667 8 9	1,951 6 0	31st Dec., 1899	Receipts Expenditure Interest on Capital Loss on Working	1,298 10 11 2,022 15 3 724 4 4 1,425 0 0	2,149 4 4
31st Dec., 1890	Receipts Expenditure Interest on Capital Loss on Working	494 9 4 1,425 0 0 1,051 2 2 2,306 18 0 554 15 10	1,919 9 4	30th June, 1900	Receipts Expenditure Interest on Capital Loss on Working	1,024 2 0 1,556 12 8 532 10 8 1,425 0 0	1,957 10 8
				31st Dec., 1900	Receipts Expenditure Interest on Capital Loss on Working	1,826 0 8 1,671 11 7	

Date	Item	Amount		Amount	
30th June, 1901	Receipts	1,397 14 10		1,096 8 11	
	Expenditure	2,003 3 5		1,028 16 9	
	Loss on Working		605 8 7		
	Interest on Capital	1,425 0 0	2,030 8 7		2,252 7 10
31st Dec., 1901	Receipts	1,553 4 2		827 7 10	
	Expenditure	2,410 18 6		1,425 0 0	
	Loss on Working		877 14 4		1,853 18 1
	Interest on Capital	1,425 0 0	2,302 14 4	1,888 13 8	1,960 15 7
30th June, 1902	Receipts	1,218 19 7		535 15 7	
	Expenditure	2,094 10 0		1,425 0 0	
	Loss on Working		875 10 5		1,172 11 9
	Interest on Capital	1,425 0 0	2,300 10 5	2,070 5 0	2,322 13 3
31st Dec., 1902	Receipts	1,164 11 7		897 13 3	
	Expenditure	1,437 7 3		1,425 0 0	
	Loss on Working		272 15 8		1,669 0 5
	Interest on Capital	1,425 0 0	1,697 15 8	1,771 0 1	1,636 19 8
30th June, 1903	Receipts	928 19 1		201 19 8	
	Expenditure	2,094 2 11		1,425 0 0	
	Loss on Working		1,165 3 10		1,177 9 6
	Interest on Capital	1,425 0 0	2,590 3 10	1,566 3 0	1,903 13 6
31st Dec., 1903	Receipts	1,100 18 6		478 18 6	
	Expenditure	1,689 12 4		1,425 0 0	
	Loss on Working		538 18 10		1,534 6 3
	Interest on Capital	1,425 0 0	1,963 13 10	1,930 7 11	1,821 1 8
30th June, 1904	Receipts	994 2 9		396 1 8	
	Expenditure	1,846 2 6		1,425 0 0	
	Loss on Working		851 19 9		1,963 14 5
	Interest on Capital	1,425 0 0	2,295 19 9	2,060 9 10	2,241 15 5
31st Dec., 1904	Receipts	1,228 9 5		816 15 5	
	Expenditure	1,362 6 4		1,425 0 0	
	Loss on Working		333 16 11		1,522 18 1
	Interest on Capital	1,425 0 0	1,758 16 11	1,885 16 9	1,737 18 8
30th June, 1905	Receipts	1,020 2 10		372 18 8	
	Expenditure	1,535 15 5		1,425 0 0	
	Loss on Working		515 12 7		1,218 5 11
	Interest on Capital	1,425 0 0	1,940 12 7	1,873 9 0	2,085 3 1
31st Dec., 1905	Receipts	1,255 16 9		660 3 1	
	Expenditure	1,665 11 1		1,425 0 0	
	Loss on Working		409 14 4		1,612 16 10
	Interest on Capital	1,425 0 0	1,834 14 4	2,164 8 9	
				551 11 11	
				1,425 0 0	1,976 11 11
					£20,144 10 2

SUMMARY:— { Loss on Working £23,329 11 4
{ Interest on £57,000 Capital 56,814 18 10

May 7th, 1906.

The above is a true and correct copy of the different Ledgers.—W. GOGGIN, Secretary.

Earle Printing Works, Skibbereen.

	Pass	Parcel	Goods	Cattle	Horse	Total for period
July-December 1912	744	54	1003	216	11	£2028
January-June 1913	694	45	1019	190	13	£1961

Extract from Accounts

Payments - January 1903

	£	s.	d.
Charles McCarthy (Blacksmith)		16	10
Charles McCarthy (Blacksmith)	1	4	6
Phoenix Nut & Bolt Co.	33	9	1
'Railway Carriage'		14	6

Payments - February 1903

	£	s.	d.
Charles McCarthy (Blacksmith)		7	6
Charles McCarthy (Blacksmith)	2	0	6
Vacuum Brake Co.		12	0
Ebbw Vale Co.	110	8	0
Tangyes Ltd	8	10	9
Charles McCarthy (Blacksmith)		6	6
Charles McCarthy (Blacksmith)	1	10	0
Charles McCarthy (Blacksmith)		4	8
Tim McCarthy (for Schull Blacksmith)		15	9
Daniel Donovan (for Blacksmith)		10	0
Mary Burke	10	3	0
Michael McCarthy		5	0
Evans Engineer - salary	2	10	0
Secretary - salary	4	0	0
Engineer's Office	10	19	2

S&SR Outgoings January-June 1904

	£	s.	d.
Permanent Way	306	18	11
Buildings	3	14	1
Loco running	106	8	2
Loco repairs	230	15	1
Carriage repairs	124	14	1
Wagon repairs	40	5	0
Coaching - wages	182	19	3
Traffic expenses	42	2	2

Wages and working hours

Before World War I wages and working hours were consistent with those obtaining elsewhere in the British Isles; the day's duty was a 12-hour shift. The Company employed about forty men and boys and it was an unwritten rule that any lapse of output or behaviour would result in demotion or dismissal. Even so, it was usual for members of three generations in the same family to serve the Company; the Murphys in the Skibbereen Works were an instance.

The paternal instinct was not absent either; when J.P. Swanton, who had served as Station Master at Ballydehob since the line opened, retired in June 1912, the Board awarded him a £20 per annum pension for faithful service.

APPENDIX

Weekly wages at the date the line opened were as follows:

Employee	Location	Position	Weekly wage
Michael O'Sullivan	Schull	Station Master	20s.
James Daly	Ballydehob	Station Master	10s.
John W. Loane	Skibbereen*	Station Master	20s.
Augustine Cruise		Engine driver	22s.
James Copithorne		Guard	10s.

Statistics

The ensuing material has been extracted from the Board of Trade records in the Manchester Central Reference Library by J.S. Wilkinson, to whom I am indebted. Mr Wilkinson appends comment as a foreword to his findings, warning that 'there is a suspicious roundness of the figures for the S&S goods mileage...' in that it has been '10 per cent almost exactly of the total mileage for quite a few years. It may of course, been the case but one cannot help thinking that the civil servants at the Board of Trade in London supplied with figures might have brought out a certain Irish contrariness'.

The bar charts represent the total annual expenditure of the respective railways to which they relate, divided by the total number of miles run. The North Wales Narrow Gauge Railways and the Talyllyn Railway figures are added for comparison.

Statistics from Board of Trade Returns 1913

Four tank engines
Seven passenger carriages to carry 172 persons†
Six other coaching vehicles
Five open wagons under 8 tons or above
Ninteen covered wagons under 8 tons or above
Twenty-two cattle trucks
Four Railway service vehicles

Eight houses owned by Railway

Passengers originating on Company's system:
1st Class 1,383, 2nd Class 52,032

Originating on Company's system:
4,010 tons merchandise
4,838 cattle
52 claves
136 sheep
5,886 pigs

Coal: 380 tons carried off CB&SCR at Skibbereen
34 tons carried off ships at Schull

---

* Presumably that portion of his wages covering the WCT.
† Uniform Class   32 1st Class seats
                  120 3rd Class seats
   Composite   10 1st Class seats
                   30 3rd Class seats

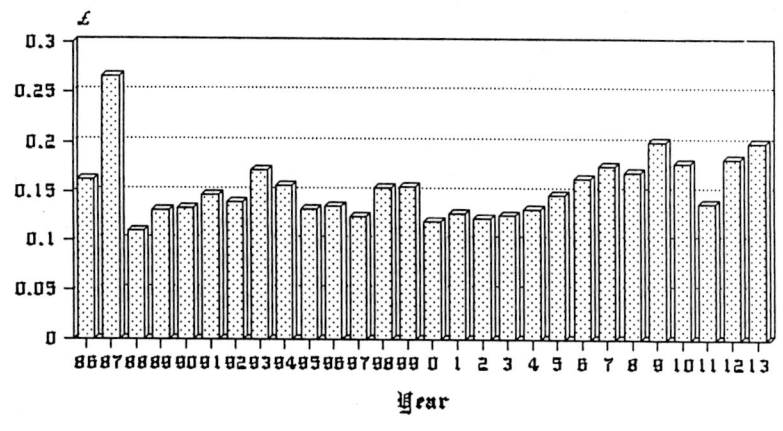
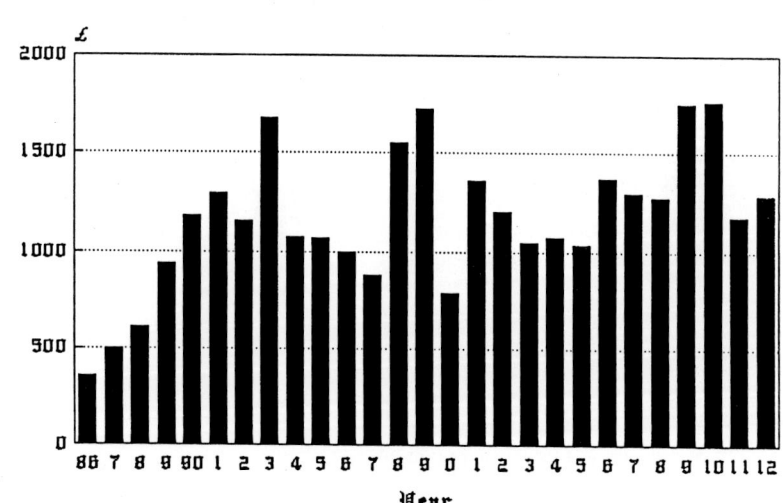

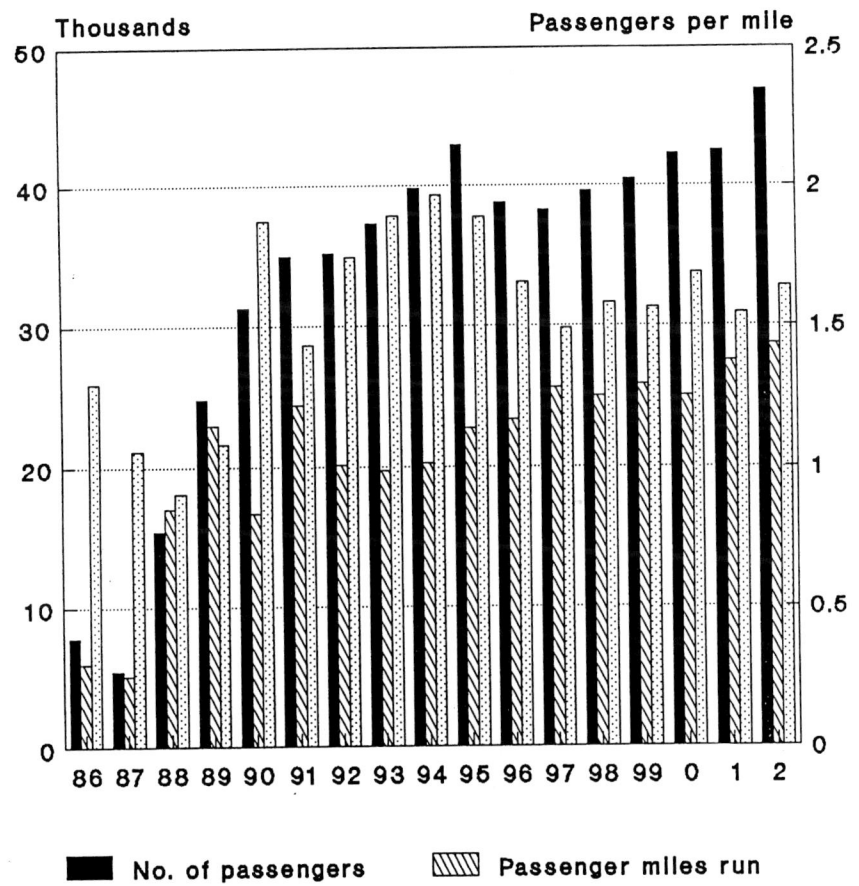

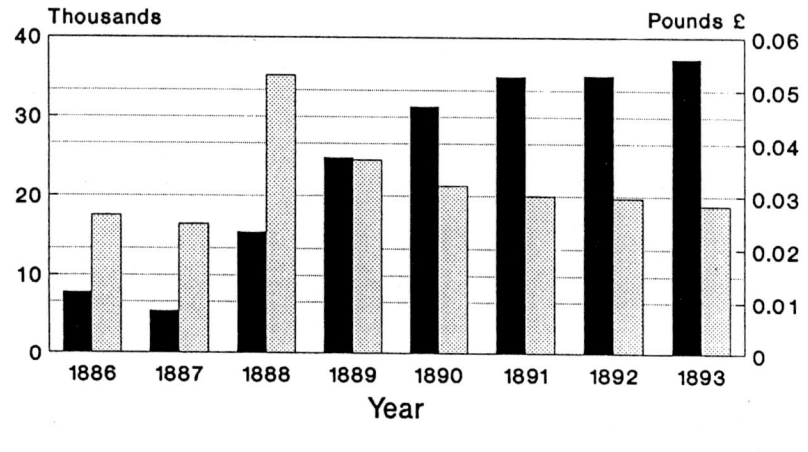
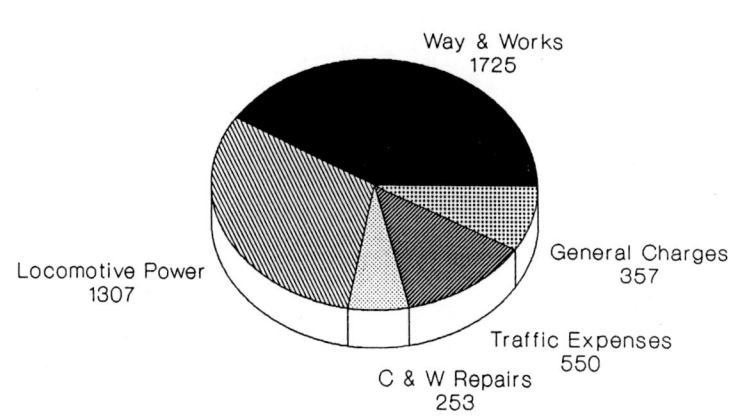

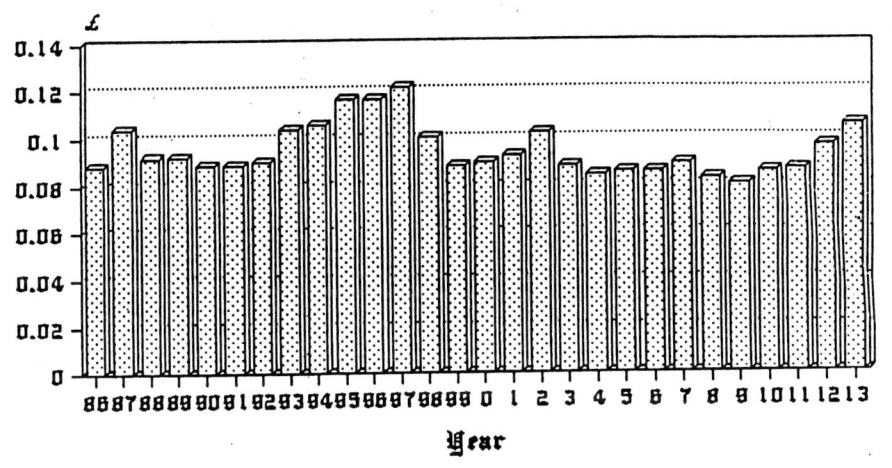
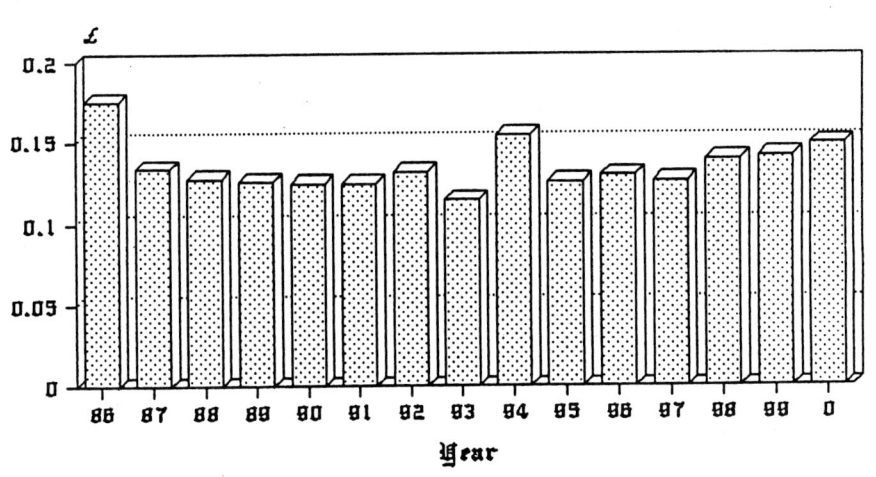

Sources, Acknowledgements and Bibliography

An Appreciation

Long-standing friends have given me generous help with the frequent problems which arose during the often-disappointing efforts to pursue sources in Ireland, bringing me to realise how fortunate we are on this side of the Irish Sea to have various places of deposit where railway history may be searched.

One reason for this is the troubled history of Ireland which has left a legacy of destroyed documents, emigration up to recent times of those who could supply recollections, and an understandable disinterest in industrial history among an essentially rural people.

The position today is much more encouraging . . . too late for this account.

Jeremy Wilkinson, Roy Thomson and Michael Morton Lloyd have made essential contributions, the last two named in the oft-contentious line drawings for which no official source exists. Jane Kennedy of The Oakwood Press has given me the encouragement to continue when my determination faltered.

The list of acknowledgments is formidable and thanks are particularly due to those Irish residents who have come to my aid over these past forty years.

To you all, my warmest thanks.

Acknowledgements of Contributors

Local history and events

Mrs Mary Mackey, Schull
Mrs Patrick McCarthy, Schull
Timothy O'Donovan, Bawnahow
John Murphy (Senr), Skibbereen
Patrick Cleary, Skibbereen
Revd Canon & Mrs G.A. Salter, Cork
Mr & Mrs John Browne, Creagh
Bernard O'Regan, Aughadown
Frank Collins, Meen Bridge
Kenneth Austin, Coosheen
Barney Bennett, Innishannon
Patrick O'Keefe, Bantry
Professor G. Tucker, Redditch

James O'Reilly, Schull
Capt. Paul Chevasse, Castletownsend
A.P. Hughes, Bantry
Niall O'Mahoney, Skibbereen
Liam O'Regan, Skibbereen
Rt Revd Dr J.A. Jagoe, Schull
Col R.G.F. Chevasse, Cappagh
Mizen Archaeological & Historical
  Society, Schull
SOUTHERN STAR Ltd., Skibbereen
Cork Archives Institute, Cork
Mick McCarthy, Abbey, Skibbereen

Line illustrations

G. R. Thomson, Winchester
Michael E. Morton Lloyd, Hereford

Railway matters

J. Cruise, Epsom
Walter McGrath, Cork
Colm Creedon, Cork
A.M. Davies, Bowdon
G.R. Thomson, Winchester

George Mahon, Dublin
Irish Railway Record Society, Dublin
J.S. Wilkinson, Wilmslow
Harold Fayle, Boscombe

SOURCES, ACKNOWLEDGEMENTS AND BIBLIOGRAPHY

Marine and mining
Roy Fenton, Wimbledon
J.S.Wilkinson, Wilmslow

Assistance in supportive matters

Rt Revd Keith A. Arnold, Olney
Roger Bird, Bristol
Paul Ivinson, Winchester

Peter Ward, Newport, Salop
Roger Bristow, Tamworth
Roger S. Carpenter, Birmingham

Photographs
The contribution is acknowledged of those whose names appear under each photograph, and for their generous help.

I have been assisted in my searches at the following locations

THE MANCHESTER CENTRAL LIBRARY
THE CORK ARCHIVES INSTITUTE
THE PUBLIC RECORD OFFICE, KEW
SKIBBEREEN PUBLIC LIBRARY
THE LIBRARY OF THE IRISH RAILWAY RECORD SOCIETY
THE SOUTHERN STAR LTD
THE WEST CORK ARTS CENTRE
CORK COUNTY COUNCIL HIGHWAYS DEPT.
THE CORK EXAMINER

Sadly, during the long preparation of this book, many of the contributors have died.

Bibliography

LANDLORDS AND TENANTS IN MID-VICTORIAN IRELAND, W.E. Vaughan, Oxford, 1994.
A TOPOGRAPHICAL DICTIONARY OF IRELAND, S. Lewis, Dublin, 1837.
A HISTORY OF THE RAILWAYS OF IRELAND, J.C. Conroy, London, 1928.
AT THE FEET OF GABRIEL, C.G. Gibson, Schull, 1953.
PROTESTANT SOCIETY AND POLITICS IN CORK 1818-1844, d'Alton, Cork, 1980.
IRELAND: INDUSTRIAL AND AGRICULTURAL, Dept of Agriculture, Dublin, 1902.
TOWARDS IRELAND FREE, Deasy, Dublin, 1973.
SOMERVILLE & ROSS, G. Lewis, Harmsworth, 1985.
A VISION FULFILLED, various, Skibbereen, 1996.
THE SPIRIT OF IRELAND, L. Doyle, London, 1935.
NARROW GAUGE RAILWAYS OF IRELAND, H. Fayle, London, 1946.
THE CORK, BANDON & SOUTH COAST RAILWAY, C. Creedon, Cork, 1986.
TRANSPORT IN IRELAND 1880-1910, P. Flanaghan, Dublin, 1969.
CAMBRIAN COASTERS, R.S. Fenton, Kendal, 1989.
THE GREAT IRISH FAMINE, various, Cork, 1995.
THE CAVAN & LEITRIM RAILWAY, by P. Flanaghan, Newton Abbot, 1966.

Also the various book titles and periodicals mentioned in the footnotes of the text.

Newspapers

The two Skibbereen newspapers (THE SKIBBEREEN EAGLE and THE SOUTHERN STAR) mentioned in the text made frequent reference to the West Carbery Tramway, especially at the time of its promotion. THE SKIBBEREEN EAGLE was a great supporter of the railway age in West Cork and the pros and cons of the West Carbery enterprise were often the subjects of editorials and heated correspondence.

THE SKIBBEREEN EAGLE began publication in 1857 and was founded by an Englishman, Elden Potter. In an area noted for its nationalistic sympathies, 'it was always stridently Imperial and loyalist in tone'.

Entirely opposite in political aspect was THE SOUTHERN STAR which commenced in 1889 (just three years after the Tramway opened) and had a nationalistic flavour). For this reason it found little favour with the-then English authority, especially so shortly after the Easter Rising of 1916 and in the 'Troubles' which followed, and to subdue its influence it was suppressed several times in 1919-20. This culminated in a Black & Tan raid on the premises, who burned its records and back numbers of the paper.

Not to be outdone, 'the opposition' did likewise at the EAGLE, and only a few older copies survived. Publication of both was resumed but when peace was restored the EAGLE, continuing its original flavour found less and less readers interested in its content. The STAR took it over in 1929 and continues to appear as a weekly paper with a combined title.

The loss of such important historical material is a severe blow to the local historian and railway researcher.

The British Library holds:

SKIBBEREEN & WEST CARBERY EAGLE or SOUTH WESTERN ADVERTISER starting with issue No. 164 in 1861 and until 1867 continued as:

WEST CORK & CARBERY EAGLE or SOUTH WESTERN ADVERTISER from 1867 to July 1870 continued as:

WEST CORK EAGLE & COUNTY ADVERTISER from August 1870 to October 1870 and from January 1871 to 1883 (Note: November and December 1870 issues are missing) continued as:

THE EAGLE & COUNTY CORK ADVERTISER from 1883 to 1899 continued as:

CORK COUNTY EAGLE & MUNSTER ADVERTISER from 1899 to 1922

Index

Abandonment Order 103.
Accident at Schull engine shed 229,231.
Accident near Schull 229.
Accident on Tralee & Dingle Rly 74,87, 88.
Acts of Parliament 7, 20, 22, 27, 28, 31, 45, 49, 64, 65, 68, 71, 73, 83, 95, 107.
Acworth, W.M. 82.
Allport, Sir James 22, 64.
Armstrong, (?) (Engineer) 73, 80.

Ballydehob 13, 14, 15, 17, 19, 27, 31, 38, 43, 45, 50, 53, 54, 56, 60, 63, 65, 67, 69, 73, 75, 81, 83, 93, 101, 122, 139 et seq., 155, 163, 187, 232-3, 235, 238, 242, 247, 249, 250, 251, 253, 260, 265.
Ballydehob Viaduct 49, 105, 143, 197.
Baltimore 6, 14, 61, 63, 66-7, 73, 92, 115, 235, 246, 250, 262.
Bandon 12,13, 20, 21, 22, 25, 31, 57, 92.
Bantry 6, 23, 27, 43, 45, 61, 63, 79, 171, 197, 203, 241, 246, 261, 262.
Barrington, William 20, 90.
Batchen, T.M. 79, 87.
BELR 63, 115.
Board of Trade 37, 46, 47, 48, 49, 51, 547, 58-61, 65, 68, 77, 80, 83, 85, 86-8, 105, 169, 223, 235, 238, 247, 271.
Board of Works 33, 73, 79, 83, 87, 88, 90, 133, 139, 141, 143, 241, 247.
Bryce, Rt Hon. James 79, 87
Burke, Daniel 73.

Carey, Richard 24, 28, 66.
Carey, William L. 72
Castletownsend 9, 65, 66, 73, 251, 252, 262.
C&BR 13, 20, 21, 24, 25, 26, 27, 28, 36, 37, 38, 43, 45, 47, 54, 57, 59, 85, 245, 247.
CB&SCR 6, 21, 63, 66, 69, 71, 74, 75, 82, 83, 85, 91, 92, 107, 119, 171, 197, 241, 250, 256, 260, 261, 266, 271.
Cheap Day tickets, introduction of 74, 242.
Church Cross Halt 50, 69, 73,121, 125, 127, 137, 166, 251, 254.
Chronology 7, 9, 13, 20, 92.
CIE 96, 97,101,103,105,183,191 et seq., 233, 245, 246.
Civil War 6, 7, 92, 95, 137, 223, 260.
Clonakilty 12, 23, 26, 27, 37, 38, 43.
CL&RLR&TCL 69-71, 197.
Clyde Shipping Co. 75, 261-2.
Committee of Management (later Board) 69-70, 72-3, 74, 82, 83, 149, 183, 191, 238, 241, 246, 247.
CONCILIATION (KENT), locomotive 179, 183.
Congested Districts (Board) 67, 261-2.
Cork city 6, 12, 13, 14, 15, 19, 20, 21, 22, 25, 45, 57, 66, 92, 101, 107, 231, 238, 261, 262, 267.
Cork City Railways 20, 107, 115.
Cork County Council 61, 69, 72, 73, 84, 87, 103, 183.

Cottam, Mick 191,197, 249.
Creedon, Daniel 80-2, 191, 203, 229, 250.
Creedon, Thomas 57, 59.
Creedon, Timothy 72, 250.
Crooked Bridge 50, 54, 73,137,139,155, 250, 251, 265.
Crookhaven 23, 24, 90-1,123.
Cross House 133.
Cruise, Augustine 58, 255, 271.
Cruise, Francis 256.
Cullinane, Henry 73.

Daly, Jack 77, 179, 233.
d'Avigdor, E.H. 24, 44, 45, 46, 47, 48, 54, 55, 66, 81, 85, 86, 88, 141.
Dick, Kerr & Co. 54, 60, 167 et seq., 191 et seq., 266.
Dorman, E.H. 28.
Dorman, J.W. 24, 25, 28, 37, 42, 46, 58-9, 245.
Dorman & Kirby 37, 42, 46.
Downes, Thomas 24, 27, 28, 31, 39, 43, 46, 58, 65.
Drimoleague 20, 25, 92,121, 235, 246.
Dunmanway 20, 22, 25, 38, 92.

Emergency, The (World War II) 13,15, 17, 97, 221, 249, 253, 254, 260.
ERIN, locomotive 11, 63, 77, 91, 96, 167 et seq., 267.
Evans, Richard 73-4, 77, 79, 82-3, 89, 179, 247.
Extension Railway (Schull) 19, 66-8, 69-71, 77, 93, 103, 105, 155, 163, 166, 229, 246, 250, 261, 262.

Fair traffic 6, 15, 26, 53, 56, 60, 81, 95, 141, 231-2, 235, 253, 254.
Fares, lists of 242-3.
Fleming, Bernard 47-8, 54-5, 57.

GABRIEL, locomotive 11, 72, 77, 80, 82, 86, 91, 167 et seq., 197, 233.
Gilhooly, James (MP) 59, 61, 63,191, 203.
Glandore 9, 24, 25, 26, 27 ,28, 29, 31, 38, 39, 42, 43, 65, 66, 68, 73.
Gloucester RC&W Co. 75, 203, 221, 266.
Goggin, William 77, 80, 93, 250.
Gradients, list of 32.
Grand Jury 7 ,22, 26, 28-9, 33, 36, 37, 39, 43, 47-8, 54, 56, 58, 61, 64, 65, 67, 69, 71, 73, 83, 84-5, 87, 88.
Great Famine 11, 13, 14, 19, 47, 121, 261, 263.
Green, Thomas & Son Ltd 187.
GSR 52, 71-2, 96-7, 133, 149, 163, 171, 177, 179, 183, 187, 191 et seq., 231, 233,240-1,246, 253,262, 266.
GS&WR 20, 25, 54, 92, 107.

Hayes, Timothy 73.
Hegarty, 'Curly' 95, 141, 233 ,234, 254.
Hollyhill 50, 60, 73, 93, 129, 133, 234, 235, 246, 250.
Hutchinson, Major Gen. 47-9, 54, 56, 58, 60, 84.

279

IDA, locomotive 11, 73, 77, 91, 167 et seq.
ILEN, locomotive 11, 81,167 et seq.
Ilen, River 15, 20, 26, 37, 42, 107, 115, 121, 252.
Ilen Valley Railway 15, 20, 21, 22, 25, 31, 37, 42, 46, 66, 79, 107.
Inspection prior to opening 49-50.
IRA 6, 93, 95, 262.

Jackson, Nathaniel 33, 56-8, 65 ,67-8.
Johnstone, J.J. 54, 58, 64.
Johnstone, J.W. 28,53-4 ,56, 58.

Kelly, J.H. 73, 149, 266-7.
KENT, locomotive 91, 93, 101, 167 et seq.
Kerr, Stuart (Co.) 81.
Kilcoe 50, 65, 69, 93, 133, 137, 139, 223, 234, 250, 260.

Land League, The 13, 46,63.
Landslide near Skibberen 223.
Last day of operation 101
'Last steaming' 103.
Levis, Dr John S. 55, 58, 66.
Levis, J.H. 25.
Lifting of track 103.
Limrick, John (JP) 28, 55, 58, 64, 66.
Lists:
  Fares 242-3.
  Level Crossings 240.
  Personnel 257-9.
  Speed restrictions 239.
  Water columns 240.
Loane, J.W. 77, 179, 271.
Locomotives sent for scrapping 103, 187.
Long Car 7, 68.
Lubbock, Sir John 45, 58, 84.

Marconi, Guglielmo 90-1.
MARION, locomotive 11, 77, 82, 167 et seq.
Market traffic 15, 17, 60, 101, 232-3, 234, 235, 254.
McCarthy, Denis 247, 249
McCarthy, Florence 73.
McCarthy, J.G. 72.
McCarthy, John 77, 179.
McCarthy, Mick 246-7, 249.
McKeon(e), Robinson and d'Avigdor 44, 46.
Meen Bridge 73, 133.
Morgan, Captain A. 28.
Murphy, Charlie 249, 253.
Murphy, Father John (priest) 27, 28, 36.
Murphy, Patrick 91, 179.

Nasmyth, Wilson & Co. 63,73,171 et seq., 266-7.
New Court Halt 47, 50, 56, 73, 123, 166, 246.
Newham, Alan 5, 45, 83 ,91, 97, 103, 139, 183, 197, 203, 234, 265.
No. 6 (unnamed) locomotive 96, 101, 103, 167 et seq.

O'Connor, Father John (priest) 77, 179.
O'Donovan, Timothy 249, 252.
Oliffe, C.T. 64.
Order of Abandonment 103.

Peckett & Sons Ltd 72, 77, 86, 173 et seq., 267.
Personnel, list of 257-9.
Pickering & Co. 221, 267.

Railway Commissioners 21.
Railways built under 1883 Act 51.
Roaring Water Bay 17, 129, 260.
Roaring Water River 129, 133.
Rosscarbery 23, 24, 26, 37, 38, 43.
Royal Commission on Irish Public Works Report 23, 64.
Roycroft, Edward 27, 73, 75, 82-7, 171, 203, 266-7.

Schull Extension Railway, see Extension Railway (Schull)
Schull Regatta 101,143, 233, 235, 250, 252.
Schull Station* 50, 52, 53, 55-7, 60, 65, 68, 69, 72, 77, 81, 91, 93, 101, 103, 115,155 etseq., 177, 223, 229, 231-3, 235, 242, 246, 249, 251, 252, 253, 254, 262, 265.
Shaw, William (MP) 25, 26, 27.
Skibbereen Station* 42, 49, 50, 52, 54, 56, 57, 60, 66, 67, 69, 72, 73, 74, 75, 80, 83, 91, 92, 93, 95, 96, 101, 107 et seq., 155, 171, 173, 177, 183, 187, 189, 231-3, 235, 238, 249, 251, 253, 254, 265, 266.
Somerville, Col J.L. (JP) 46, 58, 61.
Speed restrictions, list of 239.
Stack, Jim 77,179.
Sunday trains, discontinued 96.
Swanton, G.H. 24, 27.
Swanton, James 24, 25, 27, 58.

TCGCL 44, 46, 71.
Townsend, H.U. 31-3, 245.
TRENT, locomotive 11.

Union Hall 9, 24, 26, 27, 38, 42, 66.

Vice-Regal Commission 59, 63, 82-3, 86, 90, 173, 223, 241, 243.

War of Independence 6, 93, 266.
Water columns, list of 240.
WCR 20, 21, 25, 28, 252.
Woodlands 50, 73, 149, 151, 242.
Woods, (?) (Manager) 45,53-4
Working Results of Irish Light Rlys (1900) 90-1.
World War II (The Emergency) 13, 15, 17, 97,221, 249,253,254, 260.

---

* as 'Schull' and 'Skibbereen' appear on many pages, references are limited to those applying to the stations.